Quality Assurance for Home Health Care

Claire Gavin Meisenheimer
Health Care Consultant
Milwaukee, Wisconsin

AN ASPEN PUBLICATION®
Aspen Publishers, Inc.

1989

Rockville, Maryland
Royal Tunbridge Wells

Library of Congress Cataloging-in-Publication Data

Meisenheimer, Claire Gavin.
Quality assurance for home health care/Claire Gavin Meisenheimer.
p. cm.
"An Aspen publication."
Includes bibliographies and index.
ISBN: 0-8342-0026-0
1. Home care services--Quality control. I. Title.
RA645.3.M45   1989   362.1'4'068--dc19   88-8158
CIP

Editorial Services: Mary Beth Roesser

Library of Congress Catalog Card Number: 88-8158
ISBN: 0-8342-0026-0

Printed in the United States of America

1 2 3 4 5

To my special husband, Elliott,
to my children, Holly, Scott, and Wendy,
and to my mother, Delia Pageau Gavin

Table of Contents

Contributors xi

Foreword xiii

Introduction xv

PART I   HISTORICAL AND ADMINISTRATIVE PERSPECTIVES 1

Chapter   1—Home Care: Past Perspectives and Implications for the Present and Future 3
            Marsha K. Stanhope

            Early Beginnings 4
            Development of Home Care in the United States 5
            Home Care Today 7
            Future Prospects 9
            Summary 10

Chapter   2—Quality Assurance: Administrative Support 13
            Marilyn Harris

            Needs and Expectations for Survival and Growth 13
            Merging Clinical and Financial Data to Improve Quality of Care 15
            Analyzing Resources 18
            Summary 26
            Appendix 2-A: Field Agency Agreement 28

PART II   QUALITY ASSURANCE PROCESS 31

Chapter   3—Designing a Quality Assurance Program 33
            Claire G. Meisenheimer

            Planning: The Cornerstone of a Sound Program 33
            Assessing an Existing QA Program 34

Developing a QA Program 34
Utilization Review, Risk Management, Quality Assurance 34
Communication Flow 38
Reports and Reporting Mechanisms 38
Summary 41
Appendix 3-A: Process for Monitoring and Evaluation Activities 42
Appendix 3-B: Format for Proposed Quality Assurance Activity 44
Appendix 3-C: Quality Assurance Monitoring Activity 45
Appendix 3-D: Committee Agenda/Minutes 47
Appendix 3-E: Quality Assurance Activities Log 48
Appendix 3-F: Home Health Care Critical Incident Report 52

Chapter 4—Standards: The State of the Art 54
    June A. Schmele

Definitions 54
Approaches to Standards Implementation 55
Environment 57
Levels of Standards 57
Conclusion 62

Chapter 5—Problem Identification, Topic Selection, and Monitoring and Evaluation Methods 64
    Donna M. Wagner

Indicators: The Basis for Problem Identification 64
Group Techniques 67
Summary 70

Chapter 6—Data Collection Mechanisms 72
    June A. Schmele

Data Collection Mechanisms 73
Conclusion 79

Chapter 7—Documentation 81
    E. Joyce Gould and Paula L. Rich

Types of Documentation 82
Influences on Documentation 82
Societal Influences on the Clinical Record 84
Dealing with Societal Influences in a Clinical Situation 86

Chapter 8—Evaluating Quality Assurance Program Effectiveness 122
    G. Lorain Brault

Review of the Written Quality Assurance Plan 122
Evaluating Preparation and Completion of the Yearly Plan 122
Determining the Effectiveness of Tools/Forms 123
Reassessing Critical Quality Assurance and Risk Management Focus Issues .. 124
Evaluating the Effectiveness of the Quality Assurance Committee 125
Summary 125
Appendix 8-A: Patient Services Satisfaction Survey 126
Appendix 8-B: Physician Satisfaction Survey 128
Appendix 8-C: Referral Source Satisfaction Survey 129
Appendix 8-D: Quality Assurance Monitor Summary Form 130
Appendix 8-E: Quality Assurance Monitor/Summary; ''Do Not Resuscitate'' Monitor Summary 131
Appendix 8-F: Quality Assurance Monitor/Summary; Timely Initial Service Monitor Summary 132
Appendix 8-G: Quality Assurance Monitor/Summary; Intravenous Certification Monitor Summary 133

PART III   **Multidisciplinary Monitoring** **137**

Chapter 9 — The Staff Nurse's Perspective **139**
     Lorie E. Olson

     Commitment 139
     Case Management 140
     Staffing Patterns and Productivity 144
     Peer Review 147
     Conclusion 148

Chapter 10 — The Physician's Perspective **150**
     Paul E. Hankwitz

     Historical Forces that Shaped Today's Health Care System 150
     Home Health Care Defined 151
     Levels of Care 151
     Renewed Physician Interest in Home Care 152
     The Support of Organized Medicine for Home Health Care 152
     Monitoring Quality of Care in the Home Setting 153
     The Physician as a Member of the Home Care Team 154
     The Role of the Physician in Home Care 155
     Home Health Care 156
     Selecting a Home Health Care Agency 157
     The Role of an Agency Medical Director 157
     The Role of County and State Medical Societies 158
     The Costs of Home Care and Payment for Physician Services 158
     The Rewards of Home Care 159
     What the Future Holds 159

Chapter 11 — The Social Worker's Perspective **163**
     William E. Powell

     The Professional Competence of Caregivers 163
     Determining and Documenting the Need for Social Work Services 164
     Appropriate Social Work Referrals 164
     Documentation 168
     Teamwork 169
     Consultation 170
     Assessments of Process and Outcome 170
     Conclusion 170

Chapter 12 — The Therapist's Perspective **173**
     Christine M. Crivello

     Definition of Home Care 173
     History of Therapy in Home Care 173
     Role of the Home Health Therapist 174
     Influence of Medicare on Quality Assurance 174
     Generic Model for Quality Assurance 174
     Examples of Quality Assurance Programs in Home Care 177
     Outcome Studies in the Literature 183
     Future Considerations 185
     Conclusion 185

Chapter 13—The Pharmacist's Perspective **187**
Ilene H. Zuckerman and Madeline V. Feinberg

Drug Use and the Elderly 187
Risks and Problems of Drug Use 187
Role of the Pharmacist in Home Health Care 188
The Medication Record 190
Quality of Care and the Home Care Patient 192
Reimbursement for Pharmaceutical Services in Home Care 192
Conclusion 192

PART IV —PRACTICE ISSUES AFFECTING QUALITY **195**

Chapter 14—High Tech: Implications for Quality Assurance **197**
Lydia (Penny) Tanner

Common Characteristics of High-Tech Home Care 197
An Example of High-Tech Quality Assurance Planning: Intravenous Therapy 199
External Review Process 200
Conclusion 200

Chapter 15—Legal and Ethical Dilemmas Related to Quality Assurance **204**
Ann Helm

Ethics Committees 204
Client Rights and Responsibilities 205
Ethical Dilemmas 205
Bioethics: Application of Ethical Principles 207
Risk Management: Implications for Policy and Practice 207
Responsibilities of the Agency and the Employee 210
Admission and Discharge Policies 210
Conclusion 210
Appendix 15-A: Health Law and Bioethics Bibliography 212
Appendix 15-B: Publications of the President's Commission for the Study of Ethical Problems and
Behavioral Research 213

Chapter 16—Home Health Aide and Home Companion Program **214**
Sally Whitten

Recruitment 215
Home Companions Versus Home Health Aides 215
Training 215
Services 216
Supervision 216
Assessments 216
Marketing 217
Evaluation 217
Reimbursement 217
Summary 218
Appendix 16-A: Home Companion Job Description 219
Appendix 16-B: Home Health Aide Job Description 221
Appendix 16-C: Home Health Aide Assignment Sheet 223
Appendix 16-D: Home Companion Assignment Sheet 225
Appendix 16-E: Home Companion Program Advertisement 227
Appendix 16-F: Home Companion Program Advertisements 228
Appendix 16-G: Functional Assessment Form 229

Appendix 16-H: Home Companion Program Evaluation Form 233
Appendix 16-I: Home Companion Program Client Satisfaction Interview Form 235

Chapter 17—Role of the Family Caregiver in the Home **239**
    Lynn Rew

Role of the Family Caregiver 239
The Affirm Model 240
Potential for Abuse and Neglect 242
Strategies to Enhance Quality of Care 242
Conclusion 242
Appendix 17-A: The AFFIRM Model Booklet 245

Chapter 18—Assuring Continuity of Care: Managing the Transition from Hospital to Home **247**
    Sister Ann M. Schorfheide

Societal Forces Affecting Continuity of Care 247
The Strategies of Continuity of Care Planning 248
Barriers to Effective Continuity of Health Care 250
Discharging from Home Care: Promoting Continuity of Care 251
Conclusion 251

Chapter 19—Examples of Existing Quality Assurance Programs in Home Health Care **252**
    Donna Amblers Peters and Rhoda Regenstreif

Case Study 1: A Hospital-Based Agency 252
Case Study 2: A Coordinated Home Care Program 258
Conclusion 270
Appendix 19-A: Health Units within the Province of Alberta 272
Appendix 19-B: The Coordinated Home Care Program Statement of Philosophy 273
Appendix 19-C: Alberta Coordinated Home Care Program (CHCP) Objectives 274
Appendix 19-D: Terms of Reference for the Home Care Standards Committee 275

Quality Assurance Glossary for Home Health Care **277**

Index **283**

Contributors

G. Lorain Brault, MS, RN
President
Hospital Home Health Care Agency of California
Torrance, California

Christine M. Crivello, RPT
Rehabilitation Services of Wisconsin
A Subsidiary of InSpeech, Inc.
Wauwatosa, Wisconsin

Linda Lee Daniel, MN, RN
Associate Professor, Community Health Nursing
Chairperson, National Nursing Symposium on Home Health
   Care
The University of Michigan
Ann Arbor, Michigan

Madeline V. Feinberg, PharmBS
Assistant Clinical Professor
Director, Elder Health Program
University of Maryland
School of Pharmacy
Baltimore, Maryland

E. Joyce Gould, MSN, RN
Assistant Administrator
Director of Patient Services
United Home Health Services
Philadelphia, Pennsylvania

Paul Edward Hankwitz, MD
Assistant Medical Director
Northwestern Mutual Life Insurance Company
Milwaukee, Wisconsin
Formerly, Medical Director
Visiting Nurse Association of Milwaukee
Founding President of National Association for Physicians
   in Home Care
Board of Directors—American Academy of Home Care
   Physicians

Marilyn D. Harris, MSN, RN, CNAA
Executive Director
Visiting Nurse Association of Eastern Montgomery County
Abington, Pennsylvania

Ann Helm, RN, MS, JD
Quality Assurance Manager
Veterans Administration Medical Center
Portland, Oregon
Assistant Professor
School of Medicine
Oregon Health Sciences University
Portland, Oregon

Claire Gavin Meisenheimer, PhD, RN, CNAA
Associate Professor, Graduate Program
University of Wisconsin-Oshkosh
Oshkosh, Wisconsin
Health Care Consultant: Management/Quality Assurance
Milwaukee, Wisconsin

Lorie Edwards Olson, BSN, RN
Staff Nurse
Director of Professional Services
The Johns Hopkins Hospital
Home Care and Services
Baltimore, Maryland

Donna Peters, PhD, RN, CNAA
The Robert Wood Johnson Foundation
Program Officer
Princeton, New Jersey
Formerly, Director of Nursing
Research and Quality Assurance
The Johns Hopkins Hospital Department of Nursing
Baltimore, Maryland

William E. Powell, MSSW, PhD
Assistant Professor
University of Wisconsin-Oshkosh
Department of Social Work
Oshkosh, Wisconsin

Rhoda Regenstreif, BA
Coordinator, Long Term Care Planning
Home Care Unit
Department of Community and Occupational Health
Edmonton, Alberta, Canada

Lynn Rew, EdD, RN
Assistant Professor
The University of Texas at Austin
Austin, Texas

Paula Rich, MSN, RN
Professional Nursing Development
Philadelphia, Pennsylvania

June A. Schmele, PhD, RN
Associate Professor
The University of Oklahoma
Oklahoma City Campus-Health Sciences Center
College of Nursing
Oklahoma City, Oklahoma

Sister Ann M. Schorfheide, PhD, RN, C
Associate Professor
University of Kansas Medical Center
College of Health Sciences and Hospital
Kansas City, Kansas

Marcia Stanhope, DSN, RN
Division Director
Community Health Nursing and Administration
Associate Professor
College of Nursing
University of Kentucky
Lexington, Kentucky

Lydia (Penny) Tanner, MS, CRN
Coordinator, Quality Assurance Program
Rush Home Health Service
Chicago, Illinois

Donna Wagner, MSN, RN
Quality Assurance Manager
Upjohn HealthCare Services
Kalamazoo, Michigan

Sally Whitten, MPH, RN
Visiting Nurse Services
Calhoun County
Battle Creek, Michigan

Ilene Zuckerman, PharmD
Assistant Professor
University of Maryland School of Pharmacy
Baltimore, Maryland

Foreword

The Community Health Nursing Area of the University of Michigan School of Nursing identified a need for home health care nurses to be able to network with colleagues in order to address issues that arise within the industry. A forum was needed for nurses to address clinical, administrative, research, and educational issues of home health care. In 1985 the First National Nursing Symposium on Home Health Care was held in Ann Arbor, Michigan, sponsored by the Community Health Nursing Area of the University of Michigan School of Nursing. This symposium brought together over five hundred nurses from across the United States to discuss current and emerging nursing issues in the field of home health care. One of the major interest areas at that first symposium was quality assurance in the delivery of home care. It probably can safely be assumed that the majority of home health care agencies strive to provide quality care for clients. The question of concern is, How does an organization measure quality? Who determines quality? How can quality be assured?

Each year the number of papers concerning quality assurance in home care that are submitted to the annual nursing symposium on home health care has increased in number. This is an indication of the major concern for the quality of care and its importance in research. The Fourth National Nursing Symposium on Home Health Care in 1988 presented an expanded session on current research and interventions for quality assurance in home care.

Many of the authors of this book have presented papers concerning quality assurance in home care at one of the four national nursing symposiums. These papers and presentations have had an excellent reception by conference attendees.

There are few textbooks or reference books in the field of home care, and none focus completely on the issue of quality assurance. This book will thus meet a pressing need experienced by professionals involved in home care. It will provide a collection of papers dealing with the main issues in quality assurance and allow presentation of the knowledge and opinions of experts in the field of home health care. Assurance of quality is one of the most important issues facing the health care delivery system in this country.

In the United States, the health care system is under considerable pressure to become cost-effective while maintaining or increasing the quality of health care. This pressure is being increasingly felt in the home care segment of the delivery system. Compared with hospitals, home care represents a very small financial share of the health care dollar, but it is viewed by some third party payers as having potential for servicing a considerable number of clients and families.

Home care is often perceived and marketed as a new delivery system for health care. In reality, home care was available before hospitalization became the standard mode of treating illness. Many visiting nurse associations have celebrated their 50th or 75th anniversary in providing home care within their communities.

Home care before the mid-1960s was financed by a sliding fee scale or by limited health insurance benefits. The growth and expansion of home health care was stimulated by the advent of Medicare reimbursement. The payment sources for providing health care resulted in an increase in the number of home health agencies and in the types of such agencies. The new agencies included proprietary, nonprofit national companies and traditional visiting nurse associations.

The proliferation of new agencies in the industry presented new issues and concerns for quality of care. A wider selection of choices in the selection of a home health care agency frequently resulted in confusion among consumers. How can consumers evaluate the quality of care being provided by an agency? How can consumers determine which agency can best meet their needs when they often know very little about the services available through any home health care agency? Friedman published a book to help consumers understand home care and the methods by which services can be obtained. This is a step toward increasing the public's awareness of home care and evaluating the quality of various agencies, which is beyond the scope of many consumers.

The increasing cost of hospital care has led many providers of service and purchasers of care to look toward home care as a cost-effective alternative to hospitalization. The change in the method used by Medicare for reimbursing hospitals for patient care has had the most recent effect on the home health care industry. Patients are often acutely ill when they leave the hospital because of shortened hospital stays. The earlier hospital discharges have resulted in home care becoming an increasingly important part of the health care delivery system.

Maintaining quality in home care for an acutely ill population requires care that is more complex than ever before and the establishment of new standards for care. These new standards concern services that until a few short years ago were not even available in the hospital. The home care industry must set the standards in order to assure quality of care for consumers and to govern itself rather than be governed externally. One issue that underlies the establishment of standards and quality is the need for safe care. Is quality care equivalent to safe care or is quality care at a higher level than safe care?

The concern for quality in home care is not new and has been addressed by many different groups. One question that must be addressed is, Who defines quality care? Professionals are the ones usually expected to determine the standards, but how do professionals define and defend quality when funding sources have different standards of quality expressed through reimbursed benefits? How do professionals meet the needs of clients when funding for care is continually being reduced? It may be easy for professionals to blame funding sources for not providing adequate financial support to assure quality care. It is harder to determine just what is quality care.

Providing high-quality home care is a goal of agencies, but the selection of an agency for home care is often based on cost rather than quality. The lack of standards of comparison for quality is one reason cost is such a major factor in the selection of home care agencies.

The federal government has attempted to assure quality in home care through a certification process that an agency must complete before it can be reimbursed by Medicare. The government continues to address concerns about quality in home care and has made quality assurance a priority issue.

The home care industry is in favor of a voluntary accreditation process that would provide standards of quality developed by home care agencies and agreed upon by the profession. This is a step toward providers controlling the quality of care. An additional purpose of this voluntary accreditation would be to meet the requirements for reimbursement by Medicare and Medicaid. An accreditation mechanism that would provide deemed status and eliminate the need for state certification would also require that assuring quality in home care would be the responsibility of providers of such care.

The future success of home care will depend upon the documentation of quality care that is cost-effective and that can be understood by the consumers of home care. The challenge to nursing leaders is to develop quality assurance programs before they are developed by third party payers. The editor and the authors of this book are to be commended for addressing this important and timely issue in home health care.

Linda Lee Daniel
Chairperson, National Nursing
    Symposium on Home Health Care
Associate Professor
Community Health Nursing
School of Nursing
University of Michigan
Ann Arbor, Michigan

REFERENCE

Friedman, J. *Home Health Care: A Complete Guide for Patients and Their Families*. New York: Fawcett Book Group, 1987.

Introduction

For centuries, home health care was simply care of the sick at home provided by families. It was a component on the illness-wellness continuum that was "assumed"; it received little attention from anyone except the relatively few individuals directly involved in community and public health activities. However, with the creation of Medicare and Medicaid in 1965 as a response to "access" and the cost containment concerns that culminated in 1983 in the Medicare prospective payment system (PPS) based on DRGs, home care services have experienced a resurgence. It has also become obvious to providers and recipients alike that with the issues of the future including an aging population, a federal government (the nation's largest single purchaser of health care through Medicare) struggling to provide coverage, and continuing technological advancements, *quality* must become the central issue for those concerned with health policy.

The current and future variations on the perennial concerns for access-cost-quality require new models. Given the prospect of a financially driven health care system, the worries of consumers and payers regarding the cost-benefit performance of the system are being heightened. Answers are being sought as to whether quality of services will benefit from competitive market forces. It has become increasingly evident that the public and private sectors together must search for a more efficient health care system: a system that is responsive, progressive, and delivers quality care.

There has never been lack of perceived or real need for the monitoring of quality care; the transformation into reality has been the arduous task. Aside from economic considerations, the elusive concept of quality includes physical, psychological, functional, and social interpretations that vary with the perspective of the examiner. The term *quality* implies dis-

tinguishing characteristics that determine value, rank, or degree of excellence. Quality assurance is a process, not a goal. Quality standards are determined by experts, accountable practitioners who perform diagnostic, therapeutic, prognostic, and other health care activities that are expected to result in an improvement of their clients' health status.

While there exists a considerable literature that addresses quality assurance and evaluation techniques, there is a dearth of literature that suggests how results of monitoring and evaluation can and should cause behavioral and organizational changes. This is especially true in home health care. Compared to other components in the continuum of care, home care has a special problem regarding quality assurance. Maintaining a person at home includes supporting that person's health and functional ability in an objectively defined manner as well as preserving their personal lifestyle to a far greater extent than is possible in any other long-term care setting. To perform such activities, the provider enters the client's domain and becomes the "welcome intruder." In the absence of other observers, such as exist in acute care and other health care settings, monitoring and evaluating performance and services provided to clients becomes even more critical.

Quality Assurance for Home Health Care was written for all who are involved in the field of home health care and committed to enhancing the quality of care. It was written by and for administrators responsible for managing dynamic agencies with limited resources; quality assurance coordinators involved in designing, implementing, and evaluating programs in their agencies; educators responsible for preparing professionals to practice in the home environment and provide quality care to clients; and consultants involved in reviewing current situations, expanding the impact of research, and trying to blend the public and private sectors into a system able to provide the best care possible.

The material for this book was organized to allow multiple entry points. Depending on the reader's needs or concerns, an individual chapter or chapters will provide the information needed, using case studies, practical examples, and figures, tables, exhibits, and appendixes. Through their practical experience and expertise, the many contributors have produced information that will be useful to everyone, regardless of the differing size, social and political organizational structure, or diversity of services of the home health care agency.

Quality Assurance for Home Health Care was designed to address quality of care issues in the numerous and diverse aspects of home health care. To appreciate the growth and development of home care, the author of Chapter 1 provides a comprehensive review of care provided in the home and the implications of the past for the present and future. Only by appreciating the historical development of home care can we fully understand its importance in the current health care delivery system.

As discussed in Chapter 2, quality assurance will not succeed in any organization without the commitment and support of administration. Governing bodies, valuing their clients and providers, must dedicate sufficient resources (including people, time, equipment, and dollars) to the monitoring of quality care. Realistically, they must be capable of designing programs that merge clinical and financial data for the purpose of improving care.

Regardless of the model or system chosen to guide activities, the quality assurance process, which is described in Part II, is essentially the same. The process must begin with an assessment and clarification of beliefs and values relative to "quality." As noted in Chapter 3, professional and organizational goals must be congruent for quality assurance programs to be successful. Any agency must assess its organizational structure, be committed to its philosophy and its mission statement, and dedicate sufficient resources to fulfill its mission. Only an agency with a well-defined quality assurance program that effectively articulates and monitors its purpose can respond to the expectations and needs of the community it serves by providing appropriate programs and services.

According to Chapter 4, standards are the "explication of the desired level of quality." In order to provide an appreciation of the standards applicable to home health care, they have been classified according to agency, program, practice, and client. The author has recognized the three traditional categories of quality of care standards: (1) structural standards, which focus on organizational form, facilities, equipment, fiscal resources and management, the number and qualifications of staff, and other indices that tend to measure an agency's capacity to deliver services; (2) process standards, which focus on the actual procedures followed in delivering care and the interactions and behaviors of the provider; and (3) outcome standards, which are concerned with the end result of care, that is, whether any measurable alteration in the health or social status of the client occurred as a result of the

services rendered. Succinct summaries and selected examples with numerous references will assist the administrator, practitioner, educator, and researcher to explore integrated systems for implementing standards.

Indicators (i.e., any situation, function, or event that is reasonably frequent in the practices being studied and for which there is sound evidence that good medical care is beneficial) provide the basis for problem identification. In addition to assisting the reader in choosing high-risk, high-volume, high-benefit, problem prone aspects of care that should be monitored, the author of Chapter 5 discusses four group techniques: (1) the focus group, (2) the nominal group process, (3) quality circles, and (4) the delphi technique. These techniques can assist groups in identifying problems, setting priorities, and determining appropriate methodologies. Gaining a consensus on what is important to an agency, its practitioners, and recipients of care will contribute toward successfully monitoring and improving the critical indicators.

Although it is commonly thought that there is a lack of information regarding data collection mechanisms for measuring quality of care at home, a moderate amount of literature of a generic nature does exist that is useful for home health care. The author of Chapter 6 has provided the reader with a thorough review of those published reports that focus on practical applications and those that contain research. By building on established measures and standardizing them, agencies will discover useful tools that are both valid and reliable.

Pressures on agencies to provide evidence of quality care come from a variety of sources, for example, fiscal intermediaries, such as commercial insurance carriers and Medicare and Medicaid; state and local community funding groups; state mandates and requirements; legislators concerned with national health insurance and PROs; and professional organizations. Documentation is frequently considered the lifeblood of the organization. With accurate and appropriate documentation, payments will be received and denials will be avoided. The author of Chapter 7 provides the reader with a thorough understanding of documentation, including the whys and hows. Numerous examples of Medicare forms, plans of treatment, multidisciplinary progress notes, summary notes, a complete client's chart for reimbursement purposes, and professional documentation of practice are presented.

As noted in Chapter 8, the quality assurance process is never complete until the program's effectiveness and efficiency have been evaluated. Whether at the organizational level or at the provider-client level, it is imperative to know if the program is (1) providing direction and guidelines for selecting and evaluating critical clinical and administrative problems and (2) generating the data needed both to make decisions regarding practice and to implement corrective action within a reasonable time, thereby causing identifiable improvement in client care and provider performance. Recognizing that evaluation is a process, a means to an end, evaluation of the quality assurance program should include both formative evaluation (which assesses throughout the duration of the program how well the program is achieving its goals and objectives, with changes to improve its operation as needed) and also summative evaluation (which focuses on the attainment of agency goals and activities and their necessity or relevance for rationale decision making concerning future planning). Thus program evaluation in the quality assurance process is essential to the existence of providers and their development and growth.

The issues of quality assurance cut across the boundaries of professional parochialism and involve all disciplines. This is especially critical in home health care, where many individuals representing various professions and nonprofessional groups are accountable for providing care to clients in their homes. While autonomous in their practice, they function interdependently, each contributing a distinct part of the total service package; thus case management and quality care is contingent on communication among the various actors. Part III of this book is intended to highlight some of the major actors in this delivery system and demonstrate the unique and significant contribution each makes in caring for clients in their home.

The author of Chapter 9 elucidates the staff nurse's perspective by emphasizing the need for commitment to quality care, the agency, and professional development. Case management is thoroughly discussed, as is the significance that staffing patterns, productivity, and peer review have for assuring quality care.

The physician is the gatekeeper in home health care—the individual who "writes the order" for others to provide care at home. In Chapter 10, the author discusses the delivery system and the physician's renewed interest in home care; the roles and responsibilities of the physician, the medical director, and state and county medical societies; and the advantages and disadvantages of home care.

As a major actor in the health care team, the social worker is concerned with situations in the lives of clients that either alter the benefits of health care provided or contribute to the presenting problem(s). The author of Chapter 11 frames his discussion of structure, process, and outcome factors so as to examine the delivery and documentation of care. Concerned with the social realm that influences the well-being of the client, the social worker functions in concert with other care providers to achieve the goal of optimal physical, emotional, and social recovery for the client.

The therapist in home health care performs traditional services in a nontraditional setting, integrating the client, the caregiver, and the medical goals to attain maximum functioning. As noted in Chapter 12, the therapist becomes an active teacher, instructing clients and their families to assume responsibility for their own rehabilitation.

While home health care agencies usually do not employ pharmacists as part of their staff, the pharmacist's knowledge and skills have become increasingly important in home care. As the client population ages, the concern of clients and families about medication administration and side effects will increase, as will their desire for a general understanding regarding indications for drug therapy. The author of Chap-

ter 13 discusses the utilization of today's clinical pharmacist in monitoring the drug therapy of all clients.

While practice issues affecting quality are just as numerous in home health care as in other segments of the delivery system, the issues assume unique meaning for professionals when care is provided in the client's place of residence. In Part IV of this book, authors have addressed major issues and their impact on quality of care, commencing with high tech.

With technological advances occurring at an exponential rate in the past decade, homes can now be sites for virtually all acute care services. "High-tech" requires competent staff to provide around the clock services. As discussed in Chapter 14, agencies must employ both internal and external review mechanisms to monitor and evaluate their vendor relationships and manage risks to clients, professionals, and the agency.

Legal and ethical dilemmas related to quality assurance must be addressed in home health care. All parties involved have rights and responsibilities that must be understood so that recipients as well as providers of care can contribute to quality care by preventing or diminishing agency and corporate liability. This issue is treated in Chapter 15.

Two important nonprofessional providers of day-to-day support services in home care are the home health aide and the home companion. These providers are largely undertrained. The author of Chapter 16 gives readers an appreciation of the process one agency experienced in developing its home companion program. Comparing the roles and responsibilities of the home health aide and the home companion will assist agencies in monitoring and evaluating these individuals and understanding the contribution they can make to client care.

Often praised as a measure to contain escalating costs of health care, the shift of an individual's convalescent care from a hospital or another health care institution to the home places new demands on the client caregivers. The author of Chapter 17 discusses the burdens and strains placed on family members and, using the AFFIRM model, provides a detailed set of interventions for preparing and assisting caregivers to perform their role.

Spurred by the Medicare prospective payment system, clients are discharged from hospitals "sicker and quicker." Assuring continuity of care is critical as professionals manage the transition from hospital to home and, finally, discharge the clients from home services when they are capable of self-care. The author of Chapter 18 discusses the barriers effecting and affecting continuity of health care and outlines strategies for ensuring continuity of care and appropriate discharge planning.

Putting theory into practice can be a frustrating and time-consuming exercise for individuals who have limited time to take from daily practice and limited resources to dedicate to the overall process. Chapter 19 shares with the reader the experiences of two agencies that differ in organizational structure and in their available resources. Case Study I deals with a small hospital-based agency. The agency has (1) a conceptual practice model, that defines the scope of community nursing practice and articulates standards; (2) an organized committee structure that both facilitates and monitors compliance to the established standards and takes corrective action where indicated; and (3) an established evaluation plan that delineates the specific areas to be monitored or audited and by whom. Case Study II describes the development of a quality assurance program for coordinated home care programs in Alberta, a process characterized by local and provincial energies and perspectives working collaboratively. Among other things, the various individuals grappled with (1) establishing a quality assurance framework; (2) determining the values of clients, families, and caregivers, which resulted in related outcome criteria; (3) selecting measurement tools, scales, or items to address each of the outcome areas; and (4) pretesting the client outcome tool for reliability and validity. Both of these case studies emphasize the need for systematically evaluating the effectiveness of existing programs and for providing accurate and timely data with which providers and clients can make appropriate decisions concerning whether to maintain or change the current system. Readers will find both of these different experiences helpful in analyzing their present situations and hopefully will be able to incorporate the useful information in their settings.

The current state of knowledge about the home health care field and about quality assurance for home health care services is woefully inadequate. Home care has acquired an important position in the health care field. The major causes of the home care resurgence include (1) demographics, (2) a trend away from institutionalization, (3) an increased awareness of the potential benefits of prevention and wellness programs, (4) competitive market forces, and (5) portable technology.

Accepted definitions of quality health care must be developed by providers and recipients of services from both the private and public sectors. There must be agreement that providers will monitor and evaluate the care and services they provide and that regulators will use the data appropriately and realistically. While historically professionals in health care have been seen as the establishers of quality standards, in reality, to be successful, standards must also have input from clients, trustees of organizations, payers, and government. The peer review process is a meaningful quality function, as is client satisfaction data. Prospective payment systems or any "pricing system" for health services must be based on quality measures. Quality must not be sacrificed for financial viability. Competition in the market must be based on both quality and price as care is managed effectively and efficiently.

A combination of social developments is affecting our national life, including the aging of the population and the attendant need for chronic care and catastrophic illness insurance; the promotion of preventive care and the recognition that people have a responsibility to improve their lifestyle; the federal budget deficit; public health issues such as AIDS, the surplus of physicians, and the shortage of nurses; the push for deinstitutionalization; and the growing underutilization of hospital capacity. The future of the health care system will be determined by all of these factors, plus the irresistible development of technology and the resulting ethical issues. Providers need to *manage* the delivery of quality health care in the current finance-oriented environment, and professionals and organizations need to coexist as "colleagues." Clients need to have realistic expectations and inform policymakers and fiscal intermediaries of their wishes. Most importantly, clients need and deserve quality care; they deserve more than a minimally safe level of care which government surveys aim to address with their move to a two-tiered health system.

With home care having the potential of being a major driving force in the health care system in the next decade, quality assurance programs have never been as needed, and they can no longer only be given lip service. Quality assurance must be incorporated into daily practice—it has become our most valuable tool for survival!

Claire Gavin Meisenheimer

Part I

Historical and Administrative Perspectives

Chapter 1

Home Care: Past Perspectives and Implications for the Present and Future

Marsha K. Stanhope

Hospital Costs on the Rise. Home Care Essential for Those Needing Follow-up Posthospital Care or Unable to Afford High Cost of Hospital Care. These headlines in 1983, after the introduction of the prospective payment system for Medicare services provided in acute care hospitals, expressed the same outcry as when William Rathbone introduced in 1859 the first district nursing service in England and Lillian Wald developed in 1902 the Henry Street Settlement to provide home care for the poor in the Lower East Side of New York City. History indicates that home care's purposes are not much different today than they were in its early development. Due to economic and sociopolitical expectations, however, home care services have assumed a more prominent position in the health care delivery system.

Throughout the development of the industry, the definition of home care has become more complex and the issue of quality assurance has grown in importance. For centuries, home care was defined simply as care of the sick at home. Today, a more comprehensive definition of home care has been prepared by the Department of Health and Human Services (DHHS). A work group of DHHS has defined home health care as

> that component of a continuum of comprehensive health care whereby health services are provided to individuals and families in their places of residence for the purpose of promoting, maintaining, or restoring health, or of maximizing the level of independence, while minimizing the effects of disability and illness, including terminal illness. Services appropriate to the needs of the individual patient and family are planned, coordinated, and made available

by providers organized for the delivery of home care through the use of employed staff, contractual arrangements, or a combination of the two patterns.[1]

Quality assurance issues arose early in the development of home care services. The first attempts at assuring quality began with the use of field supervisors to monitor the work of the providers of care in the home. Early standards focused on education for nurses working in home care. Today, quality assurance issues are complex and these activities in home care agencies are often dictated by regulations of federal, state, and local government agencies.

Quality assurance involves the monitoring of patient care activities to determine their degree of excellence.[2] Quality assurance in health care can be likened to quality control in industry. The purpose of quality assurance is to set standards for care and production, to evaluate care provided and productivity of providers based on the chosen standards, and to take action to bring about change in care or productivity when they do not meet the standards.[3]

Quality assurance is particularly difficult in home care, because of the nature of the services provided. Most of the services are provided in the patient's own environment and away from the agency's facilities. A consensus among home care agencies and professional organizations has been difficult to attain regarding the parameters of quality in home care. While there are many objective aspects to quality assurance, there are also the many subjective issues that arise from the values the consumers and providers place on the services; the consumer demand for services, and the outcomes of services needed by the consumers. A stroll back through history will show the evolution of home care and quality assurance issues throughout the centuries.

EARLY BEGINNINGS

Home care, when analyzed from century to century, clearly has had its peaks and valleys, its periods of growth and its periods of decline. Visiting the sick was initially spoken of in the New Testament as a form of charity. It is reported that long before the Christian era rabbis encouraged members of the Jewish community to visit the sick in their homes to aid them and relieve them of their suffering. Phoebe is considered the first visiting nurse (reported by St. Paul).[4]

The rise of monasticism in the sixth century resulted in a more concerted effort to care for the sick in the home. One of the most important facets of a monk's work was to nurse the sick of surrounding communities.

From the Crusades came the military nursing orders and the prominent Order of Saint John of Jerusalem, which was founded in the 11th century and still in existence in 1874 in England.[5] These military nursing orders eventually developed visiting nursing services resembling the district nursing service that later was created in England. It is recorded that at the beginning of the 14th century 200,000 women working in Belgium, France, Germany, and Switzerland provided home nursing and social work services through the secular order of the Beguine.[6]

Throughout the Middle Ages important secular orders involved men, women, the rich, the educated, and those of "lowly birth" in care of the sick. During this time, people provided services for the "good of soul" and from feelings of mercy. These motives were considered honorable and were welcome in an age when cruelty and the infliction of suffering was the rule.[7] As these secular orders developed, the Church placed much pressure on them to either voluntarily or involuntarily come under the control of the Church, since for centuries past care of the sick had been deemed to belong under the purview of the Church.

The 17th century marked the beginning of the development of a new social consciousness. During this time there grew a feeling that a corporate responsibility for the welfare of the poor and the sick existed apart from any personal benefit to be derived from providing health care services. Responsibility for the care of the sick in the home began to be less of an individual matter and also less strictly confined to the Church. During this era, in 1601, the first poor law was enacted in England, bringing many positive changes and social reforms.

The work of Saint Vincent de Salle, who founded the order of the Virgin Mary, served as the model for Saint Vincent de Paul's efforts to develop nursing and social welfare in 17th century France. In 1617, Saint Vincent de Paul organized the Sisterhood of the Dames de Charite, "ladies" who visited the sick in their homes, much like modern day public health nurses. The work of the sisterhood was described as excellent in the beginning, but as the number of "ladies" increased,

difficulties arose and the performance of the "ladies" was described as "uneven." Often their husbands objected to their being exposed to the dangers of illness and impure air.[8]

Difficulties in attempting to supervise the large number of workers led to the first quality assurance measure recorded, that is, the appointment of what in the 20th century would be called a field supervisor. With the help of Mademoiselle le Gras, Saint Vincent de Paul soon realized that the productivity of the "ladies" was not at the level that he wished. After some deliberation he decided that the "ladies" were not quite the type of woman needed to care for the sick at home. He therefore solicited "healthy, hearty peasant girls of France" as the new recruits for providing care. These new recruits were initially called Servants of the Poor and worked under the Dames de Charite. This experiment worked out so well that Saint Vincent, with the help of Mademoiselle le Gras, inaugurated a training program for his workers. The first training involved advice on relationships with physicians and what would now be called principles of social work. In 1633 the Servants of the Poor became known as the Order of the Sisters of Charity. An affiliate of the Sisters of Charity, called the Sisters of Charity of St. Joseph, was created and placed under the direction of Elizabeth Bailey Seaton in July 1809 at Emitsburg, Maryland.[9]

From the latter part of the 17th century to the middle of the 19th century, rich and poor sick people alike were often cared for by overworked, ignorant, and often unprincipled women. The position of nurse was not considered one of dignity, and little effort was made to find women of good character to care for the ill. This lasted until modern day nursing was introduced by Florence Nightingale.[10] With the increase in social consciousness and the call for reform in all aspects of life in England, it was natural that nursing should share a part in these reforms. However, in spite of this new philosophy, home care was organized on such a small scale and so sporadically that it had little effect on the illness problems of those ineligible or unable to pay for hospitalization.

In 1840 Mrs. Fry, of prison reform fame, made an attempt to bring skilled nursing to the poor in England through the establishment of the Society of Protestant Sisters of Charity. In 1848 the Society of Saint Johns' House was founded as the first purely nursing order in the Anglican Church.[11] The object of this society was to raise the standard of nursing and to provide nurses not only for hospitals but for the care of the poor sick at home. However, it is to William Rathbone of Liverpool that credit is given for founding the first public health nursing association of modern times. Rathbone's wife, who died in 1859 after a lengthy illness, had been attended by a trained nurse, whose care had brought her great relief.[12] A philanthropist who had a long-standing interest in helping the poor, Rathbone asked the nurse, Mary Robinson, to engage in a three-month experiment providing home care for the poor. After one month, Robinson was so devastated by the conditions in the homes that she asked to be relieved. Rathbone persuaded her to go on, and after the remaining two months she had established such great rapport and had such good success with her patients that she asked to continue. The system of district nursing in Liverpool was based on this experiment.

During this time nurses had two purposes: to serve as attendants to the sick and to provide social reform. Rathbone recognized that the nurses must be trained for their work, that they must not interfere with the religious vows of their patients, and that they must not be almoners or social workers. Rathbone also recognized that nurses must be carefully supervised when providing care in the home. To provide supervision, Rathbone engaged "lady" superintendents, who, while not nurses, were placed in charge of each district, with the nurses directly responsible to them for the care given. These "ladies" were credited with supervising the personal services given to the patients and assisting the community to understand the aim of district nursing and its importance. Other towns and communities followed the example of Liverpool and developed district nursing services. Manchester, in the development of its service, for the first time replaced the untrained "lady" superintendents with trained nurses who supervised the work of subordinate nurses and made weekly visits to the homes of their patients.[13]

The idea of district nursing spread rapidly over England, but there was no standardization and only minimal training for the nurses in the field. In some instances, nurses were employed with only three to six months of hospital training. For other nurses, the training was even less, and they had to shoulder their heavy responsibilities with inadequate preparation. This led to an effort which met with little success: to coordinate and standardize nursing by the formation, in 1861, of the East London Nursing Society.

Failures at early attempts at standardization brought investigations into public health nursing and the establishment of the Metropolitan National Nursing Association, founded in 1875. The emphasis of the association was to employ only gentle, educated women to provide nursing care in the home, because nurses in the home were given greater responsibility in carrying out physicians' orders than nurses in hospitals. The association suggested that women of education would be able to accept this greater responsibility; that the vocation would attract women who were interested in independent employment; and that these nurses, from the ranks of educated women, would have greater influence over their patients in virtue of their higher social position and would thus enhance the image of professional nurses in the eye of the public.[14]

This new movement in district nursing gained the attention of Queen Victoria, whose efforts brought in public and private funds for the establishment of Queen Victoria's Jubilee Institute for Nurses in 1889. This institute was to prepare nurses for working with the poor sick in their homes and to extend district nursing throughout the British empire. In addition to a three-year course in the hospital, these nurses were given six months of postgraduate training in district nursing. The creation of the institute had a great impact on public health nursing and resulted in the first formal training for nurses in home care. Early efforts in home care established that hospital training alone does not equip a nurse for the duties of district public health nursing and that nursing in the home is social,

educational, and preventive work and is not only remedial or curative in the narrow senses of these terms.

DEVELOPMENT OF HOME CARE IN THE UNITED STATES

As in England in the early days, so in America were the sick cared for by nuns and sisters. The Sisters of Charity of St. Joseph was established in Maryland in 1809; the Sisters of Mercy, an order founded in Dublin in 1827 by Kathryn McCauley, came to the United States in December 1843. Formed in 1822, the Sisters of Bon Secours of Paris established an order in the United States in the 1840s. The Sisters of the Holy Cross at Le Mans, France, established in 1839, moved an order to Bertrand, Michigan, in 1844. Aside from the work of sisters and the nuns, the first organized visiting nurse work was done by the Ladies Benevolent Society of Charleston, South Carolina, founded in 1813. This society had a visiting committee of 16 ladies, who were allotted a certain portion of the city in which to visit the sick at home. When it became essential, nurses were hired by the visitors to provide nursing care to the sick at home. This society lasted well over 50 years, until the beginning of the Civil War. The society was revived in 1902 when a trained nurse was employed to carry on the work of the society.[15]

In 1832 the Lying in Charity for attending women in their homes was established in Philadelphia. In 1842 this organization was combined with a subsidiary organization called the Nurse Society. These nurses were given training to assist them in their work in the home and were supervised by an active committee of "Philadelphia Ladies." It is noted that each nurse gave 84 days alternately to the care of the rich and the care of the poor. In a private-duty-like arrangement, each nurse attended a single patient. Nevertheless, it is said that this society offered systematic nursing services to the poor at home at a time when it was very unusual to have such services.[16]

Organized visiting nursing, the precursor of modern home care, was first established in the United States in March 1877, when the women's branch of the New York City Mission first sent trained nurses into the homes of the poor sick. The first home care nurse, Frances Root, was a member of the first class to be graduated from the new training school at Bellevue Hospital.[17] The establishment of the first visiting nurses association in the United States occurred in 1885, when the Buffalo District Nursing Association was begun by Mrs. Elizabeth Marshall. In 1886 Boston formed the Instructive Visiting Nursing Association to promote health education. During this same period, Philadelphia developed a visiting nurses association that led the way for establishing a pay service. This association appointed a nurse superintendent and adopted a uniform for nurses to wear while working with patients.[18]

By 1890, some 13 years after the first nurse was sent out by the New York City Mission, 21 visiting nurses associations existed in the United States, most employing only one nurse each.[19] These associations preceded the development, in 1893, of the Henry Street Settlement, founded in New York by Lillian Wald.

Lillian Wald, an 1891 graduate of the New York Hospital School of Nursing, spent a year working at the New York Juvenile Asylum. Thirsting for more medical knowledge, she entered the Women's Medical College in New York. While there, she and a fellow nurse, Mary Brewster, were asked to go to New York's Lower East Side to lecture to immigrant mothers on the care of the sick. Through this work, Miss Wald became aware of the situation of the poor sick in this area of New York. Together, she and Mary Brewster created a nurses settlement house in one of the slum sections of the Lower East Side which became a center for the provision of visiting nurses services for the poor.

While initially Mary Brewster and Lillian Wald had to seek out the sick, word quickly spread of their services and as a result their patient population grew, with referrals coming from families and physicians. These two women provided services for all, making no distinction between those who could and could not pay. They sought to provide health education as well as care of the sick. They also sought to provide communication between patients and their physicians (for patients who had physicians). If a patient had no physician, they tried to find one for the patient. They arranged hospital treatment for those who were in need of it and made provisions for the daily comforts of bedding and bathing.[20]

By 1895 the volume of work necessitated an increase in nurses and a move to accommodations at 265 Henry Street, which later became known as the Henry Street Settlement House. The women kept data on the work they did, including the number of visits, types of care given, referral sources, disposition of cases, and diagnoses of cases. In addition to the hospital training of the nurses, each new nurse had to undergo a probation period and training under the auspices of a nurse of the Henry Street Settlement. The Henry Street Settlement was a highly organized enterprise with many departments. In addition to the nursing staff, other men and women were involved in various social and civic efforts. The model of the Henry Street Settlement suggests the model of existing home care agencies.

As the demands on public health nurses visiting in the home increased, the question of the nurses' education became more important; hospital training was not sufficient for public health nurses. The demand for nurses experienced in providing care in the home greatly exceeded the supply of trained nurses, and community after community had to begin nursing associations with untrained nurses. Undergraduate education sometimes involved an affiliation with a visiting nurses association that allowed students to leave the hospital for short periods of training in the districts. The first postgraduate course in public health nursing was offered in 1906 by the Instructive District Nursing Association of Boston. Following these very simple training programs, Columbia University, in 1910, offered the first university course in public health nursing. This set a precedent for higher education to become involved in public health nursing education.[21]

In 1909 the Metropolitan Life Insurance Company began offering home nursing services to its millions of industrial policy holders in the United States and Canada. Initially, arrangements were made with Lillian Wald and the Henry Street Settlement to provide these nursing services. By 1912 Metropolitan was offering home nursing services from 589 nursing centers. These centers provided an opportunity not only to develop payment mechanisms based on the exact cost of visits to patients, but also to engage in a number of valuable health studies and to collect data based on statistics kept by the nurses for future projections about the health care needs of the policy holders. Sixteen years later John Hancock Mutual Life Insurance Company established a similar service for its policy holders.[22]

Following the example of the Visiting Nurse Society of Philadelphia (the first to establish a pay service) and of the insurance companies, other nursing organizations began to develop pay services. In some instances payment was made on an hourly basis, by appointment, or by capitation to meet the needs of those who could pay for nursing services.[23] The introduction of payment for services marked a change in the philosophy of home nursing services—from providing services only to the "worthy" poor to providing services to people with moderate income who required continuous nursing care and household assistance.

Industrial nursing also grew out of the early visiting nurses associations. In 1895 Fletcher Proctor, one-time governor of Vermont, and Adamelle Stewart, an 1894 graduate of the Waltham Training School, introduced district nursing into several villages whose residents were employees of the Vermont Marble Company. This service was essentially a home service, with patient referrals coming from physicians.[24]

The number of public health visiting nurses in the United States increased from 136 in 1902 to 3000 in 1912. With funding from both private and public sources, visiting nurses were employed by some 810 agencies, including visiting nurse associations, city and state boards of health and education, private clubs and societies, the tuberculosis leagues, hospitals and dispensaries, business concerns, settlements and day nurseries, churches, charitable organizations, and other organizations.[25]

Although by 1911 the American Nurses' Association (ANA) and the League for Nursing Education (currently, the National League for Nursing) had already been established, public health nurses were essentially unorganized. At this time, a small group of nurses requested that the ANA and NLN appoint a joint committee to consider means of standardization for public health nurses. This committee concluded that a new national organization for public health nurses was needed to adequately meet their needs. As a result, the 810 agencies known to be employing public health nurses were asked to send delegates to an annual meeting of the two organizations held in Chicago in 1912.

The meetings continued for two days, and on the second day the National Organization for Public Health Nursing was voted into existence. Lillian Wald was its first president. The objectives of the organization were to encourage and standardize public health nursing and to further cooperation between all parties that had an interest in such nursing. The organization's first affiliation was with the American Nurses' Association. It was the first nursing organization to provide for lay as well as nursing membership, so that those engaged in directing the policies of public health nursing, such as board members and officers of local agencies, could be members and have input into the standardization of public health nursing.

The National Organization for Public Health Nursing provided for the development of standards for quality and the collection of data. Among the first committees to be appointed by the organization was one on education. This committee provided an advisory service to colleges and universities to establish guidelines for postgraduate courses in public health nursing. A statistical department of the organization strengthened the periodic census of public health nurses to adequately identify the available pool. A vocational department helped to identify nurses who were appropriate for certain positions and provided agency and individual placement services.

Statistical studies and studies of cost per visit were sponsored by the organization and the Metropolitan and John Hancock Mutual life insurance companies. These studies resulted in better methods of computing costs. It was found that improved work productivity, better supervision, and a better system of staff education steadily increased the known cost of each visit. There was considerable concern that as the price increased, the services would become too costly. However, these data had very little effect on the expansion of public health nursing.[26]

The 1920s, an economically vital period, saw continued expansion of public health nursing. Then came the dramatic crash of the stock market in October 1929 and the beginning of the financial depression in America. Public health nursing was greatly affected as the budgets of private agencies dwindled and reserve funds disappeared. At the same time, visiting nursing work became more complicated because of the social problems experienced by the patients under care and their families.

This crash ushered in an era of changing philosophy concerning the provision of home care services. Less stress was placed on quantitative growth and more on qualitative measures of care provided. However, because of staff reductions, elimination of staff educational programs, and limited supervision, quality could not be assured—at a time when the country most needed comprehensive and effective services.

At this point, the federal government provided aid to the country and began to develop a new relationship among local communities and the state and federal governments. The Federal Emergency Relief Administration provided for allocation of federal funds to states so that nursing care could be given to the employed sick receiving federal relief. The Civil Works Administration provided funds for the use of nurses who were unemployed. These nurses worked primarily for official agencies and institutions. A large number of nurses found themselves in the field of public health without preparation or experience.

HOME CARE TODAY

The system consisting primarily of one-nurse public and private visiting nurse services and the visiting nurse services of the two major insurance companies lasted into the 1940s. With the discovery of antibiotics, the implementation of immunization programs, and the development of new technologies, hospitals began to enter the home care field. The new health care discoveries were given credit for the shift of focus in health care from acute and communicable diseases to chronic illness. Hospitals became overcrowded and costs were increasing. Home care services were seen as a way to alleviate some of the crowding problems and to achieve cuts in cost.

The Montefiore Hospital Home Care Program in New York City, which began in 1947, is described as the model of modern home care. Seemingly based on a concept originally developed at the Henry Street Settlement, the Montefiore model was a comprehensive health care program providing medical, nursing, and social services directed toward the care of the chronically ill. In 1958 the program expanded to include physical therapy, vocational rehabilitation, occupational therapy, and laboratory, x-ray, and nutrition services. The program would also provide for housekeeping and homemaker services upon individual arrangement.[27]

Through the forties and fifties, home care agencies existed in random variations, including hospital-based programs, voluntary agencies, official agencies, and combination agencies. In addition, private home care agencies either were affiliated with insurance companies or were free-standing agencies. Agencies were funded through private philanthropic organizations, charitable organizations such as United Way, and official public funds.

During the 1960s, a program of "continued care" between the hospital and home was developed through the cooperative efforts of Blue Cross of New York, local hospitals, physicians, and public health nursing agencies. The purpose of the program was to provide home care after hospitalization, to reduce extended hospital stays, and to reduce costs.[28] To evaluate the quality of care provided for the Blue Cross subscribers and in conjunction with Blue Cross, Phaneuf developed a retrospective nursing process audit. Subscales of the audit were derived from the functions of nursing as stated by Lesnik and Anderson.[29] This audit instrument was one of the first instruments to be employed in public health nursing for the purpose of evaluating the quality of care.

According to many, the introduction of Medicare and Medicaid, titles XVIII and XIX of the Federal Social Security Act, had the most profound effect on the change in home care services. These 1965 amendments to the Social Security Act of 1935 set specific guidelines that home care agencies had to meet in order to be eligible for reimbursement of select services. When home care services first became allowable under Medicare, home care was defined as nursing plus one additional service. Other stipulations were placed on patient eligibility for Medicare services, such as that there be intermittent skilled care via a physician's order, homebound status, post-hospital-discharge service only, and a limited number of visits per year. Federal regulations denied services to a large number of the elderly, the chronically ill, and the disabled in need of long-term continuous care and maintenance. They reduced considerably the population of patients who could benefit from home care services and were viewed as limiting provider activities with patients.

Amendments to the Medicare program of the seventies and early eighties resulted in much needed change and helped to solve some of the problems. By 1977 there was a renewed interest in home care as a viable source of health care for meeting the potential or actual needs of some 24 million dependent elderly and disabled people.[30] Nursing visits continued to be the primary service offered to home care patients. New billing systems were introduced, regulations were rewritten to change the eligibility criteria for receiving care, the number of home care days was increased, and services were extended to cover social security recipients who were chronically disabled or had end-stage renal disease. Also, Social Security amendments in 1981 included regulatory changes that allowed the certification of for-profit, proprietary agencies and nullified the three-day hospital requirement for agency admission.

Under the Tax Equity and Fiscal Responsibility Act of 1982, the prospective payment system (PPS) for hospital reimbursement was implemented (beginning in October 1983). As projected, this PPS resulted in an increased demand for home care services, an increased number of hospital referrals of acutely ill patients, changes in patient acuity, a need to increase staff productivity to meet the service demands, and changes in provider skill level requirements. New technologies and durable medical equipment, early hospital discharge for patients, broadening the scope of health care services, more flexibility in length of hours of services, and the need to look at the changing home care regulations of the Health Care Financing Administration (HCFA) were all major issues anticipated in 1983. Initially, there was an indication that patients were more acutely ill and were being discharged earlier from the hospital and that service demand was increasing. While some indications are that the demands for service have leveled off or declined and that acuity levels may not have changed dramatically, as originally anticipated,[31] quality of care remains a major issue.

Quality Assurance

Prior to 1965 the major emphasis regarding quality assurance in home care was on the supervision of nurses in the field, the annual evaluation of agency functioning, the collection of statistical data on patients and patient care to project future needs, and nursing education requirements. With the advent of Medicare coverage for home care services, there seemed to occur a parallel emphasis on quality assurance within the system comprising such services.

Medicare introduced home care coverage in 1965; it included conditions of participation for Medicare agencies and eligibility criteria for patients, but only nominal quality assurance requirements. Medicare was interested in the evaluation of the structure of agencies and in process evaluation. However, standardization of quality assurance programs in home care was nonexistent.

About the time Medicare coverage for home care was introduced, standards of practice were being developed for health providers. In 1966, the American Nurses' Association created the Divisions on Practice in its bylaws. From the Divisions on Practice came standards of care in specialty areas in nursing. For example, standards for community health nursing practice were distributed to ANA Community Health Nursing Division members in 1973. In 1986 these standards were revised. Standards of practice in home care are now available through ANA.

In 1972, the Joint Commission on Accreditation of Healthcare Organizations (Joint Commission) clearly delineated the responsibilities of nursing in its accreditation criteria. The Joint Commission called upon the nursing industry to clearly plan, document, and evaluate nursing care. While currently accrediting approximately 1000 hospital-based home care agencies, the Joint Commission has developed specific standards for home care accreditation, effective June 1988.

In 1972 the Social Security Act was amended to establish professional standards review organizations (PSROs) and to mandate the review of delivery of health care to recipients of Medicare, Medicaid, and Maternal Child Health Benefits. PSROs were replaced by professional review organizations (PROs) as a result of 1983 Social Security amendments. The purpose of PROs is to monitor the implementation of the prospective payment reimbursement system based on diagnostic related groups (DRGs) that is used for recipients in hospitals. As of October 1, 1987, PROs initiated review of home care services as part of their mandate.

Since 1967, the National League for Nursing (NLN) has had an accreditation program for community health and home health agencies. Currently there are 100 agencies, mostly visiting nurse associations and public health departments, that are accredited under the NLN accreditation guidelines. The accreditation process is currently voluntary. However, NLN has developed guidelines for accreditation of home health agencies and, with the Joint Commission, has requested "deemed" status from HCFA to review all home care agencies requesting Medicare certification.

Approval from HCFA and DHHS would allow for uniform standardization of Medicare-approved programs for delivery of home care. It must be remembered that at this time approximately 50 percent of the agencies delivering home care are Medicare-approved agencies. While such accreditation would be a requirement for Medicare-approved agencies, private agencies could also seek this approval under a voluntary program. Such approval would make them automatically eligible for Medicare reimbursement should they desire it.[32]

Quality assurance has many facets. There are several general approaches to quality assurance; they are primarily related to agency structure and involve licensure of agencies, licensure and certification of health care providers rendering care, accreditation of agencies, certification of agencies, and education of providers. More specific approaches to quality assurance in home care are related to review mechanisms established for the purposes of reviewing processes and outcomes of care. Staff review committees and utilization review committees are specifically designed to meet these purposes. In addition, external review of agency structure and of the process and outcomes of care also occurs for Medicare-participating agencies and agencies that are required to have licensure in certain states.

Currently, approximately 33 states and the District of Columbia have licensure laws for home care, which are generally monitored by the state departments of public health or cabinets for health and human services. In addition, a number of states have regulations and standards for home care paraprofessionals. In states where licensure is required, these requirements usually parallel the conditions of participation for Medicare agencies. All states have requirements for nurse licensure and most states have licensure requirements for all other health care providers.

While currently accreditation of agencies by such organizations as NLN or the Joint Commission is not a requirement for Medicare conditions of participation or for state licensure, this is likely to change in the near future. It is anticipated that Medicare accreditation requirements will lead to parallel requirements under state licensing laws. Currently, certification is required only for those agencies wishing Medicare and Medicaid reimbursement through HCFA.

While Medicare does not have a uniform quality-assurance requirement, it is said that the Medicare conditions of participation have had the greatest effect in structuring the nature and type of quality assurance practices in home care agencies. The conditions state that all participating agencies must monitor the extent to which their services are "appropriate, adequate, effective, and efficient." At this writing, HCFA has been directed to develop a standard quality assurance program. Whether they will develop their own is still in question. If NLN or the Joint Commission are given deemed status, it is likely that HCFA will adopt the quality assurance standards of these agencies.

Throughout history there has been much debate about the education of nurses, especially for the delivery of home care services. Should home care nurses be community health nurses or should they have experience in acute and intensive care? The educational issues being debated focus on two major questions. Is community health preparation essential to give a home care nurse a broader knowledge base so that the nurse can provide a patient with promotion, prevention, maintenance, restoration, and rehabilitation services as well as provide resources to assist not only the ill member but all family members to achieve the maximum level of health possible for that family? Or is it necessary to have the nurse prepared in the high-technology skills of acute and intensive care settings in order to deliver a high quality of care primarily to the sick individual within the family?

Perhaps the solution is to offer the community health nurse ongoing staff development so that the nurse can maintain skills in changing high-tech areas and continue to provide the broad

community-based services to the total family, thus making home care more than a "skilled" service. Note that an acute or intensive care nurse is going to be less and less knowledgeable about current high technology the longer he or she is away from the hospital setting; thus additional staff development will be required for the hospital-based nurse who has come to the community, not only in high technology but in the delivery of community-based services and family care. Perhaps new configurations of personnel responsibilities can enhance the use of several types of nurses in home care.

In addition to the general approaches to evaluating the structure of agencies, such as licensure, accreditation, and certification, the specific quality assurance mechanisms in place for evaluating the structure, procedures, and outcomes of care involve internal and external review processes. (A brief outline of some quality assurance indicators is provided in Table 1-1.) These approaches are also discussed in other chapters.

FUTURE PROSPECTS

If history is a predictor of the future, home care will continue to have its peaks and valleys, depending on economic issues, consumer satisfaction, and changing health care delivery needs. Whether Medicare will continue, based on cost-effectiveness and efficiency data, to support home care as an alternative to hospital care is a question that must eventually be answered. Total payment coverage for home care for Medicare recipients or future copayment and private insurance coverage for all home care recipients will have an economic impact on agencies and patients.

Concern over the quality of health care delivered in the home, where monitoring of care is difficult, to a population that is extremely vulnerable has had negative consequences for the consumer and for the payers of services. In 1986 the Senate Select Committee on Aging held the "black box hearings" on quality in home care, during which instances of wrongdoings and deficiencies in patient care were uncovered. Fraud and abuse will be a major focus of legislators and consumers.

HCFA is calling for greater emphasis on outcome studies so as to assess the impact of home care services on patients. Health care providers have often argued that evaluations of outcomes are difficult and precarious at best. Even when a consumer has the best care possible, the outcome may not be positive. The consumers may be dissatisfied with the care, and while the result of care may be a longer life, often the quality of that life is questionable. Also, the outcome of care may not be apparent in the short term and a change in health status may be temporary. Donabedian argues that while these are concerns within the health care system, one can look beyond this and effectively measure outcome by looking at the outcomes for the total population served by an agency (including the effects of access to the service, resource allocation, and external benefits) as well as the conformity of professional performance to professional norms. In considering outcomes, one must consider mortality, morbidity, and dysfunction using a

Table 1-1 Structure, Process, and Outcome Indicators for a Home Care Quality Assurance Program

Structure	Process	Outcome
Internal	*Internal*	*Internal*
Annual agency evaluation	Application of provider standards	Clinical trials
Mission	Provider performance evaluations	Tracer evaluation
Purpose	Concurrent audit of provider care/service	Sentinel evaluation
Objectives	Retrospective audit of provider care/service	Criterion referenced patient care audits
Impact	Prospective audit of service needs	Morbidity data
Supplies/equipment		Mortality data
Administrative organization		Functional status indicators
Provider qualifications		
Facilities		
Policies and procedures		
Prospective, current, retrospective service demands/needs		
Budget		
External	*External*	*External*
Medicare certification review	Medicare review	Malpractice litigation
State licensure review	State licensure review	Joint Commission/NLN accreditation review
Joint Commission/NLN accreditation review	Joint Commission/NLN accreditation review	Patient satisfaction
PRO review	PRO review	Provider satisfaction
Fiscal intermediary review	60 day patient reauthorization	Referral source satisfaction
	Satisfaction of patients, providers, referral sources	

time series method of evaluation. In addition, home care providers and consumers must obtain some measure of the meaning of quality of life to the individual patient and family. A patient-provider transaction should be assessed based on the patient's and family's definition of quality of life.[33]

Home care continues to be a complex health care delivery service. Standards are not uniform across the nation and comparisons of agencies and care are difficult at best, because of the lack of standardization. This lack of standardization raises further questions about the lack of uniformity in cost and charges across agencies, numbers of visits per patient, and services offered, among other things. Accreditation for Medicare-approved agencies will be a requirement in the near future. This requirement can have a positive effect on all home care agencies, in that private agencies may voluntarily participate in and in that way become a part of the uniform system of home care delivery.

While nursing plus home health aide, social worker, physical therapist, speech therapist, medical services, occupational therapy, nutritional counseling, appliances, equipment, pharmacy services, and on-call physician coverage are all services provided today by home health agencies, nursing continues to be the primary service used in delivering quality home care. The argument over educational and practical experience qualifications for nurses and other providers in home health will continue to be an issue. While graduate education is addressing the need for managers, consultants, and practitioners to be prepared in home care, this type of care has not yet been treated fully at the undergraduate level.

Finally, patient mix, level of acuity, and chronicity will become major issues for home care agencies. The prediction

of increased demand for service and increased acuity level of patients after the 1983 implementation of PPS does not seem to have been accurate. There may be several reasons for this. Agencies have proliferated and the demand for service per agency may not be as great as anticipated. Referrals of patients requiring acute care and high-tech services may be going to private agencies rather than to official or voluntary agencies. Future data may show that patients requiring home care are proportionately the same number today as prior to prospective payment and that service needs are essentially unchanged. Some official agencies are seeing a switch back from the increased acuity level patients of 1983–84 to more chronic patients requiring long-term care. There may be a need to categorize home care agencies based on patient mix, acuity level, chronicity level, and services offered, much like the categorization of long-term care facilities providing inpatient services; this might provide some stability to agencies and better services for consumers.[34]

SUMMARY

The early development of home care grew out of the work of religious orders. The first attempts at the assurance of quality in home care occurred with the employment of field supervisors, the establishment of standards for training nurses in home care, and endeavors to establish standards for nurses and patients in home care. As social philosophy evolved throughout these early years, so evolved home care, which changed from being primarily under religious control into a form of secular nursing, thus paving the way for modern nursing and modern home care.

In America, as in England, home care was first delivered by sisters, nuns, and ladies' benevolent societies. Organized visiting nurse associations first developed in 1885, many with only one nurse and with a new emphasis on service for payment. With its emphasis on nursing and other services, the Henry Street Settlement, developed by Lillian Wald and Mary Brewster in 1893, was the precursor of modern home care agencies. This same era was significant for its introduction of industrial nursing, rural nursing, nurse licensure, and the involvement of major insurance carriers providing direct care and making provisions for data collection in order to assess and improve quality. In addition, through organized public health nursing, standards of care and education received greater attention.

Home care agencies of the past few decades have been controlled to a large extent by the Medicare conditions of participation and the definition of home care as intermittent, homebound, skilled care requiring the order of a physician. Quality assurance mechanisms by necessity have been related to the Medicare conditions of participation. More flexibility in Medicare requirements and licensure would allow agencies to plan new service patterns to provide a focus on long-term home care service, to continue to provide skilled service, and to show the full potential of home care as a cost-effective and efficient service delivery option. Uniform standardization will greatly enhance the movement toward home health care whose degree of excellence can be measured by valid and reliable methods.

NOTES

1. C. Warhola, *Planning for Home Health Services: A Resource Handbook*, Pub. No. (HRA) 80-14017 (Washington, D.C.: Public Health Services, Department of Health and Human Services, 1980).

2. M.J. Bull, "Quality Assurance: Its Origins, Transformations, and Prospects," in *Quality Assurance: A Complete Guide to Effective Programs*, ed. C.G. Meisenheimer (Rockville, Md.: Aspen Publishers, 1985), 1.

3. Ibid.; Regina M. Maibusch, "Evaluation of Quality Assurance for Nursing in Hospitals," in *Nursing Quality Assurance*, ed. P.S. Schroder and R.M. Maibusch (Rockville, Md.: Aspen Publishers, 1984), 3.

4. M.A. Nutting and L.L. Dock, *A History of Nursing: The Evolution of Nursing Systems from Earliest Times to the Foundations of the First English and American Training Schools for Nurses* (New York: Putnam, 1907), 1–15.

5. Mary Gardner, *Public Health Nursing* (New York: Macmillan, 1936), 3–54, 133–41.

6. Ibid.

7. Ibid.

8. A.M. Brainard, *The Evolution of Public Health Nursing* (Philadelphia: Saunders, 1922).

9. P. Kalish and B.J. Kalish, *The Advance of American Nursing*, 2d ed. (Boston: Little, Brown, 1986), 1–53, 259–289, 410–53.

10. Ibid.

11. Gardner, *Public Health Nursing*.

12. Ibid.; Kalish and Kalish, *Advance of American Nursing*.

13. Gardner, *Public Health Nursing*.

14. Ibid.

15. Ibid.; Kalish and Kalish, *Advance of American Nursing*.

16. Gardner, *Public Health Nursing*.

17. Ibid.; Kalish and Kalish, *Advance of American Nursing*.

18. Gardner, *Public Health Nursing*; Kalish and Kalish, *Advance of American Nursing*.

19. Gardner, *Public Health Nursing*; Kalish and Kalish, *Advance of American Nursing*.

20. Gardner, *Public Health Nursing*; Kalish and Kalish, *Advance of American Nursing*.

21. Gardner, *Public Health Nursing*.

22. Ibid.; Kalish and Kalish, *Advance of American Nursing*.

23. Gardner, *Public Health Nursing*.

24. Ibid.; Kalish and Kalish, *Advance of American Nursing*.

25. Gardner, *Public Health Nursing*.

26. Ibid.

27. J. Stewart, *Home Health Care* (St. Louis: Mosby, 1979), 20–23.

28. M.C. Phaneuf, "A Nursing Audit Method," *Nursing Outlook* 5 (1964): 42–45.

29. M.J. Lesnik and B.E. Anderson, *Nursing Practice and the Law* (Philadelphia: Lippincott, 1955).

30. Office of Management and Budget, *President's Proposals for Fiscal Year 1981* (Washington, D.C.: GPO, 1980).

31. R. Alford and M. Stanhope, "The Changing Scene in Home Health Care: Trends in South Carolina," *Family and Community Health* 8, no. 2 (August 1985): 66.

32. H. Heysman, "National Accreditation: Will the Home Care Industry Be Permitted to Regulate Itself?" *Home Healthcare Nurse* 5, no. 3 (1987): 5; P. Maraldo, "Accreditation: The Quality Solution for Home Care," *Nursing and Health Care*, June 1987, p. 319; U.S. Department of Health and Human Services, *Federal Register* (December 31, 1987) vol. 52, no. 251, p. 49510.

33. A. Donabedian, "Some Basic Issues in Evaluating the Quality of Health Care," in *Outcome Measures in Home Care*, ed. L. Rinke and A. Wilson (New York: National League for Nursing, vol. 1, *Research*, 3.

34. E. Phillips et al., "Public Home Health: Settling in after DRG's?" *Nursing Economics* 6, no. 1 (January-February 1988): 31.

REFERENCES

Bazer, R. "Ethics in Home Care and Quality Assurance." *Caring* 5 (January 1986): 50.

Blaha, A., and A. Smith. "Quality Assurance Medicare Standards for Home Health Agencies: A Basic Approach." *Caring* 5 (August 1986): 18.

Bohnet, N. "Quality Assurance As an Ongoing Component of Hospice Care." *Quality Review Bulletin* 8 (May 1982): 7.

Brown, J. "Homelike Care Means Quality Assurance," *American Health Care Association Journal* (November 1987): 45.

Buhler-Wilkinson, K. "Left Carrying the Bag: Experiments in Visiting Nursing, 1877–1909." *Nursing Research* 36 (January-February 1987): 42.

Daniels, K. "Planning for Quality in the Home Care System." *Quality Review Bulletin* 12 (July 1986): 247.

DeVries, R. "Hospice Care in the United States: Quest for Quality." *Inquiry* 20 (Fall 1983): 223.

Fashenpar, G. "A Management Tool for Evaluating the Adequacy and Quality of Homemaker–Home Health Aide Programs." *The Gerontologist* 32, no. 2 (1983): 127.

Gould, J. "Standardized Home Health Nursing Care Plans: A Quality Assurance Tool." *Quality Review Bulletin* 11 (November 1985): 334.

Harris, M. "Evaluating Home Care?" *Nursing and Health Care*, April 1981, p. 207.

Hughes, S. "Home Health Monitoring: Ensuring Quality in Home Care Services." *Hospitals*, November 1, 1982, p. 75.

Larson J., and N. Williams. "Quality Assurance, HMOs and Home Care." *Caring* 6 (July 1987): 13.

McCann, B., and R. Enck. "National Standards in Hospice Care." *Caring* 5 (October 1986): 28.

Matchefts, M. "New Horizons for Home Health Care: Responses to Prospective Payment." *Public Health Nursing* 4 (December 1987): 219.

Monterio, L. "Insights from the Past." *Nursing Outlook* 35 (March-April 1987): 65.

Monterio, L. "Florence Nightingale on Public Health Nursing." *American Journal of Public Health* 75 (February 1985): 181.

Mumma, N. "Quality and Cost Control of Home Care Services through Coordinated Funding." *Quality Review Bulletin* 13 (August 1987): 271.

Wagner, D., and D. Cosgrove. "Quality Assurance: A Professional Responsibility." *Caring* 5 (January 1986): 46.

Shaw, S. "Assuring Quality and Confidence in New Home Care Technologies." *Caring* 4 (January 1985): 21.

Chapter 2

Quality Assurance: Administrative Support

Marilyn Harris

Quality assurance (QA) is a term that is frequently heard in health care. What does it mean? How is it accomplished? The American College Dictionary defines the word *quality* as "a character with respect to excellence, fineness or grade of excellence." *Assurance* is defined as "the guaranteeing or making certain; a positive declaration intended to give confidence."[1] Quality assurance can be defined as the process of making certain, or guaranteeing that high quality care will be provided to clients, which will instill confidence in the product or service provided. In spite of this definition, Meisenheimer states that quality assurance is an elusive, if not frequently misunderstood, concept.[2] This is the result of the lack of a single operational definition.

A QA program is designed to demonstrate and monitor the degree to which an organization's actual performance compares with expected outcomes.[3] A QA program in a home health agency is necessary for multiple reasons, including to (1) monitor and evaluate client care; (2) identify, hire, and retain the appropriate level of personnel to meet the clients' needs; (3) meet standards established by the Medicare conditions of participation (COP), accrediting bodies, professional organizations, and the agency; (4) speak to risk management issues; and (5) address and resolve identified problems.

It is necessary to utilize multiple structure, process, and outcome criteria; to identify and measure the grade of excellence; and to have confidence in the overall procedure and final results. The agency must define what is to be measured, how measurement will be accomplished, by whom, when (daily, monthly, annually), and what is to be done with the identified outcomes (what information will be shared with whom, e.g., feedback to staff, the board of directors, the professional advisory committee, funding sources, regulatory agencies).

The format for this feedback must be clearly designed so that data can be displayed in an understandable and useful manner.

There must be administrative support to accomplish the primary goal of providing quality health care services in the home. Support must also be demonstrated through the provision of whatever time, dollars, and personnel are necessary to measure the degree of attainment of this goal.

NEEDS AND EXPECTATIONS FOR SURVIVAL AND GROWTH

Perceptions of Quality

Quality assurance is usually viewed from the perspective of client care. What is quality care? What is quality care provided in the home setting? How and by whom is it evaluated? In order to have a complete picture, myriad vantage points must be considered.

The Consumer's Viewpoint

Today's consumers—our clients and their families—are asking questions concerning their home care services. These questions concern coverage of services and financial issues. One reason is that consumers are being asked to pay a higher portion of health care costs through increased deductibles or co-insurance or to assume all payment for noncovered services.

Clients or their families may define quality as having the nurse or therapist arrive at the home before noon to provide skilled care. They may equate quality with a personal preference for a particular caregiver. Quality may also be measured from the perspective of "what I need" for a positive outcome versus "what I want and expect." Another criterion used to measure quality may be who is responsible for payment of the bill. Clients who personally pay for services may perceive quality differently than those who perceive services as being free (e.g., in the case of insurance).

To appreciate the client's perception of care, a discharge questionnaire (Exhibit 2-1) is sent to a random selection of clients or families included in the record review process each quarter. This selection process allows for two viewpoints—that of an independent reviewer and of the client or family. Discrepancies, if any are noted, are followed up by the supervisor and resolved through discussion with those responding to the questionnaire, the reviewer, and the Visiting Nurse Association (VNA) staff.

In today's health care environment, clients and families are frequently expected to participate in the care process. This is especially true in the case of hospice care, intravenous therapy, and care of ventilator-dependent clients of all ages. Data from the American Association of Retired Persons, published in *Caregivers in the Workplace Program*, indicate that family members provide 80 percent of the care needed by older relatives.[4] This causes concern among employers, who are confronted with the consequent absenteeism and stress-related illnesses. It also raises the issue of quality of care: Not only may families be incapable of meeting the responsibility to perform high-technological procedures on a 24-hour basis, but they may be trying to do so without adequate training and support.

The Third Party Payer's Viewpoint

Third party payers may define quality within a specified time frame, such as providing the subscriber home care service over a predetermined amount of time and with a specific number of visits based on a medical diagnosis. In reality, the expected progress or outcome does not always occur within these time frames. When expected outcomes do not occur within a given time frame and payment for additional visits is not available to home care providers, it seems that the payer's definition of quality is measured in terms of dollars saved rather than client services or outcomes. Professionals in any home health agency, not to mention numerous journal articles, can provide case studies that demonstrate the dichotomy between medically needed services and services for which there is available reimbursement.

Case management, a method in which an individual or organization has the responsibility for coordinating the multidisciplinary services that are provided to individuals, can lessen this dichotomy and improve quality of care. Quality assurance, one aspect of quality health care, is supported by third party payers.

The Legislative and Regulatory Viewpoint

Policymakers, both at the state and national levels, are interested in supporting the quality care concept while saving dollars overall on specific programs. Prospective payment for home care, capitation systems, and the current Medicare cost cap system are examples of existing and proposed dollar-saving contrivances.

In 1987, home health agencies were subjected to another review process related to quality assurance. Congress had mandated in 1986 that peer review organizations (PROs) (successors of professional standards review organizations [PSROs]) conduct quality assurance reviews on home health

Exhibit 2-1 Discharge Patient Questionnaire

1. Who referred you to the Visiting Nurse Association? Doctor _____ Hospital _____ Friend _____ Patient/Family _____ Other _____
2. What services were provided? Nursing _____ Home Health Aide _____ Physical Therapy _____ Speech Therapy _____ Occupational Therapy _____ Medical Social Service _____
3. Were there other services you would have liked us to provide? Yes _____ No _____
   If yes, please list: _____
4. Were instructions and/or treatments explained clearly and thoroughly? Yes _____ No _____
5. Were your questions answered adequately? Yes _____ No _____
6. Do you feel he/she considered your family's special problems? Yes _____ No _____
7. Were you satisfied with the personnel? Yes _____ No _____
   If not, why not? _____
8. Was the service what you expected it to be? Yes _____ No _____ If not, how did it differ from what you expected? _____
9. Did you have the same nurse or therapist each visit? Yes _____ No _____
   If not, did this change in personnel bother you? Yes _____ No _____
   Why? _____
10. When we ended our service to you, did you feel that patient/family needs were met? Yes _____ No _____ If not, why not? _____
11. Why was the service discontinued? Condition improved _____ Admitted to the Hospital _____ Deceased _____ Other _____
12. Would you use this service again? Yes _____ No _____
    If not, why not? _____
13. Would you recommend this service to others? Yes _____ No _____
14. Were office personnel courteous and helpful to you on the phone? Yes _____ No _____
15. Was there anything you particularly liked or disliked about this service? Yes _____ No _____ Please explain: _____
16. What suggestions would you make to improve the services? _____

Source: Courtesy of the Visiting Nurse Association of Eastern Montgomery County, Abington, Pennsylvania.

agencies and skilled nursing facilities.[5] Section 9353(c) of the Omnibus Budget Reconciliation Act of 1986 amended Section 1154, which now requires PROs to respond to all written Medicare beneficiary complaints received after August 1, 1987, concerning the quality of care provided by skilled nursing facilities, home health agencies, or hospital outpatient departments.

Val Halamandaris states that the general perception in the Congress is that diagnosis related groups (DRGs) have been a success, at least enough of a success that Medicare should continue to move in the direction of a prospective payment system (PPS) for nursing homes, home health agencies, and perhaps even physicians.[6] The federal budget reconciliation bill signed by President Reagan, on December 22, 1987, required the Secretary of DHHS to conduct a demonstration for prospective payment for home health care. Home health administrators must be involved in the development of this type of project.

Alternative payment methods are going to increase rather than decrease in importance in the future. This will also intensify the review process to which home health agencies are subjected; regulation will escalate.

The Professional's Viewpoint

From the professional's viewpoint, quality care usually means providing services in the amount needed for the client to become independent or return to a pre-illness level of functioning. The professional goal is often in direct conflict with the funding source's goal as it relates to payment for service. Home care nurses and therapists share frustration with, and concern for, the current home care reimbursement climate. Medical and technical denials of care, the limited number of authorized visits for which payment is available, and the perception of the lack of ability to deliver quality care in the stated time frames are causing home care professionals to choose other types of employment. Professionals, guided by their personal value systems and their commitment to attaining the standards of care established by professional organizations, are experiencing disillusionment with the current health care system.

The Viewpoint of Accrediting and Certifying Agencies

The site visitor from an accrediting or certifying body equates quality with having all administrative and clinical documentation completed on a timely basis and with meeting all standards at an acceptable level.

Certification is necessary for Medicare or Medicaid dollars. The certification process indicates that an agency has met minimum standards to assure client safety. There are ten conditions of participation (COP) that must be adhered to in order to participate in these federally funded programs.

Accreditation is a voluntary process. The standards include not only the basic COP standards, but also standards designed by the accrediting body that are more stringent than the COP standards.

There are many ways in which the overall quality of programs and services can be improved when an agency undergoes a comprehensive review. The National League for Nursing (NLN) accreditation process currently requires the home health agency to complete a self-study report. This provides an opportunity to examine the agency with a fine-tooth comb. It requires that policies, procedures, and actions be committed to writing. The report serves as an educational tool for board members who volunteer their time to serve, acquainting them with the agency's expectations and the roles and responsibilities of providers and consumers. It is an excellent source for orienting individuals joining the agency and is also a ready reference for staff, who frequently refer to it when writing proposals. The concern of the board and staff for quality of client care is expressed through such an accreditation process.

The Viewpoint of the Home Health Agency

From an agency's perspective, quality of care issues assume an added dimension. In addition to previously mentioned issues, all of which are crucial to survival, important considerations include the types and quality of staff needed to provide services, the agency's liability for inappropriate client care (which can result in denial of payment by third party payers), and analyses of the financial impact of all issues on agency operations.

MERGING CLINICAL AND FINANCIAL DATA TO IMPROVE QUALITY OF CARE

Home health agencies have been required to identify costs incurred by each discipline for years. This is usually done in relationship to the Medicare cost report. Since the future of prospective payment systems (PPSs) for home care is uncertain, administrators must be able to merge clinical and financial data to determine the outcomes of these aspects of a QA program.

The two main questions to be asked and answered are these: Was quality care provided from a clinical viewpoint? Was quality care provided from a financial viewpoint?

Ehrat states that in the absence of generic indicators of quality, each nursing organization must develop valid items or criteria that can measure quality care in the provider institution.[7] The Quality Assurance Policy (Exhibit 2-2), the Annual Program Evaluation Policy (Exhibit 2-3), and the Quarterly Record Review for the Home Health Aide (Exhibit 2-4) were designed by the Visiting Nurse Association of Eastern Montgomery County to include an evaluation of both clinical and financial data related to client care as well as overall administrative issues, such as program evaluation. The time frame for each activity is identified in the Quality Assurance Calendar (Exhibit 2-5).

Clinical and financial outcomes are addressed through the use of a patient classification system (PCS) (Exhibit 2-6) and

Exhibit 2-2 Quality Assurance Policy

Purpose: To systematically evaluate the quality of care rendered to individuals, families, and the community, in order to improve the quality of the care provided.

Responsible
Personnel: Nurses, therapists, social workers, members of the agency's board of directors and professional advisory committee, supervisors, administrators, and community members participate in phases of the quality assurance process.

Objectives: 1. To assess and evaluate the quality and appropriateness of care.
2. To identify deviations from standards.
3. To address and resolve identified problems.
4. To recommend methods to improve care.

Policy: As we strive for excellence in the provision of care, the agency is committed to the development and implementation of a quality assurance program. The multifaceted program encompasses an ongoing evaluation of structural, process, and outcome criteria. To ensure quality-effective, cost-effective services (within available resources) to individuals, families, and the community, we subscribe to compliance with both internal and external standards (Conditions of Participation, NLN, ANA, NAHC).

Procedure for Quality Assurance Activities

A. Quarterly Record Review

Action

Quarterly Periods

a. 1st Quarter
   May-June-July
   (Quarterly report due by 3rd Thursday in September)
b. 2nd Quarter
   Aug.-Sept.-Oct.
   (Quarterly report due by 3rd Thursday in December)
c. 3rd Quarter
   Nov.-Dec.-Jan.
   (Quarterly report due by 3rd Thursday in March)
d. 4th Quarter
   Feb.-Mar.-April
   (Quarterly report due by 3rd Thursday in June)

Annual Report Due 3rd Thursday in June.

The computer system generates a quarterly summary report which provides a numerical list of individuals serviced by all disciplines during the quarter. Based on this data, 10% of the records (7% if caseload is greater than 500) to a maximum of 50 per discipline per quarter are chosen. If the number is less than 10 cases per discipline for the quarter, all records for that discipline will be reviewed.

Records for review may be selected from the quality assurance review list. The visit register and/or the active and discharged chart files may also be utilized in the random selection process.

Recording of individual record findings and recommendations on quality assurance assessment forms will be implemented with 3 weeks notice as follows:

a. Nursing and HHA: Nursing staff, supervisors, nurse volunteers.
b. Physical therapy: PT supervisors.
c. MSS: Review with neighboring agency. Alternate locations.
d. Speech pathology: Reviewed by contractors.
e. Occupational therapy: Alternate between therapists.

Summary of findings and recommendations.

Recording of summarized findings and recommendations in:

a. Committee quarterly minutes and PAC minutes.
b. Annual report to board of directors at end of 4th quarter as part of agency's program evaluation.

Presentation of summarized findings to staff members to:

a. Identify areas of strengths and weaknesses.
b. Recommend and initiate action for the enhancement of care.

B. Quarterly Patient Questionnaires

Rationale

To assess the services provided to substantiate adherence to agency policies, internal and external standards of services for maintenance of optimal care, safety and adequate supportive services.
COP 405-1229.

Exhibit 2-2 continued

Action	*Rationale*
Following each quarterly record review, a discharge patient questionnaire is mailed to each discharged patient whose record was reviewed.	To evaluate patient satisfaction with services provided.

The QA supervisor reviews each questionnaire. If a problem area is identified, it is addressed with the appropriate employee and supervisory staff if indicated. Compliments to individuals are shared with the individual and supervisory staff when indicated.

Results of the survey are tallied and a summary report prepared and given to the executive director. These summaries may be utilized in the overall agency evaluation.

C. Unsolicited Letters

Action	*Rationale*
Unsolicited patient, family, community group letters are read and analyzed. Praise and/or problems are directed to and addressed with the appropriate persons by the QA supervisor.	The patient has the right to direct comments concerning quality of care to the agency. Comments that the writer shares about agency/services and/or personnel are reviewed and taken into consideration to praise employees and/or address and correct cited problems.

D. Annual Physician Questionnaires

Action	*Rationale*
On an annual basis, questionnaires are mailed to physicians whose patients require a recertification of a plan of treatment during a 60-day cycle. Any necessary follow-up is directed by the QA supervisor.	Encourage physicians' input as to their perception of the quality of services, since a physician who perceives the agency as providing quality care is more apt to refer his/her patients for services.

E. Utilization Review

Action	*Rationale*
Utilization is linked to the quality of services. Utilization of services will be evaluated during the quarterly review process. Refer to Utilization Review Policy.	To ensure proper utilization of all disciplines and services.

F. Annual Agency Evaluation

Action	*Rationale*
This process is the responsibility of the Professional Advisory and Agency Evaluation Committee. The board of directors, professional advisory committee, administration, and staff are involved in the evaluation process as detailed in the Annual Program Evaluation Policy. Within 90 days of the close of the fiscal year, representatives from board and PAC meet to complete the necessary worksheets. A summary of the evaluation is presented to the PAC and the board of directors for final approval and action.	COP 405-1229 To assess the extent to which the agency's programs are appropriate, adequate, effective and efficient.

G. Evaluation of Clinical Competence

Action	*Rationale*
Hiring practices are in accordance with COP 405-1202. Copies of licenses, when applicable, are on file. Certification, where applicable, (i.e., ANA certification for community health nurse) is encouraged. Each employee/volunteer is oriented to his/her roles and responsibilities. (Refer to orientation procedure manual.) Continuing education is linked to the quality assurance program to ensure that training is commensurate with quality care needs.	COP 405-1202 From a structural perspective, clinical competence and education are necessary to provide quality care.

H. Monitor & Review of Patient Outcome

Action	*Rationale*
Services are goal oriented. On selected patients, outcomes are addressed through the use of a patient classification system and nursing diagnoses. Staff must quantify goal attainment. Financial and clinical goal attainment data are available on a monthly basis through the management information system printouts. Data are analyzed on a periodic basis. Results are shared with appropriate staff members.	To evaluate goal attainment. To ensure that quality care was rendered.

Exhibit 2-2 continued

I. Incident Reports

Action

Refer to Service Policy.
Incident reports are submitted to the Director of Professional Services for analysis. Trends identified are given to the QA Supervisor for further study and follow up.

Rationale

Trends in reportable incidents are a quality assurance/risk management concern and should be studied and acted upon.

J. Study of Quality Indicator

Action

At least on an annual basis, the QA supervisor directs a study of a selected quality indicator, e.g., availability of supplies and equipment, quality of interventions, compliance with policies, procedures, and standards. This study will include data collection, problem identification, problem solving, and the implementation of solutions. A report is submitted to the Director of Professional Services and Executive Director.

Rationale

Periodic assessment of quality indicators is conducted to identify and resolve problems in structure, process, or outcome.

JY-11/87

nursing diagnoses. A PCS can be used to identify the levels of care that the client requires. Nurses select the one category or level of care that best describes that client's long-range goal. Standardized flow sheets for each of the five levels of care list the long-range goal and the subobjectives that must be addressed from a clinical perspective. Standardized flow sheets for the nursing diagnoses approved by the North American Nursing Diagnoses Association itemize the parameters that must be addressed for clients with a specific nursing diagnosis. These are considered the short-term goals. A partial listing of nursing diagnoses for Group V (terminal illness) is presented in Exhibit 2-7.

The outcomes of clinical care must be quantified so that clinical and financial data can be statistically analyzed manually or via computer (see Exhibit 2-8 and Table 2-1). It is important to build in as many aspects of the evaluation process as possible into the daily or monthly data collection process.

In addition to the evaluation of client outcomes of care, clinical care is evaluated through record review and physician and client/family evaluations of the quality of care provided.

Once the clinical data have been quantified through the use of accepted PCSs, additional statistical and financial data can be analyzed to answer the second question noted earlier: Was quality care provided from a financial viewpoint?

Ehrat states that quality care issues become more focused as lengths of stay and client mix patterns change.[8] In reality, both of these factors impact on financial outcomes. When clinical outcome data are available by multiple PCSs (e.g., rehabilitation potential, nursing diagnoses, major disease category, ICD-9), several probing questions can be answered: Was quality care provided when the client fell within "average" charge for this category of client? Did the client with a high (or low) cost, a long (or short) length of stay (LOS), or large (or small) number of visits receive quality care when compared with the "average" client? If so, what affected the cost or LOS?

When evaluating financial factors, it is important to remember that any of the above mentioned variables, such as LOS, number of visits, and so forth, may result in decreased productivity, with a resulting decrease in overall dollars to the agency. The client mix, including hi-tech clients that may require longer visits and increased and more detailed documentation, cannot be ignored. The issue of productivity will be addressed later in this chapter.

The findings of the combined evaluation of clinical and financial outcomes have been described in other publications.[9]

ANALYZING RESOURCES

Among the major concerns of administrators are the quantity and quality of human and financial resources available to them as they fulfill their obligation to monitor client care.

Human Resources

The quality of an agency's programs and services depends on its having a qualified and adequate staff to provide care. To ensure the development of competent individuals with a strong and flexible scientific base for practice, home care agencies must collaborate with educational institutions.

Service-Education Collaboration

The partnership between education and service must reflect congruency between philosophies of education; what constitutes appropriate learning experiences to achieve the student's goals and objectives while maintaining the integrity of the home care agency (see Appendix 2-A: Field Agency Agreement). Opportunities must be agreed upon that foster leadership and management skills and allow students from all

Exhibit 2-3 Annual Program Evaluation Policy

Definition of Program Evaluation

Program evaluation is the systematic collection and analysis of information necessary to assess agency effectiveness, quality, and efficiency relative to accepted performance measures and standards and to guide agency planning for the provision of health care to those it serves.

Goals of Agency Evaluation

A. To assess and improve the quality of agency programs and services.
B. To assure the relevance of all agency programs and services to community needs.
C. To accomplish and maintain overall agency accountability for programs and services.
D. To document and facilitate the prudent utilization of resources in the operation of agency programs and services.
E. To achieve and maintain the relevance of agency programs and services to the agency mission.

Uniform Program Evaluation Criteria

A. Scope

 1. The annual program evaluation will include an assessment of all programs and services offered by the agency both directly (i.e., by employed staff) and through contract in a twelve-month period comprising the program year.
 2. The annual program evaluation shall address the following elements of the agency: (I) administration and organization; (II) staffing; (III) programs and services; and (IV) the status of future agency plans bearing on service delivery and/or quality.
 3. The annual program evaluation will provide for an assessment of the adequacy, appropriateness, effectiveness, efficiency, and competency of health care delivery to agency patients and other service beneficiaries.

B. Responsibility

 1. The procedure for the Annual Evaluation specifies which personnel, group, or committees participate in the process.
 2. The board of directors, professional advisory committee, administration, and staff are involved in the evaluation process.

C. Required Annual Reviews

 1. The annual program evaluation will document and appraise the conformance of agency program operations with policies established by the board of directors and approved by the professional advisory committee.
 2. The annual program evaluation will include an assessment of patient care activities through a review of clinical records performed on an appropriate sample basis in relation to the Clinical Record Audit and Utilization Review functions of the agency.
 3. The annual program evaluation will provide a basis for assessing overall agency program operations in terms of economy and efficiency in relation to cost-containment and cost-effectiveness.

D. Format and Organization

 1. The annual program evaluation will be presented in a written format indicating those involved, general methods and procedures, specific findings or results, and any comments regarding corrective action or recommendations for further improvement.
 2. The annual program evaluation report will also address the disposition of any specific findings or recommendations presented in previous agency evaluation reports.

E. External Feedback

 1. The annual program evaluation process will involve a formal method of determining patient satisfaction with the services provided by the agency. Comments should be gathered directly from the patients or their representatives.
 2. The annual program evaluation process will include a means of collecting information on agency program performance from the physicians of patients served by the agency.
 3. The annual program evaluation process will provide for the collection of information from sources such as hospitals, other health care providers, social agencies, and similar entities concerning agency performance in accepting and following up referrals for service when appropriate.

F. Integration with Agency Accreditation
    The documentation requirements for initial and ongoing voluntary accreditation under the National League for Nursing are recognized as fully consistent with above stated criteria. The comprehensive self-study report that is prepared for interim and renewal of accreditation will be utilized for program evaluation purposes for the years covered.

8/80

Source: Courtesy of the Visiting Nurse Association of Eastern Montgomery County, Abington, Pennsylvania.

disciplines to come to understand the process of caring for clients and their families in a cost effective manner. By collaborating with expert home care providers and faculty, students will be socialized to function autonomously and be sensitive to current socioeconomic and political environments. Faculty knowledgeable in professional and regulatory standards must promote involvement in quality assurance activities such as

- nursing and multidisciplinary chart reviews
- reimbursement review sessions
- admission and discharge planning meetings
- employee evaluation sessions
- design and analyses of client/family satisfaction questionnaires
- development of standards of care

Exhibit 2-4 Quarterly Record Review for Home Health Aide

Client Name: _____   Date of Review: _____

Client Case No.: _____   Present Quarter: _____

Primary Nurse Name: _____   Months Included: _____

Status of Record: Active _____

        Discharged _____   _____

                                                    Signature of Reviewer

Services Involved	Yes	No	N/A	Comments
I. Assessment				
A. Does the clinical record include assessment of physical, psychosocial, and environmental needs of patient/family?				
B. Was the nursing assessment form updated upon each new plan of treatment or past each hospitalization?				
C. Were nursing diagnoses based on assessment factors?				
D. Did the primary nurse select the correct patient group on admission?				
E. If the patient's status changed, was the patient group changed accordingly?				
II. Planning				
A. Were client goals stated?				
B. Were the nursing parameters specific to the identified nursing diagnoses/problem?				
C. Was the plan of treatment (orders) current and signed by physician?				
D. Was the POT completed in accordance with agency policy?				
E. Were signed verbal orders obtained to cover any change in the plan of treatment?				
III. Implementation				
A. Was the frequency of nursing visits based on the assessment of the client's needs?				
B. Was the service provided consistent with the care plan?				
C. Does the record contain evidence that the applicable subobjectives in the patient classification/objectives system were being acted upon?				
D. Did the nurse request consultative services of other disciplines when needed?				
E. Did the nurse regularly supervise the performance of the HHA/LPN?				
F. Was the HHA consistent with client's needs?				
G. Did the nurse demonstrate evidence of his/her coordination of all services?				
H. Did the nurse hold conferences/joint visits with other services when appropriate?				
I. Did the nurse notify the physician/other team members of any significant changes in the client's status?				
J. Were service reports legible, dated, and signed?				
K. Did service reports include:				
1. Adequate information regarding the client's current condition?				
2. Specific treatments/instructions given?				
3. The date of the next visit?				

Exhibit 2-4 continued

Services Involved	Yes	No	N/A	Comments
L. Were the following forms present and updated according to agency protocol: 1. Authorization and Release Form?				
2. Medicare Termination letter?				
3. HHA Plan of Care?				
4. Family Information Sheet?				
M. Does the record contain evidence that medications were checked for significant side effects and indications?				
N. In the opinion of the reviewer, were services: Appropriately utilized?				
Overutilized?				
Underutilized?				
IV. Evaluation A. Were patient/family responses to nursing intervention documented?				
B. Were necessary modifications in the care plan made based on the nurse's evaluation?				
C. If discharged from nursing service: 1. Was discharge a logical development of the care plan and client goals?				
2. Does the record contain a description of the patient/family change in knowledge, understanding and/or behavior as the result of the nurse's intervention?				
3. Was there evidence of the client's goals having been met?				
4. Was the discharge summary present and accurately completed?				
5. Were the nursing diagnoses on the discharge computer summary consistent with those on the problem list?				
6. Were the service codes (group # and goal attainment) listed on the discharge computer summary consistent with the evidence found in the record?				
7. Was the physician notified of client's discharge?				

Source: Courtesy of the Visiting Nurse Association of Eastern Montgomery County, Abington, Pennsylvania.

Collaborating and confronting the issues of quality education will produce competent practitioners who can assess the needs of intellectually and culturally varied clients and families, establish goals for outcomes, and determine successful interventions. Students who can think critically, exhibit self-confidence and leadership abilities, understand the "business" environment, and willingly accept social responsibilities will emerge with a competitive advantage as "high-tech, high-touch" practitioners.

Because clients require various types and levels of care, the agency must utilize personnel with different educational preparation. It is a given that competent professionals and support personnel provide care in accordance with a physician's plan of treatment (POT) and the individual client's needs. In order to accomplish this, the agency's board and administration must establish personnel policies that address employment criteria, staffing patterns, and other factors that contribute to quality care.

Employment Criteria

Employment criteria must be established and adhered to for all levels of personnel. Job descriptions should be available to staff during the interviewing process and must include all expectations for performance. The current requirements of professional and government organizations for professional and support personnel must also be included. Once an individual is hired, a copy of the job description should be signed by the employee to confirm understanding of and an agreement to the expectations; it should then be placed in the individual's personnel file.

Support personnel who are involved in direct care to clients, such as home health aides, must complete or show evidence of

Exhibit 2-5 Quality Assurance Calendar

	Jan	Feb	Mar	Apr	May	Jun	Jul	Aug	Sep	Oct	Nov	Dec
Utilization review and record review	X	X	X	X	X	X	X	X	X	X	X	X
Record review summary			X			X			X			X
Annual Record Review Summary						X						
Patient questionnaires mailed			X			X			X			X
Patient questionnaires follow-up	X			X			X				X	
Analyze unsolicited letters	X	X	X	X	X	X	X	X	X	X	X	X
Physicians' questionnaires mailed	X											
Physicians' questionnaires analyzed		X	X									
Begin study of quality indicator	X											
Evaluation of clinical competence	X	X	X	X	X	X	X	X	X	X	X	X
Monitor and review of patient outcomes	X	X	X	X	X	X	X	X	X	X	X	X
Incident report follow-up	X	X	X	X	X	X	X	X	X	X	X	X
Annual agency evaluation					X NLN			X FY				

Source: Courtesy of the Visiting Nurse Association of Eastern Montgomery County, Abington, Pennsylvania.

having completed an approved training program to meet the Medicare COP standards. It is important to consider the quality factor as it relates to the other support staff (e.g., receptionists, billing personnel) who are indirectly involved in client care but are included when quality is measured by clients and payers. The client's first experience with the agency is usually with the receptionist; this interaction frequently determines whether there are positive or negative expectations regarding other agency personnel. A client's perception of quality may begin at this stage in the process of care.

Staffing Patterns

Closely related to the employment criteria is the identification of the level of professional needed to carry out the mission of the agency. Does the agency require an individual practitioner who is licensed and also certified in specialty areas such as pediatrics, oncology, geriatrics, or psychiatry? Does this certification have to be granted at the state or national level? Administrators must be familiar with the many certifying organizations and know what level of professional is needed to meet state and federal certification and accreditation requirements.[10] Another factor to be considered is whether additional financial remuneration will be available if there are additional credentials. Unless financial or other rewards are clearly evident, employees may not perceive accreditation and certification as important.

In many home health agencies there are a limited number of higher level positions because of the size of the agency. In order to retain staff, it may be necessary to consider a method of encouraging, recognizing, and rewarding those individuals who continue to provide direct care. Del Bueno described a clinical ladder as a hierarchy of criteria intended to provide a means for evaluating and developing professional nurses who provide direct care to clients.[11] While most of the published material addresses clinical ladders in acute care settings, Whitney and Jung describe a clinical ladder program that is specifically for a home health agency and includes four levels of clinical nurse performance standards.[12] Administrators must be involved with staff in identifying performance standards for each level, assigning a dollar value to the achievement of stated goals, and describing how nurses move from one level to another.

Staff productivity is very important in home care, since the current reimbursement basis is the cost per visit. Multiple factors impact on the productivity of staff. Travel-related variables include weather, detours, traffic, and distance between clients. Client-related variables include the clients' living arrangements and learning abilities, the levels of care required on specific visits, conferences, and telephone time. Work-related variables include student assignments, staff meetings, documentation of client care for professional and reimbursement purposes, and the agency's reporting requirements.

One event that has impacted productivity was the introduction of Medicare Plan of Treatment Forms 485, 486, and 487, in September 1985 (form revision occurred in 1988; see Chapter 7). At the Visiting Nurse Association of Eastern Montgomery County, productivity statistics (e.g., the average number of visits per day per staff) are monitored on a monthly basis through a computerized monthly case load summary report.

Productivity data from April 1985 were used as a base line for determining the impact that the introduction of these new

Exhibit 2-6 Abbreviated Description of Patient Classification System*

Group I   *Recovery*. The patient will return to pre-illness level of functioning.
Sample subobjectives:
Patient/family will demonstrate ability to independently perform prescribed treatments/exercises.
If indicated, patient/family will demonstrate knowledge of important safety measures.

Group II   *Self-care*. The patient is experiencing an acute illness, but has the potential for returning to pre-episodic level of functioning.
Sample subobjectives:
Patient/family will demonstrate ability to assume responsibility for maintaining ongoing medical supervision.
If indicated, patient/family will demonstrate understanding of restrictions imposed by the illness or disability.

Group III *Rehabilitation*. The patient will eventually function without agency services.
Sample subobjectives:
Patient/family will demonstrate ability to assume responsibility for maintaining ongoing medical supervision.
If indicated, patient/family will demonstrate ability to independently perform prescribed treatment/exercises.

Group IV   *Maintenance*. The patient will remain at home as long as possible with on-going agency services.
Sample subobjectives:
If indicated, patient/family will demonstrate understanding of prescribed diet.
If indicated, patient/family will demonstrate knowledge of important safety measures.

Group V   *Terminal*. The patient will be maintained at home during the end stage of illness as long as possible with agency services.
Sample subobjectives:
Patient/family will receive emotional support as needed.
Patient/family will receive assistance as needed to prepare for death.

*This patient classification system is adapted from the Patient Classification/Objective System of the Visiting Nurse Association of New Haven. The VNA of Eastern Montgomery County has purchased the right to use this system.

forms had on staff productivity. As of December 1987, productivity for the nursing staff had not reached the pre-485 level. Although it is easy to explain why this has occurred (extra time is required to learn to complete a new kind of form and to complete forms regularly) and why productivity will possibly continue at this lower level (e.g., clients are more acutely ill when they return home from the acute care setting), this decreased productivity has had negative implications for the bottom line of the agency's budget.

Staffing patterns in home care have changed. In the past, home health care was attractive to many nurses because it provided a nine-to-five job. This is no longer the case. Home health agencies must have staff available to accept calls and make visits 24 hours a day, seven days a week in order to meet the needs of clients and families and to remain competitive.

Administrators are exploring new staffing patterns, e.g., full-time night call, flex-time to accommodate heavy or light client census or acuity levels, separate staff for weekends, and visits after hours. Each of these alternatives has to be assessed from a quality assurance standpoint. Questions to be asked concern the level of client care required, the qualifications of staff who apply for on-call positions, and whether full-time staff should take on-call duty (since they are most familiar with the agency's caseload, systems, policies, and so forth). The cost of each method of staffing must be analyzed and justified.

Staffing with full-time employees has benefits related to continuity of care as well as staff availability and competence. But fluctuating caseloads within agencies and the shortage of professional and support personnel have resulted in alternate staffing patterns. The use of part-time or per diem staff and a flex-time staffing pattern are now familiar to most home health agency administrators. Independent contractors are also sought to provide needed services to clients for cost-effectiveness. Cathcart, Lucas and Pancoast, and Chaloux, Martin, and Brocker have cited the advantages and disadvantages of each of these staffing patterns and the potential impact on the quality of care that is provided.[13]

Peer Review

Peer review is another important administrative process that is part of the overall quality assurance program in a home health agency. Reasons for reviewing clinical records include

- meeting the Medicare COP standards
- determining if an agency's policies and procedures are being followed
- identifying unmet client/family needs
- identifying individual and group trends related to the provision of care
- maintaining professional standards
- using findings as a basis to maintain or improve the provision of care

Although this time-consuming process is sometimes considered to be just more paper work, there are multiple benefits, including the assurance that services are provided by competent staff in a safe and cost-conscious manner. (Discussion of peer review from the staff nurse perspective occurs in Chapter 9.)

In-service or Continuing Education

In order to keep abreast of changes in professional practice and to meet Medicare's conditions of participation, inservice education and training are critical components of home care practices and administrative planning. Responsibility for participation in educational offerings jointly belongs to the agency and its professionals. Mechanisms must be established by which professionals can share information with colleagues. Program summaries (see Exhibit 2-9) should be kept by the individual responsible for education functions and placed in

Exhibit 2-7 Partial List of Nursing Diagnoses for Group V—Terminal Illness

| | NURSING DIAGNOSIS STATISTICS BY GOAL | | | | |
NURSING DIAGNOSIS (TERMINAL)	NUMBER IN GROUP	AVG TIME	AVG CASE CHARGE	AVG VISITS	AVG STAY
ACTIVITY INTOLERANCE					
INEFFECTIVE AIRWAY CLEARANCE					
ANXIETY	1	2	165	11	50
ALT IN BOWEL ELIMINATION: CONSTIPATION	43	2	130	11	36
ALT IN BOWEL ELIMINATION: DIARRHEA	1	1	80	4	11
ALT IN BOWEL ELIMINATION: INCONTINENCE	2	2	68	6	15
INEFFECTIVE BREATHING PATTERNS	48	4	260	11	32
ALT IN CARDIAC OUTPUT: DECREASED	1	2	63	5	8
ALT IN COMFORT: PAIN	98	4	215	12	31
IMPAIRED VERBAL COMMUNICATION					
INEFFECTIVE INDIVIDUAL COPING	14	2	106	11	28
INEFFECTIVE FAMILY COPING: COMPROMISED	7	2	95	14	34
INEFFECTIVE FAMILY COPING: DISABLING					
FAMILY COPING: POTENTIAL FOR GROWTH	1	6	225	20	45
DIVERSIONAL ACTIVITY DEFICIT					
ALT IN FAMILY PROCESSES	1	5	275	61	74
FEAR					
FLUID VOLUME DEFICIT					
POTENTIAL FLUID VOLUME DEFICIT					
EXCESS FLUID VOLUME	1	1	70	14	40
IMPAIRED GAS EXCHANGE					
ANTICIPATORY GRIEVING	3	3	147	12	23
DYSFUNCTIONAL GRIEVING					
ALT IN HEALTH MAINTENANCE	37	6	349	13	39
IMPAIRED HOME MAINTENANCE MANAGEMENT	3	6	273	14	45

Source: Courtesy of the Visiting Nurse Association of Eastern Montgomery County, Abington, Pennsylvania.

employee files for performance appraisal purposes, advancement, and promotion.

In short, all of the issues related to human resources—recruitment and retention, job descriptions, verification of credentials (such as licensure and certification), assignment and supervision of staff, orientation, in-service training, continuing education, ongoing performance evaluations, career ladders, and productivity monitoring—contribute to the home health agency's assurance that quality care is delivered to clients.

Financial Resources

While administrators must be concerned with the delivery and measurement of the quality of care that clients receive, they must also be concerned with the cost-effectiveness of the agency's programs and services. There is a cost associated with the time, materials, and personnel needed to reach stated goals. One of the questions to be considered is whether quality of care has been sacrificed to achieve a balanced budget.

Tonges stated that in a cost-containment atmosphere, providers must either lower their standards or find ways to provide quality care more economically.[14] This author believes that administrators must find ways to be more cost-effective, since health care providers *must not* lower standards of care. This requires providers to examine ways to decrease costs, e.g.,

alternate payment schemes for staff, such as per case, per episode, or on the basis of contracts, instead of traditional salaried or hourly patterns. We also need to use teaching tools specific to an agency's unique client populations in order to assist and augment the teaching done by the professional. There must be an increased emphasis placed on help provided by the family, volunteers, and other support personnel.

The recently published report by Arthur Anderson & Company and the American College of Health Care Executives indicates that 90 percent of the combined panels of health care executives, physicians, nurses, and trustees participating in the study agreed that by 1995

- acceptable definitions of quality health care will be developed
- providers will be better able to measure the quality they provide
- providers will monitor and report on the quality of their health care services
- regulators will use this information in connection with licensure[15]

The findings also indicated that over 70 percent of the panel

- anticipated that payments for health services will be based at least in part on quality measures

Exhibit 2-8 Nursing Diagnosis Recap

GOAL	OUTCOME	AVERAGE TIME	AVERAGE CHARGE	AVERAGE VISITS	AVERAGE STAY	NUMBER OF CASES	PERCENT OF GOAL	PERCENT OF TOTAL
1	1	5.87	380.64	8	39	243	87	
	2	5.29	314.16	6	53	31	11	
	3	3.70	250.00	7	24	4	2	
	TOTAL					278	100	7
2	1	4.59	310.40	7	34	114	69	
	2	7.53	451.65	11	35	47	28	
	3	1.68	88.40	1	2	5	3	
	TOTAL					166	100	4
3	1	6.57	461.07	10	33	2336	77	
	2	6.23	415.86	9	31	621	20	
	3	3.08	179.17	4	15	88	3	
	TOTAL					3045	100	79
4	1	11.70	745.76	16	92	93	65	
	2	10.16	610.10	14	69	44	31	
	3	5.29	247.05	5	18	5	4	
	TOTAL					142	100	4
5	1	11.65	646.25	15	38	148	68	
	2	6.76	408.73	9	24	63	29	
	3	2.65	135.00	2	3	7	3	
	TOTAL					218	100	6
TOTAL						3849		100

Goals 1–5 correspond to Patient Classification System Goals

Outcome 1 = Met all goals
      2 = Met some of the goals
      3 = Met none of the goals

Source: Courtesy of the Visiting Nurse Association of Eastern Montgomery County, Abington, Pennsylvania.

- believed that providers will sacrifice quality of care for financial viability
- believed that future capitation systems will sacrifice quality of care for financial viability

In light of these projections, it is imperative that administrators use all available resources to analyze the costs and benefits of providing quality health services in the home and find ways to achieve this goal.

Smeltzer states that cost analysis considers all resources, including personnel and materials as well as client contributions and other contributions received from inside and outside the organization.[16] Cost benefit analysis requires direct and indirect costs and benefits (or results) to be expressed in monetary terms. Costs include not only the time and salaries of personnel at all levels, but also expenditures for computer programming and equipment, monthly servicing, supplies, and building maintenance, as well as volunteer time (translated into dollar amounts) that may be associated with the QA program.

What is the benefit of the QA program? To Medicare-certified agencies it means continued federal funding. But do other third party payers ask to see an agency's QA policy?

Does the QA process result in more contracts for service because agencies can provide evidence of quality through various monitoring mechanisms? Do these added contracts enhance the agency's financial position? These questions must be answered by each agency administrator.

Partridge discussed community health administration in a cost-containment era. He states, "In the face of mushrooming pressures, constituencies, and complexities, we have but three alternatives: (1) we can muddle on with our unsatisfying,

Table 2-1 Patient Outcome Goals for Fiscal Year 1988

For each group within the Patient Classification System (PCS), the following outcomes will be attained (plus or minus 1 percent on an annual basis for overall ratio).

Group	Overall Ratio	1988 Outcome	Goal Attainment within Group	1988 Outcome
I Recovery	5%		85% Max.	
II Self-care	5		65 Max.	
III Rehabilitation	80		75 Max.	
IV Maintenance	5		70 Max.	
V Terminal	5		70 Max.	
	100%			

Exhibit 2-9 Education Program Summary

Program Title: _____

Date: _____ Type of Program: Orientation _____ Mandatory Program: _____

Time: _____ In-service: _____ Continuing Education: _____

In-house Program: _____ In-state Program: _____ Out-of-state Program: _____

Program in Response to Monitoring & Evaluation Deficiency: Yes: _____ No: _____

Name of Presenter(s): _____

Summary of Program Content: _____

_____

_____

_____

_____

_____

_____

Assessment of Program Content: _____

_____

_____

Utilization of Information Gained from Program:

Enhanced Practice: _____ How? _____

_____

Met Expectations of: HHC Agency: _____ Accrediting Agency: _____

Credentialing Agency: _____ Other: _____

Program Information Shared: No _____ NA _____ Yes (How?): _____

_____

(Signature/Position, Person Completing Form)   (Date)

ATTACHMENTS: Attendance Sheets; Program Brochure/Materials

Source: Courtesy of Claire Meisenheimer.

uneven, national performance; (2) we can succumb; or, (3) we can emerge into a tomorrow we helped fashion."[17] Home health administrators must help to assure quality care for home care clients. We can do no less!

SUMMARY

The home health agency's administrator has an important role in the QA program. The administrator must

- be accountable for quality client care
- commit time, dollars, personnel, and space to the overall process
- remain knowledgeable about QA requirements
- make changes when necessary, i.e., follow through on findings and recommendations
- work with the governing body to recruit and retain sufficient qualified staff through sound personnel policies, competitive salaries, and good working conditions
- solicit consumer input into the evaluation process
- provide support and encouragement at all levels of the agency's activities

Quality care is the result of having a philosophy, qualified staff, and sound and safe policies and procedures and perform-

ing evaluations and following through on findings with corrective actions. Agency and professional standards must be addressed. Accreditation, certification, and licensure standards for the agency must be maintained. Professional licensure and certification, orientation, in-service training, and continuing education are all necessary to assure quality care in a changing environment.[18] Many of the activities related to the provision of quality care, such as collaborating with educational institutions for providing clinical experiences, and orientation, in-service training, and continuing education for all staff involve a commitment of dollars.

A Pennsylvania Nurses' Association publication included the following formula for success: "All nursing personnel, plus commitment, plus knowledge, and involvement, equal a successful Quality Assurance Program."[19] The formula is still applicable today. In home health care, it must be expanded to include all disciplines providing care and all recipients of that care.

REFERENCES

1. *American College Dictionary,* s.v. "quality," "assurance."

2. Claire G. Meisenheimer, ed., *Quality Assurance: A Complete Guide to Effective Programming* (Rockville, Md.: Aspen Publishers, 1985), xvii.

3. E. Joyce Gould and Nancy Ruane, "Components of a Quality Assurance Program," in *Home Health Administration,* ed. Marilyn Harris (Owings Mills, Md.: National Health Publishing, 1988), 393–409.

4. American Association of Retired Persons, *Caregivers in the Workplace* (Washington, D.C.: Author, 1987).

5. "Review Responsibilities of Utilization and Quality Control Peer Review Organizations," 42 CFR, 446.70–476.143, April 17, 1985.

6. Val Halamandaris, "The Future of Home Care in America," *Caring* (October 1985): 10, 4–11.

7. K. Ehrat, "The Cost-Quality Balance: An Analysis of Quality, Effectiveness, Efficiency, and Cost," *Journal of Nursing Administration* 17 (May 1987): 6.

8. Ibid., 4.

9. Marilyn Harris, Donna Peters, and Joan Yuan, "Cost Containment: Relating Quality and Cost in a Home Health Care Agency," *Quality Review Bulletin* 13 (May 1987): 175–181; J. Buck and Marilyn Harris, "Costing Home Health Care," *Home Healthcare Nurse* 5 (November-December 1987): 17–29; Harris, *Home Health Administration*.

10. J.L. Fickerssen, "Getting Certified," *American Journal of Nursing* 85, no. 3 (1985): 265–269.

11. Dorothy Del Bueno, "A Clinical Ladder? Maybe!" *Journal of Nursing Administration* 12 (September 1982): 19–22.

12. D. Whitney and J. Jung, "A Clinical Ladder Program for Home Health Nurses," in *Third National Nursing Symposium on Home Health Care: Book of Abstracts and Presentation Outlines* (Ann Arbor, Mich.: University of Michigan, 1987).

13. Elizabeth Cathcart, "Staff Recruitment and Retention" in Harris, *Home Health Administration*, 193–95; M. Lucas and L. Pancoast, "Contract Versus Direct Staffing," in Harris, *Home Health Administration*, 195–97; D. Chaloux, S. Martin, and C. Brocker, "Flextime Scheduling," in Harris, *Home Health Administration*, 197–205.

14. M. Tonges, "Quality with Economy: Doing the Right Thing for Less," *Nursing Economics* 3 (1985): 205–311.

15. R. Umbdenstock (Ed.), *The Future of Healthcare: Changes and Choices* (Arthur Anderson & Co. and the American College of Healthcare Executives, 1987).

16. Carolyn Smeltzer, "Evaluating Program Effectiveness," in *Quality Assurance: A Complete Guide to Effective Programs,* ed. Claire Meisenheimer (Rockville, Md.: Aspen Publishers, 1985), 167.

17. K. Partridge, *Community Health Administration in a Cost-Containment Era* (New York: National League for Nursing, 1978), 10.

18. Harris, *Home Health Administration,* 16.

19. C. Boyer, *Quality Assurance: Nurses Know How* (Harrisburg, Pa.: Pennsylvania Nurses' Association, 1978), 32.

BIBLIOGRAPHY

Alt, J., and G. Houston. *Nursing Career Ladders: A Practical Manual.* Rockville, Md.: Aspen Publishers, 1986.

American Nurses' Association. *Standards: Nursing Practice.* Kansas City, Mo.: Author, 1973.

———. *Standards: Community Health Nursing Practice.* Kansas City, Mo.: Author, 1974.

———. *Code for Nurses with Interpretive Statements.* Kansas City, Mo.: Author, 1976.

———. *A Guide for Community-Based Nursing Service.* Kansas City, Mo.: Author, 1985.

———. *Standards: Home Health Nursing Practice.* Kansas City, Mo.: Author, 1986.

Crockett, D., and S. Suteliffe. "Staff Participation in Nursing Quality Assurance." *Nursing Management* 17 (October 1986): 41–42.

Devet, C. "Controlling the Quality Assurance Agenda." *Nursing Management* 17 (November 1986): 52–56.

Donabedian, A. "Quality, Cost and Cost Containment." *Nursing Outlook* 32 (May-June 1984): 142–45.

Hughes, F. "Quality Assurance in Home Care Services." *Nursing Management* 18 (October 1987): 33–36.

National Association for Home Care. *Code of Ethics.* Washington, D.C.: Author, 1986.

National League for Nursing. *Accreditation Criteria, Standards, and Substantiating Evidences: Accreditation Division for Home Care and Community Health.* New York: NLN, 1987.

———. *Policies and Procedures: Accreditation Division for Home Care and Community Health.* New York: NLN, 1987.

Osinski, E. "Developing Patient Outcomes As a Quality Measure of Nursing Care." *Nursing Management* 18 (October 1987): 28–29.

Pennsylvania Association of Home Health Agencies. *Home Health Service Provider Standards.* Harrisburg: Author, 1986.

Schmall, J. "Examination of the Concept." *Nursing Outlook* 77 (July 1979): 462–65.

Smith, P. "Quality Standards in Hi-Tech Home Care." *Caring* (September 1986): 90–94.

Wagner, D. and D. Cosgrove. "Quality Assurance: A Professional Responsibility." *Caring* 5 (January 1986): 46–49.

Wagner, D. "Quality Assurance: Issues and Process." *Caring* 5(9) (September 1986): 62–67.

Appendix 2-A

Field Agency Agreement*

THE UNIVERSITY OF PENNSYLVANIA SCHOOL OF NURSING AND <u>VNA OF EASTERN MONTGOMERY COUNTY,</u>
AGENCY

<u>1421 Highland Avenue, Abington, PA 19001</u>   mutually agree to the following plan for clinical experience until further notice. This agreement is cancellable on 30 days' written notice by either party.

I. The <u>VNA OF EASTERN MONTGOMERY COUNTY</u> will provide clinical experience for students and supervision will be
AGENCY
provided by the School of Nursing faculty. Supervision applies primarily to undergraduate students and/or as specifically agreed upon by the Agency and School of Nursing representative.

Responsibilities

A. University of Pennsylvania School of Nursing

1. Will be responsible for the selection and planning of student learning experiences in consultation with appropriate clinical staff.
2. Will be responsible for the instruction, guidance and evaluation of students' activities in patient care.
3. Will inform the AGENCY of the approximate number of students who will be having experience in nursing.
4. Will assume the responsibilities of familiarizing themselves with the policies and facilities of the AGENCY prior to the instruction of students in the clinical laboratory.
5. The University of Pennsylvania carries malpractice insurance, which covers students during course-related clinical experience in an agency, in the minimum amount of one million dollars. If proof of coverage is required, please send a written request of same to Lorrie Neiberg, Assistant Director, Office of Risk Management, 423 Franklin Building, University of Pennsylvania, Philadelphia, PA 19104-6205, with a copy of the executed agreement.

B. Agency

1. Will serve as a clinical laboratory in which nursing students may be assigned for educational experience.
2. Will provide staff time for planning with the SCHOOL faculty for student learning experiences.
3. Will provide staff time for the orientation of the SCHOOL faculty to the AGENCY'S facilities and policies.
4. Will provide conference room space for faculty and students.
5. Will provide emergency medical care within the scope of their ability for the nursing students in the event of injury or illness. Workers compensation and disability and professional liability insurance will not be provided by AGENCY. (See item II below.)

II. Students will be responsible for completing physical examinations and laboratory studies as may be required by the AGENCY. Students are responsible for carrying their own health insurance and, in the event of injury in the AGENCY, their insurance will cover the cost.

III. Publications: No material relative to this field experience may be published without the mutual consent of the AGENCY and the UNIVERSITY OF PENNSYLVANIA. Neither party shall use the names, logos, trademarks or names of employees or students of the other party in any publicity, advertising, publication or other communication without prior consent of the other.

---

*Courtesy of University of Pennsylvania School of Nursing and the Visiting Nurse Association of Eastern Montgomery County, Abington, Pennsylvania.

IV. The Trustees of the UNIVERSITY OF PENNSYLVANIA, intending to be legally bound, hereby indemnify and save harmless the AGENCY from and against any liability for personal injury, professional liability, or property damage resulting directly and solely from negligence in the clinical practice of the School's students of nursing and will reimburse your AGENCY for any costs incurred in defending litigation resulting directly and solely from such negligence.

V. The <u>VNA OF EASTERN MONTGOMERY COUNTY</u>, intending to be legally bound, hereby indemnifies and saves harmless
                   AGENCY
    the UNIVERSITY OF PENNSYLVANIA from and against any liability for personal injury, professional liability, or property damage resulting directly and solely from negligence in the clinical practice of the AGENCY's personnel and will reimburse the Trustees of the UNIVERSITY OF PENNSYLVANIA for any costs incurred in defending litigation resulting directly and solely from such negligence.

VI. _____

_____

Signed:	_____	Agency Officer
Agency:	VNA OF EASTERN MONTGOMERY COUNTY _____	
Date:	_____	
Signed:	_____	Dean, School of
Date:	_____	Nursing for the
		Trustees of the
		University of
		Pennsylvania

Quality Assurance Process

Part II

Quality Assurance Process

Chapter 3

Designing a Quality Assurance Program

Claire G. Meisenheimer

Home health care has expanded more rapidly than any other health care delivery system in history. Since the explosive growth has only been recent, the formal, regulated part of the health delivery system is in its infancy. Home health care has been slow to institutionalize quality assurance (QA) programs because this dynamic field is continually adapting to new technologies, the requirements of sicker clients (as a result fluctuating payment schemes), and the delivery of services in diverse settings. For these very reasons—and because of the demand for cost-effective, quality care by clients, fiscal intermediaries, and professional providers themselves—home care agencies are seeking ways to define and monitor the quality and appropriateness of the care they provide.

To assure that a home care agency's commitment to providing high-quality, appropriate, and cost-effective care is met, it becomes necessary to design a comprehensive, well-coordinated QA program that is flexible, effective, and efficient in monitoring and evaluating client care and clinical performance with resolution of identified problems. The design of such a program requires a planning period, during which time program goals and objectives are clearly defined and an assessment of the existing structure, services, and activities occurs. This allows the QA plan to become a realistic and useful framework for conducting monitoring and evaluating activities.

The QA standards of the Joint Commission on Accreditation of Healthcare Organizations (Joint Commission), the National League for Nursing (NLN), and the American Nurses' Association (ANA) emphasize the importance of planned, systematic, and ongoing monitoring and evaluation activities and the provision of a framework for conducting these activities. It is expected that within this framework the responsibilities of each discipline or service for monitoring and evaluating be clearly delineated.

PLANNING: THE CORNERSTONE OF A SOUND PROGRAM

Though the actual design of a program may be delegated to an individual or group, extensive input must be received from all individuals currently or potentially involved in the quality assurance program. Their inclusion will provide broader perspectives, a clearer understanding of the relationship of the individuals and their practice's (or service's) monitoring activities to the agencywide QA program, and increased commitment to and participation in the program. Persons knowledgeable about and interested in QA should spearhead the efforts. Regardless of whether the agency is small, with only one person versed in QA, or large, with many knowledgeable individuals, success requires that the person(s) responsible for instituting a QA program must have authority from, and be appropriately supported by, the board of directors and administrative staff.[1]

The QA program should receive direction from the agency's philosophy or mission statement. The program's purpose should address the rights of clients to quality health care and to assure the proper utilization of resources by competent practitioners. Goals, which are stated in broad terms, reflect the program's purpose; objectives, which are derived from goals, can then be written in specific, realistic, and measurable terms related to the eventual achievement of the goals. Objectives concern (1) the achievement of an optimum level of care cost-effectively and safely, (2) compliance with relevant standards of care, (3) methodologies employed to monitor care, and (4) the integration of the QA program with other agency processes and programs. Unlike goals, objectives may periodically change; new ones are written as old ones are achieved or cease to be appropriate.

Following the establishment of the agencywide goals and objectives, individual disciplines or services within the agency have the opportunity to determine their unique goals and objectives as well as specific time frames. Objectives must reflect the individuality of each discipline or service in its provision of care. Allowing sufficient time to achieve consensus is crucial, so that all individuals are committed to expending the resources, energy, and time necessary to provide a system of accountability. Program goals and objectives provide both direction and a concrete foundation for evaluating the status of any existing program and the development of any future program.

ASSESSING AN EXISTING QA PROGRAM

QA activities do exist in every home health care agency. However, the comprehensiveness of a QA program, its effectiveness, and its efficiency need to be periodically reviewed and evaluated.[2] To understand the concept of QA, that is, the measurement of the level of care provided and the mechanisms to improve it, all individuals involved must appreciate how the external standards of licensing, accreditation, and certification imposed on an agency function in concert with the internal standards the agency wishes to impose on itself in order to project its accountability to society. With this understanding, individual disciplines and services can clearly define, implement, and evaluate a program unique to their agency. In order for this to occur, the availability and appropriateness of resources such as staff, facilities, and fiscal support need to be reviewed.

The purpose, scope, roles and relationships, and effectiveness of the QA program can be assessed by responding to several broad questions:

- Does the program have a clearly written plan based on the agency's philosophy or mission statement?
- Are the program's goals and objectives clearly stated in specific, realistic, measurable terms and are they achievable with available resources?
- Does the program meet all the requirements of various external review bodies, i.e., Medicare conditions of participation (COP), standards of the Joint Commission and various professional organizations, state practice acts, and credentialing and other state and federal standards?
- Is a complete cycle that begins with values clarification, problem identification, and so forth, and ends with sustained problem resolution described in the program plan?
- Are there sufficient resources and support systems available (e.g., persons knowledgeable in the QA process, including measurement tool design and analysis, fiscal provisions, and computers)?

- Is there appropriate coordination and integration of all related committees and agency operations (e.g., utilization review, risk management, billing, and marketing)?
- What program strengths need highlighting?
- What program weaknesses require change?

Although a program may include all of the necessary technical features, its effectiveness and efficiency may be limited by a lack of involvement and commitment. Thus, a questionnaire similar to that shown in Exhibit 3-1 and distributed to all individuals in an agency may help bring to light perceptions and attitudes that need to be addressed prior to initiating any QA program. The questionnaire, which can be returned anonymously in order to reduce respondents' fears of reprisal, is designed to elicit a Yes/No response with an expectation for comments. It can also serve as an educational tool to enhance greater understanding of the full scope of QA.

Analysis of the data should identify misinformation or misperceptions regarding QA and also identify monitoring practices that are performed effectively and those that need strengthening. Duplication in activity, overlap or lack of authority and responsibility, utilization of standards, and approaches for enhancing integration and coordination of activities should be detected during analysis of the data. Taking time to thoroughly assess the agency staff's understanding of and commitment to QA during the planning and development stages will decrease the time and resources needed as well as increase the effectiveness and efficiency during the implementation and evaluation phases of the program.

DEVELOPING A QA PROGRAM

Because each home health care agency is unique in terms of purpose, size, client populations, services provided, and resources available, the QA program should outline its unique purpose, goals and objectives, program scope and integration, and committee structures (including roles and responsibilities). The objectives of the plan should focus on clinical care of clients, involve objective assessment, and include expectations of improvement in client care.

Utilizing the data gathered from the extensive assessment as well as the appropriate standards and suggested formats established by the various review bodies, including professional organizations, the Joint Commission, Medicare, PROs, and other state and federal groups, a QA program (such as the one outlined in Figure 3-1 and described in Exhibit 3-2) should evolve to manage the risks to clients and the agency, combine a spectrum of activities and professional practices, and demonstrate viability and accountability to the community.

UTILIZATION REVIEW, RISK MANAGEMENT, QUALITY ASSURANCE

While monitoring and evaluation activities are central for the QA committee, other committees are concerned with these

Exhibit 3-1 Quality Assurance Program Assessment

Dear Members of the ⸺⸺⸺ Home Health Care Agency:

This assessment has been designed as a means for you to evaluate our current quality assurance program. As you know, quality assurance—planned, systematic, ongoing monitoring and evaluation of client care and clinical performance—is only as effective as we make it.

Please place an X in the Yes/No columns and provide explanations or suggestions of *who, what, where,* and *when* in the Comments column.

	Yes	No	Comments
A. Does the current quality assurance plan			
1. refer to the organization's philosophy?			
2. refer to the organization's goals/objectives?			
3. describe the purpose of the quality assurance program?			
4. clearly define its goals/objectives?			
5. delineate the scope of care and services provided?			
6. define the program's scope, including integration of all committees?			
7. address the question of authority?			
8. identify person(s) or position(s) responsible for coordinating the program?			
9. describe the quality assurance committee's			
a. purpose/function?			
b. membership?			
c. chairperson?			
10. identify committees interfacing with the quality assurance committee?			
11. delineate lines of communication?			
12. encourage multidisciplinary monitoring and evaluation?			
13. address confidentiality?			
14. include a plan for periodic evaluation?			
B. As a result of quality assurance efforts, do you think			
15. you appropriately utilize standards established by			
a. professional organizations?			
b. the Joint Commission?			
c. state or federal government?			
16. your practice of care has improved?			
17. your documentation has improved?			
18. client care has become more cost-effective?			
19. client satisfaction has increased?			
20. your job satisfaction has increased?			
21. staff performance appraisals are more effective?			
22. your time and involvement is worthwhile?			
23. risks of litigation for our agency have decreased?			
24. orientation and continuing education programs are more relevant?			
C. Additional comments:			

Name and department/service (optional)

activities as well. Two major contributing committees focusing on administrative issues are the utilization review (UR) committee and the risk management (RM) committee. The primary purpose of the utilization review committee is to assess the necessity of care prior to services being provided, during care, and after care. Utilization review is useful in defining and controlling costs through cost-efficient use of services. By providing explicit criteria for admission to the

Exhibit 3-2 Quality Assurance Program

Preface

The _____ Home Health Care Agency believes that quality assurance implies the distinguishing characteristics that determine the value or degree of excellence and the mechanisms to efficiently and effectively monitor and evaluate the client care and services provided by competent professionals with appropriate resources. We believe that every client is entitled to optimum health care and that every employee should be individually motivated to contribute maximally toward achieving such care. This motivation can best be nurtured in an environment supportive of excellence, fiscal accountability, and positive change.

Program Purpose

To assure the quality, appropriateness, and necessity of client care by establishing structure, process, and outcome criteria to prospectively, concurrently, and/or retrospectively identify, initiate, and assess corrective actions for known and potential problems.

Program Objectives

1. To assure the delivery of client care at the optimal level of quality and in a safe manner.
2. To utilize externally and internally designed standards to monitor and evaluate professional practice and services provided to clients.
3. To design effective mechanisms for problem identification, assessment, resolution, and evaluation of client care.
4. To ensure that professional competency and practices are routinely and reliably monitored and evaluated.

5. To develop effective systems for the documentation and dissemination of quality assurance activities and findings to appropriate persons and/or committees.
6. To provide mechanisms including educational opportunities by which all agency members may become knowledgeable and participate in quality assurance activities.
7. To ensure the inclusion of fiscal accountability and cost containment responsibility in the provision of client care.
8. To provide mechanisms for the integration of risk management, utilization review, and other agency activities in a comprehensive quality assurance program.

Program Scope and Integration

All members of the _____ Home Health Care Agency are committed to the Quality Assurance Program. Following their orientation to the problem-focused approach to monitoring and evaluation (see Appendix 3-A), they are expected to participate in the evaluation of their clinical practices or the services they provide to clients. The program focuses on the monitoring and evaluation of all activities, functions, and standards, including, but not limited to, clinical practice, education, and administration. Due to the comprehensive nature of client care and services, the Quality Assurance Program will be facilitated and coordinated by the Quality Assurance Coordinator. (See Display.) Quarterly and annual summaries of monitoring activities will be reported to the Administrator, the Professional Advisory Committee, the Board of Directors, and other person(s) and committees as appropriate.

Display Quality assurance program chart

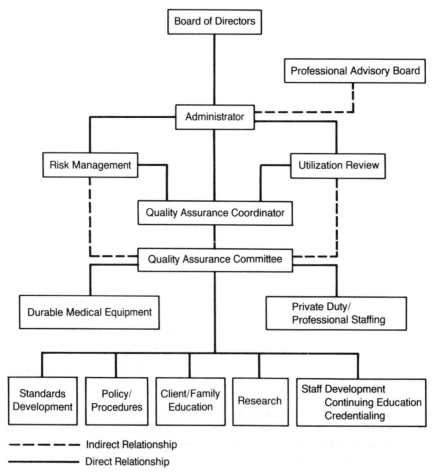

Exhibit 3-2 continued

Program Authority and Responsibility

Upon reviewing reports from the Quality Assurance Committee, Risk Management Committee, and Utilization Review Committee, the Professional Advisory Committee (PAC), comprised of professional and lay persons from the community and the agency and concerned with administrative issues and the provision and coordination of services, provides recommendations to the Board of Directors. The Board of Directors assumes final authority and responsibility for quality of care and professional practices, including

- approval of summaries of monitoring and evaluation activities
- approval of changes in activities, functions, and/or standards emanating from monitoring and evaluation activities
- recommendations concerning monitoring and evaluation activities
- review of proposals for monitoring and evaluation activities that may be costly, time consuming, or require client, family, or physician consent

The Quality Assurance Committee

The Quality Assurance Committee assumes responsibility for the central coordination and facilitation of all quality assurance monitoring and evaluation activities. Activities of other committees and services are reported to this committee through the Quality Assurance Coordinator, who is the major staff person on the committee. This committee meets on a monthly basis, unless pressing issues of quality require more immediate attention from the members.

The purpose of the Quality Assurance Committee is to

- review proposed monitoring and evaluation activities to prevent unnecessary duplication and to assist in identifying potential multidisciplinary studies (Appendix 3-B: Format for Proposed Quality Assurance Activity Form)
- facilitate and coordinate all activities
- assist in generating and coordinating suggestions for activities
- assist in designing effective mechanisms for problem identification and prioritizing, assessment, resolution, and follow-up evaluation
- coordinate a schedule of monitoring activities based on their impact on client care and services
- assist in selecting/developing criteria for monitoring activities
- assist in utilizing appropriate mechanisms to aggregate data relevant to practice and performance so that patterns and trends are discernible
- review all monitoring activities and make recommendations for corrective action to the individuals involved or to the administrator of the agency, as appropriate (Appendix 3-C)
- facilitate multidisciplinary studies between disciplines and services when care or performance issues affect more than one area
- establish a ''study'' calendar in response to agency goals or individual disciplines and services, including topics and responsible persons
- coordinate intramural educational opportunities relevant to quality assurance and continually inform everyone in the agency of pertinent extramural offerings
- evaluate annually and modify as necessary the agency quality assurance program with regard to its effectiveness and efficiency in integrating all professional disciplines and services and addressing issues of quality concerning client care and professional practice

Quality Assurance Committee Members

The members of the quality assurance committee include the chairpersons (or their designees) of all agency committees and services related to the provision of client care and professional practice. Among such committees and services are the following:

- medical director/appropriate physicians
- nurses representing various clinical areas of practice
- social services
- occupational therapy
- speech therapy
- physical therapy
- respiratory therapy
- pharmacy
- clergy
- utilization review
- risk management
- durable medical equipment
- private duty/professional staffing
- contracted services
- standards development
- policy/procedure
- client/family education
- staff development/credentialing
- research
- marketing

Each member of the committee is expected to represent his or her constituency and report activities occurring in his or her area of practice. As a resource person to constituents, each is expected to assist in identifying, prioritizing, and analyzing problems, developing resolutions, and providing appropriate feedback. Each is expected to encourage multidisciplinary monitoring and evaluation activities.

All members of the committee shall have equal votes and be recognized by the agency and their colleagues for their valuable contribution to the quality assurance process.

Quality Assurance Coordinator

The Quality Assurance Coordinator must be knowledgeable about quality assurance and its broad implications for home health care and also understand the structure and functioning of the organization. The Coordinator serves as the focal point of the Quality Assurance Program and provides the support services necessary for executing the program by

- providing appropriate secretarial support and technical assistance
- assisting staff in identifying topics and focusing studies
- assisting staff in determining the number and type of criteria needed to measure standards and by helping to write them
- assisting staff in determining the types and sizes of samples
- assisting staff in developing and utilizing efficient data-gathering procedures, methods, and systems
- assisting staff in aggregating, analyzing, and interpreting data, including computer facilitation
- assisting staff in preparing and displaying data in meaningful formats for those responsible for decision making
- coordinating activities to avoid duplication of efforts
- assisting with orientation and continuing education
- preparing thorough, reliable, and timely reports (quarterly, annually, and as requested)
- assisting with the annual review of the quality assurance program
- preparing agendas for meetings with committee input (Appendix 3-D: Committee Agenda and Minutes Report Form), disseminating meeting notices, and keeping all members of the agency apprised of quality assurance monitoring and evaluation activities relating to their areas of practice or service

Exhibit 3-2 continued

- serving as a liaison and a resource person to the Risk Management Committee and Utilization Review Committee
- serving as a liaison and resource person to the Professional Advisory Board and Board of Directors
- maintaining a log of all quality assurance activities (Appendix 3-E)
- maintaining all data in a confidential manner

Confidentiality

All data relating to quality assurance activities will be maintained in a confidential manner. All requests for information will be individually screened; only individuals directly involved in the monitoring or evaluation activities or individuals representing accreditation, certification, and other review bodies will be permitted access to documents, as appropriate. Exceptions will be determined only by the Administrator of the agency.

---

agency, continuation of services, and for discharge, utilization review can contribute significantly to providing only appropriate services as well as to preserving the agency.

The risk management committee focuses on all risks to which an agency is exposed in order to protect the agency's income and assets. While historically agencies have pursued risk management through safety programs, insurance coverage, and asset management, the likelihood of litigation against a home health care agency is increasing as complex technology increases, reimbursement for services diminishes, and professionals practicing in clients' homes are forced to decrease their time with clients and families.[3] Policies and procedures must be written to take into account the probability that some compensable event will occur in the areas of clinical care and personnel and financial management, not to mention criminal activities and those indirectly related to care.[4] Risk management emphasizes the importance of generating appropriate, accurate, and thorough documentation, having competent and credentialed staff coordinate care, and providing detailed and easily understood client/family educational materials. Incident/accident reports (Appendix 3-F) provide a mechanism for communicating deviations from desired results, procedures, or conditions. Documenting and addressing such events in a precise, thorough, and timely fashion frequently may prevent further action by an employee or a client or family in a grievance procedure.

By integrating QA, utilization review, and risk management, home health care agencies can establish a balance between the QA goal of monitoring and evaluating client care and professional practice and the utilization review goal of eliminating the cost of excessive or unnecessary care, thus protecting the agency's income and assets.

COMMUNICATION FLOW

The process of problem identification, resolution, reporting, and feedback should follow a set pattern and responsibilities within the process should be assigned. While external review bodies do not require specific numbers and kinds of monitoring and evaluation activities, there should be an expectation that each discipline and service, either individually or jointly with other disciplines and services, will engage in such activities at least annually (or as predetermined by the QA committee). Problems may be identified and reported according to the process illustrated in Figure 3-1.

REPORTS AND REPORTING MECHANISMS

Reports and reporting mechanisms, written and oral, provide the communication links vital to the success of a QA program. The process of communicating both positive and negative findings of QA activities involves an understanding of the organizational structure and the interrelationships of roles and responsibilities of various committees and individuals. QA reports are intended to provide pertinent, accurate, and timely information to decision makers for the purpose of comparing performance with pre-established standards—the ultimate goal being to improve the quality of care. Such reports are a professional's or agency's guarantee of accountability to the public that practice is congruent with professional, state, and national standards and mandates (e.g. ANA, NLN, Joint Commission, National Home Caring Council for Homemaker-Home Health Aide, Department of Health and Human Services' Conditions of Participation, etc.).

Reporting mechanisms may be in different formats (e.g., a highly structured format, as in the case of incident reports [Appendix 3-F], or a narrative format[5] [Appendix 3-C]). A report may be simply a verbal sharing of findings at a meeting or a verbal sharing followed by a written report in which participants are expected to provide additional information and potential solutions to problems. A report may be intended for an individual's files and as a source for future reports. According to Lieske, a QA report should include

- a statement of the topic (or problem) and the objectives of the study
- an explicit description of relevant data
- a delineation of the conclusions and recommendations
- the identification of corrective actions, the person(s) responsible for each action, and the date when each action is to be completed; succinct recommendations with time frames provide the basis for later focused evaluation of problem(s)[6]

QA reports are only useful when they provide the reader with a clear understanding of the issues. They should be written concisely, present a logical sequence of events, and have proper punctuation and grammar. In order to objectively present data, visual aids such as diagrams, histograms, bar graphs, and statistical tables are especially useful when clearly labeled and self-explanatory.

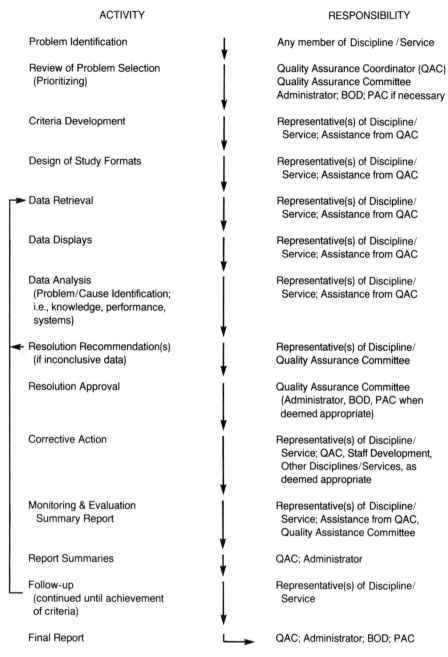

ACTIVITY	RESPONSIBILITY
Problem Identification	Any member of Discipline / Service
Review of Problem Selection (Prioritizing)	Quality Assurance Coordinator (QAC) Quality Assurance Committee Administrator; BOD; PAC if necessary
Criteria Development	Representative(s) of Discipline/ Service; Assistance from QAC
Design of Study Formats	Representative(s) of Discipline/ Service; Assistance from QAC
Data Retrieval	Representative(s) of Discipline/ Service; Assistance from QAC
Data Displays	Representative(s) of Discipline/ Service; Assistance from QAC
Data Analysis (Problem/Cause Identification; i.e., knowledge, performance, systems)	Representative(s) of Discipline/ Service; Assistance from QAC
Resolution Recommendation(s) (if inconclusive data)	Representative(s) of Discipline/ Quality Assurance Committee
Resolution Approval	Quality Assurance Committee (Administrator, BOD, PAC when deemed appropriate)
Corrective Action	Representative(s) of Discipline/ Service; QAC, Staff Development, Other Disciplines/Services, as deemed appropriate
Monitoring & Evaluation Summary Report	Representative(s) of Discipline/ Service; Assistance from QAC, Quality Assistance Committee
Report Summaries	QAC; Administrator
Follow-up (continued until achievement of criteria)	Representative(s) of Discipline/ Service
Final Report	QAC; Administrator; BOD; PAC

Figure 3-1 Communication Flow Chart

Reports may be scheduled weekly, monthly, quarterly, annually, or according to some other timetable. A daily report might consist of a summary of all inquiries regarding an agency's services (Exhibit 3-3). Weekly reports might summarize some of these data and also census by type and number of clients, hours of care provided by each discipline, medical and nursing diagnoses, and so forth, in order to determine the resources required for providing services, including the type and number of personnel with appropriate skills based on client case mix requirements.

Monthly and quarterly reports, useful for evaluating and comparing data from one time period to another, may summarize chart audits or incident reports. Reviews noting all medication errors and adverse drug reactions or staff and client accidents or injuries occurring in the home should be reported to the risk manager as well as to the QA coordinator; the ordering physician should be alerted to medication-related problems. Utilization review data determining the medical necessity for ongoing intermittent skilled care provides decision makers with information necessary to assure appropriate utilization of services to meet client needs and plan for timely discharge.

Annual reports are expected by the board of directors, the professional advisory committee, state surveyors, and any other group that needs to evaluate the agency's past accomplishments or is responsible for guiding future actions and

Exhibit 3-3 Daily Intake Report

Date: _____

Total Number of Inquiries: _____

Code:
Referral Source:
H = Hospital
NH = Nursing home
MD = Physician
S = Self (newspaper, brochure, etc.)
FC = Former client
O = Other

Payer:
T-18 = Medicare
T-19 = Medicaid
PP = Private pay
O = Other

Outcome:
Info = Information
Adm = Admission
Ref = Refused
O = Other

Name/Address/ Phone No.	Zip Code	Service Requested	Staff Required					Referral Source						Payer				Outcome				Reason Refused/ Comments
			RN	LPN	HHA	Therapy	Other (List)	H	NH	MD	S	FC	O (List)	T-18	T-19	PP	O (List)	Info	Adm	Ref	O	

Source: Adapted with permission of Monica Hart, Former Director of Patient Services, Medical Placement Services, Inc.

decisions. Each component of the QA program should be addressed in the annual report. A QA log (Appendix 3-E) is essential for tracking monitoring activities and facilitating reporting.

Systematic communication of QA, risk management, and utilization review activities through reports and reporting mechanisms requires an understanding of the organizational structure. The operational lines of authority and the interrelationships of the various program components provide feedback loops to assure quality of care. Unlike the medical record, QA documents are not admissible evidence in a court of law, since they are not integral to the provision of client care. They are, however, integral to the provision of *quality* client care. Regardless of their function and their various formats, they must be timely, concise, thorough, and understandable if they are to be useful.

SUMMARY

The home health care agency's QA program is designed to monitor and evaluate the degree to which professional practice and client care compare to expected outcomes. Each agency, whether a free-standing organization or part of a larger corporate structure, must determine whether to centralize its QA program or to decentralize and design specific strategies appropriate to each distinctive service. Assuring the quality of client care encompasses all components of agency operation,

including providing services; hiring competent and appropriate personnel in sufficient numbers; accepting and discharging clients appropriately; educating clients and families; and maintaining fiscal integrity through efficient and effective resource utilization. Specific job descriptions identifying qualifications and expected performance levels and clinical and administrative policies and procedures are critical for defining quality care and performance. The concept of quality to which an agency subscribes is an integral part of all activities, such as the agency's philosophy statement, goals and objectives, marketing plans, and personnel and fiscal management. Only through a well-defined, coordinated, comprehensive approach can a home health care agency operationalize its definition of quality and meet the public mandate to provide quality care.

NOTES

1. Claire Meisenheimer, "Designing a Quality Assurance Program," in *Quality Assurance: A Complete Guide to Effective Programs*, ed. Claire Meisenheimer (Rockville, Md.: Aspen Publishers, 1985), 73.

2. Meisenheimer, 74.

3. Joy Gould, "Litigation Risk Management: Home Care Challenge," *Caring* 5 (September 1986): 74.

4. Gould, 76.

5. Anna Marie Lieske, "Reporting Mechanisms," in *Quality Assurance: A Complete Guide to Effective Programs*, ed. Claire Meisenheimer (Rockville, Md.: Aspen Publishers, Inc., 1985), 133.

6. Lieske, 134.

Appendix 3-A

Process for Monitoring and Evaluation Activities

Client and professional practices will be monitored by defining structure, process, and outcome criteria measured by prospective, concurrent, and retrospective monitoring and evaluation activities. Emphasis will be placed on known or suspected problems relevant to

- clients and the quality of their care
- professional practitioners and their practice
- clinical and administrative services that cannot be justified as appropriate under specific circumstances

Problem Assessment

In order to identify and select alterations from the expected occurrence, a validation of the existence and extent of the problem and its nature, complexity, and characteristics must be based on the utilization of:

- multiple data sources
- valid criteria established by individuals knowledgeable about quality assurance and the problem under investigation
- an appropriate sample

Multiple data sources may be internal or external to the agency. Internal data sources may include, but are not limited to,

- clients' charts
- risk management activities, including incident/accident reports
- committee/service reports
- client/family surveys (interviews, questionnaires)
- letters of complaint
- performance appraisals
- findings by medical, nursing, and other professionals that are relevant to client care
- audits (prospective, concurrent, retrospective)

- utilization review findings
- classification systems
- staff research and literature reviews
- peer or credentialing reviews
- clinical supervisory conferences
- financial data
- observation

External data sources may include

- professional organizations and review bodies (e.g., Medicare, Joint Commission, NLN, ANA, PROs)
- fiscal intermediaries

Valid criteria include objective, specific, and measurable definitions regarding the structure (definitions of the organizational, personnel, and managerial environment), process (definitions of the actions and behaviors of providers on behalf of client), and/or outcome (definitions of the end result of care) of client care or clinical practice. Criteria must be readily available, easily abstracted, and valid.

For an appropriate sample, the quantity and quality of the "cases" assessed must be representative of the problem under review in order to estimate extent of the problem (frequency of compliance).

Problem Selection and Prioritizing

Problems should be selected when

1. resolution would have a positive impact on client care and/or professional practices
2. resolution can be obtained within available resources

Prioritizing problem selection should depend on the impact on client care and/or professional practices. The following should be taken into account:

- quantity of persons involved or potentially involved
- duration of problem

- number of disciplines or services involved
- assessment and resolution of time requirements
- staff motivation
- political environment, including accreditation surveys, regulatory agencies, fiscal intermediaries, medical staff, and governing bodies
- cost-effectiveness due to resolution

Problem Causes

Problem causes may be related to

- knowledge—deficiency in theory or practical (technical) information
- performance—deficiency in behavior/practice in spite of appropriate knowledge; requires further investigation to determine reasons for noncompliance (e.g., attitude, habit, rewards)
- systems—organization, administrative, or environmental factors preventing appropriate performance (e.g., the inappropriate management of resources such as staffing, equipment, and finances may cause problems)

Corrective Actions

Strategies to remedy problems that are correctable should describe

- all actions required to resolve causes involving knowledge, performance, and/or systems
- measurable objectives for each action, including the degree of expected change among persons or situations and the time limitations
- persons responsible for implementing actions
- the time frame for resolving the problem

Evaluation and Reaudit

The determination and documentation of problem resolution should include

- an indication of the extent of desired change
- an inventory of available resources and practical limitations
- an estimate of the impact on client care and/or professional practice
- reassessment activities, including the time frame and dates, sample size, individuals responsible, and methodology

The process of problem assessment through problem evaluation may be repeated until sustained resolution occurs.

Appendix 3-B

Format for Proposed Quality Assurance Activity

Date:

To: (Quality Assurance Coordinator)
      Quality Assurance Committee

From: (Individual/Discipline/Service)

1. Identify problem or suspected problem:

2. Describe rationale for problem selection:*

3. List individuals/groups/services involved in problem:

4. Identify type of assistance needed to study problem:

Recommendations of Quality Assurance Coordinator/Committee:

Date:

---

*See the section on problem selection and prioritizing in Appendix 3-A.

Appendix 3-C

Quality Assurance Monitoring Activity

Suspected Problem: _____   Person(s) Collecting Data: _____
_____   Discipline/Service Involved: _____
Rationale for Problem Selection: _____   Time Frame: _____ to _____
_____

Assessment (Data Source/ Extent of Problem)	Causes of Problem (Knowledge, Performance, Systems)	Corrective Action

Quality Assurance Monitoring Activity (Page 2)

EVALUATION: (Date(s), Methodology for Remonitoring, Responsible Person(s))

_____   _____
        (Quality Assurance Coordinator)   (Date)

Submitted to Quality Assurance Committee
Committee Review/Recommendations:

_____
                (Date)

Appendix 3-D

Committee Agenda/Minutes

Committee: _____	
Agenda for Meeting on: _____ Time: _____ Place: _____	
1.	
2.	
3.	
4.	

Minutes Date: _____ Time: _____ to _____ Place: _____ Recorder: _____	Members Present: Excused/Unexcused: (Sign-in Sheet Attached) Guests:

Topic	Speaker	Discussion	Action

Appendix 3-E

Quality Assurance Activities Log

Discipline/ Service Involved	Date Study Initiated	Responsible Person(s)	Suspected Problem	Selection Rationale

Quality Assurance Activities Log (Page 2)

Assessment/ Data Sources	Problem Causes (Study Results)	Corrective Action(s)	Date(s)

Quality Assurance Activities Log (Page 3)

Responsible Person(s)	Date Submitted to QA Committee	Action Taken	Date Submitted to Administrator/Action

Quality Assurance Activities Log (Page 4)

Follow-up Recommendations	Date/ Responsible Person(s)	Date/ Final Resolution	Effect of Resolution on Client Care/ Professional Staff

Appendix 3-F

_____ Home Health Care Critical Incident Report

An incident is any occurrence, accident, or event that: (a) is not consistent with normal client care or the routine operation of the agency; (b) did or could result in an injury to a client or employee, or in damage or loss of property; and (c) could result in litigation against the agency and/or employee.

Policy: To ensure timely completion and review of incident reports, thus reducing the likelihood of litigation.
Procedure: 1. Any agency staff member witnessing an unusual incident involving a client or employee must complete an incident report.
            2. Documentation should:
               a. include all client's and witnesses' observations and actions taken.
               b. be written using factual, nonjudgmental statements.
            3. Upon completion of the report by the person witnessing the incident, the report should be forwarded to the Chairperson of the Risk Management Committee. Appropriate action will be taken and reports will be submitted to the Administrator, and the Quality Assurance Coordinator/Quality Assurance Committee.
            4. Incident reports are confidential and will only be discussed with those involved.
            5. An employee's personnel record will not contain any reference to incident reports completed by the employee. No employee will be terminated for a nonmalicious, unintentional incident, but failure to report an incident may be grounds for disciplinary action.

_____ Home Health Care Agency
Critical Incident Report

Date of incident: _____   Time of incident: _____
Location of incident: _____   Report completed by: _____
Name of person(s) involved: _____
Witnesses: _____

Objective narrative of incident, apparent cause, and other pertinent details:
_____
_____
_____
_____
_____

(for more space attach separate sheet)

Description of identified problem(s) resulting from critical incident:

_____
_____
_____
_____

All corrective actions taken and by whom: _____
_____
_____
_____ Date: _____

Submitted to Risk Management Chairperson/Committee   Date: _____

Reviewed by: _____   Problem resolved _____   Problem not resolved _____

If not resolved, corrective actions taken and by whom: _____
_____
_____
_____ Date: _____

Results of corrective actions: _____
_____
_____
_____

Submitted to Administrator   Date: _____

Problem resolved _____ Problem not resolved _____ If not resolved, recommendations for corrective action: _____
_____
_____
_____

Resubmitted to Risk Management Chairperson/Committee   Date: _____

If resolved, impact of resolution on client care/professional practice:
_____
_____
_____

Recommendations if not resolved:
Discontinue monitoring and evaluation _____ Reasons: _____
_____
_____

Continue activity for interval problem solving _____
Continue activity for constant problem solving _____
Responsible person(s): _____
Time period: _____
_____

_____   _____
(Signature, Chairperson Risk Management)   (Signature, Agency Administrator)

Date: _____   Date: _____

Date of completed incident report: _____

Chapter 4

Standards: The State of the Art

June A. Schmele

Standards, although sometimes elusive, are simply the explication of a desired level of quality. What is not so simple is the recognition and articulation of the values that lead to the selection of the particular approach and content of any standards implementation program. The ultimate goal of such a program is, of course, to improve the quality of care. Thus it is imperative to establish agency consensus about values, definitions, approaches, and measures.

The purpose of this chapter is to present both a brief account of several approaches to standards implementation and an overview of the various standards that are most applicable to home health care. The description and discussion of the various aspects of standards could alone easily fill a large volume. For purposes of this chapter, a relatively succinct summary, together with selected examples and accompanying references, will suffice, giving readers a broad overview and directing them to the resources in which more detailed accounts are available. The classification system that will be used for grouping information comprises *agency, program, practice,* and *patient*. This is a manageable framework, although these are not necessarily mutually exclusive categories. The arrangement of topical categories is not meant to have any hierarchical significance. The goal is for this chapter to incorporate approaches, contents, and resources that will assist the administrator, practitioner, educator, and researcher in exploring integrated systems of standards implementation.

The author perceives that the emphasis on standards of quality has been mitigated by the current emphasis on comply-

ing with regulatory guidelines upon which reimbursement is contingent. This focus is frequently in opposition to the focus on recognized professional standards. The ideal standards implementation program, then, would encompass and integrate both professional and reimbursement requirements and ultimately improve the quality of care.

DEFINITIONS

Standards are defined in many ways, and thus semantic problems continue to exist. For example, when a plea is made for "standards in home care," there are probably as many different interpretations as there are listeners. There is value in simply recognizing this semantic problem, which then legitimizes asking clarifying questions that will lead to common understanding, at least within the agency setting.

Donabedian, probably the most recognized authority on quality assurance, describes this semantic problem in the following passage:

> Unfortunately we have used these words in so many different ways that we no longer clearly understand each other when we say them. But we have used them for so long that we are not at liberty to abandon them entirely, so as to begin all over again. Besides, what better new words would we find to say what we need to say? Our most reasonable course of action, therefore, is to see whether we can clarify the existing nomenclature, encrusted and misshapen though it may be with the barnacles of careless past usage.[1]

He further suggests that we put aside the words themselves and focus on the presence of discrete, clearly definable, and pre-

The author would like to acknowledge Katherine Scimeca, R.N., B.S.N., for assistance in the preparation of this chapter, and Karen Stolte, R.N., Ph.D., and Marilyn Seiler, R.N., M.S.N., for their critical review.

cise measures of certain phenomena, measures that can be assessed as to their presence or absence. A comprehensive definition of quality of care illustrates Donabedian's point of view on this matter. "The definition of the quality of care involves specification of three things: (1) the phenomenon that is the object of interest, (2) the attributes of the phenomenon on which a judgment is made, and (3) the criteria and standards for rating each attribute on a scale that ranges from the best possible to the worst."[2]

Standards and Criteria

The Joint Commission on Accreditation of Healthcare Organizations (Joint Commission) offers an implicit definition of standards. Standards should

- relate as directly as possible to the quality of care and the quality of the care environment
- represent a consensus of experts on the state of the art of health care
- state to the extent possible objectives and not mechanisms to meet objectives
- describe aspects of care or related functions that are surveyable
- be reasonable[3]

The Joint Commission defines the measurable aspects of the standards as "required characteristics" rather than criteria.

The National League for Nursing (NLN) provides the following definitions: a criterion "describes the variable to be measured" and a standard "specifies the level of achievement a provider must abide by in order to become accredited."[4]

The American Nurses' Association (ANA) defines standards as an "agreed upon level of excellence" and criteria as "statements which are measurable and which reflect the intent of the standard."[5]

For purposes of this chapter, the preceding ANA definition of standards and criteria will be used. Of necessity, any discussion of standards implicitly refers to criteria as well. For example, the ANA has as a standard that "the nurse uses health assessment data to determine nursing diagnoses." One of its criteria is that the nurse generalist "communicates the nursing diagnoses obtained during health assessment to appropriate members of the health care team."[6]

Structure, Process, Outcome

The commonly accepted framework for standards and criteria comprises structure, process, and outcome; this framework was first described by Donabedian in the 1960s. He defines structure as the "relatively stable characteristics of the providers of care, of the tools and resources they have at their disposal, and of the physical and organizational settings in which they work." Process is described as the "set of

activities that go on within and between practitioners and patients." Outcome is "a change in a patient's current and future health status that can be attributed to antecedent health care."[7] In spite of the fact that structure, process, and outcome make up a commonly accepted framework, the value of measuring each of the components of the framework remains somewhat controversial. Historically, structural measures have been emphasized, probably because of the ease in establishing quantifiable measures for such things as physical, financial, and human resources. During the past several years there has been increasing emphasis on process. However, now there is a movement toward outcome as the measure of choice. The debate goes on, probably because the cause and effect relationships among the three components are not clearly established. Perhaps the best approach is to measure all three components of quality and to continue to explore the relationships among them.

APPROACHES TO STANDARDS IMPLEMENTATION

Development of standards is an inherent part of any quality assurance (QA) program. At the outset of the program, time should be spent considering exactly which systematic approach to QA will be used. The selection of a specific approach will give direction and form to the program as well as provide evaluation points along the way. It will specifically show what relationships standards and criteria have to the QA program. Brief overviews of some of the best-known approaches are presented below. The reader is directed to other sources for further information.

The Joint Commission Monitoring and Evaluation Model has the following nine steps:

1. Assign responsibility.
2. Delineate the scope of care.
3. Identify important aspects of service.
4. Identify indicators.
5. Establish criteria.
6. Collect and analyze data.
7. Take actions to resolve identified problems.
8. Assess the action and document improvement.
9. Communicate relevant information to the organization-wide quality assurance program.[8]

In this model, steps two through five deal with identification and development of standards. The remaining steps (six through nine) direct the implementation of the standards using the quality assurance process.

The recently developed NLN Model for Developing Client Outcome Program Objectives (COPOs) implies a systematic approach to the development and use of standards:

1. Define the problem.
2. Define the outcome.
3. Define the population.

4. Define the numbers.

5. Design the evaluation mechanism.[9]

This study approach is directed toward particular patient groups and shows much promise as a manageable step-by-step approach to developing patient outcome standards. For a detailed description, the reader is referred to a recent issue of *Caring*.[10]

The ANA conceptual model, based on Lang's work, identifies seven steps in a circular model that may be entered at any point.[11] Lang's model, depicted in Figure 4-1, is straightforward and has stood the test of time. This model has also been used as the basis for many other approaches.

Schmele's Standards Implementation Model, which integrates several approaches, includes ten steps in a linear plan that has a feedback loop for the evaluation phase. Schmele's model is shown in Figure 4-2. Although its approach is generic, this model has been applied step by step in some detail in the home health setting.[12] It emphasizes the importance of staff ratification or involvement in formulation of standards and criteria. The value of using standards and criteria for various uses, such as performance evaluation and staff development, is also stressed.

In putting a comprehensive and integrated standards implementation program into place, it will be helpful to select a systematic approach such as one of those described above. Certainly the identification of common terminology, values, and mission is essential to the successful development and maintenance of standards. In addition, it is vital to give consideration to the forces outside of the agency.

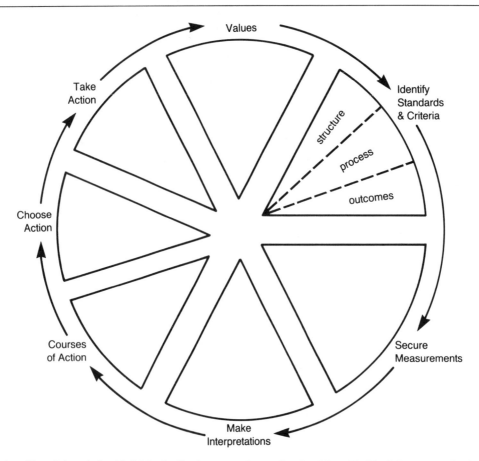

Figure 4-1 The American Nurses' Association Model for Quality Assurance. *Source:* Reprinted from *Workbook for Nursing Quality Assurance Committee Members: Community Health Agencies,* p. 111, with permission of American Nurses' Association, © 1982.

Step I	Step II	Step III	Step IV	Step V	Step VI	Step VII	Step VIII	Step IX	Step X
Explore Values	Select Standards	Develop Criteria	Determine Criteria Usage	Select Study Method	Develop Tool	Plan Study	Gather Data	Interpret Data	Take Action

Figure 4-2 Schmele's Standards Implementation Model. *Source:* Reprinted from *Journal of Nursing Quality Assurance,* Vol. 1, No. 2, p. 45, Aspen Publishers, Inc., © February 1987.

ENVIRONMENT

The changing social forces in society have resulted in the current fluidity in the health care system. In order for any system of standards to keep pace with societal demands and the concomitant competing emphases, much administrative sophistication is required. It is essential to consider current political, economic, legal, and social trends and issues and to incorporate them into a well-planned, systematic, and realistic approach to the management of quality. Strategic planning calls for the incorporation of this content into the formulation and implementation of standards.

Probably one of the most significant documents addressing the environment in which the home health care industry exists is the well-known review of the home care field prepared by the American Bar Association under the auspices of the Select Committee on Aging. The *"Black Box" of Home Care Quality* is considered a beginning step in documenting inadequacies in the present system of quality assurance in home care.[13] This report, as well as other current legislation directed toward mandatory standards, patient rights, and quality reforms, is especially illuminating on the political climate surrounding home health care.

The economic environment is reflected in the increasing Medicare payment denials. This could result in "treating the record," which would be detrimental to professional standards.

From a legal perspective, Shinnick emphasizes the importance of standards and their implementation, especially in the area of high-tech care. According to long-established precedent, health care personnel are required to answer to standards that exist in the community: "A person is judged in accordance with what a reasonable person with similar training would have done under the same circumstances."[14] Northrop addresses the issue of legal liability and raises the question of what the applicable standard will be (since the care is rendered in the client's own home, where the patient is less dependent regarding decisions about nursing accountability).[15]

The voice of the consumer in the home care arena is becoming increasingly important. Legislation, consumers' rights, and advisory boards are all mechanisms that emphasize the role the consumer has in relation to various levels of standards in home care.

LEVELS OF STANDARDS

Agency Standards

There are various mandatory and nonmandatory standards inherent in state licensure laws, regulations for government reimbursement programs, and accreditation processes. Although these "standards" may not always be referred to as such, they are inherent in laws, rules, regulations, conditions of participation, guidelines, etc. Each of the major sources of agency standards will be considered.

State Regulation

Licensure. Licensure for a home health agency is defined as the process of procurement of state permission to engage in the delivery of home health care services to the public. A state licensure law contains minimum operational standards and serves as a basis to control agency practice. According to Flanagan, the common areas of regulation (enforced by the state regulatory body) are (1) skill of personnel, (2) required scope of services, (3) compliance with all state and federal laws, (4) appropriate liability, and (5) appropriate record-keeping.[16] At present, 36 states are covered by a licensure law, according to the *State Licensure Book* compiled by the National Association for Home Care.[17] The minimum licensure standards vary from state to state; however, in most states the law is closely aligned with conditions of participation for Medicare certification. The *"Black Box" of Home Care Quality* contains a comparative analysis of the major components of the licensure acts of the various states.[18]

Certificate of Need (CON). The Health Planning and Resource Development Act of 1974 (PL 93-641) established a mechanism at the state level to determine the need for new health services, which would then have to meet state CON requirements. Spiegel defines CON as "a granting of permission by the state to operate a home health agency in a specific area, provided the applicant proves the need for the agency in terms of the need criteria established in the law or regulations."[19] Several states currently have CON laws for home health agencies (Spiegel notes that in some other states the CON requirements are contained within the licensure law). Both Spiegel and Flanagan provide a good summary of the controversial nature as well as the questionable outcomes of CON legislation.

Paraprofessional Regulation and Certification. Along with the growth of homemaker and home health aid services, some states have passed legislative initiatives that require the adherence to regulatory standards in order to gain provider certification. One example of such a program is the homemaker and home health aid training and certification program in Connecticut, which calls for adherence to "reasonable standards of health, safety, and comfort of patient."[20] The Community Nursing and Home Health Division of the Bureau of Health System Regulation, Department of Health Services, is responsible for this regulatory program.

Another state initiative especially directed toward regulation of homemaker-home health aide programs is the formation of the New Jersey DHS Commission on Accreditation for Home Care. This agency is embarking on a state accreditation program in which standards will deal with uniform screening, recruitment, and employment practices, appropriate supervision of aides, and defined case management procedures for all paraprofessionals.[21]

Accreditation

Accreditation is considered a voluntary process; it is defined by the ANA as "the process by which an agency or organization evaluates and recognizes an institution or program of study as meeting certain predetermined criteria or standards."[22] There is currently much emphasis on accreditation for home health agencies. Both the NLN and the Joint Commission are reviewing and extending their programs. Currently, both programs are requesting to be deemed as national accrediting bodies whose decisions would then be recognized as determining whether a provider met the requirements for Medicare certification. The approval of these requests is anticipated in the near future and will have far-reaching implications both for the accrediting bodies and for the home health agencies. As changes occur, the major source of regulation of quality is likely to be the standards and criteria of these accrediting bodies. If Medicare conditions of participation are subsumed under the accreditation standards, there will be increasing emphasis upon accreditation. In some states it is likely that the accreditation standards will subsume both state licensure standards and Medicare standards. Thus accreditation could become the single major regulatory force. The author does not intend to judge the merits of this situation; the results remain to be seen. Summaries of the accreditation programs of the NLN and the Joint Commission follow.

National League for Nursing. The accreditation program of the NLN was jointly initiated in 1966 with the American Public Health Association as a result of mutual concerns about nursing services delivered outside of the hospital, extended care, and nursing homes. In 1974 the program was expanded to include all disciplines delivering home health services. Currently, the accreditation program is known as the Community Health Accreditation Program (CHAP), which recently became a subsidiary of NLN. CHAP is authorized as an independent governance structure for the accreditation program.[23] The broad community-based scope of standards contain the following major components:

1. strategic planning and marketing
2. organization and administration
3. program
4. staff
5. overall provider evaluation[24]

An example of the NLN criteria and standards is shown in Exhibit 4-1, which presents the Strategic Planning and Marketing standard.

The supporting documents for the accreditation process are *Accreditation Criteria, Standards, and Substantiating Evidences* and *Policies and Procedures*.[25] The accreditation process includes a self-study report, site visit, professional review panel, and a board of review. The listing of NLN-accredited agencies is published annually in the January issue of *Nursing and Health Care*.[26] In 1987, there were 87 accredited agencies. Although previous NLN accreditation standards dealt largely with structure and process, at present there is a major thrust toward outcome-oriented evaluations. Currently, according to Wilson, new standards for paraprofessionals are being developed for 1988 implementation. Future projected additions include high-tech, complex, and hospice care.[27]

Joint Commission. Home health care accreditation for hospital-based units has been part of the Joint Commission hospital accreditation program since 1974. The standards are contained in the *Accreditation Manual for Hospitals*.[28] Since 1986 the Joint Commission has been involved in an intensive program of developing and field-testing new standards that will be the basis for the accreditation program for both hospital- and community-based home health agencies. This new Joint Commission accreditation program began in early 1988. Program components include high-tech infusion, durable medical equipment, homemaker, home health aid, and skilled

---

Exhibit 4-1 Example of National League for Nursing Criteria, Standards, and Substantiating Evidence for Home Care: Strategic Planning and Marketing

Criterion 1. The provider assesses the community served and develops a mission statement which reflects attention to current and anticipated community needs.

STANDARD	EVIDENCE
S1.1 The provider assesses the community served using staff and consumer input. • assessment data includes: demographic variables health status indicators community resources	E1.1 Briefly summarize sources of information used in assessing the community. Data sources may include: • published references of demographics and community health status indicators; • community news releases; • information from community forums or professional meetings. Have examples of sources of information available for site visitors review.

Source: Accreditation Criteria, Standards, and Substantiating Evidences by National League for Nursing, © 1987.

professional care. Standards are included in the following areas:

1. patient/client rights and responsibilities
2. patient/client care
3. safety management and infection control
4. home care record
5. quality assurance
6. management and administration
7. governing body
8. home health service
9. pharmaceutical services
10. personal care and support service
11. equipment management[29]

An excerpt of the Joint Commission standards for the topic area of Patient/Rights and Responsibilities is provided in Exhibit 4-2.

In addition to *Home Care Standards for Accreditation*,[30] which became available in early 1988, the Joint Commission is also developing a manual of survey guidelines to be used as an observation guide for home visits.[31] The survey process will include observations of the patient and staff in the home, patient and staff interviews, and an audit of clinical records to assess the quality of administrative/management activities and clinical performance.[32]

National Home Caring Council. An accreditation program for homemaker and home health aid services is conducted by the National Home Health Caring Council. Standards are considered minimum and exist for the protection and safety of the consumer and buyer. There is a total of 11 standards, with major consideration given to structure, staffing, service, and community. There is a strong emphasis on the training requirement for homemakers and home health aids. The accreditation program is in keeping with state and federal requirements.[33]

Exhibit 4-2 Example of Joint Commission on Accreditation of Healthcare Organization Standards for Home Care: Patient/Client Rights and Responsibilities

Standard I	The patient/client has the right to make informed decisions regarding his/her care.
Standard II	There is continuity in the care provided by the home care organization.
Standard III	All information concerning patient/client care is treated confidentially.
Standard IV	The patient/client is informed upon admission of the home care organization's mechanism for receiving, reviewing, and resolving patient/client complaints.
Standard V	The home care organization honors patient/client rights and informs the patient/clients of their responsibilities, if any, in the care process.

Source: Copyright 1988 by the Joint Commission on Accreditation of Healthcare Organizations, Chicago. Reprinted with permission.

Agency Certification

Medicare. Title XVIII of the Social Security Act includes the provision of federal reimbursement for home health services to the elderly and those who meet certain disability requirements. In order to participate in this program, a home health agency must meet the minimum standards contained in the conditions of participation.[34] These conditions involve 12 major areas:

1. compliance with federal, state, and local law
2. organization, service, administration
3. group of professional personnel
4. therapy service
5. acceptance of patients, plan of treatment, medical supervision
6. skilled nursing service
7. therapy services
8. medical social services
9. home health aid service
10. clinical records
11. evaluation
12. outpatient physical therapy or special pathology services

After meeting these conditions an agency becomes certified and is required to have an annual evaluation thereafter to maintain certification. According to Blaha and Smith, structure is the major focus of the requirements; process is dealt with to a lesser degree and outcome standards are negligible.[35] Standards are included for each of the areas listed above and in many cases criteria are explicitly or implicitly included. For a detailed delineation of the conditions of participation, the reader is referred to a comprehensive discussion by Webb.[36] The reader may also want to refer to a discussion by Hughes on the internal and external monitoring mechanisms that are inherent in the Medicare guidelines.[37] Home health agencies are subject to additional external reviews by the fiscal intermediary and by state surveyors as well. The reviews serve the purpose of monitoring compliance with state licensure, federal certification, and reimbursement guidelines.[38] The Omnibus Budget Reconciliation Act of 1986 calls for professional review organization services to extend to home care to ensure that home health care received by Medicare recipients is medically necessary and within professionally recognized standards of quality. The Health Care Financing Administration mandated that by October 1987 all home health agencies were required to have contracted with PROs and established a procedure for reviewing records. By July 1988, all PROs were required to ensure the quality of posthospital care.[39] The importance of developing standards and criteria to ensure that care is appropriate, necessary, and adequately documented is quite clear.

The Medicare conditions of participation are frequently the basis for state licensure laws, and thus their influence extends beyond the 6,000 Medicare certified agencies.[40] Consequently, these minimum requirements form the basis of most quality assurance programs, each of whose primary objective is likely to be reimbursement for services.

Title XIX, Title XX, and the Older Americans Act. The Medicaid program (Title XIX) is a combined federal and state health assistance program for low income persons. Limited home health services are provided by this program, with wide variance between states. For example, annual home health reimbursement ranged from $8,159 in Oklahoma to $522,958,000 in New York in 1984.[41] There is little in the literature about state certification for these programs. However, according to Sabatino, the Medicare conditions of participation also apply to state-administered, Medicaid-covered services.[42]

The Social Services Block Grant (Title XX) and the Older Americans Act are the major federal funding sources for nonmedical home-based care. Neither of these programs impose standards for this care.[43]

Program Standards

Model Standards

The model standards program promulgated by the American Public Health Association is a recognized source of standards for programmatic areas, including home health and especially in the public health system. *The Model Standards: A Guide for Community Preventive Health Services* is based on a report concerning 1990 health objectives for promoting health and preventing disease, and it has a section on home health services that consists of process and outcome objectives and the accompanying indicators.[44] This document was developed as a collaborative project of the American Public Health Association, Association of State and Territorial Health Officials, National Association of County Officials, United States Conference of Local Health Officers, and Department of Health and Human Services Public Health Service Centers for Disease Control.

Other Sources

Standards have been developed by other agencies and disciplines for some of the more specialized home care services. For example, the standards for respiratory therapy home care focus on need, medical records, equipment, and evaluation.[45] Spiegel also discusses various sources of standards for high-tech care, such as the American Society for Parenteral and Enteral Therapy, which has developed standards for nutritional support; the National Intravenous Therapy Association, which promulgates standards for intravenous therapy; and the journal *Drug Intelligence and Clinical Pharmacy*, which offers implicit and explicit standards dealing with antibiotic therapy at home.[46]

Private Insurance

There is limited information in the literature about the role of standards to legitimize insurance coverage for home health.

Implied standards put forth by insurance companies are based on standard practice as well as Medicare, with some companies leaning more toward Medicare guidelines. Increasingly, insurance companies are using case managers to decide on case handling. Even though standards may not be explicitly defined with this approach, of necessity they are implicit in the case management process.

Practice Standards

Individual Licensure

The basic minimum competency standards for members of a profession are usually represented by state licensure, which is defined as ''the process by which an agency of government grants permission to persons to engage in a given profession or occupation by certifying that those licensed have attained the minimal degree of competency necessary to ensure that the public health, safety, and welfare will be reasonably well protected.''[47] For example, the State Nurse Practice Acts contain the guidelines for one who practices as a registered nurse. Other disciplines may also be regulated by the requirements of state licensure.

A practice act, the basic document of standards that will be applied in cases of legal liability, may be somewhat special in the case of home care. Northrop addresses the issue of liability in the home care setting as well as the need to ascertain what the applicable standards of care will be.

> It is difficult to calculate the weight a court or jury will place on the fact that the patient is being cared for in his or her own home rather than in an institution, where traditionally the patient is more dependent, in decisions about nursing accountability. The nursing care setting does relate to the applicable standard of care in that a nurse is expected to act in a reasonable and prudent manner *under the circumstances* . . . Two assumptions will be tested: that medical-surgical nurses can go into home health care without consideration for the difference in setting, and that public health nurses won't need more medical-surgical skills for the more acutely ill patient . . . The home health nurse should be held to the same standard as any other *home health nurse* (not hospital or public health nurse alone, but a new configuration).[48]

Northrop's view of standards of practice for the ''new configuration'' has profound implications for the home care nurse. (Legal issues in home health care are further discussed in Chapter 15.)

Code for Nurses. An additional consideration for the professional nurse regarding ethical standards of practice is found in the ANA's *Code for Nurses with Interpretive Statements*. The ethical considerations mainly involve patient or client rights.[49]

ANA Standards

One of the most important sources for practice standards is the recently published *ANA Standards for Home Health*. The standards therein are based on the *ANA Standards for Community Health Nursing Practice* developed in 1973 and revised in 1986.[50] The ANA recommends that the two sets of standards be used in conjunction. The format of the standards for home health differentiates structure, process, and outcome standards. The process standards also differentiate the practice of the generalist (Baccalaureate preparation) and the specialist (master's preparation). The 12 topic areas and their related standards are shown in Exhibit 4-3. If there is a strong specialty focus in the home health practice, the ANA nursing specialty standards could be applied in addition to the home health standards, for example, in the psychiatric, maternal-child, and oncology areas. For a complete listing of the nursing specialty standards, the reader is referred to the ANA publication catalogue.[51]

Individual Certification

Excellence in specialty practice areas is recognized by individual certification, which is defined as "the process by which a nongovernmental agency or association grants recognition to an individual who has met certain predetermined qualifications specified by that agency or association. Such qualifications may include: (a) graduation from an accredited or approved program, (b) acceptable performance on a qualifying examination or series of examinations, and/or (c) completion of a given amount of work experience."[52] ANA certification is one of the most widely recognized programs for acknowledging excellence in the practice of nursing. There are 19 areas of certification, 7 of which require a bachelor's degree. For each of the 19 areas there are special qualifications. Several of the specialty areas of certification are particularly significant for home health (e.g., community, gerontology, maternal and child, and nursing administration).[53] In addition to the ANA, there are other certifying agencies that recognize excellence in nursing in areas related to home health. One noteworthy program is the rehabilitation certification given under the auspices of the Association of Rehabilitation Nurses.

Exhibit 4-3 American Nurses' Association Standards of Home Health Nursing Practice

Standard I.   Organization of Home Health Services
   All home health services are planned, organized, and directed by a Master's-prepared professional nurse with experience in community health and administration.

Standard II.   Theory
   The nurse applies theoretical concepts as a basis for decisions in practice.

Standard III.   Data Collection
   The nurse continuously collects and records data that are comprehensive, accurate, and systematic.

Standard IV.   Diagnosis
   The nurse uses health assessment data to determine nursing diagnoses.

Standard V.   Planning
   The nurse develops care plans that establish goals. The care plan is based on nursing diagnoses and incorporates therapeutic, preventive, and rehabilitative nursing actions.

Standard VI.   Intervention
   The nurse, guided by the care plan, intervenes to provide comfort, to restore, improve, and promote health, to prevent complications and sequelae of illness, and effect rehabilitation.

Standard VII.   Evaluation
   The nurse continually evaluates the client's and family's responses to interventions in order to determine progress toward goal attainment and to revise the data base, nursing diagnoses, and plan of care.

Standard VIII.   Continuity of Care
   The nurse is responsible for the clients' appropriate and uninterrupted care along the health care continuum, and therefore uses discharge planning, case management, and coordination of community resources.

Standard IX.   Interdisciplinary Collaboration
   The nurse initiates and maintains a liaison relationship with all appropriate health care providers to assure that all efforts effectively complement one another.

Standard X.   Professional Development
   The nurse assumes responsibility for professional development and contributes to the professional growth of others.

Standard XI.   Research
   The nurse participates in research activities that contribute to the profession's continuing development of knowledge of home health care.

Standard XII.   Ethics
   The nurse uses the code for nurses established by the American Nurses' Association as a guide for ethical decision making in practice.

Source: Reprinted from *Standards of Home Health Nursing Practice* with permission of American Nurses' Association, 2420 Pershing Road, Kansas City, Missouri, © 1986.

Client/Patient Standards

There is little question that consumerism has had a large impact on the development and implementation of standards of quality. Donabedian, Sabatino, and McClure are just a few of the health care authorities who have recently made this point.[54] In addition, there is strong organizational support for the consumers' viewpoint on issues of quality. Among the relevant organizations are the American Association of Retired Persons, National Council on Aging, National Consumers League, Hastings Center, Joint Commission, NLN, and ANA.

According to Donabedian, consumers gauge care with respect to the:

- ease of access
- amenities of the setting
- nature of the interpersonal relationships
- effectiveness of the technical care[55]

Standards and criteria could be developed to reflect these key measures as well as consumers' short- and long-term goals.

The American Association of Retired Persons suggests that current quality controls are deficient and that standards should exist in the following areas:

- caregivers
- needs assessment and planning
- case management
- patient bill of rights
- proper role of government[56]

Other sources of standards for safe, humane, and publicly acceptable home health care are the various patient bills of rights, such as the one put forth by the NLN.[57] The first set of newly developed Joint Commission standards addresses patient rights and responsibilities in such areas as informed decision making, continuity of care, confidentiality of information, the care process, and problem solving and grievance mechanisms.[58] The Joint Commission's standards for hospice care and the American Hospital Association's patient bill of rights will contribute to the incorporation of patient rights into the policies and procedures of home care agencies.[59] Although patient bills of rights may not be legal documents, they present accepted standards of care from a legal perspective.

USES

When well chosen and well formulated, standards become an extremely valuable management tool and can be used for various functions, such as

- client care evaluation
- client assessment and planning

- case management evaluation
- evaluation of documentation
- staff orientation and development
- performance appraisal
- peer review
- program evaluation

It is likely that a specific tool would be needed for each separate function. It is a relatively straightforward procedure to combine standards and criteria into a usable tool with whatever format and rating scale is appropriate.[60]

CONCLUSION

There is a vast amount of literature available that directly or indirectly provides a basis for a standards implementation program in home care. In addition, agency policies and procedures will contribute significantly to the program of standards. In this chapter, an effort was made to bring together what were perceived to be the most important resources related to standards. Admittedly, some key items may have been missed, but hopefully those included will provide the essentials necessary to an understanding of a comprehensive program of standards directed toward quality management in home care. The ideal standards implementation program will integrate agency values and mission, mandatory and reimbursement standards, and standards of the profession in such a way that the right of clients to quality services will be clearly upheld.

NOTES

1. Avedis Donabedian, *Explorations in Quality Assessment and Monitoring* (Ann Arbor, Mich.: Health Administration Press, 1982), vol. 2, *The Criteria and Standards of Quality,* 7.

2. Avedis Donabedian, "The Quality of Medical Care: Methods for Assessing and Monitoring the Quality of Care for Research and for Quality Assurance Programs," in *Health—United States* (Hyattsville, Md.: U.S. Department of Health, Education, and Welfare, 1978), 111.

3. James Roberts and Regina Walczak, "Toward Effective Quality Assurance: The Evaluation and Current Status of the JCAH QA Standard," *Quality Review Bulletin* 10 (January 1984): 9.

4. National League for Nursing, Accreditation Division for Home Care and Community Health, *Accreditation Criteria, Standards, and Substantiating Evidences* (New York: National League for Nursing, 1987), 39.

5. American Nurses' Association, *A Plan for Implementation of the Standards of Nursing Practice* (Kansas City, Mo.: Author, 1975), 16.

6. American Nurses' Association, *Standards of Home Health Nursing Practice* (Kansas City, Mo.: Author, 1986), 9.

7. Avedis Donabedian, *Explorations in Quality Assessment and Monitoring* (Ann Arbor, Mich.: Health Administration Press, 1980), vol. 1, *The Definition of Quality and Approaches to Its Assessment,* 81; ibid., 79; ibid., 82–83.

8. Joint Commission on Accreditation of Hospitals, *Monitoring and Evaluation in Nursing Services* (Chicago: Author, 1986), 18–19.

9. Lynn T. Rinke, *Outcome Standards in Home Health. State of the Art* (New York: National League for Nursing, 1988), 47.

10. Lynn T. Rinke and Alexis A. Wilson, "Client-oriented Project Objectives," *Caring* 7, no. 1 (1988): 25–29.

11. American Nurses' Association and Sutherland Learning Associates, *Workbook for Nursing Quality Assurance Committee Members: Community Health Agencies* (Kansas City, Mo.: Authors, 1982), 111.

12. June A. Schmele, "A Method to Implement Nursing Standards in Home Health Care," *Journal of Nursing Quality Assurance* 1, no. 2 (1987): 45.

13. American Bar Association, *The "Black Box" of Home Care Quality,* Report presented by the chairman of the Select Committee on Aging, House of Representatives, 99th Cong., 2d sess., Publication no. 99-573 (Washington, D.C.: GPO, August 1986).

14. Larry Shinnick, "Home Care Standards Present Unique Medical and Legal Challenge," *AARTimes,* April 8, 1984, p. 70.

15. Cynthia Northrop, "Home Health Care: Changing Legal Perspectives," *Nursing Outlook* 34, no. 5 (September-October 1986): 252.

16. E. Michael Flanagan, "Certificate of Need and Licensure," in *Home Health Administration,* ed. Marilyn D. Harris (Owings Mills, Md.: National Health Publishing, 1988), 97.

17. National Association for Home Care, *State Licensure Book* (Washington, D.C.: Author, 1986).

18. American Bar Association, *The "Black Box,"* 63–79.

19. Allen D. Spiegel, *Home Health Care,* 2d ed. (Owings Mills, Md.: National Health Publishing, 1987), 260.

20. Helen K. Mercier, "Homemaker-Home Health Aide Service, Training and Certification in Connecticut," *Caring* 5, no. 4 (1986): 44.

21. Kenneth R. Dolan and Jean Holtz, "The Commission on Accreditation for Home Care in New Jersey," *Caring* 5, no. 4 (1986): 49–50.

22. American Nurses' Association, *Plan for Implementation,* 8.

23. *News from NLN* (Publication of National League for Nursing), October 9, 1987.

24. National League for Nursing, Accreditation Division for Home Care and Community Health, *Accreditation Criteria, Standards, and Substantiating Evidences* (New York: Author, 1987).

25. Ibid.; idem., *Policies and Procedures* (New York: Author, 1987).

26. National League for Nursing, "Home Care Agencies and Community Health Services Accredited by NLN October 1987," *Nursing and Health Care* 9, no. 1 (1988): 55–56.

27. Alexis Wilson, telephone conversation, November 20, 1987.

28. Joint Commission on Accreditation of Healthcare Organizations, *Accreditation Manual for Hospitals—1988* (Chicago: Author, 1987), 53–62.

29. Joint Commission on Accreditation of Healthcare Organizations, *Home Care Standards for Accreditation* (Chicago: Author, 1988).

30. Ibid.

31. Joint Commission on Accreditation of Healthcare Organizations, *Draft of Survey Guidelines* (Chicago: Author, 1987).

32. Barbara A. McCann, "A Patient-oriented Survey Process in Home Care: Can We Assume Quality Care? (Presented at American Public Health Association Annual Meeting, New Orleans, October 20–21, 1987).

33. Nancy Robinson, "Standard Setting and Accreditation," *Caring* 5, no. 4 (1986): 34–39.

34. Department of Health, Education, and Welfare, Social Security Administration, "Conditions of Participation for Home Health Agencies," *Federal Register* 38, no. 135, Part III, Subpart L, July 16, 1973, 18978.

35. Arlene J. Blaha and Anne S. Smith, "Medicare Standards for Home Health Agencies: A Basic Approach," *Caring* 5, no. 8 (1986): 18–20.

36. Peggy R. Webb, "Adherence to Conditions of Participation," in Harris, *Home Health Administration,* (1988): 61–79.

37. Susan L. Hughes, "Home Health Monitoring: Ensuring Quality in Home Care Services," *Hospitals* 56, no. 21 (1982): 74–80.

38. Deloris G. Griffith, "Blending Key Ingredients to Assure Quality in Home Health Care," *Nursing and Health Care* 7, no. 6 (1986): 301–2.

39. "PROs Told to Review Services by HHA, SNF," *OFPR News* (Publication of Oklahoma Foundation for Peer Review), September 1987, pp. 1, 8.

40. Merit C. Kimball, "Senate Shores up Home-Care Benefits," *Health Week* 1 (November 9, 1987): 8.

41. Spiegel, *Home Health Care,* 189.

42. American Bar Association, *The "Black Box,"* 32.

43. Ibid.

44. American Public Health Association, *Model Standards: A Guide for Community Preventive Health Services.* 2d ed. (Washington, D.C.: Author, 1985), 77–79.

45. "Standards for Respiratory Therapy Home Care," *AARTimes* 7 (November 1983): 41–42.

46. Spiegel, *Home Health Care,* 79.

47. American Nurses' Association, *Plan for Implementation,* 8.

48. Northrop, "Home Health Care," 256.

49. American Nurses' Association, *Code for Nurses with Interpretive Statements* (Kansas City, Mo.: Author, 1985).

50. American Nurses' Association, *Standards for Home Health* (Kansas City, Mo.: Author, 1986); idem., *Standards of Community Health Nursing Practice* (Kansas City, Mo.: Author, 1986).

51. American Nurses' Association, *Publication Catalog* (Kansas City, Mo.: Author, 1987).

52. American Nurses' Association, *Plan for Implementation,* 8.

53. American Nurses' Association. *Professional Certification Catalog* (Kansas City, Mo.: Author, 1988).

54. Avedis Donabedian, "Health Policy Forum II: Quality of Care in a Competitive Environment" (Presented at American Public Health Association Annual Meeting, New Orleans, October 20–21, 1987); Charles P. Sabantino, "The 'Black Box' of Home Care Quality" (Presented at American Public Health Association Annual Meeting, New Orleans, October 20–21, 1987); Walter McClure, "Health Care for People as for Profit" (Presented at American Public Health Association Annual Meeting, New Orleans, October 20–21, 1987).

55. Donabedian, "Health Policy Forum II."

56. Joanna Chusid and Lucy Theilheimer, "Standards Needed to Improve Home Care Quality," *The American Nurse,* May 1987, pp. 9–18.

57. "Patient Bill of Rights," *Executive Director Wire* (Publication of National League for Nursing), January-February 1988.

58. Joint Commission on Accreditation of Healthcare Organizations, *Draft of Proposed Standards* (Chicago: Author, 1987).

59. Joint Commission on Accreditation of Healthcare Organizations, *Hospice Standards Manual* (Chicago: Author, 1987). American Hospital Association, "Statement on a Patient's Bill of Rights," *Hospitals,* February 16, 1973, p. 41.

60. Schmele, "Method to Implement Nursing Standards," 45.

Chapter 5

Problem Identification, Topic Selection, and Monitoring and Evaluation Methods

Donna M. Wagner

One of the most challenging aspects of implementing a systematic approach to quality assurance is determining what constitutes quality home health care. Although the literature is replete with definitions of quality and quality assurance, the structural framework is based on the premise that quality is defined by each home care program through its standards, policies, and programs. Therefore, the agency can base its quality assurance program on requirements already delineated in its organizational structure. These requirements, when carefully analyzed, can produce indicators of quality.

INDICATORS: THE BASIS FOR PROBLEM IDENTIFICATION

Individual health professionals have used indicators as a basis for evaluating the quality of their practice for quite some time. An indicator is a *situation, function*, or *event* (e.g., hiring an employee, teaching a patient, administering medications) that is reasonably frequent in the practices being studied and for which there is sound evidence that good medical care is beneficial. Indicators are characterized by criteria that reflect maneuvers known to result in more good than harm when correctly applied or more harm than good when inappropriately applied, or both. Use of indicators assumes that appropriate recordkeeping is a component of the home health services. This is not an unreasonable assumption, as home health care recordkeeping must be specific yet comprehensive for reasons of reimbursement, certification, and licensure. Quantitative scores for the adequacy of care for specific indicators are obtainable by standardized review of client records and other administrative documentation.

Indicators can be developed for any area of home health care. The group that develops the indicators should consist of representatives from the area or specialty for which the indicator will be used. Later in this chapter, methodologies for group delineation and decision making will be explored.

Quality indicators or important aspects of care can be categorized in many ways. Donna M. Wagner, in *Managing for Quality in Home Health Care: Effective Business Strategies*, describes a system for categorization that involves three main areas: employment, client care, and administration.[1] These broad categories can be subdivided into more specific elements to be monitored. These elements include, but are not limited to, the following:

- Employment
  —Recruitment and retention: measures relating to the successful recruitment and retention of competent providers (caregivers/service workers)
  —Employee injury reports: information revealing the impact on employee productivity of incidents and accidents involving employees and volunteers
  —Orientation and training: measures relating to the skills and expertise required to meet care and program standards and maintain caregiver competence
  —Provider competence: measures relating to job descriptions, performance evaluations, credentialing, privileging, and selection of appropriate clinical interventions
- Patient care services
  —Standards of care: measures delineating the expectations for care provided directly to patients (e.g., IV management, functional assessment, etc.)

—Continuity of care: information revealing the process of coordinating clinical services between settings and among providers

—Case management: measures relating to the agency's definition of case management (i.e., the initial assessment, planning, intervention, and evaluation of each patient)

• Administration

—Referral/intake process: measures relating to admission criteria, sources of referrals, structure of the intake process, and payment for services

—Agency standards: statements or policies delineating the scope, function, and purpose of various services (e.g., nursing, physical therapy, occupational therapy, etc.)

—Policies and procedures: statements defining the activities and methods for delivering services in the clinical, fiscal, and support areas

—Patient satisfaction: measures describing patient and family perceptions of overall service

—Productivity: standards defining the efficient allocation of available resources

—Incident reports: information revealing the impact on patient care of incidents and accidents involving patients

—Agency/program evaluation: measures describing the attainment of stated objectives

—Utilization review: information justifying the appropriateness and necessity of services

—State licensing requirements: information revealing compliance with state licensing requirements (where applicable)

—Federal certification: information revealing compliance with conditions of participation

—Voluntary accreditation: measures describing the requirements for accreditation

Each of the three main categories can be monitored from a clinical, fiscal, and support service perspective. From each of these perspectives, the subcategories relevant to the appropriate area of responsibility are selected. For example, all of the subcategories can and should be monitored from a clinical service perspective, while patient satisfaction, program standards, policies and procedures, program evaluation, referral and intake procedures, and productivity are subcategories also appropriately monitored from a fiscal service perspective. This delineation can also be made from a support service perspective, depending on the size and structure of the home care agency. This approach promotes ownership by all members of the agency, for the quality assurance program will become integrated in all aspects of the organization.

Problem Identification

To facilitate problem identification, each subcategory must be further broken down into specific activities. Generally these

activities are well-defined in the agency's policy, protocol, and procedure manuals. These specific activities can be measured and, when evaluated, will assist in problem identification. Each of the above categories will be considered below. Some subcategories will be discussed more than others, as space does not permit in-depth exploration of each. (Nor does it allow for a comprehensive list of activities, which would be virtually endless.)

Employment

This category will include those indicators that relate to typical personnel or human resource functions. As home health care providers, it is our duty to demand polished skills, solid knowledge, professional ethics, commitment to caring, and acceptance of the attitudes of all those in our employ at every level of skill, performance, and responsibility. Many activities within the employment and human resource utilization process can be measured when suspected problems exist or are monitored on an ongoing basis to prevent problems from developing. Some of the activities within the identified subcategories are described below.

• *Recruitment and retention.* Activities include those undertaken to secure qualified employees for the agency, for example, determining the employee skills required to meet client needs, identifying applicants, developing screening criteria, testing for knowledge and skills, developing interviewing techniques, verifying credentials and education, developing job descriptions, determining the performance evaluation methodology, providing recognition for excellent performance, and developing and upgrading skills. Each agency will have specific methods for accomplishing these activities. Quality assurance monitoring will be easier at those agencies where the procedures for these activities are very well defined. Examples of how these activities can be measured follow.

—Agency standard. All RN applicants will complete a written competency test after screening for required experience and credentials. Measurement will take place via review of personnel records of applicants, including those hired, for evidence of test results.

—Agency standard. All applicants who qualify by experience, education, and competency test requirements will be interviewed.

—Agency protocol. Applicant interviews will be conducted using a targeted selection question approach to determine dependability, ability to function independently, reactions under stress, professional judgment, sensitivity to the elderly, integrity, and self-awareness. Responses will be documented.

Recruitment and retention activities can all be measured for compliance by auditing new employee personnel records for evidence of documentation of the various parameters.

- *Employee injury reports*. Among the activities that can be measured are the use of proper reporting mechanisms, timeliness of reporting, follow-up actions, determination of circumstance of injury, determination of lost time, etc.
- *Orientation and training.* Within this subcategory such activities as orientation, on-the-job training, and in-service education can be evaluated relative to employee and client needs.
- *Caregiver competency*. These activities could include monitoring the certification process for specialty nurses or aides and various kinds of credentialing.

Patient Care Services

- *Standards of care*. Standards of care must be updated periodically to keep abreast of the changes in treatment modalities and new techniques. Often standardized care plans are used by agencies, and they too must be updated, along with the standards of care. Expected outcomes can be measured and can yield topics for study.
- *Continuity of care*. In this area, both staff availability and staff capability to meet patient needs can be monitored. Patient access to care and service can be monitored (e.g., the average number of visits per day and per employee, the length of visits, and the average number of visits per patient by discipline). Also, the degree of need for bilingual employees for non-English-speaking patients can be evaluated.
- *Case management*. The myriad activities that go with assessment, planning, intervention, and evaluation are monitored in this subcategory. Activities related to timeliness, procedures, documentation, and communication are but a few.

What activities should be used to measure or evaluate is always an agency-specific decision. Each agency must determine what impacts quality the most in that particular setting. In some agencies, payer sources—through contracts for service—may have a great impact on what activities are measured. In some cases, the payer may specify not only what should be reviewed from a quality perspective, but how often reviews should occur and what sources should be used to collect data. In situations where an agency has no licensure requirements, contractual agreements, or accreditation requirements and is primarily reimbursed through private sources, there is great opportunity for creativity in devising ways of measuring quality.

When does an identified deviation from a standard become a problem? This is the major question asked by most agency administrators who bring quality assurance into their organizations. The author's experience has been that few licensing or accrediting bodies will give a precise percentage or threshold. Given that standards are developed based on the values of the agency, each agency must also determine if 100 percent compliance is realistic or if something less is acceptable. The important thing to remember is that criteria for evaluation and thresholds should be realistic and attainable. If they are not

attainable, the agency staff will see quality assurance as a paper exercise and of no value, for the results will always be negative. If the thresholds are never attained, despite seeming to be realistic, perhaps the agency's standard is too high. It is also important to remember that the selected percentages of acceptable compliance (or thresholds) can be changed if warranted.

To illustrate the above, an agency might have a standard that states, "All home care employees will be supervised by a registered nurse via on-site visitations every 30 days." Upon review and audit, it is discovered that only 75 percent of the employees are supervised by on-site visits every 30 days. Seventy-five percent compliance would not seem acceptable to most agency administrators, since the standard indicates every employee should be supervised by on-site visits every 30 days. After studying the reasons for the 25 percent deviation, the agency may determine that every employee should still be subject to on-site visits, but 30 days is an unrealistically short interval; the agency may decide to change it to 60 days. Another alternative would be to specify that certain levels of staff are to be supervised every 30 days and other levels every 60 days. Restudy of the new standard and measurement of the activities that uphold that standard are necessary to determine if the change made a difference and what its impact on quality was.

Administration

This category includes those activities involving the operation and management of the agency functions. It is larger than the others, as it contains all subcategories that do not fit into the other two.

- *Referral/intake process*. In this subcategory, some of the activities evaluated might include assessing the kind of information obtained on referral, checking the qualifications of those obtaining and interpreting the referral information, assigning case managers, coordinating with patients, and communicating referral information. Following is an example of how one of these activities could be monitored.
  —Agency standard. Each patient referred to the agency will be contacted by the case manager or office coordinator within 24 hours of referral.
  —Agency protocol. Skilled care cases will be contacted by a case manager as soon as possible after referral. Personal care cases will be contacted as soon as a caregiver is scheduled or within 24 hours. Measurement of these activities can occur by reviewing the case manager's assignment log against the patient intake form where timeframes are recorded. The clinical record can also be reviewed for presence of the required documentation.
- *Agency standards*. Activities that can be measured include timely reviews of standards, updates of criteria, and evaluations for relevance to agency functions and service needs of the communication process, the imple-

mentation process, and the monitoring process. An example of how these activities can be monitored follows.

—Agency standard. Agency protocols and procedures will be current for all services provided by the agency.

—Agency procedure. At year end, procedures and protocols will be reviewed. New procedures that are required will be established by each department for each service provided. Each department head will submit the revisions on the appropriate form for administrative approval by January 30 of the new year. Evaluation of the revised procedures and protocols submitted against the current ones will yield the measures needed. Evaluation could be extended to include specific components of the procedure (e.g., equipment needed, skills needed, teaching parameters, format, documentation requirements, etc.).

- *Patient satisfaction*. Most agencies use patient satisfaction questionnaires to evaluate patient response to services. Results of these patient satisfaction questionnaires can lead to information for further study.
- *Productivity*. Patient classification systems, diagnosis-based classification systems for costing services, etc., can be used as a basis for measuring productivity.
- *Incident reports*. Timeliness, accuracy of completion, extenuating circumstances, and proper follow-up can be measured and evaluated.
- *Agency program evaluation*. This Medicare requirement has many mandated components. Each of those can be evaluated for accuracy, timeliness, and appropriate completion.
- *Utilization review*. The utilization review and the clinical record review process can be evaluated for its value to the organization and its effectiveness. Is it collecting the correct or required data? Is the service area still appropriate and the population served? Has analysis taken place consistently within the utilization review process and have changes resulted from the process?
- *State licensing requirements*. More and more states are requiring licensure for home care operations. Each has specific requirements that must be met. Findings from these state surveys to determine the degree of compliance with these requirements produce topics for future study.
- *Federal certification*. The conditions of participation of the Medicare program set out certain requirements. Survey results can yield topics for further study.

Pretesting

New or previously developed indicators should be pretested. Pretesting helps to determine the feasibility of the indicators in the environment in which they are to be measured. Can episodes (e.g., medication errors or patient falls) be found? Can the criteria be applied (1) to arrive at a score or rating, (2) to train abstractors, and (3) to conduct inter- and intraobserver agreement studies with the abstractors? It is always unfortunate if problems are detected only after a study is completed. Training and pretesting should be done under conditions as similar as possible to those of the main study.

Quality assurance monitoring in home health care can often be done with existing personnel. The author's experience suggests that the abstractors should be health professionals. Abstractors are the link between the quality assurance committee and the home health care professional or service under review.

Indicators can be used in the evaluation of innovative health care programs, such as the introduction of new professionals or other changes in organizational or financial aspects of home health care. Indicators can also be used in continuing education. The bringing together of health professionals for the purpose of specifying criteria can be educationally useful in itself. More important, the criteria then can be applied to client charts retrospectively. The results of the review of client charts constitute important feedback for the continuing education process. Indicators can also be associated with criteria useful in assessing the impact of continuing education; for example, prospective studies that assess the care provided following involvement in continuing education activities. Indicators provide a means of selectively identifying areas requiring improved performance.

Among the important objectives of using indicators as an approach are the following:

- to identify providers who are practicing at an unacceptable level generally or in specific areas
- to designate remedial actions to correct the deficiencies identified
- to ensure that the remedial actions have been effective

Quality assurance involves both quality of care assessment (e.g., the "results" of the review of patient charts and the scoring of indicators) and subsequent changes in the behavior of those involved so as to correct deficiencies. Changes in behavior are more likely to occur if the health professionals are willing to study the reviews of their practices (for their own educational benefit) and if they are motivated to alter their method of managing patients. The use of indicators has the potential for successfully dealing with educational needs and public accountability.

GROUP TECHNIQUES

To facilitate problem identification, a process must be followed that will produce the desired results as efficiently as possible. Unlike in the case of hospitals, detailed regulations or guidelines for selecting subjects of studies do not exist. Home care providers are currently allowed to establish their own priorities in selecting individual topics for conducting required quality assurance studies. While content considerations are helpful (e.g., health care outcomes and procedures and client feedback protocols), the decision process by which topics for study are selected and prioritized is of great importance. (For example, who determines topics? Who sets priorities? What data are examined? What values are important and how are final judgments made?)

Regardless of the techniques used, some guidelines should prevail. When critical decisions are made arbitrarily by one individual, the information base for deciding is usually limited and the required value judgments remain implicit, unchallenged, and the biases of that individual often predominate. To enhance the process, individuals who work well together and represent various functional areas of the organization (e.g., nurses, social workers, therapists, administrators, technicians, office personnel, and a respected lay person to represent client interests and values) should be included. These individuals differ in their perspectives and knowledge regarding local issues, such as the level of present personnel performance, workloads, interpersonal relations, quality of services provided, and community expectations. Such issues can prove as important as technical factors in identifying deficiencies and analyzing the likely benefits and costs of a recommended project.

In preparation for any type of group process, the following should be reviewed by team members:

- the agency's philosophy or mission statement (which provides direction for services and programs)
- a current description of providers and staff
- demographic characteristics of clients served
- a list of the clients presenting complaints
- a list of final diagnoses
- utilization statistics
- claims review statistics
- topics previously studied for quality assurance purposes
- reprints of literature relevant to priority setting
- annotated quality assurance bibliographies

These materials are helpful in developing prerequisite skills and a common level of understanding of quality assurance and for suggesting and analyzing topics relevant to the home care agency, the staff, and the consumers.

Four group process techniques that have been used extensively in many settings can also be used in home health care. They are (1) the use of focus groups, (2) the nominal group technique, (3) the use of quality circles, and (4) the delphi technique.

Focus Groups

A focus group can provide an efficient method for identifying issues of quality care. By centering on a particular issue with all the involved persons, the issue, together with all the associated subissues (including the impact on client care or the agency itself), can be thoroughly discussed.

An informal provider discussion, such as a discussion among nurses concerned that diabetic clients are being discharged before the client education program can be completed, could lead to a joint evaluation by physicians, nurses, and clients. The debate whether the diabetic program requires modification might include input from the clients, for example, their views on whether they were adequately instructed in self-care for their diabetes and what their continuing needs may entail. Another focus group might include therapists concerned about the increasing difficulty in obtaining state-of-the-art equipment for their clients.

Such focus groups purposely constructed and convened by the quality assurance coordinator or another suitable person for the express purpose of identifying issues for study provide an effective and inexpensive problem identification method that can be instituted by home care organizations of any size. Inclusion of clients and families can create a new and broader practical perspective.[2]

The Nominal Group Technique

A structured selection process often used by health care organizations is a variation of the nominal group process described by Delbecq, Van deVen, and Gustafson.[3] This "brainstorming" process ensures that everyone participates, not just those who speak the loudest and fastest.

For purposes of establishing consensus and priorities, the composition and size (five to nine) of the topic team is important. Having at least five members versed in clinical and administrative performance, including a consumer, ensures a broad base of experience and knowledge regarding the organization and potential problems; having less than ten members avoids unwieldy group dynamics and inefficient use of meeting time.

The goal of a nominal group meeting is to develop a list of cost-effective topics; prioritize them according to their importance to the agency, staff, and consumers; and make recommendations regarding additional data, literature, or consultations needed to make final decisions about which quality assurance topics are worthy of study.

The procedure for conducting this meeting is as follows.

1. *Introduction*. The quality assurance coordinator clarifies the purpose of the meeting, describes the tasks before the group, indicates the timing of the session, and answers general questions. The concept and the target issues, as well as the framework for establishing priorities, are discussed.
   - All members of the group are eligible and expected to contribute any idea they believe is relevant.
   - Each idea will be recorded as worded by its author (with minimal editing).
   - There will be no criticism or judging of ideas.

- No idea will be stricken or revised, but alternate ideas or variations will be accepted and recorded as new ideas.
- The above rules will prevail until the leader suspends them by calling for discussion and clarification of the ideas.

2. *Topic Nominations.* The coordinator distributes blank cards to participants and elicits ideas in writing from each team member regarding his or her perceptions of problem areas related to the agency, providers, and the provision of care.

3. *Collation of Topics.* The coordinator requests each team member to recommend one problem on his or her list. The coordinator records the problem on a flip chart or blackboard that is visible to the whole group. The process continues for two or three rounds until the most promising topics from individual lists are on the master list or until 10 or 12 leading topics are recorded.

4. *Topic Clarification.* Four dimensions of each topic are then clarified by the team member suggesting the topic. The member describes as precisely as possible its impact on clients, on health problems, and on providers and what care or service changes would be needed to effect improvement. This discussion should serve to elaborate, to defend, to dispute, and to suggest categories for the items or to synthesize similar items into one.

5. *Weighting.* The coordinator asks each team member to rate each topic on the master list on a scale from one to five (with five being high), according to their judgment of quality assurance cost-effectiveness. The coordinator reminds the participants that an achievable benefit must be judged in terms of the evidence that the target benefit is achievable, the health care technology involved is efficacious, and effecting improvement, if outcome deficiencies are confirmed, is feasible. The importance of verifying current outcome deficiencies and projecting the likelihood that improvement can be achieved will make the time and expense of the total project worth the effort.

6. *Ranking and Prioritizing.* In round robin fashion, the coordinator marks the rank given by each team member on the flip chart next to each item (e.g., 5, 3, 1, 3, etc.). Items receiving the highest scores are further discussed to determine whether there is a consensus among the group and to elicit team judgments concerning the feasibility of items in terms of quality assurance activities and the benefits achievable within the limits of acceptable project costs.

For each topic selected and approved by the agency's executive board or another approval-granting body, qualified staff should be appointed to initiate the quality assurance project. The nominal group process, by facilitating the contribution of each team member, provides a meaningful educational experience when innovative topics are generated.

Quality Circles

Another approach to setting priorities, identifying problems, and selecting topics involves quality circles. Using quality circles solves problems by ensuring higher quality services while providing for employee participation, and there is no need for organizational changes or additional full-time personnel. Quality circles offer a variety of other benefits, including (1) increased productivity, (2) greater employee involvement in problem solving, (3) higher morale and job satisfaction, and (4) reduced absenteeism and turnovers.

Each quality circle team consists of seven or eight members representing both management and staff and is usually led by an employee chosen by the team. Meeting on a regular basis and kept informed of the quality concerns and problems causing the greatest resource strain, the team can quickly identify where it should be focusing its efforts. The team is used to make the actual improvements in quality.

The quality assurance coordinator has a pivotal role in developing the team concept and is responsible for

- training team leaders and team members in problem-solving skills
- initiating team projects
- assisting the team leader and other members to make oral and written presentations to management
- following up with management to facilitate management decisions on team recommendations

Spending sufficient training time on developing critical problem-solving and teamwork skills increases quality team effectiveness. With the team's ability to identify problems and their causes, gather and tabulate data, and recommend improvements, the implementation of solutions is usually assured and productivity enhanced.

As quality circle members generate ideas in brainstorming sessions, the following criteria are helpful in evaluating ideas:

- Does this group have control over the situation? Is the group causing or contributing to the problem?
- Can the group take before and after measurements regarding the problem?
- Is the problem solvable or reducible?
- Would management support a recommendation addressing the problem? If the recommendation is conceptual? Financial?

As part of the quality assurance process, quarterly reports should be submitted to the quality assurance committee by the quality circle. The quality assurance committee members can assist in identifying resources and acting as liaisons with other standing agency committees.

The Delphi Technique

Because the delphi technique does not require face-to-face group contact, large home care agencies or corporations with

agencies or satellites in different geographic areas could benefit from applying it. This technique, a formalized approach to
soliciting and incorporating staff members' perspectives, uses
repeated rounds of questionnaires for re-evaluating and bringing about a gradual convergence of opinion. In regard to
gathering staff input for quality assurance, this technique has
several advantages: The anonymity of all respondents is pre-
served, all ideas are thought to have equal merit, large numbers of staff can participate, and, most importantly, priorities
of the staff and not just the quality assurance committee are
recognized. There is a need with this technique to make a
commitment to act on the results and to devote time to refinement of the questionnaire. Without this, staff will perceive the
task as a token effort to gain their participation without really
putting any value on their input. The ability to draw on
expertise for topic selection and methodology design from a
communitywide or even larger base is of obvious worth in
increasing the validity and generalizability of studies and
recommendations.

SUMMARY

Regardless of the mechanism used for problem identification, topic selection, and methodologies, the most essential
determinant is the fundamental view of the quality assurance
program as a process or a product. The value of professional
staff engaging in meaningful self-examination should not be
underscored by the quantities of data produced or number of
problems identified.[4]

Just as the array of available approaches has increased, so
has the pressure to balance expenditures of resources against
the anticipated value to the agency, the profession, and the
client. The presentation above of the variety of philosophical
perspectives and the range of evaluation techniques is intended
to provide an overview of the alternatives from which quality
assurance leaders must choose if they want to achieve progress
toward excellence in client care.

NOTES

1. Donna M. Wagner, *Managing Quality in Home Health Care* (Rockville,
Md.: Aspen Publishers, 1988), chap. 11.

2. Richard E. Thompson, "A Method for Identifying Quality Assurance
Issues/Problems," in *Quality Assurance in Hospitals*, ed. Nancy O. Graham
(Rockville, Md.: Aspen Publishers, 1982), 76–78.

3. A.L. Delbecq, A.H. Van deVen, and D.H. Gustafson, *Group Techniques
for Program Planning: A Guide to Nominal Group and Delphi Processes*
(Glenview, Ill. Scott, Foresman, 1973).

4. Catherine Wilbert, "Selecting Topics/Methodologies," in *Quality
Assurance: A Complete Guide to Effective Programs*, ed. Claire
Meisenheimer (Rockville, Md.: Aspen Publishers, 1985), 125–26.

REFERENCES

ASQC Quality Circles Technical Committee. *The Quality Circle Process:
Elements for Success.* Milwaukee, Wis.: American Society for Quality
Control Publications, Quality Press, 1982.

Baker, Frank. "Quality Assurance and Program Evaluation." *Evaluation and
the Health Professions* 6 (June 1983).

Bergman, R. "Understanding the Patient in All His Human Needs." *Journal
of Advanced Nursing* 8, (1983): 185–90.

Bradley, D. "Employee Credentialing: A Quality Assurance Tool." *Journal
of Quality Assurance* 6, no. 4 (1984): 19–20.

Brook, R.H. *Quality of Care Assessment: A Comparison of Five Methods of
Peer Review.* Publication no. HRA-74-31000. Rockville, Md.: U.S.
Department of Health, Education, and Welfare, Health Resources Admin-
istration, 1973.

Combs-Orme, T., J. Reis, and L.D. Ward. "Effectiveness of Home Visits by
Public Health Nurses in Maternal and Child Health: An Empirical
Review." *Public Health Reports* 100 (September-October 1985): 490–99.

Cook, Michael H. "Quality Circles—They Really Work, but. . ." *Training
and Development* 36 (January 1982): 4.

Crockett, Davy, and Sue Sutcliffe. "Staff Participation in Nursing Quality
Assurance." *Nursing Management*, October 1986.

Daniels, Kaye. "Planning for Quality in the Home Care System." *Quality
Review Bulletin* 12 (July 1986): 247–51.

Decker, C.M. "Quality Assurance: Accent on Monitoring." *Journal of
Quality Assurance* 18, no. 1 (1986): 14–17.

Dietz, James W., and James L. Phillips. "The Quality Assurance Committee
in the Hospital Structure." *Quality Review Bulletin* 1980.

Drummond, Katherine, and Judith Muenchow. "Minding Your P's (Person-
nel) and Q's (Quality Assurance) for a Successful Homemaker-Home
Health Aide Program." Presented at the Annual Meeting and Homecare
Exhibition of the National Association for Home Care, New Orleans,
September 1986.

Evers, H.R. "Key Issues in Nursing Practice: Ward Management II." *Nursing Times* 78 (1982b): 25–26.

Evers, H.R. *Key Issues in Nursing Practice: Ward Management II.* *Nursing Times* 78 (1982b): 25–26.

Fine, P.R., and S.R. Better. "Assessment and Evaluation of Home Health
Team Activities." *International Journal of Rehabilitation Research* 2
(December 1979): 507–8.

Geldbach, Patricia L., Walter F. Klein, and Rusti C. Moore. "Quality
Control Circles Solving OR Problems." *AORN Journal* 34 (December
1981): 1029.

Gonella, J., L. Miller, H. Smithline. "Identifying Patient Care Problems by
Analyzing Critical Indicator Data." *Quality Review Bulletin* 9 (1980):
16–22.

Gordon, M. "Determining Study Topics." *Nursing Research* 29, no. 2
(1980): 83–87.

Grau, Lois, "What Older Adults Expect from the Nurse." *Geriatric Nursing*
5 (1984): 14–18.

Griffin, A.P. "A Philosophical Analysis of Caring in Nursing." *Journal of
Advanced Nursing* 8 (1983): 289–95.

Health Care Financing Administration. *Conditions of Participation for Medicare.*

Hirschfeld, M. "Home Care versus Institutionalization: Family Care-Giving
and Senile Brain Disease." *International Journal of Nursing Studies* 20
(1983): 23–32.

Holmes, Joan. "Pride in Service: A Motivational Approach to Quality Hospi-
tal-Based Home Care." Presented at the Annual Meeting and Homecare
Exhibition of the National Association for Home Care, New Orleans,
September 1986.

Hutchins, David. *Quality Circles Handbook.* Milwaukee, Wis.: American
Society for Quality Control Publications, Quality Press, 1985.

Jewell, Linda N., and H. Joseph Reitz. *Group Effectiveness in Organizations.*
Glenview, Ill.: Scott, Foresman, 1981.

Kitson, Alison L. "Indicators of Quality in Nursing Care: An Alternative
Approach." *Journal of Advanced Nursing* 11 (1986): 133–44.

Knudson, Maureen. "Teamwork: The Crux of Multidisciplinary Audit." *Quality Review Bulletin* (1978).

Maser, Marjorie. "Mount Sinai Invests in Quality Circles." *Health Services Manager* 15 (February 1982): 12.

Mottet, Elizabeth A. "Monitoring Is Only the Beginning." *Journal of Nursing Quality Assurance* 1 (May 1987): 23.

National Association for Home Care. "GAO Evaluates Expanded Home Care Services." *Caring* 2 (January 1983): 4–5.

Purgatorio-Howard, Kathy. "Improving a Quality Assurance Program." *Nursing Management* 17 (April 1986): 38–41.

Schackenberg, L.A., B.E. Cooper, M.B. Derrick, P.M. Nobles, and R.B. Kellett. "Quality Assurance: A Team Approach." *Caring* 2 (September 1983): 23–24.

Scherman, S.L. *Community Health Nursing Care Plans: A Guide for Home Health Care Professionals.* New York: Wiley, 1985.

Schreiber, Kari. "Quality Outcome Indicators As Institutional Measurements." Presented at the Tenth Annual Conference of the National Association of Quality Assurance Professionals, Las Vegas, October 1985.

Smeltzer, C.H., A.S. Hinshaw, and B. Feltman. "The Benefits of Staff Nurse Involvement in Monitoring the Quality of Patient Care." *Journal of Nursing Quality Assurance* 1 (May 1987): 1.

Waszak, John J. "Adapting QC's to Health Care: Some Special Challenges." *Hospital Progress* 63, no. 8 (1982): 47–48, 63.

Weinstein, Edwin L. "Developing a Measure of the Quality of Nursing Care." *Journal of Nursing Administration* 6 (1976): 1–3.

Westfall, U.E. "Nursing Diagnosis: Its Use in Quality Assurance." *Topics in Clinical Nursing* 5 (January 1984): 78–87.

Williamson, J., F.J. Hudson, and M. Nevins. *Principles of Quality Assurance and Cost Containment in Health Care: A Guide for Medical Students, Residents and Other Health Professionals.* San Francisco: Jossey-Bass, 1982.

Zimmer, J.G., A. Groth-Juncker, and J. McCusker. "A Randomized Controlled Study of a Home Health Care Team." *American Journal of Public Health* 75 (February 1985): 134–41.

Zimmer, J.G., and A. Groth-Juncker. "A Time-Motion Study of Patient Care Activities of a Geriatric Home Care Team." *Home Health Care Services Quarterly* 4 (Spring 1983): 67–78.

Chapter 6

Data Collection Mechanisms

June A. Schmele

It is commonly thought that there is a lack of information regarding data collection mechanisms used to measure quality of care in home health. However, this view may be mistaken, as there is a moderate amount of literature available on this subject, including literature on generic measures. Generic measures have potential for testing and use in home health. The published reports are generally of two types: those focusing on practical application with little or no reference to reliability and validity and those of a research nature, which may have little or no reference to practical application.

There may be several reasons why it is difficult to access data collection mechanisms specifically for home health. The major reason is that these reports are widely dispersed throughout the literature. Even though many approaches are being successfully used in practice, they may not yet have been published. In other instances, even when there has been publication, the specific data collection mechanisms may have been tangential to the major purpose of the article and consequently not addressed in detail.

Further, some of the research focusing on quality measurement in home health is in the beginning stages and may not yet be developed to the point of practical application in a field setting. There is a recognized need in both practice and research to develop clear, straightforward, easily administered measures that will be both valid and reliable. One move in this direction is to recognize the need to build upon established measures and to standardize them.

It is encouraging to consider current state-of-the-art data collection mechanisms and to see an increasing emphasis on them, which is probably due to the rapid environmental changes in the home health milieu. The impetus for measurement of quality is clearly seen in the legislative arena and among such groups as the National Association for Home Care (NAHC), National Hospice Association, American Association of Retired Persons (AARP), Joint Commission on Accreditation of Healthcare Organizations (Joint Commission), National League for Nursing (NLN), and American Nurses' Association (ANA). One gets the message that if the profession does not develop, test, and promulgate valid and reliable measures of care, such measures will be externally imposed upon the home care field.

One of the reasons that there may be a lack of concerted and coordinated efforts to establish measures of quality is that frequently there is limited integration within home health agencies of the quality assurance (QA) program, the standards implementation program, and data collection. Each of these is often seen as isolated, with an emphasis on itself to the exclusion of the other programs. It is the author's view that it would be helpful to see QA, standards, and data collection within the total context of a QA system that uses criterion measures to collect data in order to determine the degree to which standards have been met, thus "assuring" quality. One exception to this might be when data collection is being done strictly for research purposes. However, even then the application to practice should not be neglected.

The major purpose of this chapter is to present an overview of methods of data collection, to review selected structure, process, and outcome measurement approaches, and to summarize selected composite resources. It is acknowledged that

The author wishes to acknowledge Katherine Scimeca, R.N., B.S.N., for her assistance in the preparation of this chapter and Karen Stolte, R.N., Ph.D., for her critical review.

this is not an exhaustive review. However, the selected approaches and resources are representative. Hopefully this overview will serve as a resource to readers and direct them to pursue their interest in specific areas in more detail.

DATA COLLECTION MECHANISMS

The term *data collection mechanism* will be used broadly to refer to sources of data, methods of gathering data, and criterion measures as well as tools or instruments. For purposes of this chapter, data collection mechanisms will be equated with quality measurement mechanisms.

Definitions

It is recognized that there are semantic differences involving key words, ideas, and concepts. The definitional framework for this chapter is as follows:

- *Standard*. A statement of excellence reflecting the current state of practice based on knowledge and experience.
- *Criterion*. An observable measure that reflects the accomplishment of the standard. Generally, there are several criterion measures for each standard. In most instances the criterion measures make up the items in the tool or instrument. These items need to be measurable, valid, reliable, and acceptable.
- *Structure, process, and outcome*. The widely accepted components of different aspects of quality.
  —*Structure* denotes resources (organization, physical, human, financial, etc.).
  —*Process* denotes activities that are carried out to render care.
  —*Outcome* denotes the final result of the care.
- *Measures*. Criteria assembled in the form of a tool or instrument.
- *Data*. Information.

Data Sources

There are various data sources (origins, derivations) that can be used to collect information about quality of care. The source used will depend upon the quality component (structure, process, or outcome) that has been selected for study, as well as the source accessibility and availability, time and personnel requirements, and cost of accessing. The most common sources of data include

- clinical records (patient/client and agency)
- care plans
- referral forms
- agency operational records
- agency policies and procedures
- patients/clients
- families
- nurses
- other professionals
- paraprofessionals
- home visits
- nurse-patient interactions

It is important to give careful consideration to the selection of the data source. The value of the data as a measure of quality will be contingent upon the reliability of the source as a reflection of care given. For example, if clinical records do not accurately represent the care given, this source would fail as a true measure of quality. In such cases, it may be most appropriate to use more than one data source; the clinical record and the nurse-patient interaction during a home visit may together constitute the most comprehensive source of data.

Gathering data from one or more additional sources may support or augment the original source by providing additional information with which to explain and interpret data. On the other hand, one data source may contradict or negate another data source, and this would require additional sources to gain the required information for determining the quality of care. An examination of the methods used may also be warranted to determine the process or technique best able to gain appropriate, valid, and reliable data.

Methods

Various methods (procedures, processes, techniques) of data collection can be used. The following are among the methods most recognized (note that they vary in complexity):

- *Audit*. A review of clinical records used to determine the presence or absence of predetermined criteria. (A retrospective audit deals with the clinical record after discharge from the service, while a concurrent audit is accomplished while the client or patient is still receiving services.)
- *Peer review*. A professional of equal standing reviews the quality of care.
- *Direct observation*. The patient or the nurse is viewed by a participant or nonparticipant observer.
- *Interview*. A formal or informal conference or meeting held for the purpose of determining quality.
- *Supervisory evaluation*. A review of performance by a supervisor.
- *Self-evaluation*. A review of performance by self.
- *Checklist*. A "laundry list" of characteristics predetermined as measures of quality of care.
- *Criteria mapping*. Clinical protocols, shown on a flow diagram, that specify a strategy of care.[1]

- *Staging*. A method used to investigate the antecedents of adverse outcomes.[2]
- *Patient satisfaction survey*. An assessment of patients' opinions about care.
- *Sentinel*. An epidemiological approach in which factors contributing to disease, disability, or complications are monitored.[3]
- *Tracers*. Criteria are developed for the management of problems having an impact on patients' health in a specified population group.[4]
- *Trajectory*. A cohort with distinguishing characteristics is followed through the health care system, with happenings being noted at various junctures as well as at the termination of care.[5]

Measures

Using the classification framework of the quality components of structure, process, and outcome, selected representative quality measures will next be considered. Frequently measures have criteria dealing with more than one of the components; thus placement may be somewhat arbitrary. In some instances it is not clear what the major components are. The intent of classifying is simply to establish some semblance of order among the various data collection measures, which are brought together from widely scattered sources.

Structure

Structure components largely measure an agency's resource capability to provide certain services. Structure measures, of all the quality assurance components, are probably least often cited in the literature. The reason for this may be that many of the structure standards are found in the guidelines for licensure, accreditation, and certification, which frequently include implicit or explicit criterion measures. Thus, the accreditation self-study forms and survey report forms could in themselves be considered the measures. For example, the Medicare certification form and the NLN accreditation self-study report serve to measure capability to provide services. In addition, the Joint Commission criteria supporting each standard are stated as "required characteristics" and include a five-point Likert-type rating scale for each criterion item. This scale has value in determining compliance and could also be used with other criteria as well:

1. Substantial compliance: consistently meets *all* major provisions of standard or required characteristics
2. Significant compliance: meets *most* provisions
3. Partial compliance: meets *some* provisions
4. Minimal compliance: meets *few* provisions
5. Noncompliance: fails to meet provisions
6. Nonapplicable: does not pertain[6]

Other sources of structure data are agency reports, clinical records, and various repositories of demographic data. Since in many instances structure criteria are considered to be the most observable and quantifiable, a checklist approach to determine the presence or absence of specified resources may work very effectively.

Much structure data is included in annual, monthly, and day-to-day agency records, which provide important information. Unfortunately, there is no standardized data gathering and analysis format. The NAHC is extremely concerned about agency inability to systematically gather, analyze, and use structure data at local, regional, and national levels.[7] Consequently, a major NAHC effort is being directed toward the establishment of a national minimum data set that would be useful at all levels.

Process

Generic approaches to process measurement, although developed in the 1960s, have potential for current usage. The Quality Patient Care Scale (Qual pacs), developed by Wandelt and Ager, is a method of concurrent appraisal of nursing care, with the primary focus on the patient.[8] The Phaneuf Nursing Audit uses retrospective review of the patient's records.[9] The Slater Nursing Competency Scale is an observational tool for measuring the quality of an individual nurse's performance.[10] Phaneuf and Wandelt have more recently summarized their work and discussed its potential for current usage.[11] The Slater scale has recently been tested in home health by Schmele and Hough.[12] It shows promise for this setting, although major drawbacks are the amount of preliminary teaching required for the observer and the time expenditure involved.

Hegyvary and her associate have legitimized the nursing process itself as a measure of quality of care.[13] The credibility of this approach rests on the assumption that the nursing process is the special domain of nursing. Although Hegyvary's work was done in the acute setting, the conceptual application is transferable to home health. Curtis and Simpson, Mackie and Welch, Lillesand and Korff, and others have developed approaches based on the nursing process but for use in the acute care setting.[14]

The nursing process framework as a basis for instrumentation has also been studied in the community setting. A Canadian study by Cradduck utilizes the Craig Audit Tool.[15] Schwab and Pierce report the development and testing of an instrument based on the nursing process and used to assess clinical nursing practice in a rural decentralized case management system for chronically ill children.[16] Schmele reports the development and testing of an instrument based on the nursing process in the community setting. The Schmele Instrument to Measure the Process of Nursing Practice in Community Nursing Service (SIMP) is a three-part instrument that uses three data sources (observation, record, and patient); each part focuses on the elements of the nursing process (assessing, planning, implementing, and evaluating).[17] Representative items from SIMP are shown in Exhibit 6-1. This instrument has also been tested in a home health setting[18] and is currently being further refined and tested in several other home health

Exhibit 6-1 Representative Items from the Schmele Instrument to Measure the Process of Nursing Practice in Community Nursing Service

---

Part I—Nurse Client Interaction (Observation)

Assessment
3. Did the nurse validate with the client the reason for the visit?
4. Was there family involvement in the visit (family either is present or nurse asks questions about the family)?

Planning
1. Was a short-term goal (until time of next visit) established?
3. Did the client participate in goal setting?

Implementation
4. On a scale of 0 to 4, how do you rate the frequency of the nurse's reinforcement of client and family strengths?
5. During the visit was the time for the next visit established?

Evaluation
1. Was any mention made by the nurse of the nursing care goal (set at previous visit)?
2. Was the client's progress toward nursing care goals discussed with the client?

Part II—Client Record (Audit)

Assessment
2. Does the data base include documentation of a physical assessment?
4. Is there documented evidence that a nursing diagnosis (problem situation in which the nurse can intervene) was made during the first visit?

Planning
1. Is there evidence of a short-term goal (until time of next visit)?
3. Is there documentation of action plans (steps to be taken) to meet the goal?

Implementation
1. Is there documentation about what was done during the visit?
2. Is there documented evidence of teaching that was done during the visit?

Evaluation
1. Is there documented evidence of progress toward goal accomplishment?
2. Is there documented evidence of reassessment during this visit?

Part III—Client Perception (Survey Questionnaire)

Assessment
1. How satisfied were you that the nurse listened well to what you said today?
2. How satisfied were you that the nurse understood what your main health problem was?

Planning
1. Were you involved in deciding what things you are expected to do for your health before the next visit?
3. Did you help determine what changes you would try to make to maintain or improve your health?

Implementation
2. How well do you understand what you need to do to keep healthy?
4. Do you feel that you learned something new about your health?

Evaluation
1. Did you and your nurse discuss your health progress since your last visit?
5. Did you feel that you had a chance to discuss any health care concerns that you wished to?

NOTE: Response choices vary with items.

Source: Copyright 1985 by the Joint Commission on Accreditation of Healthcare Organizations, Chicago. Reprinted with permission.

---

settings throughout the country.[19] Schmele's current work is a refinement of her earlier work on the observational portion of the instrument, and it involves home health field testing of the Schmele Instrument to Measure the Process of Nursing Practice in Home Health (SIMP-H).[20]

Davidson discusses the development of a format for concurrent and retrospective home health evaluation, which includes both the subacute and maintenance phase of care.[21] She also includes a complete set of criteria, exceptions, and data retrieval instructions for the diagnostic category of juvenile diabetes mellitus. This format and criteria set would provide a framework and model for similar program implementations.

Other approaches specifically in home care include the development of a home care risk management program by Tehan and Colegrove.[22] They recommend the development of assessment items to determine the risk factors associated with specific programs. For example, they propose a set of risk factors for evaluating an intravenous antibiotic administration program. It is relatively straightforward to transform these assessment factors into standards or criteria, which then could be used as quality measures for this specific program.

There is currently a major focus on whether documentation is adequate for both reimbursement and quality. However, objectives of the QA studies may not necessarily be congruent. Two approaches that include the enumeration of guidelines (criteria) for documentation are those of Holloway and the staff of *Caring*, the official publication of the NAHC.[23]

Wright and Wheeler report the use of a microcomputer in a community setting to audit clinical records based on pre-established nursing standards adopted from the Army Nurse Corp and the ANA Standards of Community Health Nursing. The standards and criteria deal with following major aspects of the nursing process:

1. data collection
2. nursing care problems
3. nursing care goals
4. nursing care plan
5. nursing actions
6. reassessment of patient progress[24]

This approach entailed review of the records and data entry (which required approximately three minutes per record). A computerized QA system has even more potential if the records were previously computerized.

Koerner studied selected correlates of job performance using the Job Description Index (JDI), the Leader Behavior Description Questionnaire (LBDQ), five state board licensure examinations, and the Job Performance Measures (JPM) as process measures of care documented on the clinical record.[25] (The JPM was based on the ANA Standards of Practice.) Although the study revealed negative correlation between independent variables and the dependent variable of job performance, further study of job performance as a process measure is merited. Koerner concludes that records may not reflect the actual delivery of care. Wiseman describes the participative approach used in the development of criteria for home health intravenous therapy and hyperalimentation.[26] These criteria encompass structure, process, and outcome measures.

The Foundation of Record Education of the American Medical Records Association, under the project directorship of Miller and the sponsorship of the W.K. Kellogg Foundation, has completed a home care client record project that established model forms and comprehensive guidelines for client home care record documentation.[27] The documentation guidelines include requirements of Medicare, the Joint Commission, NLN, and the National Home Caring Council (NHCC). The project resulted in a handbook for record documentation and management, including model forms and guidelines. In addition, this work has important implications for home health care minimum data collection needs.

The Ad Hoc Committee, Respiratory Care Section, American College of Chest Physicians, has developed guidelines for home care management of the long-term mechanically ventilated patient.[28] Major topic areas include (1) medical assessment, (2) critical factors for patient selection, (3) discharge criteria, and (4) respiratory care for ventilator-assisted infants, children, and adults. The comprehensive set of policies, procedures, and guidelines could serve as a model for anyone wishing to develop a similar program.

Outcomes

There is an increasing emphasis on studying outcomes of home health care. One of the major drawbacks of this measure of quality is that an outcome can rarely be directly related to the process, because there is a multitude of intervening variables in the home setting. Further, in multidisciplinary situations, there is difficulty relating the outcome to the "process" of a specific discipline. However, in this age of cost containment, the importance of outcome should not be underestimated. Both the ANA and, more recently, the NLN have developed step-by-step procedures for guidance through the process of developing outcome criteria.[29] Much of the instrumentation presently available to determine outcome measures is found in the reporting of research. Selected examples will be cited.

In the early 1980s, Barkauskus studied the effectiveness of public health nursing home visits on the postpartum conditions of mothers and infants. She utilized the Post Partum Interview Questionnaire (PIQ) to measure health and service utilization and the Home Observation for Measurement of the Environment (HOME) to measure social, emotional, and cognitive support.[30] Although the findings revealed only minimal differences between home-visited and non-home-visited families, these two instruments may be usable as quality outcome measures.

Stanwick and his associates, using a sample of 156 respondents, engaged in evaluation research concerning the outcome of postpartum public health nursing visits.[31] Although the study suggested that the visits did not show the anticipated differences in the accomplishment of visit objectives, it did address the development of outcome objectives related to confidence, knowledge, skills, and motherhood.

The well-known work of Brooten and her colleagues dealt with the outcomes of early hospital discharge and home followup of very-low-birth-weight infants. Although the experimental group of infants was discharged 11.2 days earlier than the control group, there were no significant differences between the two groups in several simple outcome measures, such as rehospitalization, acute care visits, failure to thrive, child abuse, foster placement, and developmental quotient.[32] By means of this study, the additional outcome measure of lowering cost due to early discharge was demonstrated.

Home care was viewed as a system by Day.[33] The entry was viewed as input, service usage as throughput, and exit characteristics as output. The outcome measures of service usage and discharge status were studied retrospectively from the records.

Studies have been undertaken to develop instruments to measure outcomes pertinent to home care. One example of this is the work of Choi and his associates in which the Health-

Specific Family Coping Index (HSFCI) was tested.[34] During this research another coping scale, the General Aptitude Family Coping Index, was developed to assess measurement accuracy. High correlations were noted between the two scales, showing the congruence between the two outcome instruments.

The outcome measure of quality of life is being increasingly studied. The work of Padilla deals with the development of a multidimensional quality of life index (QLI), which was developed specifically for the patient with cancer.[35] Additional work using the QLI has been done by Ferrell, who uses it as an outcome measure for pain management in home care patients with cancer.[36]

Gould has developed standardized nursing care plans based on nursing diagnoses. The patient-centered goal is the desired outcome standard for each diagnosis, while the nursing orders represent process measures.[37]

Sorgen reports on an outcome-focused program that was developed to evaluate the quality of care and support services. After the development of a conceptual framework based on systems theory, structure, process, and outcome measures were developed in the following areas:

1. pain management
2. symptom control
3. physiological health status
4. ADL
5. instrumental ADL
6. sense of well-being
7. goal attainment
8. knowledge
9. application of knowledge [38]

Votava and her colleagues have developed outcome criteria for home care of the ventilator-dependent patient, specifically for tracheostomy care and positive pressure ventilation.[39] The report of this project includes the complete set of criteria in a useful format.

After reviewing 12 studies of the effect of home health care on outcomes, Hedrick and Inui suggest that home care services have little or no impact on the outcomes of mortality, patient functioning, and nursing home placement.[40] These authors point out the need for additional methodologically sound research that deals with the outcome effectiveness of home care.

Daubert's Patient Classification Outcome Criteria System (PCO) calls for the classification of all home health care patients into one of five categories according to their rehabilitation potential.[41] The system is designed to emphasize assignment of patients into one of five mutually exclusive categories. Each category has predetermined program objectives and subobjectives that relate to outcome criterion measures. These measurable objectives provide outcome measures of program effectiveness. Further work, adopting these outcome measures, has been reported more recently by the VNA of Eastern Montgomery County (Pennsylvania), where Harris, Peters, and Yuan have related these outcome measures to cost.[42]

In a description of the QA program at the Hospital Home Health Care Agency of California, Daniels describes a discharge summary tool and Recommended Quality Guidelines.[43] The latter tool includes the domains of admission, treatment/discharge, and general management of home care, and it has potential for adaptation and use in other agencies.

A recent study by Benefield is directed toward developing productivity standards for staff in the home health setting.[44] Further work is being done to relate these productivity measures to cost.

The Easley-Storfjell productivity model provides for the analysis of the caseload of home health nurses.[45] Analysis of productivity is based on activities, time, and complexity.

LaLonde, the principal investigator for a three-year federally funded research study conducted in collaboration with the Home Care Association of Washington, has reported the findings of this study to date. The major focus of the study was to identify several outcomes that were perceived as the most important by home care representatives. The measures of taking medications, general symptom distress, discharge status, functional status, and caregiver strain have been reported as valid outcome measures that have potential for use in home care agencies.[46]

Current research includes that of Peters, who has developed the Community Health Intensity Rating Scale (CHIRS); this is a resource consumption model directed toward determining the care requirements of patients. The framework utilized for this model includes the nursing process; the domains of environmental, psychosocial, physiological, and health behaviors; and 15 parameters of these domains.[47] Quality assurance is just one of the areas of potential application, according to Peters. The researchers are now in the process of taking the content of each parameter and developing standards of care, which will then be developed into an audit tool.

Although the major focus of the well-known federally funded Omaha Visiting Nurse Association study was to develop a patient classification system, the refinement of the system includes protocols of care as well as measures of quality. Tools developed in this study include the Intervention Scheme, which deals with process, and the Problem Rating Scale for Outcomes.[48]

Stephany describes the development and testing of a QA tool that includes criteria for assessing the physical comfort of patients and families, emotional and spiritual support, and education about terminal illness and hospice care.[49] In keeping with accreditation programs of both the National Hospice Association and the Joint Commission, Stephany invites other agencies to use or adapt this instrument.

Fashimpar reports the development, testing, and utilization of the Homemaker-Home Health Aide Program Evaluation Questionnaire by the Visiting Nurse Association in Dallas.[50] This tool is a patient self-report survey and provides a method to evaluate the adequacy and quality of service, the homemaker-client relationship, accomplishment of objectives and the homemaker-home health aide job performance. The

68-item questionnaire is included in the article by Fashimpar and has potential for use in other agencies as well.

Note that there are other major federally funded studies in process that will directly or indirectly lead to development of outcome measures of care. Dr. Virginia Saba of Georgetown University is developing an acuity classification method to predict resource requirements and ultimately to measure outcome on discharge.[51] Abt and Associates, under contract to the federal government, are analyzing the vast data source contained in Medicare documents.[52] Shaughnessy, at the University of Colorado, has compared home health and nursing home data and is anticipating the further study of outcome measures of care in the home.[53]

Traditionally, QA programs evaluating quality of care have relied on standards generated by professionals or on scientifically based judgments that attempt to measure the extent to which standards are met. However, growing public awareness of health care issues, such as safety and cost of care, has prompted health care professionals to acknowledge the need for active consumer participation in evaluating quality of care. The opinions of health care consumers have become increasingly important to providers, for evaluation data is now finding its way into accreditation criteria and the legislative forum. Monitoring the quality of health care can be assessed in part by using patient satisfaction measures as quality assurance outcome criteria.[54] However, using patient satisfaction instruments in this way has been fraught with a variety of theoretical and methodological problems.[55] Patient satisfaction has many and varied dimensions of conceptualization. Among the dimensions are quality of care, delivery of services, patient-provider interaction in the utilization, contact, and the selection of providers.[56] Inadequate definition of the concept of satisfaction frequently has been cited as the underlying problem with instrument validity. An additional problem with patient satisfaction measures is the built-in tendency toward responder bias. It is anticipated that, for whatever reason, patients are generally reluctant to express a lack of satisfaction.

Risser's early work on patient satisfaction resulted in the development of the Risser Patient Satisfaction Scale, which measures the extent to which nursing actions take place in the ambulatory setting. The domains of study were (1) technical professional, (2) intra-interpersonal, (3) trusting relationship, and (4) education relationship.[57] Hinshaw and Atwood adapted Risser's scale for use in the inpatient setting.[58] Oberst made a major contribution in the study of patients' perceptions of quality and satisfaction in the development of a conceptual framework of "expectations" and the introduction of the visual analogue scales to this area of study.[59] A more recent refinement of the Risser scale for hospitalized patients has been made by La Monica, Oberst, and their associates.[60]

Although it is fairly well established that many home health agencies do use opinionnaires to determine the satisfaction of their patients, there is little evidence in the literature of the use of valid and reliable measures. Preliminary work in this area was done by Schmele, who developed and tested a patient

satisfaction questionnaire for home health. The domains of study were the elements of the nursing process.[61] Reeder has recently integrated the work of Risser, Hinshaw, and Atwood and of Schmele in the development of the Client Satisfaction Survey (CSS), which is specifically for home health and based on the nursing process.[62]

Resources

One of the obstacles to becoming knowledgeable about state-of-the-art data collection mechanisms in home health is that the required resources are diverse, widely dispersed, and often not published. Successful efforts, many of them recent, have been made by authors and editors to remedy this situation. Some of the generic and specific major resources are discussed below.

Kane and Kane's compendium of assessment measures for the elderly includes many data collection instruments, some of which may serve well as outcome measures.[63] Major areas of measurement are (1) physical functioning, (2) mental functioning, (3) social functioning, and (4) multidimensional functioning. In addition to the discussion of tool reliability and validity, a bibliography is included that pertains to use of each instrument.

A new release, *Measuring Health*, by McDowell and Newell, brings together 50 subjective instruments, many of which lend themselves to the measurement of quality, especially outcome.[64] Topical areas represented are (1) functional disability and handicap, (2) psychosocial well-being, (3) social health, (4) quality of life and life satisfaction, (5) pain, and (6) general health. Each of the topic areas is succinctly summarized by the authors. A standard comprehensive format is used to review each of the instruments.

Corcoran and Fisher have compiled a collection of 125 measures of clinical practice, which they term Rapid Assessment Measures.[65] These instruments are classified according to (1) adults, (2) children, and (3) couples and families, and they are also cross-indexed by problem area. Selected instruments from this volume offer promise as valid, reliable, and easily administered outcome measures.

Outcome measures specifically tested for home care are described in LaLonde's *Quality Assurance Manual of the Home Care Association of Washington*.[66] Measures that have been tested in the home care setting include (1) discharge status, (2) general symptom distress, (3) taking medication as prescribed, (4) caregiver strain, and (5) functional status. Information on the development and testing of two additional instruments, Physiological Indicators and Knowledge of Diagnosis/Prognosis, will later be added.

The Joint Commission has recently published an anthology entitled *Quality and Home Health Care: Refining the Tradition*, which includes several contributions dealing with data collection methods.[67]

Perloff is the principal investigator in a federally funded project at the University of Pennsylvania.[68] The goal of this comprehensive project is a computerized health instrument file.

A three-volume NLN series, recently released, provides guidance to selected major works of the current literature dealing with outcome measures. Volume 1 is specifically directed to the research aspect of quality measurement. Volume 2 includes a critical selection of both published and unpublished practical approaches to the measurement of outcomes in community-based nursing services. Volume 3 consists of a meta-analysis of the works published in volumes 1 and 2, with a focus on public policy.[69] Volume 3 also contains the step-by-step method of implementing client outcome program objectives. This series promises to be a valuable contribution in the area of outcome measures of quality.

CONCLUSION

The challenge of establishing valid, reliable, and easily administered tools to measure quality of care in home health still exists. The debate about structure, process, and outcome continues. Historically, the change in emphasis from structure to process and then to outcome is easily seen, as is the current impetus toward the use of outcome measures. However, it is still valuable to look at structure (which determines an agency's ability to deliver the care) and process (which deals with the care that is delivered). None of the three components exists alone, so perhaps the most important challenge is to establish relationships among them. A second challenge is to find a way to integrate the regulatory measures with the professional measures so that both quality of care and the financial integrity of the agency are ensured. Yet another challenge is to move toward standardizing these data collection mechanisms so that the resulting standardized data may come to have a major influence on policy decisions and ultimately on quality of care.

It is encouraging to see the various important activities that are occurring in the area of quality measurement. These activities should cause rapid and long-awaited advances. Hopefully, the many concerted efforts of practitioners, educators, and researchers will lead to the development, testing, and use of standardized data collection mechanisms that will be valid, reliable, and practical to use in the home care setting.

NOTES

1. Avedis Donabedian, *Explorations in Quality Assessment and Monitoring* (Ann Arbor, Mich.: Health Administration Press, 1985), vol. 3, *The Methods and Findings of Quality Assessment and Monitoring: An Illustrated Analysis*, 330.

2. Ibid., 310–27.

3. Marcia Stanhope and Jeanette Lancaster, *Community Health Nursing: Process and Practice for Promoting Health*, 2d ed. (St. Louis, Mo.: Mosby, 1988), 240.

4. Ibid., 239–40; Donabedian, *Methods and Findings*, 310–27.

5. Donabedian, *Methods and Findings*, 310–27.

6. Joint Commission on Accreditation of Healthcare Organizations, *Accreditation Manual for Hospitals—86* (Chicago: Author, 1985), ix.

7. Joanne Handy, "Data or Die" (Presented at National Association for Home Care 1987 Annual Meeting and Homecare Exhibition, Washington, D.C., October 10–14, 1987).

8. Mabel A. Wandelt and Joel Ager, *Quality Patient Care Scale* (Detroit, Mich.: Wayne State University, 1970).

9. Maria C. Phaneuf, *The Nursing Audit: Profile for Excellence* (New York: Appleton-Century-Crofts, 1972).

10. Mabel A. Wandelt and Doris Slater Stewart, *Slater Nursing Competencies Rating Scale* (New York: Appleton-Century-Crofts, 1975).

11. Maria C. Phaneuf and Mabel A. Wandelt, "Three Methods of Process-Oriented Nursing Evaluation," *Quality Review Bulletin* 7, no. 8 (1981): 20–26.

12. Beverly L. Hough and June A. Schmele, "The Slater Scale: A Viable Method for Monitoring Nursing Care Quality in Home Health," *Journal of Nursing Quality Assurance* 1, no. 3 (1987): 28–38.

13. Sue T. Hegyvary, "Nursing Process: The Basis for Evaluating the Quality of Nursing Care," *International Nursing Review* 26, no. 4 (1976): 113–16.

14. Betty J. Curtis and Linda J. Simpson, "Auditing. A Method for Evaluating Quality of Care," *Journal of Nursing Administration* 15, no. 10 (1985): 14–21; Larry C. Mackie and James W. Welch, "Quality Assurance Audit for the Nursing Process," *Nursing Times* 78, no. 42 (1982): 1757–58; Kathryn M. Lillesand and Sarah Korff, "Nursing Process Evaluation: A Quality Assurance Tool," *Nursing Administration Quarterly* 7 (Spring 1983): 9–14.

15. Geraldine Cradduck, "Quality of Nursing Care: How It Is Affected by Public Health Care Delivery," *Nursing Papers* 17, no. 4 (1985): 20–29.

16. Sallyann Schwab and Patricia Pierce, "Assessment of Clinical Nursing Practice in a Rural Decentralized Case Management System," *Public Health Nursing* 3 (June 1986): 111–19.

17. June A. Schmele, "A Method for Evaluating Nursing Practice in a Community Setting," *Quality Review Bulletin* 11 (April 1985): 115–22.

18. June A. Schmele, "A Comparison of Two Process Measures of the Quality of Nursing in Home Health" (Presented at the American Public Health Association Conference, New Orleans, October 18–22, 1987).

19. Phyllis Reeder, correspondence, University of Illinois at Chicago, Chicago, Ill., 1986; Mildred G. Owings, correspondence, University of North Carolina, Chapel Hill, N.C., 1986; Margo M. Burrows, correspondence, University of Wyoming, Laramie, Wyo., 1987.

20. June A. Schmele, "The Comparison of Process Measures of Quality of Nursing Care in Home Health" (Oklahoma City, Okla.: University of Oklahoma, 1987), mimeographed.

21. Sharon V. Davidson, "Community Nursing Care Evaluation," *Family and Community Health* 1, no. 1 (1978): 37–55.

22. James Tehon and Sharon Colegrove, "Risk Management and Home Health Care: The Time Is Now," *Quality Review Bulletin* 12, no. 5 (1986): 179–86.

23. Vonicha M. Holloway, "Documentation: One of the Ultimate Challenges in Home Health Care," *Home Healthcare Nurse* 2, no. 1 (1984): 19–22; National Association of Home Care, "Documentation Guidelines in Home Health Care," *Caring* 6, (August 1987): 51.

24. Charles Wright and Peggy Wheeler, "Auditing Community Health Nursing," *Nursing Management* 15, no. 3 (1984): 40–42.

25. Beverly L. Koerner, "Selected Correlates of Job Performance of Community Health Nurses," in *Outcome Measures in Home Care*, ed. Lynn T. Rinke, vol. 1 (New York: National League for Nursing, 1987), 129–44.

26. Michelle Wiseman, "Setting Standards for Home IV Therapy," *American Journal of Nursing* 85, no. 4 (1985): 421–23.

27. Susan Miller, "Home Care Project Survey Data, Part III," *Journal of American Medical Record Association*, 56, no. 12 (1985): 25–28.

28. Walter J. O'Donohue et al., "Long-term Mechanical Ventilation: Guidelines for Management in the Home and of Alternate Community Sites" (Report of Ad Hoc Committee, Respiratory Care Section, American College of Chest Physicians), *Chest* 90 (July 1986): 1–37.

29. American Nurses' Association, *Guidelines for Review of Nursing Care at the Local Level* (Kansas City, Mo.: Author, 1976); Lynn T. Rinke and Alexis A. Wilson, eds., *Outcome Measures in Home Health Care*, vol. 2 (New York: National League for Nursing, 1987).

30. Violet H. Barkauskus, "Effectiveness of Public Health Nurse Home Visits to Primiparous Mothers and Their Infants," *American Journal of Public Health* 73 (May 1983): 573–80.

31. Richard S. Stanwick et al., "An Evaluation of the Routine Postnatal Public Health Nurse Home Visit," *Canadian Journal of Public Health* 73, no. 3 (1982): 200–205.

32. Dorothy Brooten et al., "A Random Clinical Trial of Early Hospital Discharge and Home Follow-up of Very-Low-Birth-Weight Infants," *New England Journal of Medicine* 315, no. 15 (1986): 934–39.

33. Suzanne R. Day, "Measuring Utilization and Impact of Home Care Services: A Systems Model Approach for Cost Effectiveness," in Rinke, *Outcome Measures in Home Care*, vol. 1, 109–27.

34. Thomas Choi, LaVohn Josten, and Mary Lou Christensen, "Health-specific Family Coping Index for Noninstitutional Care," in Rinke, *Outcome Measures in Home Care*, vol. 1, 161–65.

35. Geraldine V. Padilla and Marcia M. Grant, "Quality of Life As a Cancer Nursing Outcome Variable," in Rinke, *Outcome Measures in Home Care*, vol. 1, 169–85.

36. Betty Ferrell and Cheryl Wisdom, "Quality of Life As the Outcome of Pain Management: Testing a Conceptual Model" (Accepted for presentation at the Annual Meeting of the Oncology Nursing Society, Pittsburgh, April 1988).

37. Joyce E. Gould, "Standardized Home Health Nursing Care Plans: A Quality Assurance Tool," *Quality Review Bulletin* 11, no. 11 (1985): 334–38.

38. Lois M. Sorgen, "The Development of a Home Care Quality Assurance Program in Alberta," *Home Health Care Services Quarterly* 7 (Summer 1986): 24–25.

39. Kathryn Votava, Tamsan Cleveland, and Katharine Hiltunen, "Home Care of the Patient Dependent on Mechanical Ventilation: Home Care Policy Development and Goal Setting Using Outcome Criteria for Quality Assurance," *Home Healthcare Nurse* 3, no. 2 (1985): 18–25.

40. Susan C. Hedrick and Thomas S. Inui, "The Effectiveness and Cost of Home Care: An Information Synthesis," *Health Services Research* 20, no. 6, pt. 2 (February 1986): 851–80.

41. Elizabeth A. Daubert, "A Patient Classification Outcome Criteria System," in *Home Health Administration*, ed. Marilyn D. Harris (Owings Mills, Md.: National Health Publishing, 1988), 300–311.

42. Marilyn D. Harris, Donna A. Peters, and Joan Yuan, "Relating Quality and Cost in a Home Health Care Agency," *Quality Review Bulletin* 13, no. 5 (1987): 175–81.

43. Kaye Daniels, "Planning for Quality in Home Care System," *Quality Review Bulletin* 12, no. 7 (1986): 247–51.

44. Lazelle E. Benefield, *Home Health Care Management* (Englewood Cliffs, N.J.: Brady Communications, 1987).

45. Judith L. Storfjell, Carol E. Allen, and Cheryl E. Easley, "Caseload and Workload Analysis in Home Health Care," in Harris, *Home Health Administration*, 322–33.

46. Bernadette LaLonde, "Assuring the Quality of Home Care via the Assessment of Client Outcomes," *Caring* (January 1988): 20–24.

47. Donna Peters, "A Patient Classification System for Home Care" (Tape from the National Association for Home Care Annual Meeting and Home Care Exhibition, Washington, D.C., October 10–14, 1987).

48. Karen S. Martin and Gary L. Bargstadt, "The Omaha System: Client Problems, Outcome, and Interventions," abstract in *Health Care: For People or for Profit? Proceedings of the American Public Health Association* (Washington, D.C.: American Public Health Association, 1987).

49. Theresa M. Stephany, "Quality Assurance for Hospice Programs," *Oncology Nursing Forum* 12 (May-June 1985): 33–40.

50. Gary A. Fashimpar, "A Management Tool for Evaluating the Adequacy and Quality of Homemaker-Home Health Aide Programs," *Gerontologist* 23, no. 2 (1983): 127–31.

51. Storfjell, *Home Health Administration*, 322–33.

52. Handy, "Data or Die."

53. Peter Shaughnessy, "Home Health Research: Differences between Home Health Agencies and Nursing Homes in Terms of Case Mix and Outcomes" (Presentation of American Public Health Association, New Orleans, October 18–22, 1987).

54. Ada Sue Hinshaw and Jan R. Atwood, "A Patient Satisfaction Instrument: Precision by Replication," *Nursing Research* 31 (May-June 1982): 170–75.

55. Elaine L. LaMonica et al., "Development of a Patient Satisfaction Scale," *Research in Nursing and Health* 9, no. 1 (1986), pp. 43–50.

56. Phyllis Reeder, "Development of an Instrument to Measure Client Satisfaction" (Unpublished manuscript, University of Illinois at Chicago, 1987).

57. Nancy L. Risser, "Development of an Instrument to Measure Patient Satisfaction with Nurses and Nursing Care in Primary Care Settings," *Nursing Research* 24, no. 1 (1975), pp. 45–52.

58. Hinshaw and Atwood, "Patient Satisfaction Instrument," 170–75.

59. Marilyn T. Oberst, "Patients' Perceptions of Care," *Cancer* 53, no. 10, pp. 2366–73.

60. La Monica et al., "Patient Satisfaction Scales," 43–50.

61. Schmele, "Evaluating Nursing Practice," 115–22.

62. Reeder, "Instrument to Measure Client Satisfaction."

63. Rosalie A. Kane and Robert L. Kane, *Assessing the Elderly: A Practical Guide to Measurement* (Lexington, Mass.: Rand Corp., 1981).

64. Ian McDowell and Claire Newell, *Measuring Health. A Guide to Rating Scales and Questionnaires* (New York: Oxford University Press, 1987).

65. Kevin Corcoran and Joel Fisher, *Measures for Clinical Practice: A Source Book* (New York: Free Press, 1987).

66. Bernadette LaLonde, *Quality Assurance Manual of the Home Care Association of Washington* (Edmonds, Wash.: Home Care Association of Washington, 1986).

67. Joint Commission on Accreditation of Healthcare Organizations, *Quality and Home Health Care: Redefining the Tradition*, ed. Karen Fisher and Karen Gardner (Chicago: Author, 1987).

68. Evelyn Perloff, "Health Instrument Data Base" (Unpublished paper of a federally funded project in progress, University of Pittsburgh, Pittsburgh, Pa.).

69. *Outcome Measures in Home Care* (New York: National League for Nursing, 1987), vol. 1, ed. Lynn T. Rinke; ibid., vol. 2, ed. Lynn T. Rinke and Alexis A. Wilson; ibid., vol. 3, ed. Lynn T. Rinke.

Chapter 7

Documentation

E. Joyce Gould and Paula L. Rich

Documentation is an essential and inherent part of delivering high-quality home health care. Documentation facilitates clear, concise, thorough, and accurate clinical diagnostic reasoning and clinical decision making regarding treatment options. "Since thinking is mainly a verbal activity, careful writing and clear thinking support each other."[1] Therefore, the most important reason for documenting an encounter with a patient is that writing stimulates the clinicians' thinking processes at each step of care delivery, enabling them to choose what is best for each patient. The critical thinking processes that are the hallmarks of professional judgment and care are incomplete until a clinician subjects the assessment, plan, intervention, and evaluation to the rigors of writing. This view of documentation implies that patient care is adversely affected when documentation is omitted or cursory.

Certain patient situations, such as life-threatening anaphylaxis, mandate that the clinician complete the thinking process and establish a written protocol before care is needed. At the other end of the spectrum, certain patient situations may be encountered so regularly that it is more efficient to design a written treatment protocol for all patients who have the same problem. In either circumstance, the documentation in the individual patient record focuses on adherence to the accepted protocol, the individual patient's response to treatment, and the reason for any deviation from the pre-established routine.

The current literature for health care professionals and home health agencies focuses on other aspects of documentation.[2] Much has been written about the documentation necessary for procuring reimbursement. Some health care professionals view the clinical record as a celebration of a patient's progress toward health, a method of communication among professionals, or a data set for future exploration. Others claim that documentation is a meaningless ritual, a protection from legal action, or nothing more than a government requirement.

Societal and cultural expectations also influence the health care professional's need to document. State governments mandate that health care providers maintain certain records for each patient. In order to process payments, insurance companies, Medicaid, and Medicare demand specific written evidence of patients' illnesses and the treatments they have received. Consumers frequently have used the courts to try to make health care professionals accountable for patient outcomes. In these instances, health care providers often rely on written records to support their claims of having acted prudently. Researchers who seek to improve patient care recognize that clinical records provide a wealth of information that can be analyzed to develop new knowledge to benefit future patients.

The time and effort devoted to documentation has increased in recent years as many forces converged to require that all health care professionals document their patient care activities. Insurers, governments, and courts are important new audiences that regularly command access to patients' clinical records. Each of these makes so many demands for specific types of documentation that the concept of documentation as a necessary ingredient for quality home care is overshadowed. Making accurate clinical decisions requires time and effort. Illuminating and analyzing the problem in writing is necessary to develop an appropriate plan and to support the actions taken by the clinician.[3]

TYPES OF DOCUMENTATION

Documentation in the clinical record should consist of a written description of pertinent data about the patient's condition, a meaningful interpretation of the patient's situation, and a comprehensive plan outlining how the health care provider will interact with this specific patient. The written record serves as a tool to plan for continuity of care among the many professionals caring for one patient. Documentation related to the clinical care of the patient at home usually consists of seven separate types:

1. the physician plan of treatment
2. discipline-specific care plans for each service the patient receives
3. clinical progress notes for each discipline for each visit (includes assessment, intervention, evaluation)
4. miscellaneous:
   - conference notes
   - telephone calls
   - consultant notes
   - supervisory notes
5. the discharge summary
6. reports to third party payers
7. incident reports

INFLUENCES ON DOCUMENTATION

There are three societal forces that govern what information is included in each of the seven types of documentation. Professional standards, legal influences, and fiscal imperatives imposed by third party payers represent different perspectives that must be taken into account when including information in each patient's clinical record. Sometimes these viewpoints coincide and sometimes they present divergent or conflicting demands. Understanding the chief concerns of each of these forces will assist the clinician in knowing what to document.

Professional Standards

The standards developed by each of the health professions are based on similar principles—principles that differentiate professional practice from lay activities. Each profession defines its specialized knowledge and its relationship to these central principles. For example, each profession collects data about the patient, but the types of data collected will vary according to the profession. The nurse and the physical therapist are both concerned with how well the patient can ambulate. However, the nurse probably will be most concerned with whether the patient can ambulate well enough to perform the activities of daily living safely. The physical therapist's area of focus will overlap the nurse's, but the physical therapist will go beyond the functional level to examine each component of the gait pattern.

The principles or chief concerns guiding professional practice determine a logical process starting with assessment and progressing to diagnosis, planning, intervention, and evaluation. The individual and collective notations in the patient's chart must reflect that all health professionals caring for the patient performed the activities appropriate for

1. collecting data
2. analyzing and interpreting data
3. identifying problems
4. planning interventions
5. providing care based on the plan
6. evaluating the patient response to care

The type and amount of data collected are based on the health care professional's education and experience. There will be a variation in the categories of data collected and the level of detail addressed within each category. Clinicians must collect data of sufficient range and depth to comply with their respective profession's practice standards.

Professionals of all disciplines use their unique knowledge base to sort the collected data into meaningful clusters of cues. Carnevali states, ''One's discipline-specific training and experience then, tends to pre-set the cues one will notice, the vocabulary that will be used to describe cues, and the diagnostic concepts that will be used to organize, classify and explain the data as well as the diagnostic labels that will be assigned.''[4] Documentation by clinicians must demonstrate attention to the cues considered important by their own professions.

A health care professional identifies problems by drawing inferences from the cue clusters to arrive at a meaningful clinical judgment regarding the patient problems to be addressed while the patient is receiving care from the home health agency. Documentation must identify the specific patient problems each discipline will address in the course of treatment. The problems must be ones that fall within the scope of practice for each profession.

Each discipline must complete the clinical decision-making process to determine which of the many intervention options are appropriate for an individual patient. As part of this process, the clinician and patient should mutually agree to the outcome goals expected as a result of treatment.

The health care professional must carry out all treatments consistent with accepted clinical procedures. Although variations in technique exist, there is an abundance of procedural protocols, current practice-oriented literature, and research findings that collectively form a yardstick for measuring whether the care provided falls within the bounds of accepted practice.

The professional must continually reassess the patient to determine whether the treatment is having the desired effect, whether the patient has developed new problems that must be addressed, and whether there are any untoward responses to treatment. The new data must be analyzed to identify significant changes that require altering the plan of care.

Professional standards define minimum criteria for proficiency in job performance. They enable judgment as to whether quality care was provided. Documentation in the clinical record is geared to verify that these minimum standards were met.[5] Some of the following professional organizations have both general practice standards as well as standards specific to home care: the American Nurses' Association, National Association of Social Workers, American Occupation Therapy Association, American Physical Therapy Association, and American Speech and Hearing Association.[6]

In addition to these professional groups, there are certifying and accrediting mechanisms that promulgate standards for a home health agency's entire operation. These standards also speak to professional practice and specify documentation requirements. The accrediting bodies that develop standards relevant to home care are the Joint Commission on Accreditation of Healthcare Organizations, National League for Nursing (NLN), Medicare, and Medicaid.

Legal Influences

In the event of a legal action, the courts require evidence that the care given to a patient met accepted professional standards of practice. The clinical record must be able to withstand scrutiny in court. Following specific guidelines gleaned from previous decisions (case law) will enable the clinician to produce a written document that can serve as credible evidence in a legal proceeding. The following guidelines address both the content and technique of documentation:[7]

1. *Content guidelines*:
   - Use objective terms. Describe your findings and interventions in specific, measurable terms.
   - Avoid subjective terms like *good*, *fair*, *poor*, and *well*.
   - Do not include personal opinions.
   - Describe what you saw, heard, and did.
   - Avoid generalizations such as "patient slept well."
   - Describe the patient's response to treatment.
   - Present information in a logical format.
   - Keep records current: Note changes in the patient's condition and subsequent modifications in your interventions.
2. *Technical guidelines*:
   - Write legibly.
   - Do not obliterate any entry by erasing, using white out, covering with a label, or blacking out.
   - Put a single line through a charting error, write the word *error*, and initial and date the notation.
   - Use only abbreviations from your agency's list of approved abbreviations.
   - Sign all notes with your first initial, full last name, and title.
   - Put a line through any blank space on a line.
   - Do not leave blank spaces between entries.
   - Do not squeeze information between entries already in the chart.
   - Enter the full date (month, day, year) and time for each patient encounter.
   - Write notes in ink.
   - Record the patient's full name and identification number on each page.

Many health disciplines have succeeded in establishing their scope of practice through state licensure laws. However, there is variation from state to state regarding which disciplines are licensed, what are the qualifications for practice, and what parameters define the limits of practice for each licensed discipline. The state practice laws indicate which services a discipline may provide independently and which ones require a physician's order before a member of that profession may legally perform the intervention. Therefore, professionals must be aware of the laws governing their own discipline in the state in which they practice. Professionals must document that the care they provide is consistent with the appropriate state laws governing their practice.

Fiscal Imperatives

Cost containment and cost-effectiveness are the key concerns driving third party payers in the eighties. Frequently, the physician is the identified gatekeeper for gaining access to payment for care provided to the patient. Insurers usually require that physicians order the services of other health professionals to assure that the services rendered to the patient are medically necessary to treat an illness or injury. Historically, most payers have insured acute care. Furthermore, Medicare, Blue Cross and Blue Shield, and commercial insurers (Aetna, Prudential, etc.) make limited payments for services that must be performed by a professional. Such services frequently are referred to as "skilled care." Finally, reimbursement by insurers is generally limited to those services that are reasonable in frequency and duration. Insurance rarely covers long-term care, chronic care, health maintenance, health promotion activities, or personal care.

Since most health insurance policies are negotiated individually by employers, their policies for covered services vary widely. Employers and insurers are designing new ways to control health care expenditures. Co-insurance and deductibles are traditional mechanisms which dissuade excessive use of covered services. The ways in which insurers control expenditures include

- requiring pre-authorization
- mandating second opinions prior to surgery

- limiting access to inpatient care
- eliminating coverage for nonessential procedures
- expanding outpatient coverage
- establishing a ceiling on the amount of covered service
- authorizing payment only to approved providers

A thorough investigation of the patient's insurance coverage prior to initiation of care will enable the clinician to determine whether the care needed by the patient meets the criteria established by the insurer. After completing this step as part of the assessment phase, the clinician must document thoroughly how the patient met the criteria established by the insurer. The plan of care should reflect the integration of the appropriate fiscal restraints and the pertinent professional standards. When these two forces conflict, the clinician must develop and document a legally defensible compromise strategy. Documentation throughout the course of treatment must demonstrate adherence to the insurer's protocol in order to secure payment.

SOCIETAL INFLUENCES ON THE CLINICAL RECORD

Professional standards, legal influences, and fiscal imperatives dictate what is documented in each section of the record. Exploring the requirements for each type of documentation in the home care clinical record will clarify the influence of these forces.

The Physician's Plan of Treatment

The plan of treatment must include all appropriate medical orders for the care of the patient. Two separate forces determine the specifics included in the physician's plan: legal requirements and third party payers. Previous court decisions, professional practice standards, and state practice acts for each licensed health profession are the sources of legal influence on the content of the physician's plan of treatment.

Many practice acts require that licensed health professionals obtain a physician's order before they initiate specific activities. A written order that includes the type, frequency, and duration of prescribed interventions provides proof of legally acceptable physician's orders. In addition, the documentation should indicate that the orders were obtained prior to implementation.

Third party payers vary in the extent of documentation required from the physician to obtain reimbursement for home health services. Many insurers will not pay for a service unless it is ordered by a physician. However, cost containment strategies often prevent payment solely on the basis of a physician's order. The physician must provide additional information to demonstrate that the ordered services are both reasonable and necessary for the treatment of the illness or injury.

Home care professionals sometimes have difficulty differentiating between the legal and fiscal constraints that demand physician's orders. Frequently, the home health professional may legally perform the necessary patient care without a physician's order, but reimbursement for the services is possible only if a physician prescribes the care. Many state nurse practice acts permit a nurse to perform cardiopulmonary assessment without a physician's order. Even though an insurance policy covers this care, insurers generally stipulate that the following two conditions are met before payment is made: (1) the clinical record must reflect that the patient suffered a recent acute cardiac or pulmonary problem that remains unstable and (2) there must be a written physician's order directing the nurse to perform the cardiopulmonary assessment.

Discipline-Specific Care Plans

Professional standards specify or imply that health care professionals develop a plan of action to meet a patient's needs. Some third party payers have adopted this professional standard as a prerequisite for reimbursement. The home care professional first assesses the patient to identify specific problems amenable to intervention. Each discipline determines the acceptable terminology for describing problems within its own scope of practice.

A patient who has a medical diagnosis of a recent cerebral vascular accident will have problems that require the care of a multidisciplinary team. The nurse may diagnose an alteration in nutrition related to inability to chew food. The physical therapist may note that the patient exhibits loss of balance to the left side during ambulation. The occupational therapist may recognize that the patient is unable to perform one-handed dressing techniques. The speech therapist may determine that the patient is unable to follow instructions because of receptive aphasia. The medical social worker may uncover that the patient has a fear of falling and is thus prevented from performing the prescribed exercise program.

After completing the assessment and identifying problems, the home care professional and the patient mutually agree on the goals to be achieved as a result of the professional's interventions. The clinician then designs a course of action that addresses the patient's problems and enables the patient to achieve the identified goals.[8]

The clinical record should contain a plan of care for each service provided to the patient. Each plan consists of three separate sections: (1) the patient problem, (2) the plan of action for solving or mitigating the problem, and (3) the expected status of the patient after the clinician's intervention. These plans are essentially road maps to guide the clinicians and the patient from the time of admission to the agency (problem identification), through the course of treatment (planned interventions by the clinicians), until discharge (goal achievement). Frequent reviews of these road maps will enable the clinicians to guide the patient toward the desired goals. These plans of care are relatively static, but the clinicians should review and revise the three sections of each plan based on information gathered while caring for the patient.

Clinical Progress Notes

Professional standards, legal influences, and fiscal imperatives all mandate that a clinician write a progress note for each encounter with the patient. Writing progress notes is a necessary component of quality care, because it demands rigorous analysis and precise thinking that the clinician may not otherwise devote to each patient in the course of a harried day of home visits. Documenting the patient encounter prompts the clinician to complete the following four steps:

1. Organize the information gathered during the patient encounter.
2. Determine which information is important.
3. Decide what action is needed.
4. Celebrate the patient's progress while highlighting the remaining deficits.

During a patient encounter, the clinician uses a variety of methods to gather information intuitively, randomly, and deliberately. This information includes data about the patient's physical, psychosocial, emotional, and spiritual needs. Clinicians use their professional experience and education to organize this mass of information into a coherent set of cue clusters or patient problems.

The health care professional then determines the relative importance of cue clusters. This process is extremely complex, because the clinician must integrate the demands arising from professional standards, legal requirements, and fiscal imperatives to determine what to include in the progress note. Deviations from the plan of care and obstacles that prevent adherence to the pre-established plan require thorough documentation. Full description of these events may assist in justifying payment and avoiding successful litigation for malpractice.

The clinician must next decide which problems require action, what is the appropriate action to take, and what is the proper time to initiate action. These decisions constitute a refinement of the plan of care in order to correct deviations, overcome obstacles, and resolve new problems that may deter the patient from reaching the identified goals.

Finally the clinical note must include an evaluation of the patient's progress toward meeting the goals. Fiscal imperatives usually require documentation that the patient's status remains unstable. Professional standards, legal influences, and fiscal imperatives mandate an accurate description of the care provided by the clinician. Documentation that covers how the patient has improved as a result of care, the patient's level of performance on return demonstrations, and the patient's perceptions of the problem and of the care provided will assist in satisfying all three kinds of societal requirements.

The clinical progress notes should *not* merely repeat information included in the physician's plan of treatment or the discipline-specific plan of care. Rather, the progress notes should provide a detailed picture of patient's needs and clinician's actions. Third party payers and legal entities scrutinize these progress notes to determine adherence to professional standards and compliance with insurance coverage criteria. When writing each clinical note, it may be helpful to answer a series of questions to assure that the note satisfies professional standards, legal influences, and fiscal imperatives (see Table 7-1). Expending the effort to write a clinical note that concisely addresses each of these questions will enhance the quality of care for the patient, promote fiscal viability for the home health agency, and reduce the possibility of successful litigation.

Miscellaneous

The clinical record should include other information related to the patient's care. This information may or may not be based on an encounter with the patient. Consultants sometimes make a home visit to the patient, but they sometimes instead review the information in the chart. In either case, their evaluation and

Table 7-1 Clinical Progress Note Questions for Consideration

Professional Standards	Legal Influences	Fiscal Imperatives
Does the patient or caregiver have the knowledge and ability to carry out the necessary care until the next visit?	What would a prudent home care professional do in similar situation?	Is the patient's condition unstable?
What observations are pertinent and necessary to describe the patient's problems and needs?	Is the care consistent with recognized professional standards?	How does the patient's condition compare to the last visit?
What specific actions must the clinician initiate to address the patient's needs and problems appropriately?	Is the care within the legally defined scope of practice for this professional?	How does the patient's current status meet the payment criteria established by the third party payer?
What types of coordination and follow-up are necessary?	Does the individual clinician have the necessary education and experience to safely perform the required care?	Did the care require the skills of a licensed health professional?
What is the evidence that the patient learned what was taught by the clinician?	Is the care consistent with the physician's orders?	How is the patient progressing toward the established goals?
Does the care reflect the most current or effective method of care?		
Was the care individualized to meet the patient's particular needs?		

recommendations should be integrated into the chart. The clinician's progress notes should incorporate the pertinent information provided by consultants.

Following a similar process for conferences with members of the multidisciplinary team or with staff of other agencies will demonstrate coordination of care. Documentation of conferences with a clinical or administrative supervisor also provides information relevant to the patient's care. Phone calls to the patient, other agencies, the physician, and insurers require appropriate documentation in the clinical record.

The documentation of conferences, consultations, and phone calls can substantiate adherence to professional standards, create an argument for procuring reimbursement, and strengthen the defense in event of litigation.

The Discharge Summary

Agency policy and third party payers dictate the format and content of discharge summaries. It is important to describe the patient's status at the time of admission, the services provided, and the patient's status at the time of discharge. The summary should describe other significant factors that influenced the course of treatment. The length of the report and the amount of detail vary according to the requirements of the third party payer. Obviously, the summary must be consistent with the information in the plans of care and the clinical progress notes.

Reports to Third Party Payers

Insurers vary significantly in the types of reports they require. Some demand that information be submitted on forms designed by the insurer; others permit the agency to send the requested information on its own forms. Some demand a copy of the entire clinical record; others are satisfied with reports at specific intervals throughout the period when care is given. Attention to the report requirements of third party payers has gained importance, as the reports are critical for securing reimbursement for services provided. The clinician must complete these reports accurately in order to assure the fiscal integrity of the home care agency.

Incident Reports

Unusual events or patient injuries that occur during the course of treatment should be documented in the patient's chart. It is advisable for the clinician to evaluate and document the patient's status after any incident. However, the full description of the event and information gathered during fol-

low-up should be documented on a separate report. The clinician must report the incident and promptly file the report with the person responsible for risk management within the agency. Other types of incidents are documented according to agency policy and may not be included in the patient's record.

DEALING WITH SOCIETAL INFLUENCES IN A CLINICAL SITUATION

To illustrate how one agency meets the mandates imposed by professional standards, legal influences, and fiscal imperatives, the following example is presented. The information describes the care provided to a fictitious patient. Six types of documentation are included.

1. *Physician's plan of treatment.* Two different formats are shown: HCFA 485 (Exhibit 7-1), required by Medicare, and the agency's plan of treatment (Exhibit 7-2), which is used for other insurers.
2. *Discipline-specific plan of care.* Care plans for nursing (Exhibit 7-3) and physical therapy (Exhibit 7-4) are illustrated. This particular agency has standardized nursing care plans (Exhibit 7-3), which are individualized to address the needs of a specific patient. The physical therapist writes each care plan by completing the appropriate section on the form. *Note:* The clinician must develop the plan of care after completing the initial evaluation or assessment.
3. *Clinical progress notes.* The nursing history and assessment form (Exhibit 7-5) and physical therapy evaluation form (Exhibit 7-6) are specialized formats for the initial visit. The clinical note form (Exhibit 7-7) is used by all disciplines. This particular format includes prompters to remind clinicians to document the information needed to satisfy professional standards and third party payers. The information taught by the nurse is documented on the teaching plan section of the standardized nursing care plan. However, the patient's response to the teaching is written in the appropriate section of the clinical progress note.
4. *Miscellaneous.* Consultant's notes, telephone calls, and supervisory conferences are documented on the appropriate sections of the clinical note.
5. *Discharge summary.* Two formats for discharge summaries are included (Exhibits 7-8 and 7-9). The formats vary based on the requirements of third party payers.
6. *Reports to third party payers.* A completed update for section 15 on HCFA 486 illustrates the type of information required by Medicare (Exhibit 7-10).

Exhibit 7-1 Plan of Treatment (Example 1)

Department of Health and Human Services Health Care Financing Administration			Form Approved OMB No. 0938-0357

HOME HEALTH CERTIFICATION AND PLAN OF TREATMENT

1. Patient's HI Claim No. 000-12-3456	2. SOC Date 07/22/88	3. Certification Period From: 07/22/88 To: 09/22/88	4. Medical Record No. 000831	5. Provider No. 39-1234

6. Patient's Name and Address COLORA, JOHN 123 MAPLE AVE ANYTOWN, PA. 18755	7. Provider's Name and Address. ANYTOWN HOME HEALTH AGENCY ANYTOWN, PA.

8. Date of Birth: 02/01/18	9. Sex [X] M [ ] F	10. Medications: Dose/Frequency/Route (N)ew (C)hanged

11. ICD-9-CM	Principal Diagnosis	Date
562.10	RUPTURED DIVERTICULUM	07/06/88

TYLENOL WITH CODEINE # 7 q 4h PRN PAIN (N)

12. ICD-9-CM	Surgical Procedure	Date
48.62	COLOSTOMY	07/06/88

COUMADIN 2.5 mg qd (N)

13. ICD-9-CM	Other Pertinent Diagnoses	Date
820.90	FRACTURED (R) HIP	07/13/88
451.	(R) FEMORAL THROMBOPHLEBITIS	07/15/88

VITAMIN C 500 mg qd (N)

14. DME and Supplies N/A	15. Safety Measures: AMBULATION PRECAUTIONS WITH WALKER

16. Nutritional Req. NO ADDED SALT, LOW FIBER	17. Allergies: NKA

18.A. Functional Limitations

1 [ ] Amputation	5 [ ] Paralysis	9 [ ] Legally Blind
2 [ ] Bowel/Bladder (Incontinence)	6 [ ] Endurance	A [ ] Dyspnea With Minimal Exertion
3 [ ] Contracture	7 [X] Ambulation	B [X] Other (Specify)
4 [ ] Hearing	8 [ ] Speech	PAIR (R) LEG & ABDOMEN

18.B. Activities Permitted

1 [ ] Complete Bedrest	6 [X] Partial Weight Bearing (R) LEG	A [ ] Wheelchair
2 [ ] Bedrest BRP	7 [ ] Independent At Home	B [X] Walker
3 [X] Up As Tolerated	8 [ ] Crutches	C [ ] No Restrictions
4 [X] Transfer Bed/Chair	9 [ ] Cane	D [ ] Other (Specify)
5 [X] Exercises Prescribed		

19. Mental Status:	1 [X] Oriented	3 [ ] Forgetful	5 [ ] Disoriented	7 [ ] Agitated
	2 [ ] Comatose	4 [ ] Depressed	6 [ ] Lethargic	8 [ ] Other

20. Prognosis:	1 [ ] Poor	2 [ ] Guarded	3 [ ] Fair	4 [ ] Good	5 [X] Excellent

21. Orders for Discipline and Treatments (Specify Amount/Frequency/Duration)

RN - ASSESS V.S., SKILLED OBSERVATION, SKIN CIRCULATION AND INTEGRITY, NUTRITIONAL STATUS, MEDICATION USE AND EFFECTS, TEACH COLOSTOMY CARE, DIET, FLUID INTAKE, SAFETY MEASURES, DISEASE PROCESS, SIGNS AND SYMPTOMS OF COMPLICATIONS, ACTIVITY/REST REGIME, MEDICATION REGIMEN. 5x/WK x 1 WK, 3x/WK x 1 WK, 2x/WK x 2 WKS, 1x/WK X 2 WKS.

PT - EVALUATION, THERAPEUTIC EXERCISE, GAIT TRAINING, TRANSFER TRAINING, ACTIVE EXERCISE, RESISTIVE EXERCISE, PARTIAL WT. BEARING 50% (R) LEG. 2x/WK x 9 WKS.

22. Goals/Rehabilitation Potential/Discharge Plans

RN - The patient will DEMONSTRATE UNDERSTANDING OF MEDICATION REGIMEN NECESSARY TO CONTROL PAIN. The patient will demonstrate ability to MANAGE COLOSTOMY REGIMEN INDEPENDENTLY. THE PATIENT WILL BE ABLE TO MANAGE THERAPEUTIC SELF CARE REGIMEN TO CONTROL THE DISEASE PROCESS. (CONT 485)

23. Verbal Start of Care and Nurse's Signature and Date Where Applicable: 7/21/88 E Joyce Howe RN MSN

24. Physician's Name and Address Robert Carpet, M.D. 80 WINDING DR. SAMETOWN, PA. 18756	25. Date HHA Received Signed POT 8/2/88	26. I [X] certify [ ] recertify that the above home health services are required and are authorized by me with a written plan for treatment which will be periodically reviewed by me. This patient is under my care, is confined to his home, and is in need of intermittent skilled nursing care and/or physical or speech therapy or has been furnished home health services based on such a need and no longer has a need for such care or therapy, but continues to need occupational therapy.
27. Attending Physician's Signature (Required on 485 Kept on File in Medical Records of HHA) Robert Carpet MD	Date Signed 7/28/88	

Form HCFA-485 (U4) (4-87)

Source: United Medical Services, Inc. Reprinted by permission of United Medical Services, Inc.

Exhibit 7-1 continued

Department of Health and Human Services Health Care Financing Administration				Form Approved OMB No. 0938-0357

ADDENDUM TO: ☒ PLAN OF TREATMENT ☐ MEDICAL UPDATE

1. Patient's HI Claim No. 000-12-3456	2. SOC Date 07/22/88	3. Certification Period From 07/22/88 To: 09/22/88	4. Medical Record No. 000837	5. Provider No. 39-1234
6. Patient's Name COLORA , JOHN			7. Provider Name ANY TOWN HOME HEALTH AGENCY	

8. Item No.	
12 (CONT.)	®️ HIP PINNING 7/13/88 ICD9 code 81.69
22 (CONT.)	RN CONT. Rehab Potential GOOD FOR COMPREHENSION AND ADHERENCE TO MEDICAL REGIMEN WITHIN 6 WEEKS. PT the patient will safely perform transfers independently. the patient will ambulate safely on even and uneven surfaces for maximum distance within limits of his condition. the patient will independently ascend and descend stairs. Rehab Potential good for complete return to independent level of functioning within 16 weeks. DISCHARGE PLANS - Patient will be discharged when independent in management of care. Patient will be discharged to self care with followup by physician.

9. Signature of Physician Robert Carft MD	10. Date 1/28/88
11. Optional Name/Signature of Nurse/Therapist E Jayre Harde RN MSN	12. Date 7/22/88

Form HCFA-487 (U4) (4-87)   PROVIDER

Exhibit 7-2 Plan of Treatment (Example 2)

PLEASE SIGN AND RETURN

Referral Source _Amy Rourke RN_

Insurance Coverage _Aetna_

Insurance Number _000-12-3456_

United Home Health Services
Div. United Medical Services, Inc.
5308 Rising Sun Avenue, Philadelphia, PA 19120
(215) 329-3550

Plan of Treatment For _07/21/88_ To _09/19/88_   Adm # _000837_

Patient Name _Colora, John_

Address _123 Maple Ave_

City _Any Town_   State _PA_   Zip _18755_

Phone _325-9164_   Age _62_

Primary Diagnosis _Ruptured Diverticulum 07/06/88_

Secondary Diagnosis _Fractured (R) Hip 07/13/88_

Therapeutic: _(R) Femoral Thrombo Phlebitis 07/15/88_

Goals: _Pt. will function without agency assistance._
Pt. will regain full function RLE.
Pt. will maintain bowel function.

Diet: _No Added salt, low fiber_   Fluid Restrictions: _None_

Allergies: _NKA_

Physician _Robert Carpet, M.D._

Address _80 Winding Dr._

City _Sametown_   State _PA_   Zip _18756_

Phone _279-0183_

Hospital or ECF _Somewhere Hospital_

Dates of Stay From _07/06/88_ To _07/21/88_

Prognosis: ☒ Good   ☐ Fair   ☐ Poor   ☐ Guarded

Diagnosis Known By: ☒ Patient   ☒ Family   ☐ Neither

Functional Limitations: _Partial weight bearing (R) Leg_

Mental Status: ☒ Oriented   ☐ Confused
☐ Depressed   ☐ Over Anxious
☐ Other

Activity Allowed: _Up as tolerated._

Safety Measures: _Walker_

MEDICAL SUPPLIES NEEDED

☐ Dressing/Surgical Supplies   ☐ Catheter Supplies
☒ Others (list) _Colostomy Supplies_
☐ Bed   ☐ Commode   ☒ Walker   ☐ Cane

SKILLED NURSING CARE

☒ Monitor Vital Signs   ☐ Dressing: _____
☐ Respiratory Status   ☐ Cardiac Status
☒ Proper Hydration   ☒ Skin Condition
☐ Enema-Fleet or S.S.   ☐ Neuro Checks
☐ Laxative   ☐ Observation: _____
☐ Fecal Impaction
☐ Foley Catheter Care
  Cath. Size _____   FR _____ CC
  Change _____   PRN   Other _____
☐ Irrigation Solution: _____
  Frequency _____   Amt. _____
☐ No Irrigation
☐ Bowel and Bladder Training
☒ Teach Applicable Phases of Care: _Disease Process_
☒ Colostomy Care: _Skin and Stoma Care_
☒ Establish & Supervise Home Management Program _Activity/Rest_
☐ Decubitus Care:
☒ Nutritional Status _____   ☒ Diet Instruction _____
Frequency _5x/wk x1_   Duration _6 wks_   Reevaluate _6 wks_
_3x/wk x1, 2 x_

MEDICATIONS: ☒ Supervise and Review; Instruct in Side Effects,
Observe Special Effects of:

Tylenol c̄ codeine #3 t q4h prn pain

Coumadin 2.5 mg qd.

Vitamin C 500 mg qd.

Call MD if 110/60(BP 180/100; 12(R) 26; TEMP)100 F
Blood Work as Needed _to be done in physician's office_
Increase or Decrease Frequency of Visits When Judged Necessary

I certify that this patient is under my care, home-bound except when
receiving outpatient services and requires intermittent skilled nursing,
physical therapy or speech therapy

Initial Certification ___X___   Recertification _____

Sign: X _____

Print Name: _Robert Carpet, MD_

☒ PHYSICAL THERAPY EVALUATION & TRAINING

☐ Range of Motion & Passive Exercise (Assistive)
☒ Resistive Exercise   ☐ Postural Drainage
☐ Muscle Reeduction   ☐ Breathing Exercise
☒ Gait Training   ☐ Balance Training
☒ Transfer Training   ☒ Wt. Bearing Status: _Partial wt. (R) leg_
☐ Massage   ☐ Family Training
☐ Home Exercise Program   ☒ Other _Evaluation_
Frequency _2x/wk_   Duration _8 wks_
Reevaluate _in 8 wks_

SPEECH – LANGUAGE EVALUATION & TRAINING

☐ Oral Muscle Reeduction and Swallowing
☐ Aphasia Therapy
☐ Other
Frequency _____   Duration _____
Reevaluate _____

OCCUPATIONAL THERAPY EVALUATION & TRAINING

☐ Strengthening   ☐ Homemaking
☐ Coordination Training   ☐ Splinting
☐ Adaptive Device Training   ☐ Family Training
☐ Endurance Training
☐ Energy Conservation
☐ Joint Conservation
☐ Self Care Training
☐ Cardiac Task Monitoring
☐ Visual/Perceptual Training
Frequency _____   Duration _____
Reevaluate _____

HOME HEALTH AIDE	MEDICAL SOCIAL SERVICE
Frequency _____	Frequency _____
☐ Personal Care	Duration _____
☐ ADL	☐ Evaluation
☐ Other _Refused by pt._	☐ Referral Services
and wife	☐ Psychosocial
	☐ Counseling
	☐ Supportive Casework
	☐ Long Range Planning

~~HOME/ENVIRONMENT~~ _Surgical Procedures:_
Colostomy 07/06/88
ORIF 07/13/88

Conditions to be reported to M.D.:
S/S of Bleeding.

Exhibit 7-3 Nursing Care Plan

Nursing Care Plan for *Colora, John*   ADM. # *000837* Date *7/22/88*

Nursing Diagnosis: Alteration in method of *bowel elimination* due to surgical intervention: *temporary colostomy*

_____

Goal: Patient/~~S.O.~~ will maintain bowel function.

NURSING ORDERS

1. Irrigate colostomy as ordered _____ *N/A* _____
2. Assess for signs of infection, obstruction or bowel dysfunction.
3. Instruct patient/S.O. in care and maintenance of an ostomy: *7/25 Hollister 1st choice cut-to-fit pouch - 2¼" pattern in home* *7/22 Hollister 3" 2 piece system with Karaya seal*

4. Consult with clinical nurse specialist for difficult or unresolved patient needs. *7/23 consult E Cross RN, E.T.*

_____

_____

Nurse's Signature: *Paula L. Rich RN.*

Teaching Plan

Contributing Objectives	Dates Instructed *1988*														Goal Date
Patient/S.O. Will	7/22	7/23	7/24												Date Accom.
Demonstrate ability to remove appliance.	I/C/N	S/E	E												7/26 / 7/24
Demonstrate ability to cleanse stoma.	I/C/N	I	S/E												7/26
Demonstrate ability to inspect skin.	I	I/E	S/E/N												7/30
Demonstrate irrigation procedure (if ordered) a) application of irrigating appliance b) filling of irrigating bag with solution c) lubrication and insertion of nozzle d) release of clamp and flow of solution e) clamping of tubing and removal of nozzle		N/A													

© United Medical Services 1983   E. Joyce Gould, RN, MSN

Exhibit 7-3 continued

Nursing Care Plan for: _Colora, John_   Adm. # _000837_

Teaching Plan

Contributing Objectives	Dates Instructed *1988*															Goal Date / Date Accom.
Patient/S.O. Will	7/22	7/23	7/24													
Demonstrate application of appliance. *See pp. 12–16 " Living with Your Colostomy"*	I/C	I/S/N	I/S/N													8/1
Know methods to alleviate pain and discomfort.	I	I/E/N	E													7/30
Explain dietary precautions and importance of nutritional balance.	I	I/N	I/N													8/1
Understand feelings of embarassment, loss of self-esteem and loss of former method of bowel function.	D	D														7/30
Understand the need for balanced periods of rest and activity in order to promote healing and mobility.	I	I/R/E														7/30
INITIALS	PLR	PLR	PLR													

KEY

I = Instruction   E = Evaluation   N = Narrative   C = Care Given   D = Discussion   S = Supervision

Initials	Signature	Title
PLR	*Paula L. Rich*	RN

© United Medical Services

Exhibit 7-3 continued

Nursing Care Plan for _Colora, John_   ADM.# _000837_ Date _7/22/88_

Nursing Diagnosis: Alteration in nutrition due to _less than body requirements_ _intestinal surgery_

Goal: Patient will achieve therapeutic food intake.

NURSING ORDERS

1. Assess patient's current and past food intake (amount, preferences, frequency).
2. Instruct patient/S.O. in recommended diet (specify): _no added salt_ _low fiber_
3. Give patient positive reinforcement in following diet plan.
4. Initiate discussion with patient/S.O. to clarify his perception of food needs.
5. Discuss methods to prepare food for easier ingestion.
6. Provide patient education materials:_____

7. _Plan meals for 1 week with wife._

7/22 8. _Pt. to record intake x24 hrs._

9. _Include high calorie, high protein, Vitamin C rich foods._

Nurse's Signature: _Paula L. Rick RN_

Teaching Plan

Contributing Objectives	Dates Instructed _1988_												Goal Date
Patient/S.O. Will	7/22	7/23	7/24										Date Accom.
List patient's food preferences which are included in prescribed diet.	I	D	D										7/24 / 7/24
Describe how to read packaged food nutrition labels to determine if conforms to diet.		I											7/30
Identify foods to be avoided and why.	I	I	D										8/5

E. Joyce Gould, RN, MSN

Exhibit 7-3 continued

Nursing Care Plan for: _Colon, John_   Adm. # _000837_

Teaching Plan

Contributing Objectives	Dates Instructed 1988															Goal Date
Patient/S.O. Will	7/22	7/23	7/24													Date Accom.
Discuss how to prepare food to enable patient to eat it.	N/A															
List alternatives to manage symptoms. ↑ fluids to 2 qts/day		I	D/E													7/30
Accept and listen to instruction concerning patient education materials. *Hospital diet plan*	I	I	E													7/24 / 7/24
Plan menu for 1 wk. consistent with diet Rx		C/N	E													7/30
INITIALS	PLR	PLR	PLR													

KEY

I = Instruction   E = Evaluation   N = Narrative   C = Care Given   D = Discussion   S = Supervision

Initials	Signature	Title
PLR	Paula L. Rich	RN

© United Medical Services

Exhibit 7-3 continued

Nursing Care Plan for *Colora, John* ADM.#*000837* Date *7/22/88*

Nursing Diagnosis: Impaired physical mobility related to a
traumatic injury to bone and tissue.

Goals: ① Healing will occur.
② Patient will attain optimal function of traumatized
extremity.

NURSING ORDERS

Hx ℗ femoral
thrombophlebitis

① Assess extremity for signs of impaired circulation.
2. Assess immobilizing device for proper fit and application.
③ Assess skin integrity.
④ Instruct in proper elevation of extremity.
⑤ Evaluate safety in transfers and maintain range of motion in
uninvolved extremities.
⑥ Instruct in safe use of assistive devices.
⑦ Evaluate personal care needs and arrange appropriate intervention.
⑧ Obtain Occupational Therapy/Physical Therapy orders when
indicated.
⑨ Coordinate Occupational Therapy/Physical Therapy Services
with Registered Nurse and Home Health Aide Services for an
optimal therapeutic regime.
⑩ Reinforce prescribed home exercise program.
11. Evaluate long-term planning needs and refer to Medical
Social Service if indicated and ordered.
⑫ Assess nutritional status.
⑬ Assess bowel and bladder status.

⑭ *Instruct in ankle pumping exercises 10x q 1 hr.*

⑮ *Assess lower extremities for pain, redness, swelling &*
presence of Homan's sign

Nurse's Signature: *Paula L Reid RN*

Teaching Plan

Contributing Objectives	Dates Instructed											Goal Date	
Patient/S.O. Will	7/22	7/23	7/24										Date Accom.
List signs of impaired circulation: edema, cyanosis, coolness.	I/E	E	E									7/30	
Identify symptoms of impaired skin integrity or infection.	I	D/E	D/E									7/30	

© United Medical Services 1984   Joan Wargo, RN, BSN

Exhibit 7-3 continued

Nursing Care Plan for: *Colora, John*   Adm. # *066837*

Teaching Plan

Contributing Objectives	Dates Instructed																Goal Date
Patient/S.O. Will	7/22	7/23	7/24														Date Accom.
Demonstrate ability to apply sling, immobilizer, and to elevate extremity.	N/A	—	—														
Demonstrate safe transfer techniques.	I/E/N	I/E/N	E/N														7/30
Participate in personal care to indicated level of activity.	E	D/E	D/E														9/15
Demonstrate an understanding of prescribed home exercise program.	PT	PT	PT D														9/1
Accept necessary services to obtain an optimal therapeutic regime with long-term planning considerations.	—	—	—														
List measures to insure adequate bowel and bladder function.	See alteration in bowel function care plan																
Demonstrate an adequate understanding of nutritional needs to promote healing.	See alteration in nutrition care plan																
INITIALS	PLR	PLR	PLR														

KEY

I = Instruction   E = Evaluation   N = Narrative   C = Care Given   D = Discussion   S = Supervision

Initials	Signature	Title
PLR	*Paula L Rik*	RN

© United Medical Services

Exhibit 7-3 continued

Nursing Care Plan for *Colora, John* ADM.#*000837* Date *7/22/88*

Nursing Diagnosis: Alteration in *coagulation of blood*, due to chemical intervention to present formation of obstructive clots in blood vessels.

Goals: (1) Patient/significant other will understand anticoagulant therapy.
(2) Patient/significant other will comply with prescribed medication regime.
3. Patient will receive scheduled venipunctures.

NURSING ORDERS

1. Schedule prothrombin times with laboratory.
2. Report laboratory results to physician.
(3) Instruct patient/significant other in aspects of anti-coagulant therapy.
(4) Instruct patient/significant other in sign and symptoms requiring medical intervention.
(5) Observe for unusual reaction to coumadin, e.g., penile infection.
(6) Instruct patient/significant other in emergency care for bleeding.

Pro-time to be drawn by physician during office visit or otherwise scheduled by him.

Nurse's Signature: *Paula L. Rich R.N.*

Teaching Plan

Contributing Objectives	Dates Instructed *1988*													Goal Date	
Patient/S.O. Will	7/22	7/23	7/24											Date Accom.	
Receive scheduled venipunctures.	N														
State self-care activities to prevent bleeding: a) never double dose if dose forgotten, b) report any falls, c)brush teeth carefully with soft toothbrush d) not take over-the-counter drugs, e) not take aspirin, f) avoid using sharp knives, g) wear shoes or slippers at all times, h) use electric razor; shave often.	I/N	I	D											7/30	

© United Medical Services 1985   Joan Wargo, RN, BSN and
                                        Ann Marie Jordan, RN, BSN

Exhibit 7-3 continued

Nursing Care Plan for: *Colora, John*   Adm. # *000837*

Teaching Plan

Contributing Objectives	Dates Instructed *1988*													Goal Date
Patient/S.O. Will	7/22	7/23	7/24											Date Accom.
Be able to state measures to control bleeding: a) Use clean white cloth to apply pressure for 5 full minutes. b) Elevate affected area above level of heart, if possible. c) If bleeding persists past 5 minutes, go to emergency room, no matter how small wound may look.	I	D/N/E												7/24 / 7/23
Identify signs and symptoms requiring medical intervention: bloody urine, bloody/black stools, nosebleeds, bleeding gums.	I/N	D	D/E											7/24 / 7/24
INITIALS	PLR	PLR	PLR											

KEY

I = Instruction   E = Evaluation   N = Narrative   C = Care Given   D = Discussion   S = Supervision

Initials	Signature	Title
PLR	Paula L. Rich	RN

© United Medical Services

Exhibit 7-4 Physical Therapy Evaluation and Care Plan

PHYSICAL THERAPY EVALUATION AND CARE PLAN

Name _COLORA, JOHN_   Medical Record No. _000837_

ROM   BOTH UPPER EXTREMITIES (UE) & (L) LOWER EXTREMITY (LE) WITHIN FUNCTIONAL LIMITS. (R) LE = 75° HIP FLEXION; 10° HIP ABDUCTION; HIP EXTERNAL ROTATION 5°. HIP INTERNAL ROTATION TO 15° → LEG RESTS IN THIS POSITION; (R) KNEE −15° → 90° FLEXION; ANKLE WITHIN FUNCTIONAL LIMITS.

STRENGTH   STRENGTH IS GOOD IN BOTH UE & (L) LE, (R) LE DEMONSTRATES FAIR⊕ HIP FLEXION; FAIR⊖ HIP ABDUCTION; POOR HIP INTERNAL & EXTERNAL ROTATION; (R) KNEE FLEXION FAIR ⊕ & (R) KNEE EXTENSION FAIR⊕; (R) ANKLE GOOD.

SHORT TERM GOALS
1) INDEPENDENT BED → CHAIR TRANSFERS
2) TOILET TRANSFERS WITH MINIMAL ASSISTANCE
3) AMBULATE WITH WALKER & INDEPENDENTLY ≈ 30'
4) ↑ AROM OF (R) LE TO 90° HIP FLEXION, 15° HIP ABDUCTION; 15° EXTERNAL ROTATION ↑ AROM (R) KNEE 0° → 90° FLEXION.
5) ↑ (R) LE STRENGTH FAIR → GOOD

LONG TERM GOALS
1) INDEPENDENT TRANSFERS & AMBULATION WITH CANE AMBULATORY DISTANCES ≈ 75' → 100' INDEPENDENTLY

PROGRAM
1) AAROM & AROM (R) LE
2) TRANSFERS
3) STANDING BALANCE ACTIVITIES c̄ WALKER

5) GAIT TRAINING

FREQUENCY   2X/WK

Duration   8 WKS

R Brown LPT
Physical Therapist

Exhibit 7-5 Nursing History and Assessment

United Home Health Services

Div. United Medical Services, Inc.
5308 Rising Sun Avenue, Philadelphia, PA 19120
(215) 329-3550

NURSING HISTORY AND ASSESSMENT

Date 7 / 22 / 88

NAME _Colors, John_   ADM.# _000837_   (M) F

GENERAL APPEARANCE _66 y.o. white male is no acute distress wearing hospital gown & lying in a hospital bed._

COMPLETE DIAGNOSIS _Ruptured diverticulum 7/6/88_
and date of onset _R intertrochanteric fractured hip 7/13/88 sustained while hospitalized_

PAST HEALTH HISTORY _Denies any medical problems prior to hospitalization_

SURGERIES _temporary colostomy 7/6/88 R hip pinning 7/13/88_

MEDICATION USAGE AND UNDERSTANDING (see medication sheet for current meds) _Pt & family have many questions about purpose of medications. Unaware of reason he is on coumadin, its side effects, or precautions. Denies previous use of any O.T.C. medications_

PROSTHESES (DENTURES) (UPPER) (LOWER)   PACEMAKERS   HEARING AID   LIMBS _____

    other: _____

PATIENT TO BE SEEN BY OTHER HEALTH CARE SERVICE: YES   NO
    (if yes, indicate name)
       Physical Therapy: ✓ _____
       Occupational Therapy: _____
       Speech Therapy: _____
       Medical Soc. Ser.: _____
       Home Health Aide: _____
       Other: _____

© United Medical Services 1983

Exhibit 7-5 continued

UNITED HOME HEALTH SERVICES   NURSING HISTORY AND ASSESSMENT   Page 2

Patient's Name _Colora, John_   Adm # _000 837_

	PARAMETER	Nor.	Abn.	Not Asses.	DESCRIBE / MEASURE
SKIN	color	✓			
	condition	✓			
	temperature	98° P.O.			
	turgor	✓			
HEAD	hair	✓			male pattern baldness
	scalp	✓			
EYES	appearance	✓			
	vision		✓		wears bifocals
EARS	hearing	✓			
MOUTH	teeth		✓		full dentures - no trouble chewing
	gums			✓	
	tongue	✓			
NECK	appearance	✓			
	mobility	✓			
CHEST (auscultation)	right upper				Clear
	right lower				
	left upper				
	left lower				
	respiration	20			
HEART	apical pulse	86			regular
	radial pulse	86			
	blood pressure	150/88			⒧ arm sitting 144/80 ⒭ arm sitting 136/70 ⒭ arm standing
BREASTS	self exam		✓		
EXTREMITIES	upper	✓			
	lower		✓		⒭ leg weak & mobility
	joints	✓			
	nails		✓		toenails thickened
PERIPHERAL CIRCULATION	temperature: right	✓			
	left	✓			
	color: right	✓			
	left	✓			
	edema: right		✓		
	left	✓			
	pedal pulses: right	✓			strong bilaterally
	left	✓			
DEFORMITIES AND/OR CONTRACTURES					
RANGE OF MOTION	right upper extrem.	✓			
	left upper extrem.	✓			
	right lower extrem.		✓		
	left lower extrem.	✓			
BALANCE	sitting	✓			
	standing		✓		needs assistance
BED ACTIVIES	turn over	✓			
	come to sitting pos.		✓		needs minimal assist
TRANSFERS	bed	✓			
	chair or wheelchair		✓		needs assist of 1 to steady
	toilet		✓		uses bedside commode
	tub		✓		unable

Nurse's Signature _Paula L. Reich R.N._   Date _7/22/88_

Exhibit 7-5 continued

UNITED HOME HEALTH SERVICES   NURSING HISTORY AND ASSESSMENT   Page 3

Patient's Name __Colora, John__   Adm # __000837__

	PARAMETER	Nor.	Abn.	Not Assess.	DESCRIBE / MEASURE
GENERAL	fatigue	✓			
	weight change	✓			
	communication Prob.				none
	able to relate to care provider	✓			
	understanding/acceptance of diagnosis	✓			States "I had a hole in my
	emergency plans: 911	✓			bowel" to describe reason for
	MD	✓			surgery, but has many
	Family	✓			questions about activities allowed.
MENTAL/ EMOTIONAL STATUS	alert	✓			Colostomy pouch + flange last
	oriented: time	✓			changed 7/21 in hospital.
	person	✓			
	place	✓			
	apprehensive	Yes			especially about walking
	confused	no			
	depressed	no			
	lethargic	no			
	angry/hostile	no			
	cheerful	Yes			
	reliable	Yes			
SAFETY PRECAUTIONS	scatter rugs	no			
	clutter on floor	no			
	stairs with handrails	Yes			
	adequate home lighting	Yes			
	smoking in bed	no			does not smoke
	water heater below 120°	Yes			
	fire escape plan	Yes			
	smoke detectors	Yes			
	multiple door locks	Yes			
	bathroom safety: Grab-bars	no			
	Non-skid mat	Yes			
	safe neighborhood	Yes			
ALLERGIES	food	} NKA			
	drug				
	inhalants/soaps etc.				
HABITS	smoking pks/day	no			never smoked
	alcohol drinks/day	Yes			1 mild drink / wk.
	addicting drugs	no			
SLEEP	initial disturbance	Yes			difficulty sleeping since
	terminal disturbance				admission - feels exhausted +
	use of drugs	no			unable to cope with colostomy
NUTRITIONAL STATUS	appetite	✓			care, incisional pain worse at
	# meals/day	3			night.
	dietary habits	→			Dislikes use of added salt - uses
	special diet: No added salt, low fiber				canned vegetables + eats
	fluid				luncheon meat sandwiches daily.
	food likes: favorite vegetables →				broccoli + cauliflower
	understands special diet	no			"what are gas producing foods?"
	complies with special diet			to be evaluated	

Nurse's Signature __Paula L. Reid RN__   Date __7/22/88__

© United Medical Services 1983

Exhibit 7-5 continued

UNITED HOME HEALTH SERVICES	NURSING HISTORY AND ASSESSMENT				Page 4

Patient's Name _Colora, John_   Adm# _000837_

	PARAMETER	Nor.	Abn.	Not Assess.	DESCRIBE / MEASURE
ADL	eating	✓			
	grooming		✓		needs assistance with
	bathing		✓		back + legs
	toileting		✓		
	dressing		✓		
	household act.	✓			
	meal preparation	✓			wife + daughter perform
	shopping	✓			
	laundry	✓			

		YES	NO	Not Assess.	DESCRIBE / MEASURE
MOBILITY	independent		✓		
	stairs			✓	unable
	assistance of 1	✓			needs moderate assist for
	assistance of 2		✓		balance
	cane		✓		
	walker	✓			
	brace/prosthesis		✓		
	wheelchair		✓		
	bedridden		✓		
RESPIRATORY	cough		✓		
	sputum		✓		
	dyspnea		✓		
	wheezing		✓		
	shortness of breath		✓		
	oxygen		✓		
	IPPB		✓		
GASTRO-INTESTINAL	anorexia		✓		
	nausea		✓		
	vomitting		✓		
	diarrhea	✓			always had problem with
	constipation		✓		diarrhea "off + on"
	bowels	colostomy			soft, semi formed brown stool
GENITO-URINARY	incontinence		✓		
	complaints		✓		
	nocturia x/night		✓		
	HX. infections		✓		
	vaginal discharge	N/A			
NEUROLOGY	memory loss		✓		
	orientation	✓			
	ability to communicate	✓			
	fainting/dizziness		✓		
	mood/affect	optimistic / appropriate			
	gross coordination		✓		
	numbness/tingling	✓			occasional tingling ® leg
	headache		✓		
	paralysis/paresis		✓		
	seizures		✓		
	PAIN	✓			® leg + abdominal incision intermittent. Fears "getting hooked on drugs"

Nurse's Signature _Paula L. Rih RN_   Date _7/22/88_

Exhibit 7-5 continued

UNITED HOME HEALTH SERVICES   NURSING HISTORY AND ASSESSMENT   Page 5

Patient's Name _Colora, John_   Adm # _000837_

Skin: note any decubiti, rashes, incisions, scars, abrasions, laceration, hematomas, jaundice, etc.

:   Temperature — warm and dry
                       cool and clammy
                       moist and perspiring
                       other_____

#1 Stoma – 2½" diameter – no excoriation
   on stoma or skin

#2 6" healed midline incision —

#3 6" incision – edges approximated,
   5 steri – strips in place (2 superior,
   1 central, 2 inferior)

Initial Needs: ① Skilled nursing –
teach care of colostomy, diet,
purpose & side effects of medications,
assess pain & teach appropriate
pain management.
② P.T. – safe transfers & ambulation with walker, muscle
strengthening & conditioning.
Pt & wife refuse home health aide services

Family involvement with care: Wife is a healthy, willing, primary
caregiver. Daughter lives 2 miles away & will assist with
household chores, errands, transportation to physician, but
cannot assist with direct care because she works full time.
Son helped move furniture to adapt 2-floor home to 1st
floor living, but returned to his home 600 miles away.

Nurse's Signature: _Paula L. Reich RN_   Date _7/22/88_

Exhibit 7-5 continued

UNITED HOME HEALTH SERVICES
MEDICATION FLOW SHEET # _____

Name _Colora, John_   Adm # _000 837_

Allergies, reactions, idiosyncracies : _____ N K A _____

DATE ORDERED	PRESCRIPTION DRUGS	7/22	7/23	7/24														
	DATE OF VISIT — YEAR 19 88																
7/21/88	TYLENOL c̄ CODEINE #3 ī Q4H PRN PAIN	I	I/N	D/E/N													
7/22/88	COUMADIN 2.5mg qd.	I/N	I/E/N	D													
	NON-PRESCRIPTION																
7/21/88	VITAMIN C 500mg qd	I	D	D													
Initials		PLR	PLR	PLR													

CODE: C – CARE   D – DISCUSSION   I – INSTRUCTION
        S – SUPERVISION   N – NARRATIVE   E – EVALUATION

Signature   _PLR   Paula L. Rich RN_

Exhibit 7-5 continued

UNITED HOME HEALTH SERVICES

GENERAL FLOW SHEET – ____________

Name *Colora, John* Adm # *006837*

PARAMETERS	DATE OF VISIT – YEAR 19*88*														
	7/22	*7/23*	*7/24*												
Acceptance/Understanding	*fair N*	*fair*	*good*												
Diet: *Lo fiber, no added salt*	*I*	*I/N*	*D*												
Medical Follow-Up:	*7/25*	*–*	*–*												
Reporting of Problems	*I/N*	*I*	*D*												
Objective Assessment:	[redacted]														
Temperature															
Pulse Apical/Radial			*See Clinical notes*												
Respirations															
B.P.															
Auscultation/Lung R.		*Cl*	*Cl*												
Lung L.		*Cl*	*Cl*												
Skin Integrity	*See admission assessment*	*N*	*N*												
Edema		*ō*	*ō*												
Weight		*–*	*166*												
Exercise Regime		*aab*	*aab*												
Transfer Ability		*mod Ⓐ*	*mod Ⓐ*												
Ambulation:		*5'*	*10'*												
Assistive Devices		*walker*	*walker*												
A.D.L.															
feeding		*self*	*self*												
personal care		*self + wife*	*self*												
household activities		*wife*	*wife*												
Safety		*E*	*E*												
Initials	*PLR*	*PLR*	*PLR*												

CODE:
C – CARE D – DISCUSSION
I – INSTRUCTION S – SUPERVISION
N – NARRATIVE E – EVALUATION

INITIALS	SIGNATURE	TITLE
PLR	*Paula L. Reck*	*RN*

Exhibit 7-5 continued

UNITED HOME HEALTH SERVICES

GENERAL FLOW SHEET

Name _Colora, John_   Adm # _000837_

PARAMETERS	DATE OF VISIT — YEAR 19 88															
	7/22	7/23	7/24													
Compliance with Regime	—	good N	good N													
Subjective Assessment:																
Appetite	fair	good														
Bowels	N	N														
Bladder	no prob.	no prob.														
Sleep/Rest	poor N	N														
Emotional Status	calm	calm														
Activity Tolerance																
S.O.B.	c̄	c̄														
D.O.E.	sl	sl														
Special Procedures:																
Stoma cleansing		I/C/N	I/C/N													
Change pouch	I/C	S/N	S/N													
Change flange	—	I/C/N	I/S/N													
Empty pouch	I/E	I/S	—													
Ⓡ lower extremity:																
Pain	c̄	c̄	c̄													
Redness	c̄	c̄	c̄													
Edema	c̄	c̄	c̄													
Homan's sign	absent	absent	absent													
Initials	PLR	PLR	PLR													

CODE:	C – CARE	D – DISCUSSION	INITIALS	SIGNATURE	TITLE
	I – INSTRUCTION	S – SUPERVISION	PLR	Paula L. Rice	RN
	N – NARRATIVE	E – EVALUATION			

Source: United Medical Services, Inc. Reprinted by permission of United Medical Services, Inc.

Exhibit 7-6 Physical Therapy Evaluation Form

United Home Health Services

Div. United Medical Services, Inc.
5308 Rising Sun Avenue, Philadelphia, PA 19120
(215) 329-3550

PHYSICAL THERAPY EVALUATION

PATIENT NAME: *Colora, John*   RECORD NO.: *006837*
PATIENT ADDRESS: *123 Maple Ave.*   S.O.C.: *7-22-88*
PATIENT PHONE: *555-4608*   PHYSICIAN: *Dr. Carpet*
DIAGNOSIS: *Intertrochanteric fracture ® hip + ORIF 7/13/88*
7/6/88 colostomy

	Max. Ass't.	Mod. Ass't.	Min. Ass't.	Close Super	Far Super	Indp.	COMMENTS
Wheelchair Level	N/A						DATE *7/23/88*
Propulsion							
Management							*Pt. admitted for*
Bed Activities							*P.T. to pinned ® hip*
sup to sit			error re ✓	✓			*for fracture sus-*
sit to sup			✓	✓			*tained from fall*
feet up			✓				*while hospitalized.*
feet down			✓				*Pt. had colostomy*
roll (R)				✓			*during admission.*
roll (L)				✓			
Transfers							*Pt required minimal*
to bed			✓				*assistance in bed*
from bed			✓				*mobility and moderate*
to chair		✓					*assistance in transfers*
from chair		✓					*due to weakness*
to tub	⟩ NOT						*from recent illness.*
from tub	ASSESSED						*Decreased strength*
to toilet		✓					*of ® lower extremity*
from toilet		✓					*(LE) as well as*
to standing		✓					*incisional pain.*
from standing		✓					
Ambulation							*Pt. able to ambulate*
walker				✓			*c̄ walker & minimal*
quad cane							*assistance of toe*
st. cane							*touch ® LE.*
crutches							
stairs up							
stairs down							
outside							
	Excel.	Good	Fair	Poor	Ass't Req.		*Balance is fair⁺ as*
Balance							*Pt. has tendency*
sitting		✓					*to lean back*
standing			✓⁺				*when standing.*
Orthotic Devices	SLB	LLB	AK	BK	AE	BE	

Exhibit 7-7 Clinical Note

CLINICAL NOTE

Service: (RN) PT, OT, ST, SW, Other _____
(Circle appropriate discipline)

Patient Name: Colora, John		Record #000837	Time 1PM	Date: 7/22/88

Activity: ☒ Visit *initial* ☐ Telephone Call   ☐ Conference   ☐ Other _____

Action taken/changes made in last visit plan:

Vital Signs	B/P		Lying	Sitting	Standing	RP 86	T 98
		R		144/80	136/70	AP 86	R 20
		L		150/88			

Patient Problems, Professional Observations & Interventions (include teaching and care given): See admission
assessment, nursing care plans, + flow sheets. Pt + wife + dgt. have questions
about prognosis & nature of both colostomy + hip pinning procedures. Unsure
how to manage colostomy although they state that some pre-discharge teaching
was done. Pt unaware of reason he is receiving coumadin, its action, side
effects, or precautions. Pt + wife instructed in diet list given to them at
hospital re low fiber foods. Pt requested to keep written 24 hr. food
intake to discuss at next visit. Began medication instruction —
instructed in general purpose of all medications with special emphasis on
bleeding precautions for coumadin. Pt denies any knowledge of follow-up
blood tests, but does report that blood was drawn daily at hospital.
Instructed pt. to take pain medication as ordered for pain + HS to
improve sleep pattern.

Patient/significant other's Response to Interventions: Pt + wife stated appropriate steps
for emptying colostomy bag + importance of reporting blood in stools or
urine or headaches to physician immediately.

Progress toward goals: Pt + wife easily overwhelmed with new information.
Will need to progress slowly with teaching by introducing only one
new thing at each visit.

Deficits Remaining: Colostomy care, medication knowledge, mobility

Communication with: ☒ agency staff   ☐ physician   ☐ other
Describe: TC to R. Brown LPT to communicate referral information. Will make
initial visit on 7/23/88.

Plan and date of next visit: Revisit tomorrow to have pt. + wife demonstrate
changing colostomy bag. Continue medication + diet instruction
Contact M.D. to clarify coumadin order + need for lab. work.

Paula L. Reich R.N.
Signature   Title

Exhibit 7-7 continued

CLINICAL NOTE

Service: (RN) PT, OT, ST, SW, Other _____
(Circle appropriate discipline)

Patient Name: Colora, John	Record # 000837	Time 3:30 PM	Date: 7/22/88

Activity: ☐ Visit ☒ Telephone Call ☐ Conference ☐ Other _____

Action taken/changes made in last visit plan:

Vital Signs	B/P		Lying	Sitting	Standing	R P _____	T _____
		R				A P _____	R _____
		L					

Patient Problems, Professional Observations & Interventions (include teaching and care given): _____

_____
_____
_____
_____
_____
_____
_____
_____
_____
_____
_____
_____
_____
_____
_____
_____

Patient/significant other's Response to Interventions: _____
_____
_____

Progress toward goals: _____
_____

Deficits Remaining:

Communication with: ☐ agency staff ☒ physician ☐ other _____
Describe: TC to Dr. Carpet: Pt to take coumadin 2.5 mg. daily — had ® femoral thrombophlebitis while hospitalized. He will obtain pro-time

Plan and date of next visit: on each visit. — first appt. 7/25/88
_____

Paula L. Reik   R.N.
Signature   Title

Exhibit 7-7 continued

CLINICAL NOTE

Service: (RN) PT, OT, ST, SW, Other _____
(Circle appropriate discipline)

Patient Name: Colora, John		Record # 000837	Time 9:30 AM	Date: 7/23/88

Activity:	☒ Visit	☐ Telephone Call	☐ Conference	☐ Other _____

Action taken/changes made in last visit plan:

Vital Signs	B/P	Lying	Sitting	Standing	RP 82 regular-T 98
	R		146/80		
	L				A P ___ R 18

Patient Problems, Professional Observations & Interventions (include teaching and care given): See flow sheets and nursing care plans. |Pain| Pt reports he is stile tired due to poor sleep. Took only Tylenol c codeine HS. State Ⓡ leg & abdominal pain is evening – "couldn't stand it any longer" so he took med at bedtime only. Instructed in principles of pain management: take med before pain is too severe & take it as ordered until pain controlled. Explored his fears of "getting hooked". Instructed in other measures to relieve pain & enhance sleep: hot cocoa HS, reading or watching TV in bed, back rub. Instructed that constipation is major side effect of tylenol c codeine & to increase fluid to 2 qts daily. |Colostomy leakage| at inferior surface of flange where skin surface is uneven. Suture line intact without fecal contamination. RN reviewed flange change procedure on pg. 15 of "Living With Your Colostomy" & then demonstrated stoma cleansing & flange application while wife read procedural steps. |Knowledge deficit| Continued instruction in therapeutic diet & planned several meals for this week with wife. |Mobility| Transferred from hospital bed to high, firm upright chair with assistance from wife & nurse. Abdominal & Ⓡ leg incisions – approximated edges, no redness or swelling noted.

Patient/significant other's Response to Interventions: Pt did not record intake, but recall consistent with meal plan discussed. Pt emptied pouch x2 using bedside commode with wife's assistance since last RN visit. Pt able to remove appliance, cleanse stoma & apply new pouch with verbal assistance. Recalled coumadin side effect "bleeding" & would "apply pressure" to any cut or scratch.

Progress toward goals: Both pt & wife seem motivated to assume total care of colostomy. This will be enhanced when pt. able to ambulate safely to 1st-floor bathroom. Both were upset with appliance leakage.

Deficits Remaining: Incisional pain which inhibits sleep, ambulation, colostomy appliance change

Communication with: ☒ agency staff ☐ physician ☐ other _____
Describe: Conference with Marci Mann RN supervisor to discuss colostomy leakage & flange adherence difficulty. Approved referral to enterostomal therapist if acceptable to pt.

Plan and date of next visit: Initial P.T. visit scheduled for this P.M. Next R.N. visit 7/24 to continue instruction in colostomy care & diet, assess pain management. Call MD re continuing pain & possible analgesic change.

Paula L. Orit — Signature   R.N. — Title

Exhibit 7-7 continued

CLINICAL NOTE

Service: RN, (PT) OT, ST, SW, Other _____
(Circle appropriate discipline)

Patient Name: COLORA, JOHN	Record # 000837	Time 4³⁰ PM	Date: 7/23/88

Activity:	☒ Visit	☐ Telephone Call	☐ Conference	☐ Other _____

Action taken/changes made in last visit plan:

Vital Signs	B/P		Lying	Sitting	Standing	RP 86	T _____
		R		134/80	120/70	AP _____	R _____
		L					

Patient Problems, Professional Observations & Interventions (include teaching and care given): _____

Ⓡ INTERTROCHANTERIC HIP FRACTURE + ORIF 7/13 BECAUSE OF FALL WHILE HOSPITALIZED. 6" INCISION HAS 5 STERI-STRIPS IN PLACE. SEE P.T. EVALUATION OF THIS DATE.
    THERAPEUTIC EXERCISES COMPLETED. AMBULATED TO BATHROOM WITH WALKER + CLOSE SUPERVISION - PARTIAL WEIGHT BEARING Ⓡ LOWER EXTREMITY. — 15' X2. INSTRUCTED WIFE IN HOW TO POSITION ELEVATED 3-IN-1 COMMODE CHAIR OVER TOILET TO FACILITATE PT'S SELF CARE. AND HOW TO ASSIST PT. TO STAND + SIT. HIP PRECAUTIONS REVIEWED WITH PT. + WIFE.

Patient/significant other's Response to Interventions: PT. VERY ANXIOUS TO AMBULATE TO BATHROOM TO PERFORM COLOSTOMY CARE. ABLE TO TRANSFER TO+ FROM COMMODE IN BATHROOM WITH MODERATE ASSISTANCE OF 1. WIFE CORRECTLY DEMONSTRATED ASSISTIVE TECHNIQUE. PT'S FEAR OF FALLING DIMINISHED BY SESSION'S END.

Progress toward goals: HIGHLY MOTIVATED PT. SHOULD PROGRESS QUICKLY. WILL PROGRESS TO QUAD CANE WHEN PHYSICIAN APPROVES WEIGHT BEARING TO TOLERANCE.

Deficits Remaining: SIGNIFICANT WEAKNESS Ⓡ LOWER EXTREMITY.

Communication with: ☒ agency staff   ☐ physician   ☐ other _____
Describe: TELEPHONE CALL TO MARCI MANN RN TO DISCUSS FINDINGS + PLAN.

Plan and date of next visit: NEXT VISIT 7/26 CONTINUE AMBULATION TRAINING, UPPER EXTREMITY MUSCLE STRENGTHENING, Ⓡ LOWER EXTREMITY ACTIVE EXERCISE.

                               R. Brown   LPT

                             Signature   Title

Exhibit 7-7 continued

CLINICAL NOTE

Service: (RN) PT, OT, ST, SW, Other _____
(Circle appropriate discipline)

Patient Name: Colora, John	Record # 000837	Time 1 PM	Date: 7/24/88

Activity:	☒ Visit	☐ Telephone Call	☐ Conference	☐ Other _____

Action taken/changes made in last visit plan: _Dr. Carpet unavailable yesterday. Pain now controlled. No need to contact MD prior to scheduled visit._

Vital Signs	B/P		Lying	Sitting	Standing	
		R		136/82		RP 82 regular _____
		L				AP _____ R 20

Patient Problems, Professional Observations & Interventions (include teaching and care given): [Bowel elimination]
Lg amount semi-formed brown stool in pouch. Pt reports leakage again yesterday. RN supervised removal of flange + pouch. Stoma pink, but 1/4" skin surface surrounding stoma reddened + macerated. Stoma now measures 2 1/4" diameter + pt. has appliance with 3" pre-cut aperture. RN instructed pt + wife in method to apply stomadhesive to fill uneven skin surfaces + to cleanse stoma + skin well at time of flange change. Pt needed verbal cueing to remove paper from karaya seal on flange before application. [Pain] Pt looks rested + less anxious. Reports taking tylenol + codeine q4h while awake with relief. States he "slept like a baby". RN reinforced previous instructions re increasing fluid intake to prevent constipation. [Mobility] RN supervised pt ambulating 10' with walker + partial weight bearing (R) leg. Both his confidence + strength are improved since 1st visit.
   Abdominal incision healed, 3 of 5 steri strips now off (R) thigh incision — edges well approximated — non tender + non reddened.

Patient/significant other's Response to Interventions: _Pt tends to move too quickly when changing appliance — skips procedural steps. Pt + wife very upset about continued appliance leakage + expressed positive feelings about enterostomal therapist involvement. Pleased with progress in initial PT visit._

Progress toward goals: _Pt gaining confidence in his ability to perform colostomy care. Independence should occur more rapidly as mobility to bathroom (+ privacy) is achieved + more appropriate appliances for needs are identified._

Deficits Remaining: _Ambulation, independence in colostomy, diet + med. management._

Communication with:	☒ agency staff	☐ physician	☐ other enterostomal therapist

Describe: _telephone call to C. Cron RN, ET to give referral + discuss case. She will see pt tomorrow AM prior to 3:30 PM physician's appt._

Plan and date of next visit: _Next RN visit 7/26 to continue instruction in colostomy care, diet + assess pain management., check outcome of 7/25 MD appt._

Paula L. Cruz	R.N.
Signature	Title

Exhibit 7-7 continued

CLINICAL NOTE

Service: (RN,) PT, OT, ST, SW, (Other) _____ E.T. _____
(Circle appropriate discipline)

Patient Name: _Colora, John_   Record # _000837_   Time _11 AM_   Date: _7/25/88_

Activity: ☒ Visit ☐ Telephone Call   ☐ Conference   ☐ Other _____

Action taken/changes made in last visit plan:

Vital Signs	B/P		Lying	Sitting	Standing	RP _____	T _____
		R				AP _____	R _____
		L					

Patient Problems, Professional Observations & Interventions (include teaching and care given): "Leaking colostomy bag". Stoma - 2¼" visible bud ⓛ UQ, + soft → brown stool. Skin - generally healthy, but some redness + maceration around stoma. Abdominal incision - 6" midline, well healed. Management: D/c 3" karaya seal + initiate first choice pouch cut-to-fit with stomahesive paste. Patient instructed to ↓ size of opening in pouch according to stoma size + modify paste application to compensate for unevenness 2° to incision line. Stoma care reviewed + taught pt. simpler regieme by performing care in bathroom. Pt. + wife instructed in pouch application. A+P of G.I. tract, surgical procedure + stoma appearance + function. Step-by-step written instructions on appliance application given to pt. with information about ordering supplies + insurance coverage.

Patient/significant other's Response to Interventions: Pt. applied pouch correctly on 1st attempt. He is very anxious to learn to become independent with his care. Emotionally accepts colostomy + feels it is little hindrance to his lifestyle.

Progress toward goals: Follow-up needed for evaluation + further teaching.

Deficits Remaining: Needs to learn skillful use of stomahesive.

Communication with: ☒ agency staff   ☐ physician   ☐ other _____
Describe: telephone call to Paula Reit RN to discuss case

Plan and date of next visit: To be followed by primary nurse.

E. Cron R.N., E.T.
Signature   Title

Exhibit 7-7 continued

CLINICAL NOTE

Service: RN, PT, OT, ST, SW, Other *Conf. to Paula Rich RN*
(Circle appropriate discipline)

Patient Name: *Colora, John*	Record # *000837*	Time	Date: *7/26/88*

Activity:	☐ Visit	☐ Telephone Call	☒ Conference	☐ Other _____

Action taken/changes made in last visit plan:

Vital Signs	B/P		Lying	Sitting	Standing	RP _____	T _____
		R				AP _____	R _____
		L					

Patient Problems, Professional Observations & Interventions (include teaching and care given): _____

Plan:

① Will continue RN visits 3 times a week until pt + wife are able to perform all aspects of care.

② Will taper frequency of nursing visits to evaluate pt's ability to adhere to treatment regimen and handle changes as they arise.

③ Will evaluate need to consult physician re ordering OT to instruct pt. in adaptive techniques regarding lower extremity dressing if ROM in Ⓡ hip does not dramatically improve by next week.

Patient/significant other's Response to Interventions: _____

Progress toward goals: *Pt progressing well with colostomy care + pain management.*

Deficits Remaining: *Major deficits in Ⓡ lower extremity strength + function.*

Communication with: ☐ agency staff   ☐ physician   ☐ other _____
Describe:

Plan and date of next visit: _____

Signature: *Marci Mann*   Title: *RN supervisor*

Source: United Medical Services, Inc. Reprinted by permission of United Medical Services, Inc.

Exhibit 7-8 Discharge Summary (Example 1)

 **United Home Health Services**

Div. United Medical Services, Inc.
5308 Rising Sun Avenue, Philadelphia, PA 19120
(215) 329-3550

SUMMARY REPORT

To: _DR. ROBERT CARPET; AND AMY ROURKE, RN, SOMEWHERE HOSPITAL_

Patient's Name: _COLORA, JOHN_   Adm # _000837_

Diagnosis: _Ruptured Diverticulum, Fx ®Hip, ® Femoral thrombophlebitis, Colostomy, ORIF_

Attending Physician: _DR. ROBERT CARPET_

SUMMARY REPORT: ☐ Interim   ☒ Discharge   Service
___/___/___ to ___/___/___   10/21/88   SN☒ PT☒ OT☐ HHA☐ ST☐ MSS☐

_RN_ – Pt. admitted with colostomy. Initial problems included pain, poor sleep, leakage around colostomy flange, and knowledge deficits regarding disease process, colostomy care, and coumadin therapy. Pt. was extremely motivated to become independent in all aspects of care. However, initially the patient and his wife were overwhelmed with new information. The teaching program was designed to introduce one new topic at each visit. All teaching was reinforced at subsequent visits. With this approach, patient was able to steadily increase his knowledge and ability to care for himself. At time of discharge from nursing on 9/1/88, patient was able to independently perform colostomy care including skin inspection, changing and emptying the bag, and modifying his dietary intake to comply with the ordered low salt, low fiber diet. His pain was resolved and his sleep patterns had returned to normal. Pt. is able to identify the S/S of bleeding to report to his physician. He will follow up care with his physician.

_PT_ At time of admission, pt. required minimal assistance in bed mobility and moderate assistance of one to transfer, ambulation was limited to 8 steps. Pt. instructed in active exercise program to increase ROM and strength. Resistive exercises and weight bearing added as program progressed. Instruction in safe use of walker. Progressed to cane as

(Continued page 2)   Signed: _Paula L. Rich RN_

Title: _Primary Nurse_

2/87   Date: _10-31-88_

Exhibit 7-8 continued

United Home Health Services

Div. United Medical Services, Inc.
5308 Rising Sun Avenue, Philadelphia, PA 19120
(215) 329-3550

SUMMARY REPORT

To: *D.R. Robert Carpet; and Amy Rauke, RN, Somewhere Hospital*

Patient's Name: *Colora, John*   Adm # *000837*

Diagnosis: ⎱
               ⎰ *see page 1*
Attending Physician:

SUMMARY REPORT: ☐ Interim   ☒ Discharge   Service

___/___/___ to ___/___/___   10/21/88   SN☐ PT☒ OT☐ HHA☐ ST☐ MSS☐

P.T. continued - strength increased. Pt. motivated to follow through on prescribed exercise program. Intermittent pain in ℝ hip required modification of the therapy program to enable pt. to comply with therapy program. Rom and strength progressed toward normal ranges. By 10/1/88, began aggressive program of stair climbing and ambulation on uneven surfaces. By 10/21/88, pt independent in all ADL. Able to ambulate without assistive devices for 75' x 2. Uses cane when fatigued. Pt. able to demonstrate home exercise program. D/c 10/21/88.

Signed: *Paula L. Rich RN*

Title: *Primary Nurse*

2/87   Date: *10-31-88*

Source: United Medical Services, Inc. Reprinted by permission of United Medical Services, Inc.

Exhibit 7-9 Discharge Summary (Example 2)

United Home Health Services
Div. United Medical Services, Inc.
5308 Rising Sun Avenue, Philadelphia, PA 19120
(215) 329-3550

Date: _10/31/88_

SUMMARY REPORT   To: _DR. CARPET and Amy Rauteleph_ From: _Paula L. Rich, RN_
SOMEWHERE HOSPITAL   Title: _Primary Nurse_

Patient Name _COLORA JOHN_   Adm # _000837_

Diagnosis _Ruptured DIVERTICULUM, FX (R) HIP, (R) FEMORAL THROMOPHLEBITIS_   Physician _Robert Carpet, MD_

☐ Recertification   ☒ Discharge   ☐ Interruption of Service
___/___/___ to ___/___/___   10 / 21 / 88   ___/___/___ Reason: _____

☒ **SKILLED NURSING CARE**   Frequency _1-5x/wk_ For: ☒ Medication Instruction ☒ Monitor Vital Signs ☐ Respiratory Status
   ☒ Establish & Supervise Home Management Program ☒ Colostomy Care ☒ Proper Hydration ☐ Cardiac Status ☐ Bowel and Bladder Training
   ☐ Foley Catheter Care ☐ Dressing ☐ Decubitus Care Other _____
   Vital Signs ☒ Stable ☐ Unstable   BP _120_/_20_ to _150_/_88_ ; P _82_ to _86_
   Progress: _D/c from NSG. 9/1/88 when pt. able to manage all aspects of colostomy care._
   Service Status: ☒ Goals Achieved ☐ Progressing toward goals _Pt. knowledgeable of S/S to report to MD regarding Coumadin therapy._
   ☐ New Goals: _____

☐ **HOME HEALTH AIDE**   Frequency _____ For: ☐ Personal Care ☐ ADL Other _____
   Progress: _____
   Service Status: ☐ Goals achieved ☐ Progressing toward goals
   ☐ New Goals: _____

☒ **PHYSICAL THERAPY EVALUATION & TRAINING**   Frequency _2x/wk_ For: ☒ Gait Training ☒ Transfer Training
   ☒ Range of Motion & Passive Exercise (Assistive) ☒ Resistive Exercise ☒ Home Exercise Program ☐ Family Training ☐ Balance Training
   ☐ Breathing Exercise ☐ Postural Draining   Other _STAIR CLIMBING_
   Progress: _At time of admission ambulated 8 steps. Now independent on even and uneven surfaces. As strength increased, progressed to stair climbing. Uses cane occasionally._
   Service Status: ☒ Goals achieved ☐ Progressing toward goals
   ☐ New Goals: _____

☐ **SPEECH — LANGUAGE EVALUATION & TRAINING**   Frequency _____ For: ☐ Oral Muscle Reeduction and Swallowing
   ☐ Aphasia Therapy Other _____
   Progress: _____
   Service Status: ☐ Goals achieved ☐ Progressing toward goals
   ☐ New Goals: _____

☐ **OCCUPATIONAL THERAPY EVALUATION & TRAINING**   Frequency _____ For: ☐ Cardiac Task Monitoring ☐ Splinting
   ☐ Visual/Perceptual Training ☐ Joint Conservation ☐ Self Care Training ☐ Energy Conservation ☐ Endurance Training ☐ Homemaking
   ☐ Adaptive Device Training ☐ Strengthening ☐ Coordination Training ☐ Family Training Other _____
   Progress: _____
   Service Status: ☐ Goals achieved ☐ Progressing toward goals
   ☐ New Goals: _____

☐ **MEDICAL SOCIAL SERVICE**   Frequency _____ For: ☐ Evaluation ☐ Long Range Planning ☐ Referral Services
   ☐ Supportive Casework ☐ Psychosocial ☐ Counseling Other _____
   Progress: _____
   Service Status: ☐ Goals achieved ☐ Progressing toward goals
   ☐ New Goals: _____

COMMENTS: _Pt. able to care for colostomy independently. Progressed in ambulation. Independent in all ADL's. Able to demonstrate home exercise program. Expects to return to work in 2-3 weeks_

WHITE COPY – OFFICE   **CANARY – PHYSICIAN**   **PINK – HOSPITAL**

Source: United Medical Services, Inc. Reprinted by permission of United Medical Services, Inc.

Exhibit 7-10 Medical Update

Department of Health and Human Services
Health Care Financing Administration

Form Approved
OMB No. 0938-0357

MEDICAL UPDATE AND PATIENT INFORMATION

1. Patient's HI Claim No.	2. SOC Date	3. Certification Period	4. Medical Record No.	5. Provider No.
000-12-3456	07/22/88	From: 07/22/88 To: 09/22/88	000837	39-1234

6. Patient's Name	7. Provider's Name
COLORA, JOHN	ANYTOWN HOME HEALTH AGENCY

8. Medicare Covered: [ ] Y [ ] N   9. Date Physician Last Saw Patient: 7/21/88   10. Date Last Contacted Physician: 7/22/88

11. Is the Patient Receiving Care in an 1861 (J)(1) Skilled Nursing Facility or Equivalent? [ ] Y [X] N [ ] Do Not Know

12. [X] Certification [ ] Recertification [ ] Modified

13. **Specific Services and Treatments**

Discipline	Visits (This Bill) Rel. to Prior Cert.	Frequency and Duration	Treatment Codes	Total Visits Projected This Cert.
RN		5 X 1WK, 3x 1WK, 2x 2WKS, 1x 2WKS.	A1, A15, A27.	14
PT		2 x 9 WKS	B1, B2, B5, B3, B2	18

14. Dates of Last Inpatient Stay: Admission 07/06/88 Discharge 07/21/88   15. Type of Facility: ACUTE HOSPITAL

16. Updated Information: New Orders/Treatments/Clinical Facts/Summary from Each Discipline

Initial nursing visit 7/22/88 - V.S. T-98, P-86, R-20, B/P 144/80. Colostomy functioning but patient and wife have minimal recall of care and are easily overwhelmed. Instructed in pouch emptying and stoma cleansing. Patient reports continuing (R) leg and abdominal incisional pain, but has not been taking analgesic as prescribed. Ambulated 8 steps with walker and moderate assistance of one. Mobility affected by pain, weakness and apprehension about falling. P.T. referral made. Will instruct in diet, medication regimen and colostomy management. Teach side effects and precautions for coumadin. (See 487 for additional information)

17. Functional Limitations (Expand From 485 and Level of ADL) Reason Homebound/Prior Functional Status

Prior to onset of this illness, patient was completely independent in all ADL's and able to leave home to work daily. Currently patient unable to (Cont 487)

18. Supplementary Plan of Treatment on File from Physician Other than Referring Physician: (If Yes, Please Specify Giving Goals/Rehab. Potential/Discharge Plan)   [ ] Y [X] N

19. Unusual Home/Social Environment

Lives in 2 story home which has been adapted to one floor living for patient.

20. Indicate Any Time When the Home Health Agency Made a Visit and Patient was Not Home and Reason Why if Ascertainable

NONE

21. Specify Any Known Medical and/or Non-Medical Reasons the Patient Regularly Leaves Home and Frequency of Occurrence

Physician visit once a month - must be accompanied by 2 people because of weakness.

22. Nurse or Therapist Completing or Reviewing Form
Paula K. Rick RN

Date (Mo., Day, Yr)
7-31-88

Form HCFA-486 (U3) (4-87)   PROVIDER

Exhibit 7-10 continued

Department of Health and Human Services
Health Care Financing Administration

Form Approved
OMB No. 0938-0357

ADDENDUM TO: ☐ PLAN OF TREATMENT ☒ MEDICAL UPDATE

1. Patient's HI Claim No.	2. SOC Date	3. Certification Period	4. Medical Record No.	5. Provider No.
000-12-3456	07/22/88	From: 07/22/88 To: 09/22/88	000837	39-1234

6. Patient's Name	7. Provider Name
COLORA, JOHN	ANYTOWN HOME HEALTH AGENCY

8. Item No.

#16 (CONT.)

P.T. Initial visit 7/23/88. Patient able to ambulate 15 feet X 2 with partial weight bearing on ⓇLE. Instructed in hip precautions. Instructed in positioning 3-in-1 commode over toilet. Required moderate assistance of 1 to transfer to and from commode. RLE = 75° hip flexion; 10° hip abduction; hip external rotation 5°; hip internal rotation to 15°. Ⓡ knee −15°−90° flexion; Ⓡ hip flexors fair ⊕ strength; fair ⊖ strength hip abductors. Ⓡ knee flexion fair ⊕ strength and Ⓡ knee extension fair ⊕. Program of AAROM and AROM ⓇLE initiated. Instructed in gait pattern for safe use of walker. Limited to flat surfaces at present. Home exercise program will be modified according to patient's pain tolerance. Will continue program until patient regains full independence in ambulation, stair climbing, and ADL's.

9. Signature of Physician	10. Date

11. Optional Name/Signature of Nurse/Therapist	12. Date
Paula L. Rich RN	7-31-88

Form HCFA-487 (U4) (4-87)   PROVIDER

Exhibit 7-10 continued

Department of Health and Human Services Health Care Financing Administration		Form Approved OMB No. 0938-0357

ADDENDUM TO: ☐ PLAN OF TREATMENT ☒ MEDICAL UPDATE

1. Patient's HI Claim No. 000-12-3456	2. SOC Date 07/22/88	3. Certification Period From: 07/22/88 To: 09/22/88	4. Medical Record No. 00837	5. Provider No. 39-1234

6. Patient's Name COLORA, JOHN	7. Provider Name ANYTOWN HOME HEALTH AGENCY

8. Item No.

#17 (CONT.) walk more than 8 steps with walker. Patient is extremely apprehensive about falling. Pt. cannot presently climb stairs.

#16 (CONT) <u>RN</u> At time of admission, patient and wife easily overwhelmed with new information regarding colostomy care, coumadin precautions, therapeutic diet, and pain management. Designed teaching program to introduce one new topic at each visit. With this approach, patient able to comprehend and retain new information. Pain and lack of sleep were difficult problems initially. With instruction, patient able to understand, accept and follow orders for Tylenol c̄ codeine to attain and maintain therapeutic blood level. Sleep returned to normal pattern once pain was relieved.

Leakage around colostomy flange was a persistent problem. RN, ET consulted and advised change to stomahesive paste and cut-to-fit pouch. Patient eager to assume responsibility for care of colostomy. Patient learning to apply pouch but requires further evaluation and instruction to assure he can independently perform procedure and resolve problems as they arise.

RN instructed patient and wife regarding purpose and action of coumadin therapy. Patient recalls that coumadin side effect is "bleeding" and would "apply pressure" to any cut or scratch.

Instruction in therapeutic diet has begun. RN planned meals with wife. Instruction in all aspects of care will continue until goals are achieved. (see next 485 for P.T.)

9. Signature of Physician	10. Date

11. Optional Name/Signature of Nurse/Therapist Paula L. Rich RN.	12. Date 7-31-88

Source: United Medical Services, Inc. Reprinted by permission of United Medical Services, Inc.

NOTES

1. Allen Weiss, *Write What You Mean* (New York: AMACOM, 1978), 8.

2. Susan C. Miller, *Documentation for Home Health Care: A Record Management Handbook* (Chicago: Foundation of Record Education of the American Medical Records Association, 1986); Elissa Della Monica, "Documentation," in *Home Health Administration*, ed. Marilyn D. Harris (Owings Mills, Md.: National Health Publishing, 1988), 273–93; Susan C. Miller, "Documenting High-Quality, Reimbursable Home Care," in *Quality and Home Health Care: Redefining the Tradition*, ed. Karen Fisher and Karen Gardner (Chicago: Joint Commission on Accreditation of Healthcare Organizations, 1987), 48–61; Marilyn D. Harris et al., "Relating Quality and Cost In a Home Care Agency," in Fisher and Gardner, *Quality and Home Health Care*, 93–99; Susan Robertson Jacob, "The Impact of Documentation in Home Health Care," *Home Healthcare Nurse* 3 (September-October 1985): 16–20; E. Joyce Gould et al., "Litigation Risk Management: Home Care Challenge," *Caring* 5 (September 1986): 74–83; Sue Reitz Perdew, "Litigation Risk Management: What the Future Holds," *Caring* 5 (September 1986): 84–88; Carolyn J. Humphrey, *Home Care Nursing Handbook* (Norwalk, Conn.: Appleton-Century-Crofts, 1986), 27–31; Diane E. Fogel, *Medical Claims Documentation Tips* (Washington, D.C.: National Association for Home Care, 1987); E. Joyce Gould, "Standardized Home Health Care Plans: A Quality Assurance Tool," in Fisher and Gardner, *Quality and Home Health Care*; 43–47.

3. Naomi Levanthal, "Making the Most of Writing Assignments," *Supervisory Management* 27 (September 1982): 17.

4. Doris L. Carnevali et al., *Diagnostic Reasoning in Nursing* (Philadelphia: Lippincott, 1984), 31–32.

5. "What You Should Know about Standards of Nursing Care," *Nursing 84* 14 (February 1984): 16F–16P.

6. Nancy I. Connaway, "Can You Meet the National Standard of Care in Home Health Nursing?" *Home Healthcare Nurse* 5 (March-April 1987): 5; Helen Creighton, "Legal Implications of Home Health Care," *Nursing Management* 18 (February 1987): 14–17; Cynthia Northrop, "Home Health Care: Changing Legal Perspectives," *Nursing Outlook* 34 (September-October 1986): 256; *Standards of Home Health Nursing* (Kansas City, Mo.: American Nurses' Association, 1986); *Standards for Social Work in Health Care Settings* (Silver Spring, Md.: National Association of Social Workers); *Guidelines for Occupational Therapy Service in Home Health* (Rockville, Md.: American Occupational Therapy Association, 1987).

7. Katherine W. Carey and Kathey E. Goldberg, eds., *Documentation* (Springhouse, Pa.: Springhouse Corporation, 1988), 12–31.

8. E. Joyce Gould et al., *Home Care Nursing Care Plans* (Rockville, Md.: Aspen Publishers, 1987), 3–4.

Chapter 8

Evaluating Quality Assurance Program Effectiveness

G. Lorain Brault

In previous chapters, the task of developing structure, process, and outcome measures to review the quality of home health service has been outlined. The same approach should be used in assessing an agency's quality assurance program. The structure review should include assessment of the written quality assurance documents, procedures, tools, and report forms. The process review should determine the effectiveness of the activities of the program by utilizing the quality assurance program's written purpose, objectives, scope, and yearly plan. Finally, the outcome review should assess whether quality of service and practice did improve measurably. As in all quality assurance activities, outcome measures are always the most difficult to design and evaluate, but outcome is the strongest measure of the effectiveness of the overall quality assurance program.

REVIEW OF THE WRITTEN QUALITY ASSURANCE PLAN

In Chapter 3 there is a section on assessing an existing quality assurance program. Review of that section will be an excellent place to start the structure review of the written plan. The key concepts to review are *comprehensiveness* and *integration*.

The plan should comply with standards of external accrediting or licensing bodies and be consistent with the mission of the agency. The plan should clearly delineate relationships with all services and departments within the agency. The committee should include representatives from all departments, not just clinical but also nonclinical services, such as education and research, community relations, finance, person-

nel, and administration. If the agency provides private duty or homemaker services, durable medical equipment, or pharmaceutical services, the appropriate departments should be represented on the committee.

The plan should also integrate all the other agency committees that have a role in providing quality. Among the committees that should be integrated in the written plan are the audit, utilization review, risk management, budget, and strategic planning committees as well as special planning task forces.

The written plan should clearly set out the responsibilities of the agency administration, the quality assurance committee, and the quality assurance coordinator. By reviewing the comprehensive and integrated outline contained in the written quality assurance plan, one can evaluate the structure of the quality assurance program.

EVALUATING PREPARATION AND COMPLETION OF THE YEARLY PLAN

The yearly plan (calendar) should be an integral part of the written quality assurance plan. As shown in Table 8-1, reports and reviews by various services, committees, and programs are scheduled in the plan, including satisfaction surveys, departmental monitoring, and the committee or program reports.

Satisfaction surveys are "outcome" studies that measure the satisfaction of consumers. While client or patient satisfaction (Appendix 8-A) is of paramount importance, physicians (Appendix 8-B) and referral sources (Appendix 8-C) should also be surveyed as consumers of home health services. Consumer satisfaction surveys can be performed frequently and

Table 8-1 Quality Assurance Committee Yearly Calendar

	Satisfaction Surveys	Department QA Monitors	Subcommittee QA Summaries Special Programs Reports*	Other Activities
January	Physician	Intermittent service		
February	Client		Audit committee	Reaudit I.V. therapy
March		Private duty/homemaker	Transfusion program	
April	Referral source		Risk management committee	
May		Hospice	Utilization review committee	Focus study phone etiquette
June		Intermittent services	Case management program	
July		Durable medical equipment	Oncology program	Re-audit 24-hour service standard
September		Finance/accounting	Risk management committee	
October			Residential care program	
November	Physician	Private duty/homemaker	Utilization review committee	
December	Client	Personnel	Strategic planning report	

*Subcommittees routinely send written reports for review at appropriate QA meetings scheduled for presentation of specific requested or scheduled issues.

Source: Reprinted with permission of Hospital Home Health Care Agency of California.

collated; they can then be reported two to four times yearly to the quality assurance committee per calendar schedule.

The second area of yearly planning concerns the departmental quality assurance monitors. The term *monitor* is broader than the term *audit*, but monitoring uses forms similar to those used in traditional auditing methodology (See Appendixes 8-D through 8-G, which contain examples of quality assurance monitor summaries). Criteria utilized in a quality assurance monitor should always be (1) relevant, (2) understandable, (3) measurable, (4) behavioral, and (5) achievable.

The third group of activities scheduled in the yearly plan includes various committee reports and new program reports. Each committee that reports to the quality assurance committee should have opportunities to provide formal scheduled reports to the committee. Additionally, the quality assurance committee should schedule the review of new programs or service lines. The strategic plan of the agency can be utilized by the committee to determine new programs and set implementation dates.

The Other Activities column in the calendar can be used to schedule re-audit or focus studies. These studies occur when a problem previously identified is scheduled for additional study later in the calendar year.

In order to evaluate scheduled progress, the agendas and minutes of the meetings conducted during the course of the year should be compared to the yearly plan and the following questions should be answered:

1. Did the committee receive and process the scheduled surveys, monitors, and reports?
2. Did all new programs submit reports to the quality assurance committee and discuss in the reports quality and risk issues inherent in operating the new program?
3. Were measures recommended by the committee to review quality and minimize risk in new programs?
4. Did the agency improve satisfaction among consumers from one survey to the next?
5. Did re-audits or focus audits bring about improved results?

If the answer to any of the questions is no, then the committee should analyze the reasons for variance. The variance analyses will assist the committee in designing the next yearly plan.

DETERMINING THE EFFECTIVENESS OF TOOLS/FORMS

The Quality Assurance Monitor

The most important tool in the quality assurance program is the departmental monitoring form. This form should be flexible enough to allow all types of studies. Generally, medical record audit forms can be adapted. The sample quality assurance monitor presented in Appendix 8-D was modified and designed to be utilized for most types of quality review. This sample form is a combination form and can be used as a measurement tool that allows review of criteria as well as a summary of measurements and recommendations for action. While it is convenient to utilize one form, two or even three forms could be designed— one to measure criteria, one to summarize criteria measurements, and one to recommend actions.

On the sample monitor, the headings and first five columns constitute the measurement tool. The following elements are included:

- the standard being reviewed
- the sample or focus of the review
- record identification (personnel, medical, financial, other source)
- the department that is performing the review
- the date of the review
- the criteria for the quality that is being measured
- the Meets Criteria measurement (generally a yes or no column)
- the expected percentage of compliance with criteria (compliance threshold)

In using the monitor as a summary tool, the same headings and columns are used and totals for meeting the criteria are recorded in the yes or no columns. Then the percentage of overall compliance is recorded for all records or item criteria reviewed.

The recommended actions based on measurements of compliance must be developed and should include responsible parties and completion dates or restudy dates. Finally, the results and recommendations should be disseminated.

The monitors that were completed for the year by departments or services should be compared to the yearly plan and the following questions answered:

1. Did all departments complete the expected number of monitors?
2. Did the criteria represent standards that are critical indicators of agency quality?
3. Are there any other key standards the committee should recommend for future departmental monitoring?
4. Was there improvement in criteria compliance shown by re-audit or focus studies?

Satisfaction Tools

Patient satisfaction, physician satisfaction, and referral source satisfaction are critical indicators of the quality of home health services. Satisfaction surveys are important outcome measurements for the home health quality assurance program.

In designing a tool, one should make it easy to understand, simple to fill out, and no more than a single page in length. Using boxes to check or numbers to circle makes the tool easier to complete. All services that send out forms from an agency should use the same measurement scale and direction of scale for ease of completion and of committee review.

In the examples found in Appendixes 8-A, 8-B, and 8-C, a four-point scale and a Not Applicable column was utilized as the primary method of measurement. The ratings ranged from "very satisfied" (4) to "dissatisfied" (1).

When the quality assurance committee evaluates satisfaction tools, there are two major issues to investigate: (1) whether there is an adequate return rate and (2) whether the level of satisfaction is at an acceptable level or improving.

When designing the sampling procedures for satisfaction surveys, an acceptable return rate should be determined. If the consumer return rates do not reach the anticipated level, new sampling methods should be designed. If the surveys demonstrate less than acceptable levels of satisfaction, the quality assurance committee and home health management must take immediate action to improve the consumer perceptions about quality.

Reporting Tools

The committee should determine a method of reporting to management and staff on an ongoing basis. A list of recipients should be developed for various reports. Methods of reporting to staff may include graphs (particularly effective with satisfaction surveys), memos, reports to staff committees, and awards to departments with 100 percent compliance on certain indicators. Other creative methods might well be devised.

Reporting to management could include minutes, summaries, and a periodic (at least yearly) evaluation of the quality assurance program effectiveness that follows the outline of this chapter. Results of the yearly evaluation should be reported to management and to the board of directors.

REASSESSING CRITICAL QUALITY ASSURANCE AND RISK MANAGEMENT FOCUS ISSUES

Incident and Action Reports

Incident reports constitute an excellent resource for the quality assurance and risk management committees in reviewing critical indicators of quality. Since incident reports should not be copied and original reports should not be utilized, the best strategy is to use an incident report summary. The summary should be submitted periodically to the quality assurance committee based on data from incidents. The sample incident report included in Appendix 8-H has a section entitled "Type of Incident" that allows for a simple summary.

Summaries of the types of incidents should be carefully reviewed and a determination made whether committee recommendations throughout the year addressed methods to reduce incidents involving patients (e.g., patient endangerment, protocol errors, patient falls, and medication errors).

Action reports (see Appendix 8-I) are generated as a result of problems, complaints, or compliments received by any staff member. Action reports may also be summarized by types of reports and compared to quality assurance committee and departmental recommendations. (For example, the types might include billing errors, clinical service complaints, switchboard or answering service problems, etc.) In comparing the summaries of key problems and risk management issues with the quality assurance committee recommendations, the committee can determine whether attention was focused on risk and problem issues described in the incident and action reports. These are issues which will clearly have an impact on the quality of care. Goals should be established that focus on reducing patient-related problems, complaints, and incidents.

Legal and Ethical Questions

As part of the yearly review, the committee could prepare a list of legal or ethical issues that have been reported in incident or action reports, perhaps including

- identified and reported elder abuse
- I.V. therapy for known drug users
- refusal of staff to treat patients with HIV infections
- Do Not Resuscitate orders in the hospice program
- threatened or pending legal actions

The quality assurance committee should determine and report whether quality assurance recommendations sufficiently addressed the legal and ethical issues. If they have not been sufficiently addressed through recommendations for educational programs, policy and procedure changes, or focus reviews, the annual quality assurance committee evaluation report (or other reports) to management should be used to identify legal and ethical issues for the next year's review activities.

EVALUATING THE EFFECTIVENESS OF THE QUALITY ASSURANCE COMMITTEE

In order to assess program effectiveness, the quality assurance committee must provide an ''outcome'' evaluation of its activities. This is most easily performed by reviewing the written plan and determining to what extent the quality assurance program goals were met (the goals should be considered one by one).

For example, one common quality assurance program goal is as follows: Company policies and procedures will address all quality issues that surface through quality assurance activities. The minutes of meetings, the recommendations or results of monitors, risk management summaries, and new program reports should be reviewed. What policy or procedural changes (additions or deletions) were recommended? After answering this question, it is simple to review company manuals to determine if the quality assurance program policy and procedure recommendations were implemented or are in process of being implemented.

Each program goal should be measured as objectively as possible, taking into account the numbers of policies com-

pleted (or not completed), the scores or percentages for satisfaction surveys, or the decrease in the numbers of protocol or medication errors.

If the quality assurance program goals are well written, they should allow objective measurement. If the goals are not objectively measurable, it should be stated in the committee's annual evaluation, with the recommendation that the goal should be rewritten in more measurable terms for next year's evaluation. In the final phase of evaluating program effectiveness, the committee should present its recommendations for changes in the overall quality assurance plan or in the quality assurance committee activities.

SUMMARY

The written evaluation of quality assurance program effectiveness is an essential step in the process of improving and maintaining high-quality service in a home health care company. Evaluation provides the quality assurance committee with an opportunity to report its successes and to make future recommendations to management. It also provides a broader perspective for the committee's own review and should not be excluded from the quality assurance process.

Structure, process, and outcome measures of the quality assurance plan and the committee's activities should be included in the written evaluation. The structure review involves evaluating the written plan and making certain that it provides the basis to operationalize the program for the home health company and that it meets all the standards of outside accrediting or licensing bodies. The process review involves evaluating the accomplishments of the committee and the company based on the yearly plan. The outcome review involves determining the extent to which the program met the goals of quality service that were established in the plan.

The program evaluation may appear to be time consuming for the committee. However, it not only assesses prior quality assurance activities but also gives clear direction for the future of quality assurance in the home health company.

REFERENCES

Joint Commission on Accreditation of Healthcare Organizations. *Monitoring and Evaluation of the Quality and Appropriateness of Care: A Home Care Example*. Chicago: Author, 1988.

Meisenheimer, C.G. *Quality Assurance: A Complete Guide to Effective Programs*. Rockville, Md.: Aspen Publications, 1985.

Miller, Susan C. *Documentation for Home Health Care: A Record Management Handbook*. Chicago: Foundation of the American Record Association, 1986.

National League for Nursing. *Criteria and Standards Manual for NLN/APHA Accreditation of Home Health Agencies and Community Nursing Services*. New York: Author, 1980.

Appendix 8-A

Patient Services Satisfaction Survey

Thank you for allowing Hospital Home Health Care Agency of California to be providers of your recent home health care. Please spend a few more moments with us by answering the following questions, which will help us learn how you see our performance. **Thank you.**

A. How satisfied are you with the care you received at home from your:

	Very Satisfied	Satisfied	A Little Dissatisfied	Dissatisfied	Did Not Use
Nurse	4	3	2	1	0
Social Worker	4	3	2	1	0
Physical Therapist	4	3	2	1	0
Occup. Therapist	4	3	2	1	0
Speech Therapist	4	3	2	1	0
Home Health Aide	4	3	2	1	0
Nutritionist	4	3	2	1	0

B. Please rate your telephone contact:

Very Prompt			Very Slow	Did Not Use
4	3	2	1	0
Very Courteous			Discourteous	Did Not Use
4	3	2	1	0
Very Helpful			Not Helpful	Did Not Use
4	3	2	1	0

C. Please rate the staff who provided your care:

Very Knowledgeable			Not Knowledgeable	No Opinion
4	3	2	1	0
Professional Appearance			Unsatisfactory Appearance	No Opinion
4	3	2	1	0
Very Courteous			Discourteous	No Opinion
4	3	2	1	0
Very Helpful			Not Helpful	No Opinion
4	3	2	1	0

D. Would you recommend our services?   Yes   No

E. We welcome your suggestions on how we can improve our services. Are there services you would like that we did not offer?

F. Please check one of the following: _____ Patient   _____ Family Member

_____ Friend   _____ Other

Optional: Completed By: _____Date: _____

If you have further comments you may call the Vice President, Patient Services at (213) 530-3800, ext. 430. Thank you.

REMOVE TAPE AND SEAL

Source: Reprinted with permission of Hospital Home Health Care Agency of California.

Appendix 8-B

Physician Satisfaction Survey

We would like to provide you and your patients the best possible service. Please help us to know how well we met your needs by completing this questionnaire.

1. How satisfied are you that your plan of care and follow-up instructions have been followed consistently:

Very Satisfied 4	Satisfied 3	Dissatisfied 2	Very Dissatisfied 1	Did Not Use 0

Intermittent Nursing Care:

4	3	2	1	0

I.V. Therapy Program:

4	3	2	1	0

Pediatrics Program:

4	3	2	1	0

Rehabilitation Program (PT-OT-SPEECH-MSW):

4	3	2	1	0

Hospice Program:

4	3	2	1	0

2. Overall, how satisfied are you with our services?

Very Satisfied 4	Satisfied 3	Dissatisfied 2	Very Dissatisfied 1	Did Not Use 0

3. We would appreciate any comments or suggestions you would like to make that would aid us in evaluating and improving our services.

_____
_____
_____
_____
_____
_____
_____
_____
_____

Thank you for answering this questionnaire. Please seal and return. If you have further comments, you may call the Vice President, Patient Services (213) 530-3800, ext. 430.

Optional: Name: _____

REMOVE TAPE AND SEAL

Source: Reprinted with permission of Hospital Home Health Care Agency of California.

Appendix 8-C

Referral Source Satisfaction Survey

We would like to provide you and your patients the best possible service. Please help us to know how well we met your needs by completing this questionnaire.

1. How satisfied are you that the physician's plan of care and your follow-up instructions have been followed consistently?

	Very satisfied			Dissatisfied	N/A
Intermittent Nursing	4	3	2	1	0
I.V. Therapy Program	4	3	2	1	0
Pediatric Program	4	3	2	1	0
Physical Therapy	4	3	2	1	0
Occupational Therapy	4	3	2	1	0
Speech Therapy	4	3	2	1	0
Hospice	4	3	2	1	0
Medical Social Worker	4	3	2	1	0

2. How satisfied are you with our organization's response to your concerns and questions?

4	3	2	1	0

3. Rate your satisfaction with the following:

Telephone System	4	3	2	1	0
Phone Referral Process	4	3	2	1	0
Liaison Nurse	4	3	2	1	0
Other _____	4	3	2	1	0

4. (a) Are you receiving the feedback you expected regarding your patients? Yes _____ No _____

   (b) If "yes," in a timely manner? Yes _____ No _____

5. Overall, how satisfied are you with our services?

	Very satisfied			Dissatisfied	N/A
	4	3	2	1	0

6. We would appreciate any comments or suggestions you would like to make that would aid us in evaluating and improving our services:

_____

_____

_____

_____

Thank you for answering this questionnaire. Please seal and return. If you have further comments, you may call us at (213) 530-3800.

Optional: Name: _____

REMOVE TAPE AND SEAL

Source: Reprinted with permission of Hospital Home Health Care Agency of California.

Appendix 8-D

Quality Assurance Monitor Summary Form

STANDARD:

FOCUS:

Identification No. _____

Department _____

Date _____

CRITERIA	MEETS CRITERIA		% OF EXPECTED COMPLIANCE	% OF ACTUAL COMPLIANCE	RECOMMENDED REMEDIAL ACTION	PERSON/DEPT. RESPONSIBLE FOR ACTION	RESULTS OF ACTION DATE COMPLETED
	YES	NO					

Source: Reprinted with permission of Hospital Home Health Care Agency of California.

Appendix 8-E

Quality Assurance Monitor/Summary; "Do Not Resuscitate" Monitor Summary

STANDARD: "DNR" Order signed by patient's attending physician will be on file in the patient's chart before patient's death.

FOCUS: 40 Hospice discharged charts, selected at random, representing Hospice patients who died while on service in 1987.

Identification No. _____

Department   Hospice _____
Date   11/87 _____

CRITERIA	MEETS CRITERIA YES	NO	% OF EXPECTED COMPLIANCE	% OF ACTUAL COMPLIANCE	RECOMMENDED REMEDIAL ACTION	PERSON/DEPT. RESPONSIBLE FOR ACTION	RESULTS OF ACTION DATE COMPLETED
Either a signed supplemental order or a signed medical treatment plan clearly stating "DNR" order will be on file in each patient chart surveyed. *Exceptions:* 1. Patient or PCG documented as desiring "full code" status. 2. MD gives verbal "DNR" order to 2 RNs before patient's death but patient dies before signed order returned.	35	5	100%	88%	Hospice Patient Care Managers to track for "DNR" orders on treatment plans. New Standard Hospice Orders to include requirement for code status orders. No patient accepted to the Hospice Medicare Benefit with a "DNR" order. Legal requirements for signed "DNR" order to be reviewed with L.A. and Orange County Hospice Teams.	Hospice Director	Remedial action reviewed with Hospice staff 2/88. Will do follow-up audit of 40-50 charts 9/88.

Note: If chart meets the criteria by "exception," indicate in "yes" column which exception qualifies it to be a positive response.

Source: Reprinted with permission of Hospital Home Health Care Agency of California.

Appendix 8-F

Quality Assurance Monitor/Summary; Timely Initial Service Monitor Summary

STANDARD: Upon receipt of a referral for home care services, the initial home
visit will be made within 24 hours or the next working day.

FOCUS: 50 active and 50 discharged charts, selected at random, representing all
three offices. The time period will be from 10/01/87 to present.

Identification No. _____

Department   Med-Surg

Date   1/88

CRITERIA	MEETS CRITERIA YES	MEETS CRITERIA NO	% OF EXPECTED COMPLIANCE	% OF ACTUAL COMPLIANCE	RECOMMENDED REMEDIAL ACTION	PERSON/DEPT. RESPONSIBLE FOR ACTION	RESULTS OF ACTION DATE COMPLETED
1. The primary service shall establish care on the next working day. *Exceptions:* *1a.* Pt/PCG refuses on that day. *1e.* No authorization. *1f.* Unable to locate patient. *1g.* Visit requested for later date by DP or patient. *1h.* MD Order for another date.	90	10	100%	90%	All offices are now tracking the scheduling and initiation of services to VP Pt. Services. Records will be kept of delays due to staff shortage and attempts made to correct.	Office Management V.P. Pt. Services	Re-audit in four months. 5/88

Note: If chart meets the criteria by "exception," indicate in "yes" column which exception qualifies it to be a positive response.

Source: Reprinted with permission of Hospital Home Health Care Agency of California.

Appendix 8-G

Quality Assurance Monitor/Summary; Intravenous Certification Monitor Summary

STANDARD: All Agency/Ventures RNs must be certified by HHHCAC for IV
Administration of antibiotics, chemotherapeutics, opiates, or continuous
subcutaneous opiates.

FOCUS: 100 discharged charts of patients who have been on service during the period of 8/87 to
12/87 for I.V. administration of antibiotics, chemotherapeutics, opiates or continuous
subcutaneous opiates with all three offices, M/S, Hospice, or Care Connection.

Identification No. _____
Department   All Nursing _____
Date   12/87 _____

CRITERIA	MEETS CRITERIA		% OF EXPECTED COMPLIANCE	% OF ACTUAL COMPLIANCE	RECOMMENDED REMEDIAL ACTION	PERSON/DEPT. RESPONSIBLE FOR ACTION	RESULTS OF ACTION DATE COMPLETED
	YES	NO					
1. All RNs providing I.V. administration of antibiotics, chemotherapeutics, opiates, or continuous subcutaneous admission of opiates have been certified to perform these procedures by HHHCAC.	99	1	100%	99%	1. Redistribution of policy/procedure on RN certification alternative to all Coordinators/ Managers. 2. In-service Coordinators/Mgrs. in utilization of same appropriately.	Director of Education	2/22/88

Note: If chart meets the criteria by ''exception,'' indicate in ''yes'' column which exception qualifies it to be a positive response.

Source: Reprinted with permission of Hospital Home Health Care Agency of California.

Appendix 8-H

Incident Report Form

AGENCY	INCIDENT REPORT	VENTURES
_____ Hospice	CONFIDENTIAL—Not Part of Medical Record	_____ DME
_____ Pt. Svcs.		_____ Consulting
		_____ Private Services

Patient	Medical Record #
Address	Telephone

Age	Sex	Diagnosis

Attending Physician	Telephone

Date & Time of Incident:	Date of This Report
Mo. Day Year Time	

TYPE OF INCIDENT:

_____ Loss/Breakage   _____ Decubitus Ulcer   _____ Attended/Unattended Fall

_____ Equip./Medical Device   _____ Refusal of Treatment   _____ Medication Error

Endangerment   Problems with Procedure   _____ Cardiac Arrest

  _____ Building Security   _____ Protocol Error   _____ Other (Specify) _____

  _____ Patient Endangerment   _____ Untoward Outcome   _____

  _____ Staff Endangerment   _____ Consent Problems

DESCRIBE INCIDENT AND/OR INJURY (IF ANY). IF NONE, STATE "NO APPARENT INJURY."

_____

_____

_____

_____

_____

_____

_____

_____

_____

_____

Observed by:

Name of Drugs taken within 8 hrs. prior to incident:	Dose	Route	Time

FOLLOW UP/NOTIFICATION:

Family	Yes _____ No _____	Who? _____	Time _____	By Whom _____
M.D.	Yes _____ No _____	Who? _____	Time _____	By Whom _____
Service Office	Yes _____ No _____	Who? _____	Time _____	By Whom _____
Equipment Vendor	Yes _____ No _____	Who? _____	Time _____	By Whom _____
Was Employee Injured?	Yes _____ No _____			

ACTION TAKEN BY PHYSICIAN:

NATURE OF INJURY:

_____ No Apparent Injury	_____ Concussion	_____ Death	_____ Other (Specify)
_____ Anaphylaxis	_____ Contusion, Cut, Laceration	_____ Fracture, Dislocation	_____
_____ Burn, Scald	_____ Contagious, Infectious Disease	_____ Sprain, Strain	_____

Witnesses (Include name and employee title or relationship to patient)

1.

2.

	Date	Time
Signature of Person Reporting		
Department Head	Date	
Reviewed by	Date	

#702 REV. 4/87

Source: Reprinted with permission of Hospital Home Health Care Agency of California.

Appendix 8-I

Action Report Form

HOSPITAL HOME HEALTH CARE COMPANIES

ACTION REPORT

Report Initiated by: _____ DATE: _____

Inquiry From: _____ Phone #: _____

☐ Patient/Client   ☐ Family Member   ☐ Physician   ☐ Other _____

Situation Identified:

Patient/Client Name: _____ Employee Name: _____

Contractor Name: _____

Account #

Or Address: _____ Payor: _____ Date Occurred: _____

Description of Situation

_____
_____
_____
_____
_____

Person Designated to Follow Up: _____

Action(s) Taken: (Sign and Date All Actions) _____

_____
_____
_____
_____
_____
_____

Outcome of Action: (Sign and Date all Outcomes) _____

_____
_____
_____
_____
_____

Reviewed by: _____   _____
              Department Head/V.P.

White: Person to Follow Up   Yellow: V.P./Dept. Head   Pink: Person Initiating
(To V.P. when complete)   of Follow Up Dept.

Form #803 Rev. (6-87)

Source: Reprinted with permission of Hospital Home Health Care Agency of California.

Multidisciplinary Monitoring

Chapter 9

The Staff Nurse's Perspective

Lorie E. Olson

The role of the staff nurse in quality assurance for home health care is essential, for the nurse, as the direct care provider and coordinator of services, is most often the health care professional that directly determines the quality of care a client receives. Often the patient's first experience or contact with a home health agency is through the nurse. This leaves the home health nurse with the important responsibility of establishing a relationship with clients and giving them confidence that the highest quality of care will be provided. Today nurses are confronted with multiple factors challenging their ability to provide quality patient care. With the implementation of DRGs and early hospital discharges, the home health nurse faces the challenge of caring for clients with increasingly complex needs. The nurse also faces an increase in consumer and community expectations regarding quality home care.[1] The home health agency has the responsibility of assuring that the staff nurse meets the mandated activities of its quality assurance criteria, but the nurse has the challenge of developing quality assurance monitoring into the daily practice of caring for clients.

The home health nurse has a unique perspective on quality assurance, as the entire nursing process is utilized to provide comprehensive care. Within the framework of primary nursing, the home health nurse becomes the client's case manager. Throughout the nursing process, the nurse, as case manager, is responsible for comprehensive patient assessment, the development and implementation of a multidisciplinary plan of care, and ongoing evaluation of the client's progress. As a professional, the nurse assumes accountability for the nursing process.[2]

Given the current economic challenges of reimbursement in home health care, the home health nurse must try to provide quality care while still meeting the demands of efficiency and productivity. The nurse cannot afford to sacrifice quality to increase productivity or productivity to increase quality.[3] The process of peer review within the home health agency can assist the staff nurse with the many components of quality assurance monitoring. The role of the staff nurse in quality assurance requires the nurse to make a basic commitment to the provision of quality care for each individual patient.

COMMITMENT

Quality Care

When a nurse chooses to specialize in home care, there must be a commitment on the nurse's part to assure quality patient care in all aspects of practice. There are many challenges to quality care in this special area of nursing. The client's value system may not always support values of quality health care. While acknowledging this, the nurse must decide to continue to provide quality care. Providing this care may be even more difficult given the stress of wondering if the extra quality measures of care provided are reimbursable. The client's environment and hazardous working conditions (e.g., sometimes having to go into high crime areas) may challenge further the nurse's ability to assure quality care. However, the nurse, having chosen this profession, must make the additional choice to provide quality patient care despite these factors.

The Agency

As an employee of a home health care agency, the nurse also makes a commitment to the organization to assure quality in the delivery of patient care. This commitment requires the nurse to be knowledgeable about the agency's mission statement. The agency's mission statement describes the goals, program objectives, and services provided by the home health agency.[4] With this understanding part of daily practice, the nurse can competently deliver the care within the scope of the agency's quality assurance program. Also, the nurse must be well informed of the job description as outlined by the home care agency in order to function appropriately within the policy standards of the organization. The home health nurse should understand that all staffing functions are carried out with a view toward meeting agency goals and objectives.[5]

The staff nurse in home care must be knowledgeable about and comply with the agency's policies, procedures, and protocols in providing daily client care. This requires a professional commitment to follow these guidelines in the autonomous practice of home care, where there are only a limited number of colleagues available to monitor the daily activities of practice. As the home care industry continues to grow, the policies, procedures, protocols, and standards must be updated to meet the evolving needs of clients. Nurses must participate in these quality assurance mechanisms by providing ongoing input into the updating of these guidelines for practice. This is especially important for staff nurses, for they have firsthand experience with clients. Manuals for standards, policies, procedures, criteria for admission and discharge, and client care must support and reflect a concern for quality and a commitment to excellence in the delivery of client care.[6] Home health nurses must be active in their commitment to excellence.

Professional Development

The home care nurse must make a commitment to continued education. Again, this challenges the nurse working in an environment where there are decreased funds available for educational opportunities. With changes in the complexity of care, the nurse needs to attend in-service training and educational programs so as to be updated on the many new therapies clients are receiving. "The home health care nurse must be a clinical expert in a variety of areas (i.e. medicine, neurosurgery, oncology, etc.), be knowledgeable in community resources and provide care within regulatory and third-party reimbursement guidelines. The nurse in home health functions independently in determining what nursing care will be provided, when it will be provided, what clinical outcomes are to be attained and when home health care services are to be terminated."[7] The staff nurse in home care then makes a personal commitment to continued education and to providing care for clients within this framework, in particular, high-quality care that meets the physical, psychosocial, emotional, and spiritual needs of these clients. Few other areas of nursing require such a comprehensive focus.

Holistic Care

When the home health nurse walks through the doors into the client's home and discovers, for example, an elderly woman discharged from the hospital after an exacerbation of congestive heart failure, the nurse must take into account the realities of the woman's environment. If the client has no food in the home, no money, has not obtained her medications, and believes strongly that "the good Lord will provide," the nurse is called upon to utilize a variety of resources to meet the client's immediate needs. After addressing the woman's physical needs and ensuring basic survival and safety, the nurse should assist the client with her spiritual needs, perhaps by praying with her or contacting the pastor of a nearby church. These additional measures are required by the nurse's commitment to providing holistic care and meeting the comprehensive needs of the client.

CASE MANAGEMENT

The trend in home health care nursing is to deliver care within the framework of primary nursing. As one agency made the transition from team nursing to primary nursing, it discovered improvements in productivity and quality of care. The impact of primary nursing in home care is another indicator of quality assurance monitoring.[8] Primary nursing is defined as a mode of organizing nursing care such that one nurse is responsible for overseeing the care of one patient during the patient's stay.[9] Primary nursing in home health care tends to evolve into case management. When a client is first referred to the home care agency, a nurse begins the management of care for this client. Case management in home care is a process whereby the nurse utilizes the nursing process to implement the care a client requires and receives and coordinates the multiple disciplines and resources necessary to meet the client's needs in the home.

This aspect of primary nursing in home care is different than in other clinical areas, because the multidisciplinary supports are not immediately available. The nurse must coordinate the other health team members to provide services in the client's home. The home care nurse has a unique and ongoing view of the client in his or her environment. As the case manager, the nurse must communicate the knowledge gained to the physician and health team, as they are not always aware of the challenges the client faces daily in the home and community. The home care nurse is active in this role as case manager and leads the health team to assure quality health care for the client.

The Initiation of Care

Case management may begin while the patient is still in the hospital. The home health nurse may participate in the patient's discharge planning process. Whether this occurs, however, is dependent on the referral source, and the role of the home health nurse is primarily to collect as much information as possible to initiate the care and assure the client will be provided for safely and adequately at home. It is important for the nurse to engage in active communication with the referral source and the physician at the onset of a case. "In home care the situation is very different. Not only are the physicians planning services for unknown settings and needs, but they also have little or no knowledge of what care is actually given."[10] Providing feedback to the physician and the referral source assures continuity of care and informs them of what the client's environmental and home care needs will be.

As the nurse prepares to make the initial visit, a telephone call to the client is advisable. This serves as an introduction and can be used to establish an appointment and verify the address for the home visit.[11] Home health care nursing differs from hospital nursing in that the nurse becomes a part of the client's terrain. The nurse must be flexible and creative in developing rapport with the client in the client's own surroundings. In the home, the client is in control and the nurse is the intruder; the nurse must be flexible in meeting the client's needs.[12] "On an initial visit, most patients are concerned with what the nurse expects of them, and what they can expect of the nurse. By the end of the visit, a foundation of trust and rapport is established, due in part, to the clarification of these expectations."[13] The home health nurse has a key role in this foundation of trust, which can be developed by clearly explaining to the client what are the roles of the nurse and the client, the available resources, and the services of the agency. It is important to stress to the client and to family members that they should play an active role in the care delivery process. As the client accepts his or her role in the health process, greater quality outcomes will result.

The home care nurse is responsible for obtaining the informed consent of the client or an available caregiver. The nurse must also inform clients of their rights as patients. The signed informed consent form and the bill of rights are tools utilized to assure clients that they will receive quality care. The home health nurse has the vital responsibility to initiate care through (1) making an appropriate introduction, (2) obtaining an informed written consent, (3) reviewing the bill of rights with the client, and (4) utilizing flexibility and interviewing skills in an effort to build a foundation of trust and begin the case management process. The home health nurse must develop effective interviewing techniques to facilitate this process.

The Nursing Process

Assessment

The nursing process, including assessment, planning, intervening, and evaluation, is a useful framework within which holistic, comprehensive care can be achieved.

As the case manager, the home health nurse begins the nursing process with the assessment. The initial assessment provides the nurse with the data needed to identify health problems and plan interventions.[14] The nurse must have good physical assessment skills in order to allow for the independent functioning in the home setting.[15] To implement quality assurance in the assessment phase, the nurse should utilize a documentation tool that allows accurate assessments of the environment, the family, the community, and the client, including the client's psychosocial and physical aspects of health behaviors. The nurse must monitor and update these assessments over time. While assessing the client, the nurse must concentrate on the establishment of a trusting relationship and the use of effective interviewing techniques. The data base becomes the tool that reflects the client's status and assists the nurse in developing quality documentation for the client's record. When someone reviews that client's record, that person should be able to read the data base and understand the overall situation of the client. The home care nurse has the responsibility of carefully obtaining the information from the client and documenting a written assessment.

Once an accurate assessment is made, the nurse is able to make appropriate nursing diagnoses and identify those problems for which nursing interventions are appropriate and those which require use of other resources. Within the reimbursement framework for home health care agencies, the nurse assesses the necessary skilled nursing interventions based on the medical diagnoses. The nurse must determine what the client's nursing needs are and consider them in relation to reimbursement and the case management plan of care. The use of nursing diagnoses in the assessment assists the nurse in making a complete assessment—with the goal being the provision of quality client care.

Planning

Once the home health nurse identifies the problems, a plan of care is formulated. As the case manager, the nurse establishes a plan of treatment and determines the need for other disciplines. Ideally, the plan of care is mutually agreed to by the client.[16] This is not always possible, and the home care nurse sometimes becomes the client's advocate in the planning process. The staff nurse formulates the plan of care and documents this individualized care plan. Care plans for home care clients require planning variables different from those used in the inpatient setting. For example, in the hospital, a client receives medications dispensed by the health care team according to a regular schedule. In the home, a client may take medications independently on a schedule compatible with the client's lifestyle. When planning a schedule for the client in the care plan, the nurse should individualize it to accord with the client's daily routine.

The care plan must state the plan of treatment, describe specific nursing interventions, and list specified goals for each nursing diagnosis. Timely documentation of the total plan of care is essential. Each goal and objective should be recorded together with its estimated time frame. The written care plan is important for ensuring that tasks are carried out, that established standards are complied with, and that there is a continuous reassessment and evaluation of the client.[17]

As the home care plan is implemented and client progress is made, there will be a need to revise the plan. The nurse must be flexible, receptive to indicators that the client is moving toward the goals, and willing to alter the plan accordingly.[18] In updating the plan, it is helpful to record actual and potential problems and the appropriate actions required for each one. As the nurse documents the case, the care of the client should be reflected in the plan of care (e.g., in the goals). It is the responsibility of the nurse, as case manager, to receive updates from the other disciplines concerning their goals for the client and to incorporate these changes in the updated plan of care. Although it is difficult for the nurse to make continuous updates in the care plan, updating is important for ensuring that quality care is rendered in the home. The initial care plan and updates provide the nurse with a framework for care. It takes less time to study the situation and plan it initially than it does to begin inappropriate nursing actions and then have to repeat the entire process. The written plan is also an essential tool in the quality assurance processes of utilization review and evaluation.

Interventions

It may appear that nursing interventions are the primary activities of the home health nurse, but in fact direct care interventions are just part of the multifaceted nursing process. Once the planning is done, the home care nurse begins to implement the interventions outlined in the plan. During each visit, the nurse utilizes interventions that are required to assist the client in meeting the goals. As the case manager, the nurse makes appropriate referrals to any other services required to meet the designated goals. This may include sending a home health aid to assist the patient with activities of daily living and personal care until the patient returns to independence in these activities. Or it may include a referral to a speech therapist to assist a patient who has aphasia as the result of a stroke. The specific interventions the home health nurse utilizes to assist the client in meeting his or her maximum health potential are numerous, but they may be categorized as (1) direct client care, (2) monitoring, (3) teaching, (4) counseling, and (5) coordinating.[19] In any intervention, the nurse is responsible for the provision of quality care to the client.

Direct Client Care. In direct client care, the home health nurse must follow the standards of the agency. The documentation of interventions must reflect compliance with the agency's procedures and protocols. While out in the field, the home care nurse is unable to refer to the standards of care manual as needed, but can contact the supervisor for the pertinent information. For direct care, the nurse can follow the standards of care for the particular nursing diagnosis. During a visit to a client who has an open lesion requiring wound care and a nursing diagnosis of "alteration in integument," the nurse would follow the protocol for alteration in integument. This may be outlined as follows: (1) provide wound care, (2) instruct client on signs and symptoms of infection, (3) position patient properly, and (4) monitor the wound for any drainage, infection, etc. By following the outlined standards of care, the nurse determines what interventions are re-

quired to achieve the desired outcomes. During the process of developing standards of care, the staff nurse must participate to assure quality interventions for direct patient care. Among other reasons, the staff nurse has the most active clinical role in client care, has primary knowledge of patient care on a daily basis, and has realistic expectations regarding the meeting of these standards.

Teaching. In home care, a client or a caregiver is often the "practitioner" who delivers the care. Teaching the client becomes an important factor in quality assurance. Comprehensive client education manuals—with detailed procedures and instructions written in lay terms—are a necessity. The home health nurse plays a key role as case manager to assure continuity within the client teaching process.

After assessing the client's learning abilities, the nurse must be flexible in the delivery of client education and take into account the client's ability to read, listen, and follow directions.[20] (This information may be obtained using a cognitive assessment tool or the mini-mental scoring system.) The home health nurse must also consider the possibility of illiteracy when making a learning ability assessment. The most important quality assurance measure for client education is to require the client to verbalize or demonstrate understanding of and compliance with the instruction.

The teaching role of the nurse is essential in home care, and to assure quality care the nurse must follow a consistent teaching plan. If the client is instructed in the hospital about one method of glucose monitoring using a particular glucose recording device but is sent home with a totally different device, the nurse must alter the teaching plan to allow instruction about the new device and at the same time assure consistency in the instructions concerning purposes, methodology, and frequency of glucose monitoring. Consistency is a quality assurance factor for all care providers. As case manager, the nurse must make certain that each caregiver is following a similar teaching plan. If the client has several nurses visiting to perform a procedure, the primary nurse should write instructions or a teaching plan for the other caregivers to follow. This will assure continuity and facilitate the client education process. The client can become confused by different instructions coming from multiple sources, and this confusion will inhibit progress toward the goal. Therefore, in home care the nurse must assure the continuity and consistency of teaching. The home health nurse must review and develop the appropriate patient education materials.

Counseling. The client in home health care should not be viewed as an isolated individual but rather as a member of a whole social or community system. The home health nurse participates in counseling activities as part of the intervention process. Families or caregivers in home care are now assuming more responsibility and caring for sicker clients; they thus need more information about illness, treatment, equipment, and rehabilitation. Clients and their families require a more sophisticated level of counseling and teaching.[21] It is necessary for the home health nurse to respond to the needs of these clients and caregivers by guiding them through the changes in the health status of the client and by utilizing available community resources as needed. Because the patient is part of the whole system of family and community, the home health nurse must be skilled in communicating with and counseling families or caregivers and accessing the community network. A certain amount of assertiveness is also an asset for a nurse dealing with the intervention of counseling.

The client may also need counseling to deal with changes in functional ability. The nurse must know the limits of his or her ability to counsel the client and be able to determine when the client requires a referral to other resources for more extensive counseling or follow-up. The client may require a social worker referral. The home health nurse would initiate this referral. Within the framework of skilled interventions for reimbursement, the nurse may neglect to document counseling interventions, but the key to quality assurance is to try to address the client's total health needs. The nurse must document any psychosocial or spiritual interventions that were provided.

Coordination. The case manager role requires the nurse to provide coordination. At present, clients discharged from a hospital require more community support and therapeutic services in order to be cared for at home. The increase in care requirements in the home has resulted in a need for various therapies, transportation arrangements, personal care services, meal preparation services, etc. In addition to locating and arranging for these services and therapies, the home health nurse is responsible for coordinating care and directing those involved toward mutually agreed upon goals.[22] In order to provide comprehensive coordination of multidisciplinary care for the client, the home health nurse is required to be well versed in available services and resources.

As the case manager, the nurse is accountable for all therapies initiated by the nurse. The nurse also has the responsibility of communicating clearly to all service providers the plan of care and the client goals. The record should indicate that multidisciplinary communication occurred. This may be facilitated by the use of a preprinted daily progress note sheet with a place for noting multidisciplinary conference (Exhibit 9-1) or a flow sheet describing all multidisciplinary communications. The progress note serves as a reminder to the home care nurse to record coordination as one of the interventions.

Home health agencies have 24 hour a day responsibility for a client followed under their plan of care. As a coordinator, the home health nurse's responsibility is to assure that the on-call system is updated and accessible for each primary patient. When a nurse is responsible for on-call duties, he or she must respond to client calls in a timely manner and provide appropriate intervention (Exhibit 9-2).

The physician responsible for the client's care must be informed of the client's progress. The home health nurse has the responsibility of reporting any changes or problems to the physician as they occur. As the case manager, the nurse is in the best position to inform the physician of the coordination of other services. As the physician generally is not aware of the client's home environment and community network, the nurse who provides care under the physician's orders must communicate to the physician the holistic view of the client's status and describe the services being used to meet the client's needs.

Evaluation

The home health nurse is in a challenging situation when evaluating the outcome for a client. Assessment of outcome has been defined as the evaluation of end results in terms of health and satisfaction. It is assumed that good results for clients are brought about, at least to a significant degree, by good care. In the Medicare program, the outcomes of nursing care are currently inferred to be the results of reimbursable care.[23] The whole aspect of the reimbursement climate confronts the home health nurse in the ability to deliver quality care. "The responsibility for preventing clients from being dropped from care precipitously or inappropriately, while capturing maximum reimbursement, is being assumed by many staff nurses in home health agencies."[24] The nurse cannot assume that good care was delivered just because it was reimbursed. The evaluation process will assist the nurse in determining effective outcomes.

The role of the nurse in evaluation of the client is critical. This is often the weakest link in the nursing process chain. The quality assurance measure that ensures quality of care is the evaluation. The assessment, planning, and interventions may all be superior, but, without a superior evaluation of their effectiveness, they may be rendered ineffective or their quality undermined or undetermined. The nurse must review the care that has been delivered and the client's evolving status and determine if the desired outcomes are being met.

The client should be evaluated as part of each visit. During delivery of care to the client, the nurse should be evaluating the client's status vis-à-vis the goals. When a goal is met, the nurse then re-evaluates the client with respect to the other goals. During each visit, the nurse assures that care is focused on the goals and documents this on the record. On the preprinted progress note (Exhibit 9-1), the nurse may record the evaluation under the sections "Progress/Status" and "Evaluation of Teaching." The nurse then re-evaluates and records the current goals. This may be recorded in the section labeled "Goals." This focuses the care on the outcomes that are to be achieved.

Discharge from the Agency. A mandated evaluation of the case, as determined by Medicare, is to occur every 60 days. This assures that the client's case will be evaluated by the home health nurse, physician, and other providers to determine if there is a need for further skilled care or if the client should be discharged. In the current reimbursement climate, determining if the client's needs are met while also assuring reimbursement is difficult. The nurse has this responsibility and must ready the client for discharge. The client is provided with the necessary information to independently continue the plan of care, to independently access the necessary resources, and to follow through with appointments with the physician.

Exhibit 9-1 Progress Note Sheet

Date: _____   Patient: _____

Time: _____   History Number: _____

Purpose of Visit: _____

S. *Patient's Reports: Medication/Treatment Status*

_____

_____

_____

_____

_____

O. Vital Signs   T _____   HR _____   RR _____   BP _____ _____ _____

   Weight _____   D-Stix _____   Measurements _____

   Physical Findings:

   General/LOC _____

   Skin _____

   Head/EENT _____

   Chest _____

   COR _____

   GU/GI/Abd _____

   Neuro/Extrem _____

   Labs _____

   Environment/Caregiver _____

   _____

A. Progress/Status _____

   Evaluation of Teaching _____

P. Interventions _____

   _____

   _____

   _____

Future Teaching _____

MD Conference _____

Multidisciplinary Conference _____

HHA Supervision _____

Return Visit _____   Goals: _____

Interventions for Next Visit: _____

Homebound _____   _____

                                              Signature

Source: Courtesy of the Johns Hopkins Hospital, Department of Home Care and Services.

The client may continue to have multiple unresolved problems that the home health nurse and health team were unable to address. However, based on the updated prioritized care plans, the ongoing evaluation and interventions, the client's or caregiver's demonstration of progress toward independence in care, and the designated outcomes, the nurse may nevertheless decide that the client should be discharged from home care. When the home health nurse terminates the case, the nurse must be certain the client is competent to contact the physician and community resources for continued care as needed.

For quality assurance purposes, the nurse must document a clear, concise summary of the client's status at discharge. An efficient agency discharge summary should be completed by the nurse that outlines the diagnoses, evaluation of care given, the client's current status, and follow-up plans of care (Exhibit 9-3). The client's medical record should reflect the completion of the nursing process. In the evaluation process, the services the client received may be reviewed to assure quality care was delivered.

STAFFING PATTERNS AND PRODUCTIVITY

The home health nurse not only is required to meet demands for quality and excellence in rendering all aspects of patient care, but also is expected to achieve high levels of produc-

Exhibit 9-2 On-Call Patient Data Base Form

THE JOHNS HOPKINS HOSPITAL
DEPARTMENT OF HOME CARE AND SERVICES

ON-CALL PATIENT DATA BASE

NAME: _____   HISTORY NUMBER: _____

ADDRESS: _____   PHONE: _____

DATE OF BIRTH: _____ SEX: _____   INSURANCE: (if needed) _____

SIGNIFICANT OTHER/CAREGIVER: _____   RELATIONSHIP: _____

ADDRESS: _____   PHONE: _____

PRIMARY NURSE: _____   HOSPITAL PAGING: ___955-6070_____

PRIMARY PHYSICIAN: _____   METHOD OF CONTACT/PHONE #: _____

SECONDARY PHYSICIAN: _____   PHONE: _____

VS: R _____, T _____, HR _____, BP _____, BP _____

CURRENT PROBLEM LIST	CURRENT MEDICATIONS

PATIENT'S CURRENT STATUS: _____

_____

_____

_____

_____

PURPOSE OF VISIT: _____

_____

_____

_____

SUPPLIES TO BE DELIVERED: _____

DIRECTIONS: _____

_____

Source: Courtesy of the Johns Hopkins Hospital, Department of Home Care and Services.

tivity. The home health nurse confronts this dichotomy daily in attempting, during home visits, to provide thorough care but in a timely manner, since usually several other visits have to be made. Besides the daily visits, the nurse's time is spent in such activities as preparation and gathering of supplies, travel, coordination of services, telephone calls, documenting, obtaining referrals, researching a health condition, processing laboratory specimens, and completing visit statistics.[25] "The key word in scheduling work activities is flexibility."[26]

Mindful of productivity requirements, the home health nurse must be flexible in the scheduling of visits. The home health nurse is an independent practitioner relying on expertise, skill, and judgment to make decisions regarding visit frequency, for example.[27] One of the most satisfying aspects of home health care nursing is the autonomy. When scheduling appointments, the nurse should consider the geographical location of clients, the intensity of care, and the projected length of visit. The nurse must develop an individualized system of scheduling that is efficient and organized. Once the home care nurse establishes a system of scheduling client visits and follow-up visits, the nurse can carry out interventions confidently, knowing that the return visit can be utilized for follow-up care.

In the course of a day, the nurse must render care efficiently during each visit. The length of a visit may depend on a multitude of factors. Lengths might range from 20 minutes for a regular visit for blood pressure monitoring to 4 hours for the administration and infusion of an antibiotic therapy. To provide quality patient care in a timely manner, the nurse must focus on the client's goals.

One strategy for saving time and improving quality is to document client care immediately after the visit. "For exam-

Exhibit 9-3 Discharge Summary

THE JOHNS HOPKINS HOSPITAL
DEPARTMENT OF HOME CARE AND SERVICES

DISCHARGE SUMMARY

Patient Name _____ Medical Record No. _____

Source of Referral _____ Date of Hospital Adm. _____ D/C _____

Services	Admission Date	Discharge Date
( ) RN		
( ) HHA		
( ) OT		
( ) PT		
( ) ST		
( ) MSS		
( ) Other, Comments		

Medical Diagnosis _____

Patient Problem	Goal Reached	Goal Not Reached	Comments

Summarize Course and Significant Events: _____

Patient's Status
V.S. _____

Physical Status: (   ) Stable   (   ) Improved   (   ) Strong   (   ) Weak   (   ) Varies
    Describe: _____

Mental Status: (   ) Alert   (   ) Cooperative   (   ) Confused   (   ) Coping Orientation _____

Activity Level: (   ) Homebound   (   ) Ambulates Independently   (   ) Bedridden
    (   ) OOB With Assistance   (   ) Ambulates with Assistance   (   ) Other _____

Adaptation/Equipment: (   ) Cane   (   ) Walker   (   ) Wheelchair   (   ) Hospital Bed   (   ) Bedside Commode
    (   ) O_2 (   ) Other _____

Diet/Fluids _____ Wt _____ (   ) Gain   (   ) Lost   (   ) Unchanged

Medication	Dosage	Frequency	Instructed	Takes as Ordered/Comments

Reason for Discharge:
1. (   ) Condition no longer requires skilled care.
2. (   ) Patient has moved out of the geographic area.
3. (   ) Patient/MD terminated services.
4. (   ) Patient transferred to another agency.
5a. (   ) Patient admitted to Hospital, name: _____
5b. (   ) Patient admitted to Long-term Care Facility, name: _____

6. (   ) Patient expired.
7. (   ) Not homebound.

Client Referrals _____
Follow-up Health Care/Appointments _____

Additional Comments: _____

JHH c: 1988
11/86
Rev: 3/88

Signature _____   Date _____

Source: Courtesy of the Johns Hopkins Hospital, Department of Home Care and Services.

ple, charting on a client's record as soon as possible after the client contact requires less time than doing it days later and having to spend time recalling what was said and done."[28] Charting on a preprinted progress note or flow sheet also assists the nurse in timely completion of documentation (Exhibit 9-1). As the nurse develops efficiency and flexibility in making home care visits, the quality of patient care will increase.

While the home health nurse needs to develop skills in time management for client visits, other components of home health nursing must also be acknowledged. One way for the nurse to review the multiple additional responsibilities involved in client care is for the home health nurse to accurately record visit statistics, length of visit, travel time, documentation time, telephone time, coordination time, conference time, administrative time, etc. This provides an accurate method of time management evaluation. When the nurse reports feeling overwhelmed with paperwork and yet is convinced the day was nonproductive, the time records will show the multiple activities that consumed indirect patient care time. It also helps to report how time is under- or overutilized and to cite areas of productivity that may be improved. It is the home health nurse's responsibility to accurately record this vital information. Not only will it benefit the nurse as an individual, but as productivity standards and patient classification systems are developed, the accurate recording of time and visit statistics will demonstrate the acuity levels of home care clients.

The home health staff nurse must take responsibility for participating in the development of systems that will identify acuity levels for client care. Given the potential for a prospective payment system to be implemented in the home care industry, the staff nurse has a central role in identifying the multiple activities that constitute patient care. The home health nurse must participate in the development of patient classification systems or acuity indices. Recording this information will assist the nurse in providing quality client care with a logical and realistic system of productivity standards.

Supplemental Personnel

To meet the demands of increased acuity in client care, a home health agency may be using supplemental personnel to provide care. The staff nurse can assure quality patient care by monitoring the actions of the supplemental or contract staff. Already pressured by the demand for increased productivity, this additional responsibility for the home health nurse can be a real challenge. The home health nurse must ensure that there exists a mechanism for reporting to the supplemental staff and informing them of the patient's status and needs. Also, to ensure consistent care to the client, the number of different nurses should be limited. Staffing patterns may vary, but consistency in the caregivers will assure continuity of care and therefore quality outcomes.

PEER REVIEW

Because the staff nurse in home care delivers the majority of client care independently, an essential tool for quality assurance is the peer review process. As in any form of client care, the practice of care must be defined and then monitored. In home care, the nurse has defined the delivery of care through the medical record; by monitoring this, the quality of patient care can be determined. Once the nurse has written the medical record, he or she is accountable. In home care, where there are virtually no other health team members witnessing the daily delivery of patient care, the client's record must be reviewed to assure quality. Yet, as has been noted,

> some nurses are offended by the idea of being judged in the review process. An open minded acceptance of the value of the record audit and utilization reviews is necessary if they are to achieve their purpose—the improvement of quality of care. For a nurse who is particularly uncomfortable with the idea of peer review, one possible solution is to ask a coworker to review the record prior to the formal review. This can help a nurse become accustomed to receiving constructive criticism and can alert the nurse to his/her own commonly made recording errors.[29]

The home health staff nurse should participate in the peer review activity of chart auditing as a learning experience.

The peer review process should include a committee consisting of staff and supervisory members, who review client records, assess the appropriateness of the care plans and interventions as documented in the record, and evaluate for the completeness of the care and the documentation. After the review process, the committee will report positive and negative documentation findings, suggest improvements consistent with the agency's standards of care, recommend any areas requiring continued education, and direct individual staff members as needed.[30] The frequency of peer reviews is determined by the agency's quality assurance standards. Closed cases can reveal general trends in care delivery and they provide staff nurses with opportunities to improve client care in the future.

Another method of peer review involves evaluating client care while the home health nurse is active in the case. This is done during regularly scheduled supervision conferences with the individual home health nurse and the clinical supervisor. Reviewing the case while the client is active provides the nurse with the opportunity to obtain administrative support and feedback regarding the case. The supervisor assists the nurse in clarifying the nurse's role and identifying any unmet needs of the client. The home health nurse should give a report on the client in a concise format, including name, age, reason for home care referral, significant history, the framework of the nursing diagnoses and plan of care, and the goals of the client (with time frames for achievement). The supervisor has the responsibility of guiding the nurse in this presentation and focusing on the client's outcomes.

At the same time, the client's record will be reviewed for timely completion of documentation, the accuracy of the plan of care, the appropriateness of interventions, and the ongoing evaluation of client goals. This review process will provide the home health nurse with frequently needed, objective support and help him or her to improve client care. The underlying assumption of this process is that the nurse's documentation is a true reflection of the situation and the interventions employed, which reinforces the need for the nurse to document accurately.[31] These measures of case and record review will improve the quality of care and contribute significantly to the agency's quality assurance components, and the home health staff nurse can play a significant role in the peer review process.

CONCLUSION

There are many ways in which the home health nurse can implement quality assurance measures in the practice of home care nursing. First, the nurse must make a commitment to provide quality holistic care as part of a general commitment to client care. Caring for clients in their homes requires a high level of dedication—because of the autonomy of the practice and the many challenges and unknown factors that are discovered when caring for clients in their own domain. Second, the nurse must make a commitment to the home care profession. This includes a commitment not only to the agency's standard for quality assurance, but also to the ongoing development of quality assurance mechanisms, such as standards of care, protocols, client classification systems, etc. The staff nurse must actively participate in the development of these tools.

As a home care nurse visiting clients in the community, the nurse must meet a variety of needs. The nurse assumes the role of case manager, providing direct care to clients and coordinating multiple therapies, services, and community resources to assist the client in meeting needs and returning to a higher level of health.

Throughout the case management process, the primary nurse utilizes the nursing process to ensure quality patient care. During the assessment phase, the nurse monitors the quality of care by an accurate assessment tool and by formulation of nursing diagnoses. To ensure quality care, the nurse then formulates a plan of care with specific client goals and time frames. While implementing the plan of care, the case manager utilizes and coordinates other disciplines, depending on the goals. Evaluation is an ongoing process whereby the nurse determines if the client is ready for discharge. The goal of providing home care is to help the client achieve his or her maximum level of independence. The staff nurse in home care assists the client in attaining this goal and ensures that the client will have adequate follow-up care with the physician and through community resources after discharge.

To provide quality care within the limitations of time and productivity demands, the home health nurse must be highly skilled in time management and organization, yet at the same time be flexible. Accurate visit and time recording will assist the nurse with accountability and in tracking acuity levels for client care. In home care, there are many additional responsibilities of the nurse besides direct care. Tasks indirectly related to care must be recorded to reflect the acuity of care that home care patients currently require. To decrease the timely process of documentation and to improve quality care, the nurse should record the visit as soon as possible after the visit. The nurse has the responsibility to try to decrease duplication of documentation and reduce overall recording time whenever possible without compromising the record.[32]

To monitor the staff nurse's delivery of care, the home care agency utilizes the peer review process. This is a learning tool for the nurse and a quality assurance tool for independent practice. The nurse must participate in the peer review process to improve client care.

The home health nurse has a multitude of responsibilities and challenges. Being mindful of the client's goal of living at home and attaining an optimum level of health and well-being, the home care nurse utilizes many skills and talents to provide quality holistic care in the autonomous practice of home health care nursing.

NOTES

1. D.M. Wagner and D.S. Cosgrove, "Quality Assurance: A Professional Responsibility," *Caring* 5, no. 1 (1986): 47.

2. C.G. Meisenheimer, *Quality Assurance: A Complete Guide to Effective Programs* (Rockville, Md.: Aspen Publishers, 1985), 259.

3. C.L. Corriveau and R.H. Rowney, "What Is a Day's Work?" *Nursing Outlook* 31, no. 6: 336.

4. S.C. Miller, *Documentation for Home Health Care: A Record Management Handbook* (Chicago: Foundation of Record Education of the American Medical Record Association, 1986).

5. National League of Nursing, *NLN Administrators Handbook for Community Health and Home Care Services* (New York: Author, 1984), 225.

6. S. Shaw et al., "Assuring Quality and Confidence in New Home Care Technologies," *Caring* 4, no. 1 (1985): 52.

7. C. Sylvester, "Home Health Care," *The Hopkins Nurse* 10, no. 1: 5.

8. L.T. Rinke, "A VNA Switches to Primary Nursing," *American Journal of Nursing* 84, no. 10 (1984): 1226–29.

9. M.R. Dear, C.S. Weisman, and S. O'Keefe, "Evaluation of a Contract Model for Professional Nursing Practice," *Health Care Management Review* 10, no. 2 (1985): 68.

10. M.O. Mundinger, *Home Care Controversy* (Rockville, Md.: Aspen Publishers, 1983), 51.

11. C.P. Elkins, *Community Health Nursing: Skills and Strategies* (Bowie, Md.: Robert J. Brady Co., 1984), 232.

12. Ibid., 232.

13. Rinke, "VNA Switches to Primary Nursing," 1226–29.

14. Elkins, *Community Health Nursing,* 43.

15. L.Z. Webb and S.M. Sundahl, "The Critical Care to Home Care Program: A Career Opportunity," *Dimensions of Critical Care Nursing* 4, no. 1 (1985): 55.

16. Elkins, *Community Health Nursing*, 43.

17. S. Stuart-Siddall, *Home Health Care Nursing* (Rockville, Md.: Aspen Publishers, 1986).

18. Elkins, *Community Health Nursing*, 88.

19. E.K. Phillips and P.A. Cloonan, "DRG's: Ripple Effects on Community Health Nursing," *Public Health Nursing* 4, no. 2: 84–88.

20. Stuart-Siddall, *Home Health Care Nursing*, 184.

21. Phillips and Cloonan, "DRG's," 84–88.

22. Ibid.

23. Mundinger, *Home Care Controversy*, 51.

24. Phillips and Cloonan, "DRG's," 84–88.

25. Elkins, *Community Health Nursing*, 371.

26. Ibid., 370.

27. Webb and Sundahl, "Critical Care to Home Care Program," 55.

28. Elkins, *Community Health Nursing*, 371.

29. Ibid., 183.

30. National League of Nursing, *NLN Administrators Handbook for Community Health and Home Care Services*, 248.

31. Elkins, *Community Health Nursing*, 182.

32. Ibid., 181.

REFERENCES

Bonstein, J., G. Robert, and J. Mueller. "Improving Agency Productivity." *Caring* 4, no. 11 (1985).

Dear, M.R., C.S. Weisman, and S. O'Keefe. "Evaluation of a Contract Model for Professional Nursing Practice." *Health Care Management Review* 10, no. 2 (1985): 65–76.

Corriveau, C.L., and R.H. Rowney. "What Is a Day's Work?" *Nursing Outlook* 31, no.6 (1983): 335–339.

"Don't Let High Productivity Standards Alarm Staff." *Hospital Home Health* 3, no. 1 (1985).

Elkins, C.P. *Community Health Nursing: Skills and Strategies*. Bowie, Md.: Robert J. Brady Co., 1984.

Knollmueller, R.N. *The Community Health Nursing Supervisor: A Handbook for Community/Home Care Managers*. New York: National League for Nursing, 1986.

Meisenheimer, C.G. *Quality Assurance: A Complete Guide to Effective Programs*. Rockville, Md.: Aspen Publishers, 1985.

Miller, S.C. *Documentation for Home Health Care: A Record Management Handbook*. Chicago: Foundation of Record Education of the American Medical Record Association, 1986.

Mundinger, M.O. *Home Care Controversy*. Rockville, Md.: Aspen Publishers, 1983.

National League of Nursing. *NLN Administrators Handbook for Community Health and Home Care Services*. New York: Author, 1984.

Petrowski, D.D. *Handbook for Community Health Nursing*. New York: Springer Publishing, 1984.

Phillips, E.K., and P.A. Cloonan. "DRG's: Ripple Effects on Community Health Nursing," *Public Health Nursing* 4, no. 2 (1987): 84–87.

Rinke, L.T. "A VNA Switches to Primary Nursing." *American Journal of Nursing* 84, no. 10 (1984): 226–229.

Shaw, S., E. John, C. McNamara, and R. Perchard. "Assuring Quality and Confidence in New Home Care Technologies." *Caring* 4, no. 1 (1985): 51–55.

Stuart-Siddall, S. *Home Health Care Nursing*. Rockville, Md.: Aspen Publishers, 1986.

Sylvester, C. "Home Health Care." *The Hopkins Nurse* 10, no. 1 (1987): 5.

Wagner, D.M., and D.S. Cosgrove. "Quality Assurance: A Professional Responsibility." *Caring* 5, no. 1 (1986): 46–49.

Webb, L.Z., and S.M. Sundahl. "The Critical Care to Home Care Program: A Career Opportunity." *Dimensions of Critical Care Nursing* 4, no. 1 (1985): 46–57.

Chapter 10

The Physician's Perspective

Paul E. Hankwitz

My first exposure to home care occurred when my father, a family physician, took me on a house call during my adolescence. The dynamics of the physician-patient relationship in the patient's home exemplified the physician's role with the art of medicine—a healing dialogue, good bedside manner, patient and environment assessment, teaching the patient and family to move them toward independence, therapeutic recommendations, and humanism.[1] That home visit was a most positive experience and it remains vivid in my memory to this day.

Much has changed in health care delivery, however, since that home visit nearly 30 years ago. We have moved from an emphasis decades ago on access and quality of care to a current concern with cost containment and the possible need to ration effective health care. As the pendulum now swings back, the call for quality assurance is again being heard, but its purpose today is to prevent the erosion of quality rather than its expansion.[2]

HISTORICAL FORCES THAT SHAPED TODAY'S HEALTH CARE SYSTEM

It is important to review the gradual reduction, until recently, of health care delivery by physicians in homes across America.[3] During the mid-eighteenth century, physicians were required to fulfill a wide variety of functions. Most physicians were trained by apprenticeship and practiced general medicine. The late eighteenth century saw an influx into the great seaboard cities of academic, intellectual physicians trained in European universities who challenged the prevalent folk medicine and the locally trained apprentice physicians. In

1765, Dr. William Shippen established the first U.S. medical school at the University of Pennsylvania in Philadelphia, and it was based on the European model. The great American physicians of the time became well-respected leaders, and in fact many were representatives to the Continental Congress and became signers of the Declaration of Independence. The model for medical care as the United States came into being was entrepreneurial fee-for-service, and little thought was given to medical services provided by local or federal government.

The nineteenth century brought attempts at public health measures and public hospitals. The latter were built largely for poor incurables, and infectious diseases ran rampant and killed many patients. Nonetheless, some hospitals in the Eastern United States became teaching facilities and established a tradition of training physicians, surgeons, and nurses within the confines of an institution. So here we find an initial de-emphasis of home care during the formative medical education process. As many as 400 medical schools were founded that lacked standardized graduation requirements and produced physicians and surgeons who had inconsistent and often inadequate education.

During the period before the Civil War, populism found widespread medical expression through the practice of lay healing, with lay "practitioners" treating with herbs, remedies, and diet. But by 1830, 13 state governments (significantly not the federal government) had passed medical licensing laws establishing trained physicians as the only legal healers. It wasn't, however, until the end of the century that a combination of state and national medical societies finally drove out much "irregular" practice. Almost all medical practice involved a fee or barter for services rendered. But many of the public preventive services were performed solely for the public good; this helped to establish a tradition of charitable medical service in the United States that prevailed among physicians until the onset of Medicaid legislation 150 years later.

In 1910, the Carnegie Commission authorized Abraham Flexner, a nonphysician, to evaluate medical education throughout the United States. The Flexner Report disclosed many of the inadequacies in medical education and resulted in a radical change in the nature of medical education, including the closing of as many as 40 percent of the "borderline" medical schools. The public demand for a new breed of physicians again led to a concentration of medical education in the laboratory and hospital rather than the home.

Since World War I, health care delivery evolved from being a system that featured the community hospital and the general physician (who viewed patients in relation to their families and society) to being a system with an incredibly complicated and bewildering array of providers and institutions. World War II brought a physician shortage, making home visits a less efficient use of physician time. Additionally, the advancement of science and technology subsequently occurred in quantum leaps, providing a vast spectrum of new drugs, diagnostic tools, and technological procedures and making caregiving much more complex than ever before. The rapid growth of high technology made hospital care generally more appropriate than the limited range of services that could be provided in the home. The I.C.U. was created, and it provided a much more "exciting" and financially viable environment than the home for providing medical care.

No longer could the general practitioner handle all health problems or keep up to date on all new knowledge. Thus, the "superspecialist" became the acceptable physician-university-institution model, outranking the nonspecialist in status and access to academic and financial rewards. Inevitably, specialization created an increasing gap in general continuing health care at the community level. We have been left with a serious contradiction between the need to provide basic health services to the entire population and the push toward specialization that results from the ever-increasing growth of institutionally based scientific and technological knowledge.

As previously noted, a major issue of the 1960s was *access* to health care; the 1970s focused on *quality* of care. During the 1980s, however, *financial constraints* have become the issue and several "forces" have thrust provision of health care services from the inpatient to the outpatient setting.

HOME HEALTH CARE DEFINED

Home health care is that component of a continuum of comprehensive health care whereby health services are provided to individuals and families in their places of residence for the purpose of promoting, maintaining, or restoring health or of maximizing the level of independence while minimizing the effects of disability and illness, including terminal illness. Services appropriate to the needs of the individual patient and family are planned and coordinated in consultation with the patient's physician and made available by providers organized for the delivery of home health care. Home health services are made available based on patient care needs as determined by an objective patient assessment administered by a multidisciplinary team or a single health professional in consultation with the patient's physician. Centralized professional coordination and case management are included. Home health care is provided under a plan of care that includes, but is not limited to, appropriate components such as medical, dental, nursing, social work, pharmacy, laboratory, physical therapy, occupational therapy, speech therapy, nutrition, homemaker-home health aide, transportation, chore, and medical equipment and supply services.[4]

LEVELS OF CARE

Generally speaking, the level of care refers to the degree of care required (1) to enhance an individual's level of functioning and/or prevent further physical dependency and deterioration and (2) to facilitate the transfer of patients, when appropriate, from expensive inpatient facilities to the home.[5]

High-Tech Acute Care

The high-technology level of home health care provides services for patients who need acute, intensive treatment and/or rehabilitation and who would otherwise require inpatient care.[6] These patients require a high degree of physician and nursing supervision and management, as well as centralized and professional coordination of treatment and services. This level of care is typically provided for a temporary serious illness and may entail coordination of such specialized services as

- I.V. therapies (antibiotics, chemotherapy, total parenteral nutrition, fluids, blood product administration)[7]
- wound care, catheter care, injections
- pre- or post-outpatient diagnostic study or outpatient surgery support
- enteral nutritional support or ostomy care
- inhalation therapy, oxygen, ventilator support[8]
- continuous ambulatory peritoneal dialysis (CAPD)
- home intervention for high risk infants[9]
- specialized therapies (physical, occupational, speech)[10]
- home back care program or traction
- in-home lab and x-rays

Long-Term Care

Long-term or maintenance level supportive home health care is appropriate for patients who are reasonably stable medically and who have attained a satisfactory level of rehabilitation. Such individuals require just periodic evaluation and regular monitoring and they only need (1) assistance with daily living activities and (2) personal care services such as bathing, dressing, light housekeeping, laundry, and meal preparation. Typically, long-term supportive care means preservation of personal independence and dignity with overall lower medical costs and postponement of nursing home placement. Government funding of long-term care has, fortunately, become a major national priority.[11]

Home Hospice Care

Home hospice services are provided to patients with terminal illnesses. These services range from nursing care for the patient to bereavement services for the family. The hospice program assists individuals and their families in adjusting to and coping with the unique aspects of terminal illness and death.

The basic justification for providing all levels of care in the home is that the conditions of patients often change. Patients tend to move back and forth in a continuum of care. They do not remain static at one level of functioning, nor do they need just one service.

RENEWED PHYSICIAN INTEREST IN HOME CARE

Along with changes in many other aspects of health care delivery, the role of the physician in home care is currently undergoing a major metamorphosis. There are at least five reasons for physician interest in the organization, delivery, and financing of home care services.[12]

First, the elderly population, suffering a high incidence of activity limitations, is expected to increase by 30 percent by the year 2025. The needs of the elderly account for more than half the services in the home, and two of the goals of home care are to reduce institutionalization and to promote independence.

Second, the recent availability of sophisticated high-technology medical equipment and therapies for safe use in the home is now allowing Americans of all ages—from technology-dependent children to the frail elderly[13]—to receive intravenous antibiotics, I.V. chemotherapy, prolonged total parenteral nutrition, I.V. rehydration, blood products, and I.V. pain managing medications in the less expensive noninstitutional home setting. Apnea monitoring permits even very-low-birth-weight infants to receive care at home. The availability of ventilators, dialysis, and other life support systems for home use continues to expand, as does the availability of a variety of rehabilitative devices and services.

Third, the implementation of the prospective pricing system (PPS), with its incentives for shorter and less costly hospital stays, has encouraged development of noninstitutional post–acute care treatment alternatives. It has been stated that some of the money saved on hospital costs under PPS should

be used for home care programs for the elderly. Diagnosis related groups (DRGs), peer review organizations (PROs), and health maintenance organizations (HMOs) have had a staggering effect on the recent health care scene.

Fourth, there has always been an overwhelming patient preference for receiving acute, long-term, and hospice care in noninstitutional settings, when possible.

Last, the number of persons with AIDS (acquired immunodeficiency syndrome) is expected to grow to more than 270,000 by the end of 1991. With anticipated improvement in length of survival, it is becoming clear that care for persons with AIDS is more feasible outside the acute care hospital, when possible. Accumulated data demonstrate a dramatic reduction in cost associated with noninstitutional management.[14]

THE SUPPORT OF ORGANIZED MEDICINE FOR HOME HEALTH CARE

In 1960, the American Medical Association's House of Delegates adopted a policy on home health care that recommended "physicians be urged to participate in organized home health care programs for any patient who can benefit from the program, and to promote such programs in their communities."[15]

In 1980, the AMA's Council on Medical Service prepared a booklet entitled *Physician Guide to Home Health Care* to assist physicians in the appropriate use of home health care services for their patients and to stimulate greater development of programs in areas that need such services.[16] In this booklet, physicians are encouraged to determine the availability of home care services in their areas by using a number of sources, including hospital discharge planning units, state and local health departments, insurance carriers, state home health care associations, and health planning agencies. Whether physicians decide to use this care component for their patients will depend on the quality of home health care services in the local area. Although the AMA has recognized a number of programs designed to monitor the quality of care provided by home health agencies, physicians are encouraged to make their own evaluations of local programs. They are also encouraged to become familiar with local home care agencies' organizational and administrative structures, their scope of services, their policies, and the qualifications of those personnel who provide care to home health care patients. Finally, physicians are encouraged to make personal contact with the local agencies' medical directors or administrators and to establish communication with other key staff.

The AMA has continued to emphasize the need for physician initiative and participation in the development and use of home health care programs. As a means to this goal, the AMA is examining how physicians can expand their practices to include home health services and how medical societies can contribute to the development, coordination, and operation of home health care programs. In the AMA's *Home Health Care*

Report, prepared in March 1987, Dr. Chavigny stated, "There is an urgent need to provide medical practice standards for medical management in the home. In particular, criteria for selection of patients for home care, for discharge planning, and coordination of care for the medical regimen delivered in the home are needed for continuing medical education."[17] She went on to state, "Home care preferably should be integrated longitudinally throughout the curriculum in all [medical education] programs regardless of medical specialty. It must apply to all age groups, including chronically ill children and adults, as well as acutely ill patients discharged from hospitals prior to complete recovery and returned to their pre-illness functional status."[18]

In April 1986, the American College of Physicians' Board of Regents approved a position paper stating that home health care today is "vastly different from what it was just five or ten years ago" and that it can be of great benefit to many elderly people and should be adequately funded by government and other programs.[19] The ACP's positions on home health care are as follows:

- Physicians need to be more involved in home health care. They should be involved in continuing assessments of the functional needs as well as the medical needs of homebound patients and should be able to advise patients on the availability and use of home health services.
- Adequate funding for home health services should be provided by Medicare, Medicaid and other health care programs to ensure that appropriate services are accessible.
- Efforts need to be made to reduce confusion about home health care coverage under Medicare and other national health care programs.
- Home health care is an option that should be available to serve patient care needs. It may not be appropriate for all patients, and its availability does not justify the denial of needed institutional care.
- Medical equipment and technologies should be reviewed for safety and effectiveness in the home care setting.
- Home health personnel who provide care should be appropriately trained and certified. The delivery of home health services should involve members of a team of health professionals that will vary according to the individual patient's needs. Certification requirements for home health agencies and reimbursement regulations that impede the provision of medical and nursing services at home should be reduced to a minimal level sufficient to maintain high quality care and discourage fraud and abuse.[20]

MONITORING QUALITY OF CARE IN THE HOME SETTING

Just what is quality medical care? One physician stated it this way. "For the physician and the patient, quality medical care can be defined as that care that has the capacity to achieve the goals of both the physician and the patient. . . . Goals can reflect that aspect of care that has been variously called *technical* or *scientific* and usually are achieved by the physician's appropriate choice of tests and therapies. Other goals refer to the nontechnical or interpersonal aspect of care, the art of medicine; these goals usually are not achieved by tests or therapies but by attention to those patient values that generated them."[21]

The AMA's *Physician Guide to Home Health Care* states,

> The quality of home health care services is an important concern to both patients and physicians. There are a number of programs designed to monitor the quality of care provided by home health agencies. To be eligible for reimbursement under Medicare and Medicaid, home health agencies are inspected to determine if they meet Medicare "Conditions of Participation." Additionally, some states assure a minimal level of quality by the licensing of home health agencies in that jurisdiction. The Joint Commission on Accreditation of Healthcare Organizations has established minimum standards for hospital based home care programs as just one requirement for accreditation of hospitals with such home care programs. The National League for Nursing directly accredits home health care agencies. Finally, the National Council for Homemaker-Home Health Aide Services, Inc. serves as the national standard setting body for homemaker-home health aide services.[22]

Brook and Lohr briefly reviewed the state of the art of quality assessment:

> When quality of care is to be evaluated, the following questions must be addressed:
> 1. Will the structure (the organizational elements of care), the process of care (what professionals do to and for patients), or the outcomes of care (what happens to patients), or some combination thereof, be evaluated?
> 2. Will the criteria used to judge care be explicit (pre-set), or implicit (subjective), or both?
> 3. Will the data come from a secondary source (insurance claims data), computerized institutional databases, individual medical records, or patients, or some combination thereof?
> 4. Will only the technical dimension of quality be assessed, or will the art of care also be examined?
> 5. Will the method of assessment be based on populations and communities or on individual patients—that is, be concerned with those who are eligible to use a service or with those who actually use a service?
>
> Research in quality assessment over the past 20 years provides at least partial answers to the above questions. We are compelled, however, to register one important caveat: There are, at best, only a handful of clinically validated criteria or standards, either in the process or the outcome domain, that can simply be taken off a shelf and

applied. Indeed, the bookcase in which to place the shelf has yet to be built.*

Expert professional review of an individual medical record, especially when evaluating the medical home care given to a technology-dependent child or frail elderly patient, is an especially valuable tool. Brook and Lohr state,

> Using this approach calls for special attention to three points: (1) assisting physician-reviewers to locate critical information by investing sufficient resources to ensure that medical records are complete, legible, and in good order; (2) choosing records for review with a relevant sample frame in mind; and (3) selecting physician-reviewers carefully, after appropriate screening and testing. Picking skilled physician-reviewers may be the central and critical step.
>
> Explicit review of the process of care, which is also typically applied to data from a clinical record, is only as good as the thought put into constructing the criteria. Methods that use branched criteria ("If X is positive, then was Y done?") are more valid than methods based on simple criteria ("Was Y done [irrespective of X]?"). The criteria-mapping method has been used more often in the outpatient than the inpatient setting.
>
> To evaluate quality of care fully requires obtaining data from the patient, as well as from the medical record. Likewise, assessing the art of care, which is especially important for patients with chronic disease, entails collecting data directly from the patient.
>
> Insurance claims data can reveal only major deficiencies in quality of care. Currently available claims data have even less application in assessing the quality of care rendered in nursing homes or by home health agency personnel.
>
> Outcome techniques are less well developed than process techniques. Outcome data by themselves are not very useful in deciding what to do about quality if it appears to be deficient. To guide quality assurance interventions, such data must be linked to process-of-care information and even structural data. For this, a coherent clinical model of disease and an organizational model of care are required, so that physicians and managers can decide how care can be improved. This requires precise enough information about how clinical care and organizational factors affect outcome so that problems can be identified quickly and accurately.
>
> To be comprehensive, quality assessment should proceed from the notion of "eligible" populations. Unfortunately, virtually all studies of quality today proceed on the basis of "user" populations.
>
> Despite the cautions noted above, we should stress that quality can be measured, not perfectly, but certainly accurately enough to make people take notice. Furthermore, nearly all quality studies over the past two decades have found important clinical deficiencies.*

---

*Reprinted from *Journal of the American Medical Association*, Vol. 258, No. 21, pp. 3138–3141, with permission of American Medical Association, © December 4, 1987.

THE PHYSICIAN AS A MEMBER OF THE HOME CARE TEAM

Traditionally, the attending physician signs orders and medical treatment plans for services and products, with most referrals to home care providers originating from the hospital discharge planner or social worker. Few physicians recognize that they have control over this referral process, which will undoubtedly become of greater importance as liability issues become more visible in the future. Typically, the physician who establishes the medical home care plan is the same physician who has had a longstanding relationship with the patient and provided ongoing outpatient medical care as well as attended the patient in the hospital setting. It is the patient's personal physician, therefore, who understands the patient's medical condition better than anyone else. The importance of the physician for continuity of patient care cannot be overemphasized, and home care should be viewed as part of that continuity. The patient receiving medical home care services must be under the supervision of the physician, and the physician must certify the patient's need for the planned care. It is only the physician who can order medical care or modify a medical home care plan of treatment.

The provision of a variety of health care services to the patient at home constitutes a logical extension of the physician's therapeutic responsibilities. At the physician's request and medical direction, the personnel who provide these home care services operate as a team in assessing and developing the home care plan, as indicated below:[23]

- The *physician* outlines the specific program of care.
- Skilled nursing service is provided by a *professional nurse*, who carries out the specific program of care prescribed by the physician. The nurse serves as a link between the patient and the physician by providing information (usually through telephone contact or periodic written reports) on the patient's progress and changes in the patient's status.
- The *clinical specialist* is a nurse, usually master's degree prepared, with specialized training in rehabilitative care, stoma care, diabetes, geriatrics, pulmonary disease, dialysis, I.V. therapy, pediatrics, oncology, hospice care, or some other specialized area.
- A *homemaker-home health aide* is a trained individual who works under the supervision of a nurse or a physical, occupational, or speech therapist. The home health aide may help with bathing and transfers to and from bed and duties may include reminding about taking medications at the proper times, limited household tasks, and helping with prescribed exercises. The homemaker's duties may include household shopping, meal planning and preparation, child care, and light housekeeping.
- Services are provided by a registered *physical therapist*, who works with the patient to regain or improve movement through exercises and other approved methods, such as a home "back care" program.

- Services are provided by a registered *occupational therapist* who helps the patient to resume the routine of daily living by instructing the patient in self-care (dressing, bathing, etc.), in homemaking, and in living more fully with limitations. The occupational therapist will suggest ways of adapting the home environment to make living at home easier for the patient and family.

- A *speech/language therapist* helps to overcome problems in communication, including speech and hearing.

- The *medical social worker* helps sort out personal, family, employment, and other problems resulting from disability or illness. This professional can assist in reaching other needed community services.

- *Psychological counseling* services are provided to the patient and family in the home setting, where socioeconomic and other factors are more readily apparent and more effectively dealt with by the therapist.

- The *dietitian* assists with specialized dietary needs and meal planning.

- The *pharmacist* may assist with educating patients and their families about medication dosage, administration, and side effects; preventing medication interaction problems; promoting improved patient compliance; and monitoring medication and I.V. therapy.[24]

THE ROLE OF THE PHYSICIAN IN HOME CARE

The AMA has stated that leadership by physicians is essential for efficiently and successfully providing high-quality home health care medical services.[25] Depending on the needs of the patient, home health care may require that many persons and organizations combine their efforts and form a health care team under physician direction.[26]

First and foremost, physicians with intent to be involved with home care must be informed of the multidimensional aspects of health care delivery in the home setting.[26,27] This teaching process should begin during the medical undergraduate years and continue through residency; it should also become an ongoing part of the continuing medical education process.[28] Physicians in home care should follow these guidelines:

- Find out about the home care services available in the community (agencies, organizations, church and volunteer groups) and the various methods by which they can be developed or improved. Also find out about medical equipment that can be used in the home—from low-tech to high-tech.

- Be knowledgeable about functional, psychological, and environmental assessment; primary prevention; home health care coordination; team management, education, and leadership; family dynamics; cross-cultural issues; informed consent, medicolegal issues, and patient's

rights; hospice, death, and dying; and discharge planning.

- Take a leadership role in initiating innovative ways to coordinate delivery of and improve access to more efficient, economic, and appropriate medical care in the home setting.

- Become familiar with the various financing alternatives that can be used in paying for home care services and become a patient advocate at the policy-making level to prevent denial of patient access to needed services.

- Establish a plan of treatment for each patient and periodically review this plan and the patient's progress with the home health personnel providing the care. Special efforts or arrangements may be needed to maintain this communication when a patient is cared for at home, because of the separation in time and distance between different services and personnel. The physician may therefore wish to support the establishment of efficient, coordinated home care management programs that have provisions for maintaining communication.

- Inquire carefully into the qualifications and competence of those designing and implementing new technologies and patient medical care plans at home.

- Encourage medical educators to integrate instruction on the proper use of cost-saving home care services into undergraduate, postgraduate, and continuing medical education teaching programs.

- Seek new approaches to reimbursement for physician services in the home. Third party payers must recognize that time and thought are needed by the physician to develop, implement, and monitor good medical plans for home care patients.[29]

Assessing the Functional Limitations of Patients

The first task when evaluating the feasibility of home health care services is to determine the individual patient's functional status and level of dependence prior to the onset of illness.[30] Then one should make assessments regarding

- the patient's awareness of the nature and extent of the health problems

- indications of realistic patient goals in relation to the identified health problems

- the patient's self-perception of dependency or independency

- the patient's desire to continue to live at home

- the patient's mental status, ability to manage own affairs, and ability to follow verbal and written instructions

- the availability of friends and neighbors of the patient for frequent contact and socialization

- the realistic concept of patient's self needs

- the patient's ability to direct others in obtaining required assistance

The next step is to consider the diseases, illnesses, or injuries responsible for the apparent need for home health care services. This step involves the following:

- identification of the patient's health problems
- evaluation of and prognosis for these problems
- expectations for future improvement and eventual stability
- methods to prevent further loss of function
- identification of appropriate and available home health care programs and services that may help prevent further loss of function and improve and stabilize the patient's functional abilities at or near pre-illness levels
- identification of medications and purpose for taking, side effects, and dose schedule

The physician should briefly assess the patient's level of functional ability to independently do basic physical activities (communicating, seeing, hearing and speaking, using the telephone, bathing, shaving, brushing teeth, dressing, eating and feeding self, getting in or out of bed or chair, going up and down stairs or outside, bowel and bladder control, using the toilet, walking) as well as home management activities (doing chores, cleaning house, doing laundry, handling money, preparing meals, driving, handling public transportation or taxi service, shopping, using house keys).[31] The need for assistance with these activities increases dramatically with age and may warrant home health care intervention to maintain a noninstitutional living situation.[32]

Physician Responsibilities

- To receive regular reports, observations, and progress notes from the health personnel providing the services.
- To answer reasonable requests for patient information that is important for provision of care.
- To sign requests for orders promptly.
- To define parameters to be contacted in regards to changes in the patient's condition and physician's availability.
- To inform the home health agency of time preferences for communication with home care staff.
- To promptly convey any complaints to the home care agency management for expeditious and acceptable correction.
- To provide explicit home care orders.
- To specify the home care agency of choice.

HOME HEALTH CARE

Advantages

- Home health care may provide more efficient use of physician's time by expanding use of the team approach.
- It expands the physician's patient base through the use of coordinated home care programs, because the physician can order all ancillary care easily through one coordinator.
- It gives the physician a comprehensive perspective of the patient and family.
- It provides an educational opportunity for house staff physicians and medical students.
- It improves continuity of health care.
- It results in the early identification of day-to-day problems and a reduction in emergency situations.
- It results in earlier discharges from the hospital and other health care institutions.
- It reduces institutional readmissions.
- It results in more rapid recovery, improved emotional well-being, and greater freedom and personal dignity, for the patient can spend time with the family in comfortable and cheerful surroundings.
- Patients are not exposed to institutional-induced illness.
- Each patient's own food tastes can be met.
- Long-term and terminal illnesses may better be cared for at home.
- The family is part of the care team.
- Home health care improves progress in the activities of daily living, with less deterioration in indices of socioeconomic functioning.
- It provides the support and understanding of visiting home care personnel.
- It allows savings to the patient and third party payer (compared with institutional care).
- It reduces unnecessary capital construction costs for inpatient facilities.
- It provides educational benefits to patients and their families, for the home is a more effective site for patient learning and motivational activities directed toward achieving a relatively independent status.[33]

Disadvantages

- Home health care burdens physicians with heavy and often unreimbursed management responsibilities (e.g., time is spent meeting supervisory demands, doing paperwork, and making lengthy phone calls).
- It may be necessary for the physician to see the patient at home rather than in the office.
- It requires the deep involvement of family members and may disrupt family functioning at the same time that it permits the family to remain technically intact.
- The indirect costs may be high when the family members' or caregivers' time and out-of-pocket expenses are considered.
- There may be a lack of coordination and communication between physician, home health agency, family, and patient.

- Quality of care delivered in the home is not easily measured, monitored, or documented.
- Third party payers may not provide reimbursement for supplies and services that are covered when provided in an institutional setting.[34]

Barriers to Acceptance and Use

Any plan in developing home health services in any area should address itself to the elimination of these barriers:[35]

- lack of physician and consumer awareness of the availability and use of home health care services in the community
- skepticism, indifference, and lack of knowledge on the part of physicians and the public
- the therapeutic orientation of the American health care system as reflected in its emphasis on episodic and crisis care
- lack of universally accepted standards for the quality of home health care
- inadequate utilization review procedures to prevent overutilization and increasing costs
- strict and inconsistent interpretations of ever-changing Medicare guidelines by fiscal intermediaries and statutory restrictions on covered services
- bureaucratic red tape arising from the myriad requirements of local, state, and federal government agencies and programs
- limited funding for the provision of a comprehensive array of home health care services
- deficiencies in program planning, development, management, and coordination
- lack of a mechanism for easily assessing patients' needs and matching them with available services
- geographic barriers that restrict or prohibit access to patients' homes (e.g., in rural areas)
- an insufficient number of personnel trained to deal with the diverse needs of patients

SELECTING A HOME HEALTH CARE AGENCY

Physicians are finally becoming aware of the tremendous legislative, economic, technological, and social forces pushing home care forward. However, more than 6,000 home health care agencies throughout the United States provide variable services of variable quality and with geographic disproportion. It is imperative that physicians take control in the home care selection process, for a physician may be at least partially liable if substandard home care services are provided under his or her direction and medical plan of care. Finding the best home care agency requires some research by the physician, but it is time well spent. Quality of care and caliber of

personnel should be overriding factors in the decision process.[36]

Questions to Consider During the Selection Process

- What is the reputation of the agency and how long has it been serving the community?
- Is the agency accredited and certified by Medicare to provide services? By the Joint Commission on Healthcare Organizations?
- Does the agency provide quality care 24 hours a day, 7 days a week? Does it respond to emergency situations at any time (evenings, weekends, holidays)?
- Does the agency offer services regardless of the patient's ability to pay and within the limits of agency funds (sliding fee payment schedule)? Will the agency continue service if Medicare or other reimbursement sources are exhausted?
- Does the agency focus on family-centered care, training the patient and family to independence whenever possible to prevent agency overutilization?
- Does an agency nurse or social worker conduct an evaluation of the patient's needs with the patient and family members in the home and in consultation with the physician to develop a treatment plan of coordinated services? Does the agency evaluator present the recommended plan and services to the physician for his review and approval prior to a final recommendation of plan and services to the patient and family?
- Does the agency provide quality professional backup staff when regular nurses or aides are ill or unavailable?
- Does the agency provide mandatory ongoing educational programs for staff?
- Does the agency have a commitment to providing access to health care, serving those in need, working with the community being served, meeting professional standards of service, providing health education and cost-effective service, and promoting an active home health care research program?

THE ROLE OF AN AGENCY MEDICAL DIRECTOR

The role of the medical director of a home health care agency may vary greatly. However, duties of the medical director often include

- being responsible for planning, coordination, and implementation of agency medical-related programs
- serving as a liaison between professional services staff and referring physicians and as a consultant to agency management and staff

- being responsible for representing the home care agency in its relationships with other agencies, institutions, the medical profession, and the public (as required)
- coordinating voluntary physician input relating to medical policies and protocols
- coordinating and participating in utilization review, quality assurance, and research programs
- serving as a consultant to home care agency administration in the development and evaluation of agency health service programs
- serving upon request as liaison between professional services staff and the patient's personal physician(s)
- representing the agency in its relationships with medical institutions in the coordination and supervision of medical student, resident, and fellowship training programs
- working with the agency educational department in developing and conducting staff educational programs
- informing the medical community of the agency's services and programs
- representing the agency before government and intermediary agencies, as appropriate, in matters pertaining to claim interpretation, regulations, and legislation

THE ROLE OF COUNTY AND STATE MEDICAL SOCIETIES

Dr. Charles Weller, former chairman of the Committee on Home Health Care of the State Medical Society of New York, has stated that "the state and county medical societies have a proper concern with the availability and adequacy of home health care services for the individuals served in its service area. These medical societies, therefore, should stimulate physician interest in, and acceptance of, home health care as an integral part of the overall continuum of care. Along with this, these societies should provide community leadership in both improving the coordination of existing home care services and stimulating the development of new services where they are needed."[37] The adequacy of community home health care services will depend not only on the actions of state and local medical societies, but also on the sound, cooperative planning efforts of many public and private health and service agencies in the community.[38] These medical societies should

- provide technical advice and assistance in developing and operating coordinated home health care programs
- encourage the public to demand insurance coverage for any needed home care service
- stimulate the development and use of home health care programs in the community—in whatever settings are considered most appropriate
- emphasize the need for medical schools and medical postgraduate training programs to educate medical students, residents, and fellows in the value and proper use of home health care programs

- emphasize in all deliberations concerning home care that effective home health care programs can offer high-quality medical care and can be an extension of physicians' services
- seek methods of reimbursing physicians for managing home health care
- stress a case management system for coordinating home health care with a central information and follow-up center
- urge the medical staffs of hospitals to form home health care committees for the coordination of discharge planning with the continuum of care
- support the concept that all home health care agencies, voluntary and proprietary, should be subject to the same controls, regulations, and standards

THE COSTS OF HOME CARE AND PAYMENT FOR PHYSICIAN SERVICES

The Health and Public Policy Committee of the American College of Physicians has developed an "issues paper" addressing the difficult topic of financing long-term care. The paper states, "Although most home health care is provided by relatives without payment, paid home care in 1982 averaged about $164 per month. At the same time, the cost of home care for elderly persons having five or six limitations in the activities of daily living was about $439 per month. Current Medicare national average home care costs are about $43 per day. Recent estimates of total annual home health care expenditures range from $4 billion to $8 billion. Forecasters have predicted that by 1990, total home care costs will be $13.8 billion and could rise to almost $25 billion by 1995."[39]

On the other side of the coin, some physicians, previously frustrated by having to complete lengthy care plans and make phone calls while referring patients to others who made all the profits, have become financially involved with home care as a potential source of investment income. This has been most successful in the lucrative for-profit, high-technology home care I.V. infusion industry, where physician ownership is not federally restricted as long as profits are not directly linked to referrals. The Health Care Financing Administration limits physician ownership of Medicare-certified home care agencies to a maximum of 5 percent of equity or profits and individual physician earnings to a maximum of $25,000 per year.[40] Other physicians have entered into joint ventures and limited partnerships. Many physicians, however, remain highly skeptical of these arrangements, fearing that payment for clinical management efforts may be interpreted as a "kickback" for patient referrals. The ethics manual of the American College of Physicians states, "The physician must avoid any personal commercial conflict of interest that might compromise his loyalty and treatment of the patient."[41]

In any event, if physicians are to fulfill their role in assuring access to necessary high-quality, cost-effective medical care for their patients in the home setting, it is imperative that physicians are adequately paid for both their cognitive and their technical efforts.

It is important for all home health care providers to define organizational purposes and character, identify strengths and weaknesses, and develop practices that generate interest and ingenuity among all employees. The goals that must be pursued include innovation, access, quality, and equity at an affordable cost.[42] A preoccupation with the bottom line, productivity, and efficiency at the expense of humane care and high professional standards, however, will put any home care provider at a competitive disadvantage.

THE REWARDS OF HOME CARE

- Home care is an important service for patients of all ages, ranging from the frail elderly to younger homebound patients.
- Home care permits the physician to assess the important "nonmedical" factors that are pertinent in the care of a homebound patient. These factors include the social support structure (formal and informal caregivers), the environmental status (hazards to safety), and the functional status of the patient (self-care).
- Physician-patient relationships may improve through enhanced communication skills and humanism displayed through home care.
- Home care reminds physicians that they are advisors and educators. Patients should be encouraged to achieve independence and maintain self-responsibility.
- Seeing patients at home can be an immensely rewarding experience for the physician. Usually the patient is very grateful, and there develops deep personal relationships between the patient, the family, and the physician.
- Many physicians have found that home care offers the potential for better control over patient care and referrals in a very competitive and restrictive health care environment.
- Home care helps the physician to be more understanding and more effective in dealing with nonphysician professionals providing home services.[43]

WHAT THE FUTURE HOLDS

As the anticipated movement of sophisticated medical services from institutions to homes continues to accelerate, physicians must be educated about the potentially unlimited spectrum of home care products and services that will become increasingly available to the patients they serve. Second, much research needs to be completed in order to critically examine the safety, quality, and cost of home care as compared to institutional care and provide the necessary data to assure that home care services will not be under- or overutilized and will meet the necessary acute and long-term health care needs of patients. Third, physicians must take a leadership role in carefully examining the pitfalls of the current expensive and often fragmented acute care–oriented health care model, for it has not effectively addressed the increasing costs and incidence of chronic disease in our society. With computerization, networking, and the explosive mobilization of high-technology health care products and services, we are witnessing an exponential growth in the list of medical therapies now available in the home setting, therapies that only a few years ago one would never dream of utilizing outside the hospital. There has never before been a time when physicians have needed to be as innovative in developing accessible and cost-effective alternative health care delivery systems as now. I believe that the remolding of home care, using physician vision, direction, and review, will be a major step toward providing the highest-quality medical care for patients at home.[44]

NOTES

1. W.W. Benjamin, "Healing by the Fundamentals," *New England Journal of Medicine* 311 (August 30, 1984): 595–97; N. Cousins, "How Patients Appraise Physicians," *New England Journal of Medicine* 313 (November 28, 1985): 1422–24; I. Rossman, "The Geriatrician and the Homebound Patient," *Journal of the American Geriatric Society* 36 (1988): 348–354.

2. R.H. Brook and K.N. Lohr, "Monitoring Quality of Care in the Medicare Program," *JAMA* 258 (December 4, 1987): 3138–41.

3. R.B. Greifinger and V.W Sidel, "American Medicine: Charity Begins at Home," in *The Nation's Health*, ed. P.R. Lee, N. Brown, and I. Red (San Francisco: Boyd & Fraser, 1984), 176–186.

4. G.B. Schwartz, "Physicians Support Home Health Care," *Hospitals*, February 16, 1980, pp. 52, 56, 65; A.D. Spiegel, *Home Health Care* (Owings Mills, Md.: National Health Publishing, 1983); N.J. Vetter, D.A. Jones, and C.R. Victor, "A Health Visitor Affects the Problems Others Do Not Reach," *Lancet* ii (July 5, 1986): 30–32.

5. Spiegel, *Home Health Care.*

6. H.G. DeYoung, "Healthcare Looks beyond the Hospital," *High Technology*, September 1985, pp. 46–51; A.I. Goldberg, "Home Care for Life-supported Persons," *Chest* 90 (November 1986): 744–48.

7. L.H. Bernstein, A.J. Grieco, and M. Dete, *Primary Care in the Home* (St. Louis: Lippincott, 1987); DeYoung, "Healthcare Looks beyond the Hospital"; P.E. Hankwitz, "Helping Physicians Feel Right at Home," *Internist*, January 1988, pp. 13–15, 23; A.C. Kind et al., "Intravenous Antibiotic Therapy at Home," *Archives of Internal Medicine* 139 (1979): 413–15; D.M. Poretz et al., "Intravenous Antibiotic Therapy in an Outpatient Setting," *JAMA* 248 (1982): 336–39; S.J. Rehm and A.J. Weinstein, "Home Intravenous Antibiotic Therapy: A Team Approach," *Annals of Internal Medicine* 99 (1983): 388–92; H.G. Stiver et al., "Self-Administration of Intravenous Antibiotics: An Efficient, Cost-effective Home Care Program," *Canadian Medical Association Journal* 127 (August 1983): 207–11; D. Corby, R.F. Schad, and J.P. Fudge, "Intravenous Antibiotic Therapy: Hospital to Home," *Nursing Management* 17, no. 8 (August 1986): 52–61; J.D. McCue, "Outpatient IV Antibiotic Therapy: Practical and Ethical Considerations," *Hospital Practice* (March 15, 1988): 208–211; D.M. Poretz, L.J. Eron, R.I. Goldenberg, A.F. Gilbert, J. Rising, S. Sparks, and C.E. Horn, "Intravenous Antibiotic Therapy in an Outpatient Setting," *JAMA* 248, no. 3 (July 16, 1982): 336–339; S.J. Rehn and A.J. Weinstein, "Home Intravenous Antibiotic Therapy: A Team Approach," *Annals of Internal Medicine* 99 (1983): 388–392.

8. Goldberg, "Home Care for Life-Supported Persons."

9. L.D. Eggert et al., "Home Phototherapy Treatment of Neonatal Jaundice," *Pediatrics* 76 (October 1985): 579–84.

10. J. Portnow and M. Houtmann, *Home Care for the Elderly* (St. Louis: McGraw-Hill, 1987).

11. Bernstein, Grieco, and Dete, *Primary Care in the Home*; Portnow and Houtmann, *Home Care for the Elderly*.

12. Hankwitz, "Helping Physicians Feel Right at Home"; M.J. Koren, "Home Care—Who Cares?" *New England Journal of Medicine* 314 (April 3, 1986): 917–20.

13. Portnow and Houtmann, *Home Care for the Elderly*.

14. K. Crossley and K. Henry, "AIDS: Implications for Long-Term Care," *Clinical Report on Aging* 1, no. 4 (1987): 1, 3, 5–6.

15. Schwartz, "Physicians Support Home Health Care."

16. American Medical Association, *Physician Guide to Home Health Care* (Chicago: R.T. Kelly, 1979).

17. K.H. Chavigny, *Home Health Report* (Chicago: American Medical Association, 1987).

18. Ibid.

19. B. Frame et al., "Home Health Care," *Annals of Internal Medicine* 105 (1986): 454–60.

20. Ibid.

21. G.E. Steffan, "Quality Medical Care: A Definition," *JAMA* 260, no. 1 (1988): 59.

22. American Medical Association, *Physician Guide to Home Health Care*.

23. K.S. Edwards, "What Do I Do with My Patient?" *Ohio State Medical Journal* 80 (March 1984): 188–91; J. Emmons, "Home Health Care: Where Does the Physician Fit in?" editorial, *Texas Medicine* 80 (August 1984): 5–6; Spiegel, *Home Health Care*.

24. P.E. Hankwitz, "MD's Focus on Home Care," *American Druggist*, June 1987, p. 64.

25. American Medical Association, *Physician Guide to Home Health Care*; Chavigny, *Home Health Care Report*.

26. Spiegel, *Home Health Care*.

27. P.W. Brickner et al., "The Homebound Aged: A Medically Unreached Group," *Annals of Internal Medicine* 82 (1975): 1–6; Edwards, "What Do I Do with My Patient?"; C.Eisdorfer, "Care of the Aged: The Barriers of Tradition," *Annals of Internal Medicine* 94 (1981): 256–60; Emmons, "Home Health Care"; Hankwitz, "Helping Physicians Feel Right at Home"; Koren, "Home Care—Who Cares?"

28. Chavigny, *Home Health Care Report*; Hankwitz, "Helping Physicians Feel Right at Home"; A. Sankar and S.L. Becker, "The Home as a Site for Teaching Gerontology and Chronic Illness," *Journal of Medicine Education* 60 (1985): 308–13.

29. Chavigny, *Home Health Care Report*; N. Shrifter, "The Role of the Physician in Home Care," *Home Health Review* 4 (December 1981): 11–14; Spiegel, *Home Health Care*.

30. R.W. Besdine, "The Educational Utility of Comprehensive Functional Assessment in the Elderly," *Journal of the American Geriatric Society* 31 (1983): 651–56; R.H. Fortinsky, C.V. Granger, and G.B. Seltzer, "The Use of the Functional Assessment in Understanding Home Care Needs," *Medical Care* 19 (1981): 489–97; J.A. Friedman, "Getting Well at Home: Health Services, Support and Consumer Tips," *Ms.*, May 1986, pp. 95–101; National Center for Health Statistics, "Americans Needing Help to Function at Home," in *Advance Data from Vital and Health Statistics*, No. 92 DHHS Pub. no. (PHS) 83-1250 (Hyattsville, Md.: Public Health Service, September 1983); T.P. Almy, "Comprehensive Functional Assessment for Elderly Patients," (Position Paper of the Health and Public Policy Committee, American College of Physicians), *Annals of Internal Medicine* (July 1, 1988): 70–72; E.G. Tangalos and P.I. Freeman, "Assessment of Geriatric Patients—Spreading the Word," (Editorial), *Mayo Clinic Proc* 63 (1988): 305–307.

31. Besdine, "Comprehensive Functional Assessment"; Brickner et al., "Homebound Aged."

32. J. Williamson et al., "Old People at Home: Their Unreported Needs," *Lancet* i (1964): 1117–20.

33. American Medical Association, *Statement on Home Health Care* (Chicago: Author, 1973); Schwartz, "Physicians Support Home Health Care"; Spiegel, *Home Health Care*.

34. L.H. Bernstein et al., "Are You Ready for the New Home Care? Home Care: Avoiding Institutionalization," *Patient Care* 19 (November 15, 1985): 20–67; Spiegel, *Home Health Care*.

35. S.J. Alger, "Physician Home Health Programs Examined," *Group Practice Journal*, July-August 1987, pp. 54–58; P.R. Alper, "Count Me Out of the Home-Care Boom," *Medical Economics*, April 15, 1985, pp. 89, 91–93; A.M. Clarfield, "Home Care: Is It Cost-effective?" *Canadian Medical Association Journal* 82 (1983): 1–6; Hankwitz, "Helping Physicians Feel Right at Home"; T.L. Louden, "Who Controls Home Care Referrals?" *Caring*, October 1985, pp. 17–19.

36. American Medical Association, *Physician Guide to Home Health Care*; Friedman, "Getting Well at Home"; Louden, "Who Controls Home Care Referrals?"; D.T. Nash, "Making Use of Home Care Services," *Geriatrics* 29 (1974): 140–43; C. Weller, "Home Health Care," *New York State Journal of Medicine* 78 (October 1978): 1957–61.

37. Weller, "Home Health Care."

38. American Medical Association, *Physician Guide to Home Health Care*.

39. J.A. Ginzberg et al., "Financing Long-term Care," *Annals of Internal Medicine* 108 (1988): 279–288.

40. K.P. O'Donnell, "Why Your Group Should Enter the Home Care Market," *Group Practice Journal*, July-August 1987, pp. 47–51.

41. American College of Physicians, "Ethics Manual," Reprinted from *Annals of Internal Medicine* 101, 1984, pp. 129–37; 263–74.

42. Clarfield, "Home Care"; T.J. Peters and R.H. Waterman, Jr., *In Search of Excellence* (New York: Harper & Row, 1982), 159; N. Shifter, "The Physician and Home Health Care—Costs Are Less and Patients Feel Better," *LACMA Physician* 110 (October 6, 1980): 23–26.

43. Brickner et al., "Homebound Aged"; J. Burton, "The House Call: An Important Service for the Frail Elderly," *Journal of the American Geriatric Society* 33 (1985): 291–93; Koren, "Home Care—Who Cares?"; O'Donnell, "Home Care Market"; A.J. Samuels, "Physicians Will Enter Home Care Practice," *Home Health Journal*, July 1985, p. 11; Sankar and Becker, "Home as a Site for Teaching"; Vetter, Jones, and Victor, "Health Visitor"; J. Williamson, "Old People at Home."

44. Bernstein, Grieco, and Dete, *Primary Care in the Home*; Hankwitz, "Helping Physicians Feel Right at Home."

BIBLIOGRAPHY

Alger, S.J. "Physician Home Health Programs Examined." *Group Practice Journal*, July-August 1987, pp. 54–58.

Allgaier, A. "Home Care Needs Physicians Who Care." *Hospital Medical Staff* 9, no. 5 (1980): 2–11.

Alper, P.R. "Count Me out of the Home-Care Boom." *Medical Economics*, April 15, 1985, pp. 89, 91–93.

American College of Physicians, Health and Public Policy Committee. "Long-term Care of the Elderly." *Annals of Internal Medicine* 100 (1984): 760–63.

American Medical Association. *Statement on Home Health Care*. Chicago: Author, 1973.

———. *Physician Guide to Home Health Care*. Chicago: Author, 1981.

Benjamin, A.E. "Determinants of State Variations in Home Health Utilization and Expenditures under Medicare." *Medical Care* 24 (June 1986): 535–47.

Benjamin, W.W. "Healing by the Fundamentals." *New England Journal of Medicine* 311 (1984): 595–97.

Bernstein, L.H., A.J. Grieco, and M. Dete. *Primary Care in the Home*. St. Louis: Lippincott, 1987.

Besdine, R.W. "The Educational Utility of Comprehensive Functional Assessment in the Elderly." *Journal of the American Geriatric Society* 31 (1983): 651–56.

Blumenthal, D., M. Schlesinger, P.B. Drumheller, et al. "The Future of Medicare." *New England Journal of Medicine* 314 (1986): 722–28.

Borders, C.R. "Are You Ready for the New Home Care? Home Care: Avoiding Institutionalization." *Patient Care* 19 (November 15, 1985): 20–67.

Brickner, P.W., T. Duque, A. Kaufman, M. Sarg, J.A. Jahre, S. Maturlo, and J.F. Janeski. "The Homebound Aged: A Medically Unreached Group." *Annals of Internal Medicine* 82 (1975): 1–6.

Brook, R.H., and K.N. Lohr. "Monitoring Quality of Care in the Medicare Program." *JAMA* 258 (1987): 3138–41.

Burton, J. "The House Call: An Important Service for the Frail Elderly." *Journal of the American Geriatric Society* 33 (1985): 291–93.

Chavigny, K.H. *Home Health Care Report*. Chicago: American Medical Association, 1987.

Clarfield, A.M. "Home Care: Is It Cost-effective?" *Canadian Medical Association Journal* 82 (1983): 1–6.

Coe, R.M., and R.F. Rustige. "Physicians' Perspective on Home Health Services." *Home Health Review* 2 (June 1979): 3–8.

Cousins, N. "How Patients Appraise Physicians." *New England Journal of Medicine* 313 (1985): 1422–24.

Crossley, K., and K. Henry. "AIDS: Implications for Long-term Care." *Clinical Report on Aging* 1, no. 4 (1987): 1, 3, 5–6.

DeYoung, H.G. "Healthcare Looks beyond the Hospital." *High Technology*, September 1985, pp. 46–51.

Donovan, R.J., Jr. "Prescribe Home Care? Now I Can." *Medical Economics* 54 (September 5, 1977): 145–50.

Edwards, K.S. "What Do I Do with My Patient?" *Ohio State Medical Journal* 80 (March 1984): 188–91.

Eggert, L.D., R.A. Pollary, D.S. Folland, and A.L. Jung. "Home Phototherapy Treatment of Neonatal Jaundice." *Pediatrics* 76 (October 1985): 579–84.

Eisdorfer, C. "Care of the Aged: The Barriers of Tradition." *Annals of Internal Medicine* 94 (1981): 256–60.

Emmons, J. "Home Health Care: Where Does the Physician Fit in?" Editorial. *Texas Medicine* 80 (August 1984): 5–6.

Fortinsky, R.H., C.V. Granger, and G.B. Seltzer. "The Use of the Functional Assessment in Understanding Home Care Needs." *Medical Care* 19 (1981): 489–97.

Frame, B., and J.A. Ginsburg. "Home Health Care." *Annals of Internal Medicine* 105 (1986): 454–60.

Freudenheim, M. "G.M. and Ford Pacts Provide Custodial Care." *New York Times*, November 2, 1987.

Friedman, J.A. "Getting Well at Home: Health Services, Support and Consumer Tips." *Ms.*, May 1986, pp. 95–101.

GAO/HRD-85-110, September 30, 1985.

Gaumer, G.L., H. Birnbaum, F. Pratter, S. Franklin, and K. Ellingson-Otto. "Impact of the New York Long-term Home Health Care Program." *Medical Care* 24 (July 1986): 641–53.

Ginzberg, E. "The Monetarization of Medical Care." *New England Journal of Medicine* 310, no. 18 (1984): 1162–65.

Ginsburg, J.A. 'Financing Long-term Care." *Annals of Internal Medicine* 108 (1988): 279–288.

Glazier, W.H. "The Task of Medicine." *Scientific American* 228, no. 4 (April, 1973): 13.

Goldberg, A.I. "Home Care for Life-supported Persons." *Chest* 90 (November 1986): 744–48.

Gray, J.A. "The Family Doctor's Role in the Care of the Elderly." *Practitioner* 228 (December 1984): 1149–51.

Greifinger, R.B., and V.W. Sidel. "American Medicine: Charity Begins at Home." In *The Nation's Health*, edited by P.R. Lee, N. Brown, and I. Red. San Francisco: Boyd & Fraser, 1984:176–186.

Grizzard, M.B. "Home Intravenous Antibiotic Therapy." *Postgraduate Medicine* 78 (November 1, 1985): 187–95.

Ham, R. "Alternatives to Institutionalization." *American Family Physician* 95, no. 1 (1980): 95–100.

Hankwitz, P.E. "A Welcome to Our Readers." *The Journal for Physicians in Home Care* 1, no. 1 (1987): 6–7.

———. "MD's Focus on Home Care." *American Druggist*, June 1987, p. 64.

———. "Helping Physicians Feel Right at Home." *The Internist*, January 1988, pp. 13–5, 23.

Hughes, S.L. "Home Health Monitoring: Ensuring Quality in Home Care Services." *Hospitals*, November 1, 1982, pp. 74–80.

Jonas, S., and K.W. Dueschele. *Health Care Delivery in the United States*. New York: Springer, 1981.

Kind, A.C., D.N. Williams, G. Persons, and J.A. Gibson, "Intravenous Antibiotic Therapy at Home." *Archives of Internal Medicine* 139 (1979): 413–15.

Koren, M.J. "Home Care—Who Cares?" *New England Journal of Medicine* 314 (1986): 917–20.

Lombardi, T., Jr. "Nursing Home without Walls: Long-term Care at Home." Report of the *New York State Senate Health Committee*, September 1986.

Louden, T.L. "Who Controls Home Care Referrals?" *Caring*, October 1985, pp. 17–19.

———. "Home Care: Six Secrets to Success." *Healthcare Executive*, May-June 1986, pp. 45–48.

Naisbitt, J. *Megatrends*. New York: Warner Books, 1984.

Nash, D.T. "Making Use of Home Care Services." *Geriatrics* (September 1974): 140–43.

Nassif, J.Z. *The Home Health Care Solution*. New York: Harper & Row, 1986.

National Center for Health Statistics. "Americans Needing Help to Function at Home." *Advance Data from Vital and Health Statistics*. No. 92 DHHS Pub. no. (PHS) 83-1250. Hyattsville, Md.: Public Health Service, September 1983.

O'Donnell, K.P. "Why Your Group Should Enter the Home Care Market." *Group Practice Journal*, July-August 1987, pp. 47–51.

O'Donohue, W.J., R.M. Giovannoni, A.I. Goldberg, T.G. Keens, B.J. Make, A.L. Plummer, and W.S. Prentice. "Long-term Mechanical Ventilation: Guidelines for Management in the Home and at Alternate Community Sites." *Chest* 90 (July 1986): 1S–37S.

Peters, T.J., and R.H. Waterman, Jr. *In Search of Excellence*. New York: Harper & Row, 1982.

Poretz, D.M., L.J. Eron, R.I. Goldenberg, et al. "Intravenous Antibiotic Therapy in an Outpatient Setting." *JAMA* 248 (1982): 336–39.

Portnow, J., and M. Houtmann. *Home Care for the Elderly*. St. Louis: McGraw-Hill, 1987.

Rehm, S.J., and A.J. Weinstein. "Home Intravenous Antibiotic Therapy: A Team Approach." *Annals of Internal Medicine* 99 (1983): 388–92.

Rowe, J.W. "Health Care of the Elderly." *The New England Journal of Medicine* 312 (1985): 827–35.

Samuels, A.J. "Physicians Will Enter Homecare Practice." *Home Health Journal*, July 1985, p. 11.

Sankar, A., and S.L. Becker, "The Home as a Site for Teaching Gerontology and Chronic Illness. *Journal of Medical Education* 60 (April 1985): 308–13.

Schwartz, G.B. "Physicians Support Home Health Care." *Hospitals*, February 16, 1980, pp. 52, 56, 65.

Shrifter, N. "The Physician and Home Health Care—Costs Are Less and the Patients Feel Better." *LACMA Physician* 110 (October 6, 1980): 23–26.

———. "The Role of the Physician in Home Care." *Home Health Review* 4 (December 1981): 11–14.

Spiegel, A.D. *Home Health Care*. Owings Mills, Md.: National Health Publishing, 1983.

Stein, R.E.K. "Providing Home Care for the Seriously Ill Young." *Business & Health*, January 1987, pp. 26–30.

Stiver, H.G., S.K. Trosky, D.D. Code, et al. "Self-Administration of Intravenous Antibiotics: An Efficient, Cost-Effective Home Care Program." *Canadian Medical Association Journal* 127 (August 1983): 207–11.

Trager, B. "Home Care: Providing the Right to Stay Home." *Hospitals* 49, p. 93.

Vetter, N.J., D.A. Jones, and C.R. Victor. "A Health Visitor Affects the Problems Others Do Not Reach." *Lancet* ii (July 5, 1986): 30–32.

Weller, C. "Home Health Care." *New York State Journal of Medicine* 78 (October 1978): 1957–61.

Williamson, J., I.H. Stokoe, S. Gray, M. Fisher, A. Smith, A. McGhee, and E. Stephenson. "Old People at Home: Their Unreported Needs." *Lancet* i (1964): 1117–20.

Chapter 11

The Social Worker's Perspective

William E. Powell

The linkage of the profession of social work with health care has spanned more than 80 years. Social work is concerned with the treatment of the whole person within the context of family and social environment. Quality assurance in the home care setting is conceptualized within this framework. Social work practitioners in the home function as part of a team of health care providers who are autonomous professionals yet dependent on each other for contributing a distinct part to the whole service package.

From a social work perspective, the provision of quality home health care may be assured by the examination of its delivery, its documentation, and the actions of the caregivers. This examination of home health care from a social work perspective will follow a general outline that includes factors subsumed into the categories of structure, process, and outcome. *Structure* refers to such factors as organizational makeup, policies, and procedures and personnel matters. *Process* refers to the delivery of the care and the interaction and coordination of the caregivers' efforts. *Outcome* refers to the effectiveness of the care that is given.

A *process concern* is one that involves the coherent delivery of home health care services. Process concerns include the nature of interdisciplinary care, teamwork, and the orchestration of the services and interventions of members of the different disciplines involved in home health care. More specific concerns include the interactions of members of various disciplines, issues of occupational boundaries and authority, and professional rivalries.

The profession of social worker has to deal with its relationship with clients, the tasks and functions that fall under its purview, and the situations in the lives of clients that either alter the benefits of health care provided or contribute to the presenting problem. The social work perspective on quality assurance includes the principle that optimal home health care cannot be delivered without some minimal knowledge of the client as a social being. Aged clients must be treated with understanding rather than mythologized and the particular patterns of health care usage among minority groups must be recognized if minority clients are to receive and benefit from home health care. Such factors influence the delivery and outcome of care.

THE PROFESSIONAL COMPETENCE OF CAREGIVERS

One structural principle of quality assurance is the assumption that all caregivers should be well trained and well educated in the field of health care and should have a commitment to maintaining their skills and expertise. They should not only understand the technical aspects of their particular field of endeavor but the nature of their clients and their social situations as well. The sites where home health care is ministered is not a controlled setting, nor is it one in which the caregiver is likely to be the major actor. Understanding one's strengths and limitations and how to use oneself and others appropriately will be invaluable in ensuring quality care.

A social worker involved in home health care should have, minimally, a masters degree (M.S.W.) and special knowledge of health care and health care systems. The social worker should be expected to learn the implications of various illnesses, both chronic and acute, for the lives of clients and their families.

Social workers are also expected to have a well-grounded knowledge of the dominant value systems of this country and of the profession and be aware of the potential for value conflicts that may impair work with clients. They should be aware of cultural characteristics that may influence the clients' responsiveness to home care or affect the clients' relationships with physicians, other helping professionals, and institutionalized health care services. These beliefs, values, and cultural characteristics may be of immense importance in clients' response to caregivers' efforts, their cooperation with the plan of care, and the efforts to prevent further problems.

Quality assurance begins with the hiring of properly trained and competent social workers. Attention paid at this point will markedly simplify later efforts to ascertain if certain procedures, contacts and interventions were done competently and comprehensively. Far too often short-sighted agencies hire minimally trained social workers or social work designees at low wages and find that enormous effort has to be expended to ensure that their efforts and their work is adequate. Such an approach is penny-wise and pound-foolish. Quality is better assured if competency is the point of departure.

DETERMINING AND DOCUMENTING THE NEED FOR SOCIAL WORK SERVICES

In the majority of home health agencies, social workers are limited in their ability to provide services due to limitations in third party reimbursement. The insurance plans that cover many persons receiving home care restrict the coverage for social services or provide for none at all. Health maintenance organizations have seemingly elected to follow the example of many insurers and restrict social services in order to limit their expenditures. Much of the utilization of social services in home health care is due to Medicare reimbursement for such services. Even for clients covered by Medicare, there is no carte blanche approval for social work services. For reimbursement purposes, it is necessary to have a physician's documentation that there are social problems which are or will be an impediment to the patient's treatment or recovery. This restriction, which shows the dominance of medicine over other health care professions, is an obstacle that must be addressed if social services are to be provided. Assuming that physicians can be convinced of the need for social work services, there must be proper documentation of goals, interventions, plans of care, and the course of treatment.

Quality assurance requires that social workers involved in home care have a demonstrated comprehension of Medicare and other insurance regulations regarding home health care, particularly their own services. They should have a demonstrated ability to define social or emotional problems and needs, relate them to clients' medical plans of care, plan their work with and for clients so that these needs are addressed, and articulate their interventions and their results. Simply put, social workers should have the ability to define their goals and efforts, the rationale for them, and the results of their efforts. They must communicate this clearly if they are to continue to

be reimbursed for their services. In the absence of clear and appropriate communication, there is likely to be a lack of reimbursement for services provided as well as a lack of recognition for the part that social work plays in health care.

APPROPRIATE SOCIAL WORK REFERRALS

In home health care it is rare that social workers generate clients for their agencies (though their peers in medical settings may do so). To make appropriate use of social workers, it is necessary that the variety of services that they can offer be conceptualized, and that the other disciplines refer appropriately (Exhibit 11-1). Measurement of quality could be determined by auditing the appropriateness of referrals based on the following topical areas for which social work services may be provided. It should be noted that referrals are subject to the "sins" of omission and commission. However, while the appropriateness of referrals can be examined, it is more difficult to determine the appropriateness of potential referrals that were not made. This is because social and emotional factors might not have been detected or noted in documentation. Structurally, quality is better assured if the agency has a well-formulated policy that dictates what information should be gathered and, based on this information, when a social work referral should be made and how quickly it should be acted upon. The carrying out of these referrals can be a process concern.

Problems

Mental Competency

If problems are suspected and clients need referrals and testing to either confirm or deny the existence of problems in this area, the social worker should be notified. If the findings are positive and indicate the likelihood of a problem that will hinder the client's medical treatment, then the social worker should work to insure treatment, protective placement, legal guardianship (when necessary), and so forth. An increasingly common problem is the existence of dementias such as Alzheimer's disease.

Nursing Home Placements

When the client's care requirements are such that a nursing home placement is indicated, then the social worker should initiate referrals to such facilities. This can include working with the family in making such a placement, planning financial arrangements, and completing the necessary paperwork. It may also be necessary to establish a guardianship and to advocate in various ways for the rights of the client.

Abused or Neglected Patients and Others

Social workers should immediately intervene in instances where the client's well-being is endangered by physical or emotional abuse from others or when the client is neglected and basic needs are not being met. Laws among the states

Exhibit 11-1 Social Work Referral Form

Problems*	Referred by: (_____)	Date: (_____)	SW: (_____)
Name: _____ Married ___ Single ___ Widowed ___ Separated ___			
Case Number: _____ Age ___ Primary Caregiver _____			
Date File Opened: _____ Financial Status: SS ___ SSI ___ VA ___ Other _____			
1. Mental competency	( )	( )	( )
2. Nursing home placement	( )	( )	( )
3. Abuse/neglect (possible)	( )	( )	( )
4. Terminal illness	( )	( )	( )
5. Caretaker concerns	( )	( )	( )
6. Unsafe environment/housing	( )	( )	( )
7. Eligibility: services/benefits	( )	( )	( )
8. Emotional/psychological status	( )	( )	( )
9. Alcohol/substance use	( )	( )	( )
10. Housing/living arrangements	( )	( )	( )
11. Adjustment to illness	( )	( )	( )
12. Crisis intervention	( )	( )	( )
13. Family relationships	( )	( )	( )
14. Future needs planning	( )	( )	( )
15. Socialization needs	( )	( )	( )
Other Problem(s): _____	( )	( )	( )

*(These represent *possible* problems as perceived by the person initiating the referral. That person should note the date of the referral and initial it; the written progress notes should detail the problem. This record is to remain in the client's chart; when this form is used, a corresponding memo to the social worker informing them of the referral is to be made. The social worker will acknowledge the referral by initialing this form and dating it as well. Additional problems should also be noted as they occur.)

vary, but immediate attention must be paid to an abusive situation to ensure the client's future health and safety. If the client is a minor or if abuse of any minor family member is detected or suspected, the social worker or other professional must immediately notify the appropriate authorities.

Terminal Illness

A terminally ill client must have various types of interventions from each of the disciplines involved. The social worker must support the other caregivers—be they other professionals or the family of the client. The social worker should engage the client in counseling that will help them deal with both the illness and the prognosis. Working with the family is strongly indicated as well.

Caretakers' Concerns

Social workers should become involved when concerns are expressed about the security or adequacy of the future care arrangements for the dependent client. Such concerns can originate with family members, friends, or caregiving personnel such as nurses and homemakers. The worker should help arrange for the future care of the client so as to ensure the client's ongoing well-being and safety.

Unsafe Environments and Inadequate Housing

Many recipients of home health care services live in housing that is hazardous, unconducive to independent living, or so problematic as to confound efforts to remediate health problems. Referrals to social workers should be made and documented when there is a reasonable indication that the living environment of the client is detrimental to the client's well-being. Included are situations where there is a likelihood of an accident in the home, a problem with household management, or such physical decay that the environment has become unsafe. The remediation of safety problems may not properly lie in the domain of the home health agency, but social workers can draw upon the expertise and services of their professional colleagues to effect changes. If needs regarding safety are not recognized or are not properly referred, they cannot be addressed and health care and medical treatment might well be impaired.

Eligibility for Other Services or Benefits

There are clients receiving home health care whose health and social situation can be improved by the prudent involvement of other social service agencies. It is entirely possible that many clients are unaware of their eligibility for some benefits and services and hence are not functioning as well as they might. A referral should be made to the social worker to assess the socioeconomic status of the client to determine whether the client is eligible for financial assistance or other services; referrals should be made accordingly. The social worker should facilitate this process as needed.

This type of social work intervention necessitates a familiarity with a wide variety of state, local, and federal social welfare programs and their eligibility criteria. In addition to governmental programs, there are a wide variety of services available from proprietary agencies and nongovernmental social agencies. The social worker should be familiar with these as well and utilize such services to augment the care provided by the home health agency.

Evaluating the Emotional and Psychological Status of Clients

When reasonable evidence exists that there is some emotional, behavioral, or psychological problem which may impair the client's ability to fully benefit from home health services or which places the client at risk for other problems, a social service referral should be made. Clients may have emotional problems that are longstanding, result from their physical illness, or are aggravated by the stress brought about by the illness. Such problems may confound the efforts of caregivers and adversely affect the well-being and safety of the client. Among these problems is the potential for suicide and other forms of self-destructive behavior.

The social worker should be knowledgeable about normal and abnormal mental processes and about reactions to illness and also have good diagnostic skills. It should be especially noted that diminished cognitive functioning is a very real possibility for the elderly client. This can occur because of the stress of the illness, a depressive reaction to the illness, physiological changes, medication side effects, and so forth. Often these changes begin subtly but become of great significance in the ongoing care of the patient. Social workers should be especially alert regarding changes in mentation among the elderly.

Referrals for appropriate psychiatric, counseling, or other mental health services should be made after a finding that problems are of such magnitude that they significantly impair the efforts of health care providers and the safety of the client. Social workers should document their efforts to facilitate appropriate mental health treatment. Documentation should include at a minimum the referral, the assessment and diagnostic indicators, and statements about the potential severity of the problem, the problem's effect on the client's medical plan of care and safety, and the actions taken to provide a remedy for the problem (Exhibit 11-2).

Alcoholism and Other Substance Abuse

Alcoholism is a problem of major proportions for both younger and older clients. In either age group, the excessive and continued use of alcohol can aggravate existing health problems and cause additional health problems. It may also exacerbate the emotional reactions to illness and become an additional stressor.

In the elderly, the inappropriate use of alcohol can result in a variety of problems, including a higher likelihood of falls, interactive effects from medications, aggravation of other health problems, gastrointestinal problems, and so forth. If the use of alcohol, medications, or other substances is deemed to be such that the client's health and safety is compromised, then referral for appropriate treatment is indicated. Such treatment may be inpatient or outpatient. An alcohol or drug abuse intervention requires close work and cooperation between the various involved disciplines as well as a good working relationship with the client and family.

Social workers should document the nature and severity of the problem, the indicators of the problem, and the referrals made. They should also arrange for the services suggested.

Housing and Living Arrangements

Often the housing situation of clients puts them at greater than average risk for illness, accident, or criminal victimization. If a client's housing situation adversely affects health care, the social worker should help the client to understand various housing alternatives and facilitate appropriate housing changes.

Adjustment to Illness

Both acute and chronic illnesses produce stress for patients and family members and stress takes its toll on the social, psychological, and physiological well-being of the client and family. Illnesses necessarily impinge upon the lifestyles of clients and alter normal patterns of behavior and relationships. The client's reaction to an illness has the potential to aggravate or create emotional and psychological problems as well as interpersonal and social problems. The social worker should be cognizant of how the client adapts to the illness, what effect the illness has on the client, and which interventions will ensure that the adjustments made to the illness do not impair the client's recovery or lead to secondary problems. Problems adjusting to an illness should be carefully and fully stated on care plans. Additionally, the types of interventions used to address such problems should be noted, as should the outcomes of such interventions.

Crisis Intervention

There is a greater than average likelihood that nonphysical problems will occur with clients who are enduring an illness and the attendant financial strain. Such problems may be unforseen, and they are sometimes of such magnitude that they affect the physical recovery and well-being of the client. In such cases, the social worker should employ crisis intervention skills to counteract negative events and help return clients to a condition where they can make optimal use of the health and medical care being rendered. The crisis should be identified and addressed and its negative effects diminished.

Successful crisis intervention requires that there is good communication among the various professionals involved in the patient's care. Accurate and comprehensive recordkeeping is also a must. For social workers to intervene in a crisis situation in a timely manner, they must have quick access to the information and insights of other involved caregivers, be able to define the problem, and work toward some resolution of the problem through involvement of the client and others.

Exhibit 11-2 Social Services Progress Note

Client's Name: _____   Date: _____
(Initial Visit)

Address: _____   Case No: _____

Principal Diagnosis: _____

Date of Referral: _____ Person Initiating Referral: _____

Reason for Referral: _____

Assessment & Diagnosis: Indicators & Background Information: _____

Potential Severity & Impact of Problem(s): _____

Affect of Problem(s) on Client's Medical/Nursing Plan of Care and Safety: _____

Plan for Problem Resolution: _____

Progress Achieved: _____

Follow-up Plans: _____

Discharge Summary (Description of Client's Condition/State of Being at Time of Closure): _____

Future Needs: None _____ Yes _____ Describe (Include Referrals): _____

Report to: Physician _____ Nurse _____
Other _____

_____   _____
(Signature, Social Worker)   (Date)

Family Relationships

In the majority of situations, the client's family is the major supplier of care and physical assistance. Knowing when and how to work with members of the client's family is essential. Conferences, teaching, and coordinated care planning with family members is necessary. Problems should be identified with and for family members, strategies worked out to address identified problems, and the results of work with the family members noted. The logic of working with the family and how this work is linked to the client's medical problems and treatment plan should be noted in the records.

Planning for Future Needs

After a client's medical condition has been addressed and the client has sufficiently recovered from the illness so that he or she no longer needs or qualifies for in-home care, the client's life still goes on. Caregivers may not be privy to the future events in their clients' lives, but they should anticipate their future care needs and likely problems and should identify and convey sources of assistance. Helping clients prepare for their own future care and for arranging for their own needs empowers them and makes them less dependent on others.

The well-being of clients does not become irrelevant when home health care is no longer being given. Quality home health services necessarily take into account anticipated future needs and situations that may interfere with the stability of the client's health. Consideration of future needs should occur from the first contact with the client and be part of the overall planning of care.

Clients' Socialization Needs

There are instances when clients, because of illness or other limitations, become socially isolated. Social isolation often may impair the client's response to the efforts of caregivers to improve his or her physical status or medical condition. Isolation may precede, accompany, or exacerbate the emotional response of the client to an illness. The lack of sufficient social contact may result, for example, in dispirited clients who are more disposed toward depression or who pay only halfhearted attention to their own well-being.

In the end, it is the clients who hold the key to their own well-being. If the caregivers detect that the client has little opportunity to socialize and that this seems to be accompanied by a general malaise, the social worker should be asked to do an assessment and to develop a plan of care accordingly. Such a plan of care can include making the client aware of resources for socializing and helping him or her select and take advantage of the various alternatives.

General Considerations

The above are some of the major areas in which social services should be employed by home health agencies. This list is not all-inclusive, and it is probable that some clients will have multiple needs. While it may be technically feasible to attend to purely physical problems, it is shortsighted to neglect social and psychological factors that might have a significant effect on the presenting medical problems and their resolution. Health problems precipitate social problems, and social factors influence the detection of, treatment of, and recovery from illness and injury.

The areas in which social workers can and should be employed are not necessarily areas in which problems are evident to physicians. While reimbursement for services is often dependent upon the physician's documentation of social factors that need to be addressed, it does not follow that any physician is capable of knowing all the social factors that impinge upon patients' lives and affect their responses to treatment. Social workers and nurses, as primary care providers in home health care, should be assertive in identifying such factors and making them evident to the physician in order that they may be properly addressed and the required work be properly reimbursed.

DOCUMENTATION

Documentation is a process itself as well as the concrete result of other processes that are undertaken to achieve some goal or outcome. Documentation must be clear, be worded appropriately, and demonstrate the relationship between the social problems identified and the medical or health problems being treated. It is entirely possible that more appropriate coverage for social work services can be obtained if social work providers can better document their work by clearly stating the problems and interventions and making the linkage of these to the medical problem obvious. It is also entirely possible that social work services can be obtained if nurses and others appropriately document problems which indicate the need for such services.

Documentation can take different forms. There is documentation on forms specifically used for communication with financing agencies (e.g., Health Care Financing Administration form number 485 for Medicare-eligible clients) and documentation that may best be described as detailed anecdotal notes and plans. Each form of documentation has its own level of specificity and format, but each should include the following components. For the purposes of this chapter, the focus will be on social work documentation. Other disciplines should determine what constitutes appropriate documentation for them.

Initial Assessment

The initial social work assessment is the basis for developing a treatment plan and ongoing work with the client. The assessment is more than descriptive; it is a problem-oriented diagnostic statement. A good assessment should include at a minimum the following:

- problems, needs, and strengths that exist in the client's social system and that can be used to construct a plan of care
- factors that obstruct the desired response of the client to medical care (these can be factors that contributed to the initial problem or influenced the severity of the problem)
- social and emotional problems that might influence either the medical condition or the effectiveness of care that is given to address the condition
- types of changes in the client's social and emotional situation that would positively influence the effectiveness of care given

Treatment Plan

Goals should be stated precisely and should be related both to the needs and problems identified as well as to the illness of the client and the physician's orders and treatment. Each goal specified should have a corresponding plan for social work treatment. The social worker's plans for intervention should be specific and demonstrate how they will address the problems and needs which have been identified. Each plan should clearly indicate why it will augment the physician's plan of care and contribute to the client's recovery. Clarity in stating the treatment plan will help to better define the social worker's role and function as well as help to ensure reimbursement for services. Such planning need not demean the social worker's right to utilize and incorporate his or her own professional judgment in diagnosing and treating clients and addressing their needs. Any competent home health care service properly uses the skills and insights of its professional staff. After the initial assessment and the development of the treatment plan, subsequent visits should be documented and progress notes maintained.

Notation of Visits, Contacts, and Progress

Notations are, or should be, billable. They must demonstrate coherence with the original treatment plan or amply illustrate situations in which the treatment plan must be amended. Client contact should be documented to include the following:

- a description of the client's condition or state of being at the time of the visit
- a statement describing the treatment and service provided during the visit (this should of course reflect skilled professional intervention)
- a notation of the progress made toward the goals defined in the treatment plan or the lack thereof (in the latter instance, causes should be noted)
- the planned intervention for the next contact (this should reflect continuity of treatment and a coherent ongoing plan of care)

Discharge Summary

When cases are closed or treatment has been concluded, a case summary should be written. Such summaries should include the following:

- a description of the client's condition or state of being at the time of closure
- a description of the effect of the treatment and social work intervention on the social and emotional problems that influenced the client's physical care and health
- notation of planning done in anticipation of future care needs and problem resolution
- notation of possibly premature discharge or problems arising from a lack of future skilled care (where appropriate)
- a summary of the social worker's views concerning the client's future functioning and well-being

These summaries should be incorporated into the medical record and officially close the social work involvement in the case. In the eventuality that cases need to be reopened, discharge summaries serve as springboards for subsequent care planning.

For the purpose of assuring quality home health care, social and emotional factors that impinge on a client's health or ability to benefit from treatment should be detected, noted, and treated. A social worker has the training and skills to ameliorate such problems and should be employed to provide these skills to clients and staff. Ignoring or minimizing such factors and neglecting to use professional social workers can often result in ineffective health care and the persistence of illness. Proper home health care includes attention to all factors relevant to a client's well-being, and the case documentation should reflect a comprehensive definition of the problem and the process of problem resolution. Documentation should demonstrate the structural dimension of referrals and reflect the processes employed and the outcomes of the work.

TEAMWORK

Caregivers must utilize teamwork in organizing their collective work. How to work as a team needs to be examined critically by both the members of a team and nonteam agency staff. While there are some quantitative measures that can be made of "team behaviors," evaluations and critiques of team working is probably most appropriately addressed qualitatively. Instructing some staff members in qualitative research methodology would help develop some techniques and procedures for monitoring the effectiveness and efficiency of team working.

There are numerous articles and publications that examine and define the concept of teamwork. In fact, the term *teamwork* has become part of the jargon of health care. However, teamwork should not be assumed to exist just because there is an absence of overt strife or interdisciplinary warfare. Working as a team demands the orchestration of efforts toward a common goal and requires more than the presumption that parallel undertakings will somehow coalesce into some grand design.

The professions of medicine, social work, and nursing have a tendency both to expand the boundaries of their professional domains and to preserve privileges and authority already attained. Most professionals have an inculcated inclination to serve as protectors of their professions. To a degree, this is as it should be. On an agency level, however, such concern for boundaries often serves less to define the standards of a profession than to sanctify power struggles. At that level, some amount of teamwork is essential if disparate caregivers are to bring coherence and effectiveness to their separate efforts. In short, teams can be more effective than the sum of their parts.

The establishment of good team working should *not* diminish the expectation that there will be appropriate accountability for professional activities. Members of different disciplines should have an awareness of each other's skills and expertise, and they should expect the best from each other. Also, while members of a team are accountable to each other, they are likewise accountable to the clients they serve. The functioning of a team should be monitored and not presumed, appropriate referrals should be generated, and each member should be expected to anticipate the information needs of other members so that appropriate communication can occur. Finally, good teamwork is orchestrated and nurtured rather than demanded.

CONSULTATION

It should be recognized that there are times when professional care providers need additional information, a different perspective on a situation, or support due to the emotional demands of caregiving. In short, care providers are human too. Ensuring quality in the process of caregiving also involves attending to the processes by which the caregivers themselves are helped to function optimally. Consultation can be defined, can be both formal and informal, and can be noted and quantified. It can be evaluated both quantitatively and qualitatively.

In providing quality home health services, it is essential to be cognizant of the needs of the professional caregivers themselves, such as the need for additional information or insights. Caregivers also need the opportunity to reframe the client's problem or living situation in such a manner that problems in ministering health care are linked with nonphysical variables. Finally, in working with the terminally ill and in similar situations, caregivers need support from others so that they can properly experience their own emotions but without losing their professional decorum and objectivity.

Social workers and others can and should consult with each other to share knowledge and perspectives. Consultation can also be of value when it is used in joint care planning with other agencies involved with the client. In whatever form consultation occurs, it should be seen as a tool for better equipping the caregivers for performing their work. The notation of consultation can be a tool for use in assuring quality in the delivery of services.

ASSESSMENTS OF PROCESS AND OUTCOME

When various processes are well documented and described, they can be measured and quantified for evaluative purposes. Additionally, the perspectives of professionals familiar with good work can be utilized to evaluate process recording, the technical manner of service delivery, types of supervision, teamwork, and so forth. This type of evaluation—the professional review of work done—rests on the premise that the practice wisdom of professionals ought to play some role in assessment. While this type of evaluation has obvious utility, there is room for bias—both favorable and unfavorable. Thus, objectivity and a thorough critique are of the utmost importance.

Outcome assessments are concerned with the benefits derived from the services provided to the clients. Benefits are important to the clients, the insurance sources, and the agency itself. For all the professional caregivers involved, including the social worker, the essential question is whether the defined problem or need was addressed and how completely. This means that the medical or social problem has to be stated as specifically as possible, as does the status of the problem at the time of termination. Using research methodology, the descriptions can be made amenable to different kinds of analysis, both quantitative and qualitative. If problems and outcomes are well defined and able to be quantified, correlational studies can be used to assess the effectiveness of different types or amounts of intervention. But this does require good documentation of different client and staff characteristics (variables) and of specific types and numbers of staff behaviors and services.

Correlation studies basically investigate the relationship between two or more factors (e.g., the number of social work visits and some measure of the client's physical well-being). Correlation studies do not provide a cause and effect explanation of any relationship found, but they can demonstrate that some relationship seems to exist between certain caregiver behaviors and certain outcomes. Since computers and good software are widely available, such studies can be done more easily and be used for purposes other than mere research.

One special frustration with correlation studies is the lack of control over factors extraneous to the immediate problems and to the care given. Nonetheless, correlation studies are valuable inasmuch as they can relate outcomes to the processes used in providing care; they can be used in conjunction with other quality assurance methods. Having someone versed in questionnaire construction help with agency documents will benefit data collection and subsequent analysis. Correlation studies can be used with other types of assessment of the results of care.

CONCLUSION

From a social work perspective, assuring quality in home health services involves a variety of factors. Included are the obvious need for a staff of professionals who can operate autonomously and use good judgement and who have the necessary technical skills to do their jobs well. Technical skills are just one factor in quality care; the conceptualization of relevant factors or variables that influence the clients responsiveness to the health care and medical services being administered should also be considered. If doing procedure A normally produces effect B, but that effect is not in fact realized, then an attempt must be made to find the extraneous factors that obstructed the effectiveness of the caregiving. It is in situations like this that thoughtfulness and good problem solving should be demanded of all caregivers. Problem solving, information gathering, and agency processes need to be made evident in documentation or by other methods. By being made explicit, quality can be better assured (Exhibit 11-3).

When nonphysical factors impede treatment or rate of recovery, social workers should be utilized. Social workers should diagnose factors in the social realm that influence the well-being of the client, develop a plan of care for diminishing

the negative influence of such factors, and work with other care providers in a concerted effort to achieve the goal of optimal physical, emotional, and social recovery.

Documentation skills are necessary both for reimbursement purposes and for communicating the various factors influencing the care of the client. Documentation skills include writing and thinking skills. They should be clear, concise, and address the problems as defined.

Finally, quality home health care is delivered by a community of caregivers. As caregivers, home health agency staff are often expected to be autonomous professionals. At times, though, there is another level of professional functioning that may best be characterized as teamwork and agency work. Quality health care is ultimately affected by the ability of the care providers to function interdependently, coherently, and with more than a modicum of support for each other. Without attention to this aspect of work, it is all too easy for autonomous care providers to become socially and professionally

Exhibit 11-3 Social Services Quality Assurance Audit

Client Name: _____
Case Number: _____
Dates: Case Opened _____ Social Service Referral _____ Acknowledged _____

| | Scaled Performance* | | | | | Problem type (#)† _____ | | | |
	POOR 1	2	AVERAGE 3	4	EXCELLENT 5		Yes	No	
1. Was a referral made via memo or other notation in the client's record? _____									
2. Was the referral acknowledged in writing (in the client's record)? a. 1–2 working days? _____ b. 3 or more? _____									
3. Was information gathering about client/family adequate? _____									
4. Was plan of care/intervention specified? _____									
5. Do the progress notes reflect the plan of care? _____									
6. Was new information discovered that was pertinent to client's well-being? _____									
7. Do progress notes reflect progress toward goals? _____									
8. Was notation made that the client is helped to develop problem-solving skills? _____									
9. Does the summary a. note the final status of the problem? _____ b. note future needs? _____ c. review the success/failure of the case plan? _____									

*The scaled performance score should reflect a critique of the worker's work (process) and the outcome of the work. A written narrative (in addition to this form) should summarize the review.

†*Problem type (#)* refers to the problem areas defined in the "Social Work Progress Note" and the "Social Work Referral Form." Each problem defined should be reviewed separately.

isolated and be able to offer little else besides their technical skills. This would not bode well for clients in complex situations and with complex needs, nor for the caregivers and their professions.

BIBLIOGRAPHY

Anderson, Scarvia, and Samuel Ball. *The Profession and Practice of Program Evaluation*. San Francisco: Jossey-Bass, 1978.

Banks, W.M. "The Black Client and the Helping Professionals." In *Black Psychology*, edited by R. James. New York: Harper & Row, 1972.

Chea, Mary Wong. "Research on Recording." *Social Casework* 53 (March 1972): 177–80.

Collins, Alice H., and Diane L. Pancoast. *Natural Helping Networks: A Strategy for Intervention*. Washington, D.C.: National Association of Social Workers, 1976.

Crane, Diana. "Decisions to Treat Critically Ill Patients: A Comparison of Social versus Medical Considerations." *Millbank Memorial Fund Quarterly: Health and Society* 53 (Winter 1975): 1–53.

Fordyce, Wilbert E. "On Interdisciplinary Peers." *Archives of Physical Medicine and Rehabilitation* 62 (February 1981): 51–53.

Freidson, Eliot. "Professional Dominance and the Ordering of Health Services." In *The Sociology of Health and Illness*, edited by Peter Conrad and Rochelle Kern. New York: St. Martin's Press, 1981.

Gruber, Murray L., ed. *Management Systems in the Human Services*. Philadelphia: Temple University Press, 1981.

Harwood, Alan., ed. *Ethnicity and Health Care*. Cambridge, Mass.: Harvard University Press, 1981.

Kadushin, Alfred. *Consultation in Social Work*. 2d ed. New York: Columbia University Press, 1985.

Levy, Charles S. *Social Work Ethics*. New York: Human Services Press, 1976.

Light, Donald, Jr. "Uncertainty and Control in Professional Training." *Journal of Health and Social Behavior* 20 (1979): 310–22.

Maldonado, David, Jr. "The Chicano Aged." *Social Work* 20 (May 1975): 213–16.

Nagi, Saad Z. "Teamwork in Health Care in the U.S.: A Sociological Perspective." *Health and Society* 53 (Winter 1975): 75–91.

National Association of Social Workers. *Standards For Social Work in Home Health Care*. Silver Spring, Md.: Author, May 1987.

Posavac, Emil, and Raymond Carey. *Program Evaluation: Methods and Case Studies*. Englewood Cliffs, N.J.: Prentice-Hall, 1980.

Rieken, Henry, and Robert Boruch, eds. *Social Experimentation: A Method for Planning and Evaluating Social Intervention*. New York: Academic Press, 1974.

Rubin, Irwin M., and Richard Beckhard. "Factors Influencing the Effectiveness of Health Teams." *Milbank Memorial Fund Quarterly* 50 (July-October 1972): 317–35.

Solomon, Barbara Bryant. *Black Empowerment: Social Work in Oppressed Communities*. New York: Columbia University Press, 1976.

Taylor, Alice L. "Case Recording: An Administrative Responsibility." *Social Casework* 34 (June 1953): 240–46.

Watkins, Julia M., and Dennis A. Watkins. "Continuum of Care as a Policy Framework for the Social/Health Care Needs of the Elderly: A State of the Art Review." *Journal of Gerontological Social Work* 6 (January 1984): 49–64.

Woy, J. Richard, Donald A. Lund, and C. Clifford Attkison. "Quality Assurance in Human Service Program Evaluation," In *Evaluation of Human Service Programs*, edited by C. Clifford Attkison, William A. Hargreaves, Mardi J. Horowitz, and James E. Sorensen. New York: Academic Press, 1978.

Chapter 12

The Therapist's Perspective

Christine M. Crivello

Although there is a great deal of information on the quality assurance activities of occupational, physical, and speech therapists and a fair amount on the activities of home care agencies, there is very little available on the activities of home care therapists. To help remedy this dearth of information, this chapter attempts to provide

- a model to use in designing a quality assurance program
- a broad overview of some of the quality assurance activities performed by home care therapists
- a summary of two home care quality assurance activities published in the literature
- ideas for future consideration

DEFINITION OF HOME CARE

The Assembly of Outpatient and Home Care Institutions, American Hospital Association, National Association of Home Health Agencies, National Home Caring Council, and Council of Home Health Agencies/Community Health Services of the National League for Nursing defined home health services as follows:

Home health service is that component of comprehensive health care whereby services are provided to individuals and families in their places of residence for the purpose of promoting, maintaining or restoring health or minimizing the effects of illness and disability. Services appropriate to the needs of the individual patient and family are planned, coordinated and made available by an agency or institution, organized for the delivery of health care through the use of employed staff, contractual arrangements, or a combination of administrative patterns. These services are provided under a plan of care which includes appropriate service components such as, but not limited to, medical care, dental care, nursing, physical therapy, speech therapy, occupational therapy, social work, nutrition, homemaker, home health aide, transportation, laboratory services, medical equipment, and supplies.[1]

HISTORY OF THERAPY IN HOME CARE

The National Center for Health Statistics reports that the first home care program was developed in Boston in 1796.[2] Prior to the 1940s, voluntary community agencies, such as the New York City Mission, and visiting nurse associations, such as those in Buffalo, Boston, and Philadelphia, began providing nursing care primarily to those who could not secure other skilled care for their illnesses. Social services, physical therapy, nutrition, and, later, home health aide services became part of home care as nurses began to seek support services and the skills of other disciplines in order to provide more comprehensive care. Hospitals re-entered the home care field in the 1940s. In 1966 the home health benefit was included in Title XVIII of the Social Security Act (Medicare), and public health departments, visiting nurse associations, and independent agencies became certified to provide home health care.[3]

The author would like to acknowledge the Visiting Nurse Association of Orange County, CA, and in particular, Lida Mooradian, P.T., M.A., for her assistance and cooperation in preparing this chapter.

The number of Medicare-certified home health agencies grew from 2,446 in 1978 to 5,247 in 1984. In 1976, 858 speech-language pathologists were providing services in home care, compared to 2,793 in 1984.[4] Because of the increased utilization of home care, concerns have been raised about the continuity and quality of care. Quality of care is an extremely critical issue given the isolated setting in which care is provided and the vulnerability of the population served (i.e., the elderly and disabled).

ROLE OF THE HOME HEALTH THERAPIST

The Community Health Section of the American Physical Therapy Association has described the role of the community home health therapist as follows: "The role of the community home health therapist is unique in that they perform traditional physical therapy services in nontraditional settings, integrating patient, care giver, and medical goals to attain maximum functions. This involves addressing ethnic, cultural and environmental conditions. The responsibility of meeting the medical goals lies primarily with the patient and care giver, with the therapist acting as a facilitator."[5]

The concept of the therapist as a facilitator who assists the patient in meeting goals is accurate with respect to the state of therapy services in home care today. The provision of therapy in home care is predominantly influenced by Medicare's reimbursement guidelines. Because of the interpretation of the Medicare guidelines by fiscal intermediaries, the role of the therapist in home care has become that of a teacher, with the patient and family assuming more of the responsibility for rehabilitation. In home care, therapy is usually provided on an intermittent basis. Therefore instruction begins immediately in a home exercise program (or in speech therapy homework) for the patient and caregiver to carry out between visits. In addition, therapy is generally short-term, requiring the patient or caregiver to maintain the gains made in therapy or make further progress.

INFLUENCE OF MEDICARE ON QUALITY ASSURANCE

Medicare regulations have also had a profound influence on structuring the quality assurance practices being used by home health care agencies. All home health care agencies that receive Medicare reimbursement are required to

1. review the appropriateness of continued care for each patient at 60-day intervals
2. conduct a clinical record review of open and closed cases on a quarterly basis
3. establish a professional advisory group that reviews policies, procedures, and clinical care
4. produce an annual evaluation of the total program of services provided[6]

A survey conducted by the Foundation of Record Education of the American Medical Record Association in May 1985 found that quality assurance activities in most agencies were primarily those required by Medicare (i.e., program evaluation and clinical record reviews). Only 25 percent of the agencies surveyed performed outcome-oriented patient care evaluation studies using objective criteria, and only 24 percent performed process-oriented patient care evaluation studies.[7]

GENERIC MODEL FOR QUALITY ASSURANCE

John C. Schmadl proposed this definition of quality assurance for nursing:

> Quality assurance involves assuring the consumer of a specified degree of excellence through continuous measurement and evaluation of structural components, goal directed nursing process, and/or consumer outcome using pre-established criteria and standards and available norms, and followed by appropriate alteration with the purpose of improvement.[8]

This definition indicates the important aspects of any quality assurance program. First, the focus of quality assurance is on the consumer or patient. The objective of quality assurance is to improve patient care and ultimately the outcome of that care. Second, the process must be continuous. The field of rehabilitation is very dynamic. A quality assurance program needs to reflect knowledge gained as a result of the current research. In addition, actions taken as a result of quality assurance studies must be monitored to ensure that improvements are sustained. Third, there are three domains of measuring quality: structure, process, and outcome. Fourth, quality assurance uses criteria, standards, and norms. Finally, a quality assurance program is not an end in itself, but must be followed by appropriate action to correct identified problems or improve patient care.

A generic model for quality assurance adapted from other sources is displayed in Figure 12-1.[9] It can be used in developing a quality assurance program for home care therapists.

Select Topic

In choosing a topic for study, Williamson et al. recommend selecting a topic with a high degree of ABNA (achievable benefits not achieved). They state that "the most significant patient care evaluation topics would be those problems encompassing interventions of proven efficacy based on reliable and valid research . . . In the absence of clinical research on which to base selection of significant quality review topics, group consensus of professionals is a reliable alternative."[10]

In addition, the Joint Commission on Accreditation of Healthcare Organizations recommends giving priority to clinical activities that affect a large number of patients, entail a

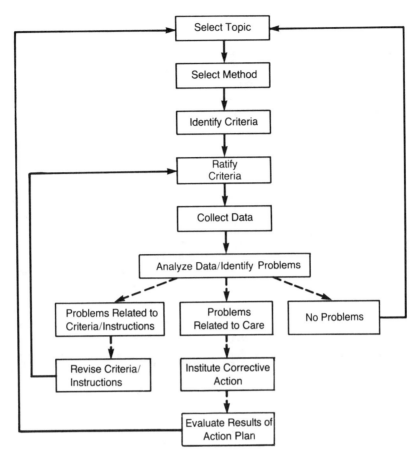

Figure 12-1 Generic model for quality assurance.

high degree of risk for patients, or tend to produce problems for patients or staff.

Select Method

A number of decisions must be made in choosing a method that will meet the objectives of the quality assurance activity. The three basic approaches to quality assurance as outlined by Donabedian are structure, process, and outcome.[11] *Structure* refers to the physical or organizational components of the health care system and of its environment. *Process* refers to the activities or procedures that take place as a part of caring for patients. *Outcome* refers to the end result of the treatment.[12] The pros and cons of the three approaches are described in the literature. John C. Schmadl suggests that it is questionable whether any one of the three approaches taken alone is a valid indicator of quality; ideally the interrelationship of structure, process, and outcome should be measured.[13]

Select Committee

The method is further defined by the type of committee that develops the criteria. The three choices to be made are these:

1. monodisciplinary versus multidisciplinary versus interdisciplinary
2. internal versus external
3. peer versus authority

Members of a monodisciplinary committee have a better understanding of their discipline and are more likely to formulate meaningful criteria.[14] However, according to Shanahan, no facet of medical science coordinates the activities of multiple care disciplines as effectively as rehabilitation medicine and no other service lends itself so well to multidisciplinary patient care evaluation.[15]

The National Professional Standards Review Council differentiates the terms *multidisciplinary* and *interdisciplinary* in the following way. Multidisciplinary studies are those in which one topic is selected and data are collected from one sample of records. Each discipline whose care is to be reviewed develops or selects its own criteria, analyzes the data relevant to those criteria, identifies any variance, and develops its own recommendations for follow-up action.

Interdisciplinary studies are those in which one committee, including members of the discipline whose care is to be reviewed (e.g., physicians, therapists, or nurses), develops or selects and agrees upon one set of criteria. These criteria are then applied to the data collected from one sample of records. The analysis of data, identification of variations, and development of recommendations are conducted collaboratively by the committee.

The interdisciplinary method can reflect the standard of professional care shared by all health care practitioners involved in that care. However, the more general the criteria, the more likely specific problems will be missed. Interdisciplinary studies lend themselves to joint professional problem analysis and resolution, role clarification, and improved interprofessional communication.[16]

The committee can be made up of persons internal or external to the agency or be a combination of the two. Professionals from outside the agency can offer new insights and objectivity. This is especially helpful for smaller agencies with only a few therapists. The committee can be made up of peers of the therapists being evaluated or of a group in authority or be a combination of the two.

Select Time Frame

The two primary time frames for a study are concurrent and retrospective. A concurrent study collects data on patients who are currently receiving care. A retrospective study collects data on patients who are discharged from a service.

There are two primary methods of collecting data. One method is the audit, which is a review of recorded materials. The second is observation, which is a direct method of gathering data.[17] Direct observation is costly and time consuming. Selective perception by the observer may also be a problem. Another major limitation of this method is that practitioners may change their usual practice when they know they are being observed.[18] The disadvantage with the audit method is that records might be incomplete and one might end up assessing the quality of the records instead of the care provided.[19]

Identify Criteria

Criteria, as defined by the *Patient Care Audit Manual* of the American Physical Therapy Association, are predetermined elements with which aspects of the quality of health care services may be compared. Criteria are developed by professionals relying on expertise and on the professional literature.[20] The manual defines seven different types of criteria:

1. *Admission*: criteria used to determine medical necessity and the appropriate level of care
2. *Discharge*: criteria used to determine the point at which care should be discontinued or transferred to another level of care
3. *Generic*: criteria that apply to a specific procedure or classification of care and whose indication for quality care is not dependent upon the patient's diagnosis
4. *Outcome*: criteria used to measure the quality of care by examining short-term or long-term results
5. *Process*: criteria used to measure specific elements of patient management

6. *Referral*: criteria that determine the appropriateness of requested services
7. *Structure*: criteria concerned with the organization of policies according to which care is delivered

Criteria can be developed from many sources, including standards of care or practice, policies and procedures, job descriptions, and lists available in the literature or in use elsewhere. The criteria chosen should be valid, important, relevant, and applicable through use of the medical record.[21]

Ratify Criteria

The criteria developed by the committee should be ratified by the therapists whose care will be reviewed. During ratification, criteria will be approved, modified, or rejected. The process includes discussing the criteria and the expected level of performance and giving instructions or explanations to the abstractor or observer.[22]

Collect Data

Which sources for data are selected depends on the topic and method chosen. Possible sources include

- medical records
- committee minutes
- incident reports
- patient/family complaints
- hospital transfer/discharge information
- patient satisfaction questionnaires
- department policies and procedures
- telephone interviews
- observer recordings
- computer-assisted studies

Data may be abstracted by medical record, clerical personnel, or therapists by using the criteria and instructions provided by the committee. The abstractor then summarizes the findings and returns the results to the committee.

Analyze Data and Identify Any Problems

All deviations from the criteria are identified. If an audit is used, records that do not meet the criteria or lack sufficient documentation are retrieved and reviewed. Upon analysis, three determinations can be made:

1. There is an acceptable variation or no problem (e.g., the deviation is due to an uncontrollable variable such as medical complications).
2. There is a problem related to the criteria or instructions. The criteria or instructions may require refinement. The

criteria should be revised and ratified, and the instructions may need to be made more specific. The process of data collection is then restarted.

3. There is a problem related to care.

Before remedial action can be undertaken the cause of the problem must be identified. Possible causes include

- insufficient staff knowledge or skills
- nonutilization of existing knowledge or skills
- inadequate number of staff
- inadequate administrative procedures or regulations
- shortage of appropriate material or equipment

Institute Corrective Action

The Quality Assurance Committee develops a remedial action plan based on the probable cause of the identified problem. The plan should specify the corrective actions to be taken, the responsible individuals, the completion time for each action, and a date for re-evaluating the results of the remedial action. The remedial action plan should be ratified by all members involved in its implementation.[23]

Evaluate Results of Action Plan

After the remedial action plan is implemented, data are collected using the same method and criteria. If the corrective action was found to be effective, the improvement of quality is documented and the cycle is begun again with the selection of a new topic.

EXAMPLES OF QUALITY ASSURANCE PROGRAMS IN HOME CARE

The generic model describes the steps involved in designing a quality assurance audit or activity. However, in approaching the challenge of quality care, one must be aware that quality permeates every aspect of operations and is not confined to the functional domain of a committee or to the administrative domain of a specific program.[24]

Visiting Nurse Association of Orange County

The quality assurance activities of the rehabilitation services department of the Visiting Nurse Association of Orange County (California) permeate every aspect of the delivery of services. They include both structure- and process-oriented quality assurance activities. In addition, the outcome of patient satisfaction is monitored through the use of a patient survey form (Exhibit 12-1). The association conducts quarterly utilization review. Topics or diagnostic groups for review are chosen by the Services Advisory Committee at its planning

meeting. The members of the Utilization Review Committee include the chairman, who is a member of the board of directors, a clinical reviewer, the director of hospice, a social worker, the director of rehab, the director of nursing, three nursing managers, three rehab managers, an outside director of speech pathology, an outside director of physical therapy programs, a pharmacist, a consumer, and a physician. Each member of the committee receives four to five records to review and comes prepared to report and discuss the care received (Exhibit 12-2). Any action recommended by the committee is reported to the area managers, who in turn relay the information to the appropriate field staff. The corrective action is recorded on the utilization review form.

Several mechanisms are in place to ensure interdisciplinary communication. Case conferences are held on selected patients. Staff meetings are held, including general meetings, rehab meetings, area manager meetings, and individual meetings. An informal two-hour meeting (core time) is held weekly to discuss various issues and policies. All field staff are required to attend and are grouped by the area of the county they serve, which facilitates interdisciplinary discussions. A flow sheet is used in the patient's home for the purpose of interdisciplinary communication on each case (Exhibit 12-3). Case coordination and teamwork are emphasized at all levels.

Hiring practices and orientation are an important part of assuring quality care. At the association, a minimum of two years of experience is required of the rehabilitation staff. Clinical competence in areas such as electrical stimulation, ultrasound, and traction is checked. A five-day orientation to services and programs and to the agency is conducted. This includes three days of joint visits. Field supervision or joint visits between rehab managers and staff is then conducted every month initially. A joint visit with field staff is made at least quarterly thereafter. Productivity is monitored daily to ensure that sufficient time during each visit is spent on patient treatment.

The Rehabilitation Services Department has standards in place for supervisory staff, including workload assignments and scheduling. The standard on workloads states that "each supervisor shall assign workload to appropriate staff and assist staff with resolving conflicts." To meet this standard, expected behaviors include, but are not limited to, the following:

- assigns workload to staff per agency procedure
- monitors clinical staff regarding appropriateness of visit frequency
- assists staff in setting priorities and necessary redistribution of their workload
- hires and schedules sufficient staff to assure coverage for all workload
- reviews workload with staff members daily and more frequently when changes are needed
- assures that all patients are seen on the day requested

A standard is in place for quality assurance. The standard reads, "Each supervisor is responsible for assurance of deliv-

Exhibit 12-1 Patient Survey Form

Dear Patient;

Our continuing goal at the VNA is to provide you with the highest level of quality home health care.

You can help us by taking a few moments to complete this questionnaire. Your observations are of great importance to us and your comments and suggestons will assist us in meeting your future needs, as well as those of other patients.

To mail this form, simply fold, seal and drop in any mailbox. Postage has been paid.

Please feel free to call our referral department if we can be of further service to you. Our patient service representative is Sharmon Steffler. She can be reached at 771-7364 between the hours of 9:30 a.m. to 11:30 a.m. Monday through Friday.

Sincerely,

Jo-Anne Andre

Jo-Anne Andre
President

VISITING NURSE ASSOCIATION
OF ORANGE COUNTY

Please (✓) check a box next to services which apply to your experiences with VNA.

	SATISFIED	NOT SATISFIED
OVERALL QUALITY OF CARE	☐	☐
NURSE	☐	☐
PHYSICAL THERAPIST	☐	☐
HOME HEALTH AIDE	☐	☐
OCCUPATIONAL THERAPIST	☐	☐
SOCIAL WORKER	☐	☐
SPEECH THERAPIST	☐	☐
OFFICE PERSONNEL	☐	☐

HOW DID YOU FIND OUT ABOUT OUR SERVICES?

☐ FROM DOCTOR
☐ FROM HOSPITAL
☐ FROM A FRIEND
☐ OTHER _____

Patient Name: _____ (OPTIONAL)

City: _____ (OPTIONAL)

This form was filled out by:

☐ PATIENT
☐ FAMILY MEMBER
☐ FRIEND

DO YOU HAVE ANY SUGGESTIONS AS TO HOW WE COULD HAVE IMPROVED SERVICE TO YOU?

_____
_____
_____
_____
_____
_____

WOULD YOU USE OUR SERVICES AGAIN OR RECOMMEND US TO A FRIEND?

☐ YES   ☐ NO

COMMENTS:

_____
_____
_____
_____

Source: Courtesy of Visiting Nurse Association of Orange County.

Exhibit 12-2 Utilization Review Form

UTILIZATION REVIEW

All Data To Be Held In Strict Confidence And Must Not Be Filed In Patient Record

SECTION I - IDENTIFYING DATA

1. Chart #_____   2. Age_____   3. Sex
                                              Male_____   Female_____

4. Referred by:_____   5. Admission Date:_____   6. Discharge Date:_____

SECTION II - CARE PLAN AND SERVICES

7. Diagnosis - Primary

8. Diagnosis - Secondary

9. Surgery and Dates

10. Limiting Conditions/Significant History

11. Initial Patient Care Plan	Present	Absent	N/A	Comments
A. Diagnosis(es)				
B. Prognosis				
C. Goals				
D. Plan of Care				
E. Symptoms & Reactions to be Observed				
F. Medications(Oral /Parenteral)				
G. Diet				
H. Medical Equip./Supplies				
I. Orders Signed by Physician				

12. Therapeutic Services	Needed Y	N	Ordered Y	N	Prov. Y	N	Rx Plan Y	N	Goals Y	N	Visit Frequency or Total Visit Duration
A. Nursing											
B. Physical Therapy											
C. Occupational Therapy											
D. Speech Therapy											
E. Medical Social Service											
F. Home Health Aide											
G. Nutrition											
H. Other											

Comments regarding therapeutic services:

Exhibit 12-2 continued

SECTION III - CLINICAL REVIEW OF SERVICES

13. Plan of Care Indicates:	Yes	No	Comments
A. Concern with patients total health needs.			
B. Coordination of service to meet patient's health needs.			
C. Family and home situation.			
D. Need for other community resources - referral if indicated			
14. If patient discharged:	Yes	No	Comments
A. Discharge summary present for each discipline?			
B. Date of discharge noted?			
C. Outcome of intervention and patient's current condition noted?			
D. Reason for discharge?			
E. Patient/M.D. notified of discharge?			
15. Case record indicates periodic re-assessment and alteration in plan of care as necessary?	Yes	No	Comments

16. Reviewer's decision and summary statement to the type and amount of services utilized:

    A. Appropriate   _____

    B. Over utilization   _____

    C. Under utilization   _____

Summary Statement:

Recommendation for follow-up:

Date:_____

                                                Reviewer's Signature and Title

Action Taken Following Review:

                                                Signature

Source: Courtesy of Visiting Nurse Association of Orange County.

Exhibit 12-3 Patient Flow Sheet

VNA — VISITING NURSE ASSOCIATION OF ORANGE COUNTY
1337 Braden Court • P.O. Box 1129 • Orange, California 92668-0129 • (714) 771-1209

PATIENT FLOW SHEET

Patient Name _____ VNA # _____ First visit date _____

Staff Assigned to Patient	Date new staff initates care	Staff Assigned to Patient	Date new staff initates care
Registered Nurse _____		Physical Therapist _____	
Home Health Aide _____		Occupational Therapist _____	
Social Worker _____		Speech Therapist _____	
Nutritionist _____			

NOTES AND COMMENTS

Date	Staff Name	

VNA-OC-122 (Rev. 5/84)

Source: Courtesy Visiting Nurse Association of Orange County.

ery of quality care to patients seen by the staff.'' In addition, each supervisor will participate in agencywide mechanisms for quality assurance.

To meet the quality assurance standard, the expected behaviors include, but are not limited to, the following:

- supervises staff by direct observation to assure clinical competency no less often than when performance evaluations are due and more frequently as needed
- provides correctional feedback to staff immediately regarding service quality
- evaluates staff regarding their patient evaluation, care plans, goals, and interventions on a regular basis
- attends, and assures that staff attends, scheduled in-service programs
- attends and actively participates in Service Advisory Committee meetings as scheduled
- submits to the service director any questions or concerns regarding delivery of service that should be brought to the attention of the Medical Advisory Committee
- shares information learned at outside educational programs with other supervisors and staff, when possible
- assists the educational coordinator with student placements and assures that cases assigned to students do not exceed their level of clinical expertise
- participates in team conferences and development of appropriate care plans to meet identified needs
- conferences with staff on a regular basis regarding their caseload management and individual patient needs

- considers educational, experiential, and personal qualifications needed to provide quality performance when hiring staff
- works within a committee framework to develop patient care standards and clinical procedures, as appropriate

In addition to these quality assurance measures, there is also a Medical Advisory Committee and a Bioethics Committee. The Bioethics Committee meets every two months and consists of the director of rehab and nursing, an administrator from a physiatric institute, a director of community education, an internist, a priest, a lawyer, and two social service directors from area hospitals. Area managers are invited to the meetings. Cases are presented and discussed at these meetings, and recommendations are shared with staff when appropriate.

Rehabilitation Services of Wisconsin

Rehabilitation Services of Wisconsin (RSW) is a therapy practice that provides physical, occupational, and speech therapy under contract with numerous home health agencies in southeastern Wisconsin. RSW conducts several quality assurance activities, including concurrent chart reviews, retrospective chart audits, on-site evaluations, and performance appraisals. All home care therapists receive a performance appraisal after the first six months, then yearly thereafter. The communication and patient care standards to be met by the therapists are outlined in Exhibit 12-4.

Exhibit 12-4 Performance Appraisal Form for Home Care Physical Therapists

---

THERAPIST—HOMECARE
PERFORMANCE APPRAISAL

The following rating scale provides the guidelines for the development of standards and criteria:

3: *Above Standard*: The individual performs above the required level.
2: *Standard*: The individual consistently performs at required level.
1: *Below Standard*: The individual frequently performs below standard.
0: *Unsatisfactory*: The individual consistently performs below standard.

Communication

In order for RSW to maintain accuracy of its records and promote quality services to the agencies it represents, it is necessary to follow through with the proper guidelines of communication.

I. *Standard: Communicates* in a timely manner with RSW office personnel regarding scheduling, confirmation of patient visits, messages and other activities.
  2: meets the standard
  0: does not meet standard
II. *Standard: Responds* to referrals within 24 hours of therapist receiving referral and sees pt. within 3 working days of RSW receiving referral.
  2: meets the standard
  0: does not meet standard
III. *Standard:* Contacts appropriate agency within 24 hours of initial evaluation.
  2: meets the standard
  0: does not meet standard

Exhibit 12-4 continued

IV. *Standard:* Conferences with agency, doctors, and other disciplines every 2–3 weeks and as needed to insure patient care is complete and documents conferences appropriately.
    3: in addition, attends case conferences, meets with agency personnel
    2: meets the standard
    1: conferences only sporadically; neglects to conference as needed
    0: no evidence of conferencing
V. *Standard:* Contacts the appropriate agency to notify them of d/c planning and to confirm actual d/c date.
    2: meets the standard
    0: does not meet standard

Patient Care

The meeting of criteria for patient care will be determined by patient questionnaires, chart audit results, manager/agency input and on-site evaluations. Quality care is the most important goal of RSW. The following are standards to be met.

I. *Standard:* Encourages and instructs patient or family in a home treatment program as an adjunct to regular therapy treatment (written home program provision is preferred but documentation of HP instruction is acceptable).
    3: 100% of patients reviewed have evidence of initial home program with update as necessary
    2: 75–99% " " "
    1: 50–75% " " "
    0: less than 50% " "
II. *Standard:* Considers and documents physical and psycho/social environment when evaluating patient.
    3: 100% of patients reviewed have evidence of above
    2: 75–99% " " "
    1: 50–75% " " "
    0: less than 50% " "
III. *Standard:* Goals set at evaluation are specific and consistent with problems and treatment plan and are consistent with reimbursement guidelines.
    3: 100% of patients reviewed meet standards
    2: 75–99% " " "
    1: 50–74% " " "
    0: less than 50% " "
IV. *Standard:* Treatment reflects skilled services, is consistent with treatment plan and goals and is consistent with reimbursement guidelines.
    3: 100% of patients reviewed meet standards
    2: 75–99% " " "
    1: 50–74% " " "
    0: less than 50% " "
V. *Standard:* Goals are upgraded as needed.
    3: 100% of patients reviewed meet standard
    2: 75–99% " " "
    1: 50–74% " " "
    0: less than 50% " "
VI. *Standard:* Discharge goals are achieved and if not met a clear statement as to why is made.
    3: 100% of patients reviewed meet standard
    2: 75–99% " " "
    1: 50–74% " " "
    0: less than 50% " "
VII. *Standard:* Plans for, suggests and assists patient in obtaining needed equipment, e.g., ambulatory devices, transfer equipment, ADL adaptations, etc.
    3: 100% of patients reviewed meet standard
    2: 75–99% " " "
    1: 50–74% " " "
    0: less than 50% " "

Source: Reprinted from *Therapist—Homecare Performance Appraisal* with permission of Rehabilitation Services of Wisconsin.

A complete quality assurance program in home care should include observation as well as other methods of study. In other practice settings, observation usually is done informally by peers, supervisors, or other health care professionals. In home care, the patient and family members are often the only observers of the care provided. They do not have the necessary objectivity and expertise to judge the quality of the care. At RSW, the on-site evaluation is carried out by a supervisor. (Exhibit 12-5 is the form used to document the findings of the observer.)

OUTCOME STUDIES IN THE LITERATURE

Occupational Therapy

A six-month retrospective chart review conducted by a home health agency in Oakland, California, was published in the *American Journal of Occupational Therapy* in November 1984.[25] Data were collected on 68 home health patients from July through December 1983. From chart review, data were gathered on diagnostic categories of patients treated by occupational therapy (Table 12-1).

Exhibit 12-5 On-Site Evaluation Form

```
ON-SITE EVALUATION
(for use by Supervisor/Manager in Home Care when making a
combined visit for purpose of staff evaluation)

Therapist: _____      Date: _____
                                 Manager: _____
Patient: _____
Dx: _____
Fx/duration: _____           _____
                                           (appropriate)
Tx time: _____                _____
                                           (appropriate)
Establishes patient rapport: _____
Incorporates family into program: _____
Scope of treatment: _____
_____
_____
Thoroughness of treatment: _____
_____
_____
_____
Tx specific to patient problems: _____
_____
_____
_____
Patient demonstrates functional progress: _____
_____
_____
Adherence to Medicare guidelines (what if not Medicare): _____
_____
_____
Additional comments: _____
_____
_____

        Source: Courtesy of Rehabilitation Services of Wisconsin.
```

The treatment consisted of an initial evaluation and goal-directed treatment, with the primary emphasis being on assisting patients in reconstructing previous activity patterns disrupted by accident or illness and in developing new patterns compatible with their present condition. Prevention and patient and family education on the home program were also essential components of the home health treatment process. The retrospective chart review revealed that the 68 patients received an average of 7.25 occupational therapy visits at an average rate of 2 visits per week (Table 12-2).

Since one of the primary goals of occupational therapy in a home health agency is to alleviate functional impairments and enable a person to remain safely at home, the outcome focused upon in the study was whether the person was able to remain at home either independently or with assistance. As seen in Table 12-3, 41 percent of the patients were able to remain at home without assistance, 38 percent required in-home assistance from another for at least one activity of daily living, 15 percent were placed in skilled or intermediate care facilities, and 6 percent expired. The author felt that diagnosis alone was not reliable for determining treatment duration. Data on the severity of the disorder or a standardized index of functional impairment would have been helpful in this review.

Table 12-1 Diagnostic Analysis of Occupational Therapy Patients

Diagnosis (Reason for Referral)	Number of Patients	Percentage with Multiple Diagnosis
Parkinson's disease	4	100
Cardiac	8	88
Other	6	83
Orthopedic	17	76
Arthritis	4	75
Postsurgical	4	75
Renal	2	50
Respiratory disease	10	50
Neurological (CVA and brain injury)	13	46
Total	68	65

Patients defined as having multiple diagnoses were those with additional disorders actually treated by occupational therapy. Neurological disorders category was the only one with less than 50% multiple diagnoses. A possible explanation for this variance is that the functional impairments caused by the neurological disorders can be so catastrophic that other conditions are either masked or treatment is not a priority.

Source: Reprinted from *Occupational Therapy in a Medicare-Approved Home Health Agency* by Anne MacRae. Copyright 1984 by the American Occupational Therapy Association, Inc. Reprinted with permission.

Table 12-2 Occupational Therapy Visits per Diagnostic Category

Diagnosis	Number of Patients	Total Visits	Average Number of Visits per Patient
Respiratory disese	10	47	4.70
Cardiac	8	38	4.75
Renal	2	10	5.00
Parkinson's disease	4	22	5.50
Other	6	34	5.67
Postsurgical	4	29	7.25
Orthopedic	17	126	7.41
Arthritis	4	30	7.50
Neurological	13	157	12.08
Total	68	493	7.25

Standard deviation = 2.57

Source: Reprinted from *Occupational Therapy in a Medicare-Approved Home Health Agency* by Anne MacRae. Copyright 1984 by the American Occupational Therapy Association, Inc. Reprinted with permission.

Multidisciplinary

A multidisciplinary outcome-oriented quality assurance program was developed by the Visiting Nurse Association of New Haven (Connecticut) and published in *Nursing Outlook* in July 1979.[26] Elizabeth Daubert writes that "the final measure of the effectiveness of service is the outcome, the actual functional level of a patient at time of discharge from service."[27] The system they developed, the Rehabilitation Potential Patient Classification System, requires the classification of all patients admitted to the agency into one of five patient

Table 12-3 Comparison of Intervention Outcomes of Single-Diagnosis and Multiple-Diagnoses Patients

Classification	Independent	Assist	Placement	Expired	Totals
Number of single-diagnosis patients	12	8	2	2	24
Percent of single-diagnosis patients	50	33	8	8	
Number of multiple-diagnoses patients	16	18	8	2	44
Percent of multiple-diagnoses patients	36	41	18	5	
Number of total patients	28	26	10	4	68
Percent of total patients	41%	38%	15%	6%	100%

Patients designated as needing assistance at home are those individuals needing the help of another for at least one activity of daily living. These assistants include family members, significant others, or non-professional paid personnel such as attendants, aides, or homemakers.

Source: Reprinted from *Occupational Therapy in a Medicare-Approved Home Health Agency* by Anne MacRae. Copyright 1984 by the American Occupational Therapy Association, Inc. Reprinted with permission.

groups according to rehabilitation potential. The primary nurse, along with any involved therapist or social worker, selects the appropriate patient group.

Each patient group has an identified ultimate program objective and a separate set of subobjectives that are applicable to all of the disciplines providing home care. The subobjectives are customized and incorporated in the patient action plan portion of the record. At the time of discharge, a discharge summary is completed; it includes information such as patient name, length of service, diagnosis(es), service program goal, goal accomplishment, reason for discharge, total visits made by each discipline, cost of each service discipline, payment source, and total cost of all services provided. The data collected provide objective evidence concerning the degree of effectiveness of the services for the population served. The data help the agency to assess the current method of delivering services and to plan corrective actions when needed. The data can uncover specific weaknesses in the agency's current method of delivering services and can be used to validate the need for funding from other sources.

FUTURE CONSIDERATIONS

In a survey of physical therapy departments that was conducted by the Wisconsin Physical Therapy Association Quality Assurance Committee in 1985, 83 percent of the home health agencies who responded indicated they were not satisfied with their present methods of assessing quality assurance.[28] Of the types of facilities that responded (i.e., hospitals, nursing homes, private practices, home health agencies, and schools), home health agencies had the largest percentage of dissatisfaction. This seems to indicate that there is a lot of room for improvement in the quality assurance activities of therapy departments in home health agencies.

A cover letter sent with the survey explained a quality assurance method developed by physical therapists in Minnesota. In this method, a panel of peers external to the department performs a peer review of an individual physical therapist or physical therapy service.[29] This or a similar method might be very useful for agencies with a small number of therapy personnel. One question raised by departments responding to the survey was whether an external peer review might not cause competitiveness among agencies. Indeed, the home health field seems to be extremely competitive—to the point where agencies are reluctant to share information even for educational purposes.

CONCLUSION

"Occupational therapists have a valuable service to offer the homebound patient; occupational therapy treatment has been successful in alleviating functional impairments, thus allowing patients to remain safely in their homes. Thus, the challenge to home care occupational therapists is to substantiate further the ability of occupational therapy to provide cost-effective quality home health care."[30] This is the challenge that we all face. Prospective payment and DRGs are on the horizon for home care. We need to be able to prove to consumers as well as to third party payers that the home care services we provide are cost-effective and high quality.

NOTES

1. I.E. Stewart, Home Health Care (St. Louis: Mosby, 1979).

2. National Center for Health Statistics, *Health Resource Statistics* (Washington, D.C.: GPO, 1974).

3. Evelyn McNamara, "Home Care—Hospitals Rediscover Comprehensive Home Care," *Hospitals*, November 1, 1982, p. 61.

4. Patricia G. Larkins, "The Delivery of Speech-Language and Audiology Services in Home Care," *ASHA*, May 1986, p. 49.

5. "Standards in Action," review and finalization of guidelines, American Physical Therapy Association Combined Section Meeting, Orlando, Fl., Feb. 3–6, 1985.

6. Susan L. Hughes, "Home Health Monitoring Ensuring Quality in Home Care Services," *Hospitals*, November 1, 1982, p. 76.

7. Susan C. Miller, "The Home Care Client Record Project: Model Forms and Comprehensive Guidelines," *Quality Review Bulletin*, May 1986, p. 188.

8. John C. Schmadl, "Quality Assurance: Examination of the Concept," *Nursing Outlook*, July 1979, p. 465.

9. Mary Ann McColl and Barbara Quinn, "A Quality Assurance Method for Community Occupational Therapy," *American Journal of Occupational Therapy* (1985): 571; Edward W. Saitz, Lily Y. Hoy, and James A. Armour, "Simplified Physical Therapy Audit," Western Pennsylvania Regional Medical Program, 1976, p. 11. Supported by DHEW Grant No. 5603-RM00041, University of Pittsburgh. Found in *APTA QA Manual* (see note no. 16).

10. John W. Williamson, Patricia Curran Ostrow, and Harriet R. Braswell, *Health Accounting for Quality Assurance* (Rockville, Md.: American Occupational Therapy Association, 1981), 9–10.

11. Avedis Donabedian, "Evaluating the Quality of Medical Care," *Milbank Memorial Fund Quarterly*, July 1966, pp. 166–203.

12. McColl and Quinn, "Quality Assurance Method," 573; Avedis Donabedian, "Criteria and Standards for Quality Assessment and Monitoring," *Quality Review Bulletin*, March 1986, pp. 99–100.

13. John C. Schmadl, "Quality Assurance," 463.

14. McColl and Quinn, "Quality Assurance Method," 572.

15. Maryanne Shanahan, "Rehabilitation Review," *Quality Review Bulletin*, November 1978, p. 5.

16. American Physical Therapy Association, *Quality Assurance Manual* (Alexandria, Va.: 1986), B7–B9.

17. McColl and Quinn, "Quality Assurance Method," 572.

18. Donabedian, "Quality of Medical Care," 173.

19. Ibid., 171.

20. American Physical Therapy Association, *Patient Care Audit Manual* (Alexandria, Va.: Author, 1980), 6.5–6.7.

21. Donabedian, "Criteria and Standards," 104.

22. American Physical Therapy Association, *Patient Care Audit Manual*, 7.

23. Kathleen M. Griffin, "Sound System, Patient Care Audit for Speech-Language Pathologists and Audiologists," *Quality Review Bulletin*, November 1978, p. 30.

24. Kaye Daniels, "Planning for Quality in the Home Care System," *Quality Review Bulletin*, July 1986, p. 250.

25. Anne MacRae, "Occupational Therapy in a Medicare-approved Home Health Agency," *American Journal of Occupational Therapy* 38 (November 1984): 721–25.

26. Elizabeth A. Daubert, "Patient Classification System and Outcome Criteria," *Nursing Outlook*, July 1979, pp. 450–54.

27. Ibid., 451.

28. Teresa Steffen and Teresa Trostmiller, "Quality Assurance: A State Survey," *Clinical Management* 7, no. 5: 28.

29. Ibid., 28.

30. MacRae, "Occupational Therapy," 725.

REFERENCES

Harris, Marilyn D., Donna A. Peters, and Joan Yuan. "Relating Quality and Cost in a Home Health Care Agency." *Quality Review Bulletin*, May 1987, pp. 175–81.

Joe, Barbara E., and Patricia C. Ostrow. *Quality Assurance Monitoring in Occupational Therapy*. Rockville, Md.: American Occupational Therapy Association, 1987.

Kulpa, Judith I. "Interdisciplinary Review in Long-term Care." *Quality Review Bulletin*, November 1978, pp. 15–21.

Larkins, Patricia G. (1987). American Speech-Language-Hearing Association, Committee on Quality Assurance. "Quality Assurance Process Indicators." Unpublished.

Larkins, Patricia G. "Determining Quality of Speech-Language-Hearing Services." American Speech-Language-Hearing Association, May 1987, pp. 21–24.

Meisenheimer, Claire G., ed. *Quality Assurance: A Complete Guide to Effective Programs*. Rockville, Md.: Aspen Publishers, 1985.

Moore, Marsha, Linda Bjork, Robin Smith, and Su-Lin Yang. "Quality Assurance in a Rehabilitation Setting." *Clinical Management* 4, no. 2: 30–32.

Mumma, Nancy L. "Quality and Cost Control of Home Care Services through Coordinated Funding." *Quality Review Bulletin*, August 1987, pp. 271–78.

Chapter 13

The Pharmacist's Perspective

Ilene H. Zuckerman and Madeline V. Feinberg

Home health agencies caring for patients usually do not provide medications. For reasons that are difficult to understand, home health care personnel usually still view the pharmacy as a retail outlet where medications are purchased. Patients and families are often left to their own resources when they need to obtain medications, and they complain of problems of medication administration, medication side effects, and a general lack of understanding regarding indications for drug therapy. Physicians play a marginal role in the care of home health patients,[1] and nurses for the most part do not have adequate training in pharmacotherapeutics to assess complicated drug regimens. Hence there is a need for the expertise of today's consultant pharmacist, who is trained to monitor the drug therapy of all patients, especially the elderly. The elderly constitute a large segment of the home health care population.

DRUG USE AND THE ELDERLY

According to the Office of Technology Assessment, drugs are the most cost-effective modality of chronic disease management.[2] However, little is known about drug action in the elderly, particularly when multiple drugs are used. Those 65 years of age and older compose 12 percent of the population, but they receive 32 percent of all prescription drugs dispensed.[3] And this does not include the use of nonprescription drugs (which unfortunately often adversely affect the outcome of therapy with prescription drugs).

The population is aging. With age, there are several factors that can alter drug efficacy. Normal changes induced by the aging process, changes due to multiple diseases and drugs, and socioeconomic changes or environmental factors all lead to greater unpredictability of drug action. Elderly females living alone are the most sensitive to adverse effects of medications, and it is they who predominate in the very old population.[4]

Aging is accompanied by impairment—vision, hearing, speech, cognitive, and physical impairment, all of which can lead to problems of medication compliance. Noncompliance adds another dimension to the difficulties of managing drug therapy in the older population.

RISKS AND PROBLEMS OF DRUG USE

In contrast to the home care setting, pharmacy services are regulated in the nursing home setting, where only 5 percent of the elderly reside. By federal law, a pharmacist must review the drug regimen of all patients receiving both skilled and intermediate care, regardless of funding sources, in order for the nursing home to participate in the Medicare or Medicaid programs. Consultant pharmacy services in the long-term care sector have been found to be clinically effective and cost-effective in these facilities,[5] yet there is currently no mandate for the pharmacist to review the drug regimen of the home care patient. In the home care setting, where there is less supervision by the health care provider, consultant pharmacy services should be available to agency staff while they are caring for patients on complicated drug regimens.

Drugs are the mainstay of chronic disease management. However, drug use may present difficulty. The disease may be exacerbated. A new illness may be superimposed. It is important to recognize that home care patients will generally be receiving oral medications. Very few of the home care population will receive "high-tech" infusion therapies, and pharmacists must be prepared to deal with the routine medications characteristically seen in chronic care.

According to a published chart review of 100 patient records of a home health agency, most patients had multiple pathologies and were prescribed multiple drugs.[6] The average drug regimen required patients to take almost eight doses of medication per day. This did not include medications prescribed "as needed" or medications that patients may have been taking which were not listed in the chart (Table 13-1).

There was virtually no information regarding nonprescription drug use; the patient record did not require this information. As noted, it is well documented that elderly persons take a substantial number of such drugs and that nonprescription drugs can have a clinically significant effect on the outcome of a drug therapy regimen.[7] (It is interesting that only 2 charts out of the 100 reviewed indicated the name of the patient's pharmacy; there was no place for this to be noted on the medication record in the chart.)

ROLE OF THE PHARMACIST IN HOME HEALTH CARE

Ninety-five percent of long-term care is provided in the community setting. Once patients are discharged from the hospital, from a nursing home, or from home care, their only routine contact with the health care system may be through the community pharmacy, where medications and health-related products are purchased. Pharmacists are increasingly aware of the need to assist these patients in adhering to their medication regimen and to monitor the medication regimen for therapeutic and adverse effects. Indeed, the community-based pharmacist with training in geropharmacy is well positioned to monitor the drug regimen. Given an adequate patient data base, coupled with computerized drug information systems, the pharmacist can provide sophisticated patient care in the community setting.[8]

Table 13-1 Characteristics of Home Care Patients (n = 100)

Mean age (range)	66.9 (23–104) years
Sex	63 women, 37 men
Number of patients living alone (n = 88)*	22 patients
Mean number of chronically prescribed prescription drugs (n = 91)*	3.8 drugs per patient
Mean number of nonprescription drugs used (n = 44)*	2.0 drugs per patient
Mean number of doses per day (excluding p.r.n. medications) (n = 91)*	7.7 doses per day
Mean number of diagnoses	3.7 diagnoses per patient

*Complete data were unavailable

Source: Adapted from *The Consultant Pharmacist,* Vol. 1, pp. 123–128, with permission of American Society of Consultant Pharmacists, © 1986.

Successful management of drug therapy may enable patients to remain in the community with some degree of functional independence. Several reasons for providing consultant pharmacy services in the home care setting are listed below:

- altered physiology
- disability leading to medication misuse
- inadequate drug therapy monitoring
- inadequate information on drug use
- increased adverse drug effects
- multiple chronic diseases
- multiple medications on a long-term basis
- multiple prescribers
- self-medication

Drug Distribution Systems

The pharmacist's role has been traditionally confined to the dispensing of medications. Everyone is familiar with the traditional prescription vial. Within the "formal" health care setting (i.e., hospitals and nursing homes), medication distribution is rigidly supervised by the pharmacist. Pharmacists have developed systems for distributing drugs to patients, and, in conjunction with nurses, they have developed comprehensive medical record systems for documentation of medication administration and treatment orders. Unit dose systems are state of the art in hospitals. In nursing homes, most pharmacists prefer a 30-dose blister card, which is a modification of the unit dose system.[9]

In home care, however, there are no systems. Visiting nurses have resorted to the egg carton or to elaborate homemade calendars to help patients and families administer medications. These are often inadequate and result in more confusion for patients.

Compliance Packaging

There are several devices, such as daily or weekly pill containers, that can assist patients and families in adhering to the doctor's orders. One such device is a miniature computerized timer built into the cap of the traditional prescription vial. The timer may ring or display the time when the next dose of medication is due.[10] Recently patented is a tabletop medicine chest with compartments specified for each medication vial. It includes a programmable computer with hard copy readout that specifies when each medication is to be taken or indicates when a medication has been missed. Such devices require a technological sophistication not commonly found in today's older population. Costs are a factor to consider as well.

ASCO Calendar Card

The ASCO* calendar card (Figure 13-1) may offer a practical and economical approach to helping patients and care-

*Automated Systems Company, 8561 Fenton Street, Silver Spring, MD 20910.

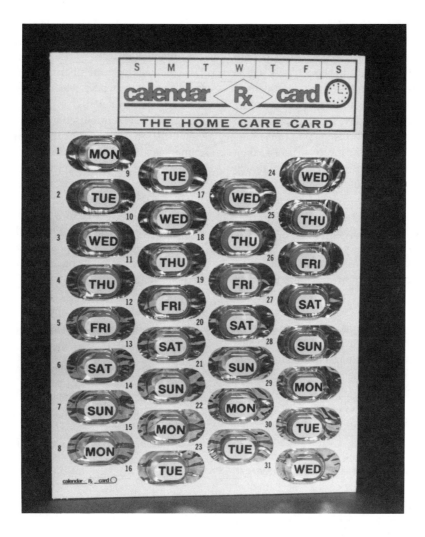

Figure 13-1 ASCO calendar card. *Source:* Courtesy of Automated Systems Company, Silver Spring, Maryland.

givers to comply with even the most complex medication regimen—and with a minimum amount of training. The calendar card has been shown to significantly improve patient compliance among an outpatient geriatric population.[11]

Consider Mrs. C. and her drug regimen (Table 13-2). Her diagnoses include congestive heart failure, arrhythmia, esophageal strictures, a history of recurrent hospitalization for arrhythmia stabilization, and some degree of cognitive impairment. She is 79 years old, lives alone in a senior citizen complex, and receives meals and light housekeeping services. The residential staff may assist Mrs. C. by reminding her to take her medications, but they are prohibited from administering medications to her by state regulation.

The ASCO calendar card is labeled for each time of the day: morning, noon, evening, bedtime. "Special" times can be written on the top of the card. Each card contains 31 large blisters with the days of the month printed next to them. All of the tablets or capsules to be taken at a given date and time are packaged within the appropriate blister. The United States Pharmacopoeia has published official guidelines for labeling

Table 13-2 Medication Regimen for Mrs. C.

Quinidine gluconate 324mg	i q6h
Klotrix 10 mEq	ii bid
Lanoxin 0.125mg	i qod
Calan 80mg	i q8h
Bumex 1mg	ii bid
Isordil 10mg chewable	1/4 qid
Coumadin 5mg	i qd
Zantac 150mg	i hs
Diazepam 2mg	i tid
Carafate 1 gram	i qid ac and hs
Gaviscon foamtab	i-ii tid pc prn gas
Diprosone cream 0.05%	apply to rash bid
NitroDur 5mg	apply i patch daily
Phenergan suppositories 25mg	i rectally q6h prn nausea

and storing patient med-paks (i.e., the ASCO calendar card and other cards designed to hold multiple doses).[12]

For the visually impaired patient, the pharmacist can punch holes into the top of the card to identify the correct time of day.

The patient begins with the first blister and, by feeling the way, proceeds down the row as the days progress.

All routinely prescribed medications, that is, those that are taken on a regular basis, are packaged and hermetically sealed into the calendar card. Only one month's supply is dispensed at a time to avoid waste. Medications to be taken every other day (or only on Sunday and Wednesday, for example) would be placed in the appropriate blister corresponding to the correct date. Half tablets are broken by the pharmacist, then sealed in the blister. Hence, the card is customized for each patient. All routine medications can automatically be filled for the patient each month, and there is no need for the patient or family to reorder these medications.

Medications to be taken only as needed (i.e., not on a regular basis) are packaged individually in separate "p.r.n." cards. These medications must be reordered, since the pharmacist cannot anticipate when the p.r.n. medications will need to be refilled. This is also true for eye drops, liquids, and ointments.

In order for the system to work, the patient must patronize a single pharmacy, because the dispensing pharmacist must have a complete record of all the patient's medication, both prescription and nonprescription. The pharmacist can then monitor the medication each time a new order is prescribed. When an irregularity is noted, the physician, visiting nurse, or family member—whoever is the appropriate caregiver—can be contacted to address the problem.

The calendar card permits quick and accurate monitoring for patient compliance. One look at a patient's cards can provide the caregiver with good evidence that the patient is taking (or failing to take) the medications as directed. The cards permit any caregiver (even a residential staff member) to assist patients in taking the correct doses, because the doses are prepackaged by the pharmacist. Thus the untrained caregiver does not have to select the correct prescription vials for the patient.

In the case of Mrs. C., the resident manager or the staff can look at the cards to assess her compliance with her doctor's orders. When a problem is noted, it can immediately be referred to the pharmacist, visiting nurse, family member, or physician. The pharmacist has a complete record of all medications. The resident manager can make a reasonable judgment about patient compliance, and steps can be taken to follow up on any problem noted.

Consultant Pharmacy Services in Home Care

Home health care providers need to be educated about pharmacy services and pharmacists need to demonstrate the advantages of their participation in the delivery of quality patient care. Home care is essentially multidisciplinary. The consultant pharmacist can play a major role as a member of the team.

Medicare guidelines currently delegate the drug-monitoring function to the nurse. Nurses are expected to supervise drug administration, to educate patients about their drug regimen, and to "identify ineffective and contraindicated medications" (Medicare conditions of participation). Reluctance to utilize a consultant pharmacist to assist in this function may be due to a lack of awareness of pharmacist expertise in drug therapy management or, worse, a fear of loss of control or authority by the nurse or physician.

Agencies are reimbursed by the number of visits, and nurses cannot afford to waste time in the delivery of services. When a complicated medication problem is identified, it would be most efficient to refer this problem to the professional with the training and expertise to solve the problem. As previously noted, the federal government believes this expertise is held by the pharmacist (this is shown by the guidelines for nursing home participation). Indeed, several nursing associations have written in support of the pharmacist-monitoring function.

The objectives of a consultant pharmacy service in home care are listed below:

- to increase patient compliance
- to decrease drug-related problems
- to enhance effective and safe use of medications
- to decrease admission or readmission to an institution

The range of consultant pharmacy services that can be offered to a home health agency is as follows:

1. pain and symptom control consultation for home hospice patients
2. medication record review
3. drug information
4. newsletter
5. home visits
6. staff in-service education
7. development of policy and procedures
8. participation in the agency's utilization review committee
9. establishment of drug-related policies and procedures
10. provision of compliance packaging

THE MEDICATION RECORD

Contents

A medication record should include complete documentation of medications and should identify patients at risk for drug-related problems. The record should include not only prescription and nonprescription medications being used, but also "other medications" in the home, including health food products that might have pharmacologic activity and medications that have been prescribed by other physicians or recommended by friends. In a home health agency, it is the nurse's responsibility to take the drug history and complete the medication record form. However, the consultant pharmacist can provide in-service education on how to take a complete drug history, and community pharmacists can be utilized by agency staff to provide more complete drug history information (e.g., prescription refill records and costs of medications).

In addition to listing medications, the medication record should indicate all prescribers, all pharmacies where medications are purchased, and the patient's functional status (e.g., mental status, physical or sensory impairments, and living arrangements). The medication record presented in Exhibit 13-1 uses a check-off format whenever possible for the convenience of both the nurse and the pharmacist. This medication record was developed and tested through a team effort by agency staff, administration, and the consultant pharmacist, and it has been adopted for agencywide use.

Exhibit 13-1 Medication Record Review Form

MEDICATION RECORD REVIEW

Patient: _____ Phone: _____ District: _____
Diagnosis: _____ Birth date: _____
Pharmacy: _____ Pharmacy Phone: _____
Allergies: _____
Pharmacy consult requested: No _____ Yes _____

Check if present (index of risk for drug-related problems):

_____ History of noncompliance   _____ Lives alone
_____ Poor nutrition   _____ History of substance abuse:
_____ Dentures/poor dentition   _____
_____ Visual impairment   _____ Hearing impairment
_____ Joint disease   _____ Paralysis
_____ Bedbound   _____ Renal disease
_____ Hepatic disease   _____ Cardiac disease

Nonprescription Medications (name, dose, route, regimen)

Cough/cold _____   Analgesics _____
Antacids _____   Ear, eye, nose, throat _____
Topical _____   Laxatives/antidiarrheals _____
Antiemetics _____   Vaginal products _____
Vitamins/minerals _____   Other _____

Date: _____   Signature: _____

Prescription Medications (name, dose, route, regimen)	Prescriber	How Long?	Date Disc.	Comments

Medication Record Review

Ideally, the consultant pharmacist should review every medication record. Since the nurse case manager often has the home care chart, it is important that the medication record be completed thoroughly upon a patient's admission to home care services. The consultant pharmacist may receive a copy of every medication record and make written comments (assessments and recommendations) when appropriate. Or the nurse can request a pharmacy consult, for example, regarding a noncompliant patient or information about a specific drug.

The pharmacy note should be entered into the patient's chart and used as information for the nurse, prescriber, or patient. A home visit by the consultant pharmacist to deal with complex situations is also an option. In any case, the consultant clinical pharmacist should be available, perhaps through a beeper arrangement, for immediate questions.

QUALITY OF CARE AND THE HOME CARE PATIENT

Two cases are presented that illustrate how consultant pharmacy services directly affect quality of care.

Case 1

The patient is an 82-year-old woman with congestive heart failure, hypertension, mitral regurgitation, and arthritis. Her medication record was routinely reviewed by one of the home health agency consultant pharmacists. Her medications are listed below:

- Digoxin 0.25 mg q.d.
- Captopril 25 mg t.i.d.
- Naprosyn 250 mg b.i.d.
- Furosemide 20 mg q.d.
- Colace 100 mg q.d.

The consultant pharmacist recommended monitoring closely for signs and symptoms of digoxin toxicity (nausea, anorexia, weight loss, depression, mental status changes, pulse changes) and contacting the clinical consultant pharmacist if digoxin toxicity was suspected. After a case conference between the consultant pharmacist and the nurse, the pharmacist called the physician to recommend holding the digoxin and ordering a serum digoxin concentration and electrolytes because of a change in mental status and anorexia. The patient was indeed digoxin toxic and hypokalemic. One week later, after administration of potassium and adjustment of the digoxin dose at home, the patient was no longer confused, appetite was improved, and the digoxin serum concentration was no longer elevated.

Case 2

Upon routine medication record review, the consultant clinical pharmacist noted that a patient with allergy to sulfa drugs received a prescription for Bactrim (trimethoprim and sulfamethoxazole). The pharmacist contacted the nurse, who was unaware that Bactrim contains a sulfanamide antibiotic. In addition, the patient had developed a rash on his fingers and arms since starting the Bactrim the previous day. The consultant pharmacist instructed the patient to hold the Bactrim, contacted the physician, and instructed the nurse to monitor the skin for exacerbation of the rash.

Both cases illustrate the multidisciplinary approach to drug therapy in the home care setting. The problem in each case was potentially life threatening. Without the intervention of the consultant pharmacist, it is probable that hospitalization, or even death, could have ensued.

REIMBURSEMENT FOR PHARMACEUTICAL SERVICES IN HOME CARE

Medicare is the largest single source of reimbursement for many home health agencies. Agencies may include the cost of consultant pharmacy services in the overhead expenses under Administrative Costs—General. Pertinent information is found in the *Medicare Provider Reimbursement Manual*, Section 2119B #2 (costs related to patient care). Consultant pharmacy services may sometimes be justified as quality assurance or staff education.

Most pharmacists need to charge a small additional fee for packaging medication in special cards, such as the ASCO calendar card described above. Pharmacists are currently seeking third party reimbursement for this service, which may ultimately result in a saving if the patient can be assisted with compliance.[13]

CONCLUSION

Once a home health agency decides to provide consultant clinical pharmacy services, it must be determined how much money the agency can afford to pay for the services. Once again, these services are reimbursable through Medicare as an allowable overhead expense. However, it may not be possible for a home health agency to budget additional overhead expenses if cost capitations have been exceeded.

Agency administrators may contact community pharmacists, the local or state professional pharmacy associations, or the regional school of pharmacy to identify qualified consultant pharmacists. Services can range from a full menu, including complete medication review, in-service education programs, and specialized compliance packaging and drug monitoring to just one or two services, depending on the needs of the agency. Exhibit 13-2 lists state-of-the-art pharmacy

Exhibit 13-2 State-of-the-Art Services Offered by Dispensing and Consultant Pharmacists*

Dispensing Pharmacy Services

Selling drug products

- prescription
- nonprescription

Providing drug packaging systems

- compliance packaging
- "reminder" devices

Providing medical equipment

- durable medical equipment
- fittings, braces, supports
- incontinence products
- ostomy supplies

Providing consultation for patients and caregivers

- prescription drug information
- nonprescription drug selection
- nutrition supplements

Providing wellness and preventive medicine

Making referrals to community resources for patients and caregivers

Providing community drug education programs

Clinical Consultant Services

Reviewing drug regimen

Providing drug information to patients and professional caregivers

Providing pharmacokinetic consultation

Prescribing (to a limited extent) in conjunction with physicians

Providing nutritional assessments

Monitoring and making recommendations concerning laboratory results regarding drug therapy

*These services often overlap depending on site of practice of pharmacist.

---

services offered by dispensing and consultant pharmacists. Indeed, interested pharmacists may take the initiative to contact home health agencies.

It cannot be emphasized enough that in order for home care to continue to be successful, care providers must choose the multidisciplinary approach, as they have already done in the long-term care sector. As long as medications continue to be a major tool of disease management, especially management of chronic conditions, the pharmacist will be an indispensable member of the home health care team.

NOTES

1. M.J. Koren, "Home Care—Who Cares?" *New England Journal of Medicine* 314 (1986): 917–20.

2. U.S. Congress, Office of Technology Assessment, *Technology and Aging in America*, 99th Cong., 1st sess., 1985.

3. P.P. Lamy, "New Dimensions and Opportunities," *Drug Intelligence and Clinical Pharmacy* 19 (1985): 399–402.

4. P.P. Lamy, "The Needs of the Elderly Patient," in *Home Health Care Practice*, ed. P.N. Catania and M.M. Rosner. (Palo Alto, Calif.: Health Markets Research, 1986), 279–88.

5. S.W. Kidder, "The Cost Benefit of Drug Reviews in Long Term Care Facilities," *American Pharmacy*, n.s. 22, no. 7 (1982): 63–67.

6. I.H. Zuckerman et al., "Consultant Pharmacy Services to a Home Health Agency," *Consultant Pharmacist* (1986): 123–28.

7. P.P. Lamy, "Nonprescription Drugs," in *Prescribing for the Elderly* (Boston: PSG Publishing, 1980), 314–44.

8. M. Feinberg, "High-Tech Pharmacy and Home Care: A Sophisticated Partnership," *Caring* 5, no. 9 (September 1986): 35–38.

9. American Society of Consultant Pharmacists, *ASCP Member Profile* (Arlington, Va.: Author, 1985). This is a survey of the leading practitioners in consultant pharmacy.

10. R.W. Gehres, "Medication Compliance Aids," *Consultant Pharmacist* 1 (1986): 218–20.

11. B.S.M. Wong and D.C. Norman, "Evaluation of a Novel Medication Aid: The Calendar Blister-Pak and Its Effect on Drug Compliance in a Geriatric Outpatient Clinic," *Journal of the American Geriatrics Society* 35 (1987): 21–26.

12. Customized Patient Medication Packages. The United Pharmacopoeia XXI, 4th suppl. (United States Pharmacopoeial Convention, Rockville, Md.: 1986): 2249–50.

13. M. Feinberg, "Drug Packaging and Medication Compliance in Home Care: The Pharmacist's Expertise," *U.S. Pharmacist Rutgers Symposium Special Supplement* (October 1987): 31–38.

Practice Issues Affecting Quality

Chapter 14

High Tech: Implications for Quality Assurance

Lydia (Penny) Tanner

Home health care agencies presently are, and in the future will be, providing care in the home that was unimaginable a decade ago. Commonly referred to as "high-tech home care," it encompasses a broad spectrum of care that was originally thought to be safe only if delivered in the hospital setting. What kind of health care should be called "high-tech" is relative to the setting. High-tech home care usually involves the delivery of the following types of services in the home:

- I.V. therapies such as antibiotics, chemotherapy, total parenteral nutrition, and blood product administration
- enteral nutritional support
- oxygen and ventilator support
- phototherapy
- outpatient support
- continuous ambulatory peritoneal dialysis

The provision of the above types of services puts the patients and the home care agency at risk and demands a staff who are not only able to competently deliver the service 24 hours a day, but also able to teach the mechanics of the care to the clients and families. Regulatory agencies, physicians, clients and families require the home care agency to deliver high-tech services safely and effectively. It is imperative that the agency has an internal mechanism for review of the care it provides. Not only will an internal review process ensure that care is delivered safely and effectively, but it will also reduce the risk to clients and to the agency itself.

COMMON CHARACTERISTICS OF HIGH-TECH HOME CARE

What are the common characteristics of high-tech home care services? Answering this question will help the agency that delivers high-tech home care to design an internal quality assurance program which will effectively evaluate the services it provides (regardless of the particular modality) and thus contribute toward the highest quality of care.

High-tech home care services generally require the following:

- home care staff who can competently deliver the particular high-tech services
- twenty-four-hour service and an effective on-call mechanism
- timely referral responses (often same day or within hours of referral)
- very accurate initial assessments of the ability of clients and families to manage prescribed treatment plans prior to discharge from the hospital and the delivery of services in the home
- accurate assessments of the ability of clients and families to deliver or monitor care once clients are in the home
- the ability to rapidly teach key components of the care to clients and families
- good, reliable working relationships with the vendors supplying pharmaceutical products or equipment
- delivery of care without incidents or complications that might seriously endanger the well-being of clients

Competent High-Tech Staff

One of the first steps for a HHCA that wants to render high-tech home care is to decide who will deliver this care. This might entail hiring staff who have prior experience in the area of high-tech, upgrading current staff skills, or contracting with another agency that has appropriate staff. Regardless of which process the agency takes to ensure that home care professionals are in place who can deliver high-tech care, it is necessary to substantiate that they are appropriately trained and to evaluate the care they provide on an ongoing basis.

The evaluation of health care professionals is often subjective and based on the reviewers' particular priorities, however objective they desire to be. Such subjectivity should be avoided in the case of high-tech care. The evaluator must use acceptable standards of care in the reviewing process. In the area of intravenous therapy, for example, standards of care have been developed by the National Intravenous Therapy Association. Whenever possible, standards of care that have been developed for the delivery of high-tech care in the hospital setting should be adapted or modified for the home care setting.

A home care agency that has its own home health care staff and also uses the services of a contracting agency must not restrict evaluation to its own staff. The staff evaluation process must encompass the appropriate staff of the contracting agency. This requires a good working relationship with the contracting agency and a mandated sharing of evaluation reports. The home care agency that uses contractual services must be apprised of the contracting agency's hiring practices and criteria, since the staff of that agency will be representing the home care agency.

Around-the-Clock Services

Home health care in the past was a nine-to-five service, with perhaps weekend coverage for certain clients. Now most home care agencies offer at least 24-hour availability by pager. The home care agency that provides high-tech care must recognize that 24-hour coverage by pager is not enough. The agency must be capable of providing visits regardless of the hour—day or night, seven days a week. Monitoring the on-call process and the agency's ability to respond to the needs of clients in a timely fashion is essential for the quality assurance program.

Referral Response Time

High-tech clients not only require same day service, but often demand that the first visit to the home occur within hours of the referral. If the visit does not occur at the time requested, a client's well-being could be jeopardized and the treatment plan might have to be altered significantly. Meeting these demands must always be a high priority for an agency providing high-tech home care.

Accurate Initial Assessment

One of the most important considerations in providing high-tech home care is the initial ability of a client or family to manage the care between nursing visits and to solve problems on an ongoing basis. Home care agencies often rely heavily on a discharge planner's or social worker's appraisal of the client or family. It is the nurse, though, who makes the first visit and has the responsibility of accurately assessing the family's ability to provide care and to solve problems. The agency must evaluate initial nursing assessments for accuracy and thoroughness. It can put itself at serious risk by continuing to provide high-tech care if the client or family is unable to manage the mechanics of care.

Ongoing Assessment and Teaching

The high-tech patient, although usually stable medically, often has the potential of going "sour" in a short time. Nursing staff providing care must be able to identify appropriate assessment parameters for the client's particular problem and treatment modality and act on the assessments in a timely fashion. It is imperative that staff providing care to a high-tech client have excellent assessment skills and can communicate their findings quickly and effectively. The agency is required to evaluate the nurses' ongoing assessments and to monitor nursing interventions for appropriateness.

High-tech clients and their families require a great deal of instruction in order to manage the care between nursing visits. Often this instruction has to occur in a relatively short period of time and is necessarily restricted to key points. The nurse must be capable of providing the client with the essential information rapidly and effectively. It is important for the agency that appropriate teaching takes place and that it is effective.

Vendor Relationships

There are many different types of vendor relationships in today's home health care market. Regardless of the type of agreement the agency has with a vendor, there must be a good working relationship, including trust in each other's ability to provide services. The home care agency that relies on a vendor to supply clients with pharmaceuticals and equipment must have confidence in the vendor's own quality assurance program. Ultimately it is the home care agency's responsibility to assure that the equipment supplied functions correctly and that the pharmaceutical products are appropriately compounded, delivered, and stored. Thus, mechanisms for ongoing review of the products and equipment supplied are necessary.

Risk Management: Incidents and Complications

Everyone in home care desires to avoid any of the untoward incidents or complications that may occur. Of all the services

provided in the home, high-tech home care puts the client at greatest risk. The wrong medication or the incorrect delivery of a medication by the intravenous route could cause irreparable harm to the client. It is absolutely essential that the home care agency monitors all untoward incidents and complications that occur in the delivery of high-tech services. All such complications and incidents should be carefully analyzed to determine the reasons they occurred, and corrective action plans should be developed immediately.

AN EXAMPLE OF HIGH-TECH QUALITY ASSURANCE PLANNING: INTRAVENOUS THERAPY

The first step in developing a high-tech quality assurance plan (once the important aspects of care have been identified) is to determine the indicators (or the measurable dimension of the quality of care) for the various aspects of care delivered. The next step is to establish the measures or criteria by which the quality of care will be evaluated. Once indicators for the aspects of care are established and the criteria developed, one must determine by what mechanism data are to be collected and monitored.

Indicators for Intravenous Therapy

Aspect: Staff Competency

Indicator: All nursing professionals who provide intravenous (I.V.) therapy in the home have had appropriate experience and training in the delivery of intravenous therapy.

Criteria:

1. The home health agency has on file documentation of the professional nurse's I.V. therapy credentials and/or documentation of specific orientation/in-service training in the delivery of I.V. therapies.
2. The adherence to home intravenous therapy standards is verified through ongoing home visits by supervisors.

Monitors:

1. Personnel records that contain a particular nurse's credentials and state all in-services training pertaining to the delivery of I.V. therapies.
2. Performance appraisals that document that the nurse used appropriate techniques in the delivery of I.V. therapy based on National Intravenous Therapy Association (NITA) standards.

Aspect: Referral Response Time

Indicator: The home care agency provided visits at the time requested.

Criterion: Visits occur at the time requested by the referral source (regardless of the time of day).

Monitors: A record of all I.V. referrals with the specified times for first visit. At least quarterly, the agency reviews response time by correlating the time of the first visit with the time requested (documentation forms should include the time of the visit and the date). Any visit that does not occur at the specified time is documented as an unusual incident.

Aspect: Accurate Initial Assessment

Indicators:

1. The initial assessment was performed by a nurse trained or certified in the delivery of I.V. therapy.
2. The correctness of the initial assessment was verified through a home visit by the nurse's supervisor.
3. The client or family was instructed on appropriate problem-solving steps and the initial mechanics of I.V. therapy.
4. The client or family has verbalized an initial understanding of the specific I.V. therapy.
5. The client or family used the pager system appropriately within the first 24 hours of care.

Criterion: All nursing professionals who deliver I.V. therapy will perform an accurate initial assessment of the ability of the patient or family to manage care and to solve problems.

Monitors:

1. Focused record review (at least quarterly) of initial nursing assessments of all clients receiving I.V. therapy.
2. Performance appraisals that document that the nurse appropriately assessed the initial ability of the client or family to manage care.
3. Specific I.V. record form that documents teaching performed during the initial home visit.
4. Documentation of unexpected visits or use of on-call pager system prior to the next scheduled visit because of an inability to manage the required care.
5. Record review (at least quarterly) of all documented telephone interventions.

Aspect: Ongoing Assessment and Teaching

Indicators:

1. Assessments and interventions are accurate and appropriate.
2. Appropriate teaching is provided during each visit.

Criteria:

1. The correctness of assessments is verified through a home visit by the nurse's supervisor.

2. Alterations occur in therapy based on the nurse's assessments and interventions.
3. The client or family is independent in the delivery of I.V. therapy by the third visit.
4. The client or family verbalizes understanding of the particular I.V. therapy.

Monitors:

1. Performance appraisals that document the nurse's ability to do a focused assessment based on the client's particular problems.
2. Record review of all nursing interventions that resulted in a change in therapy. Record review of unexpected hospitalizations of I.V. patients.
3. Identification and tabulation of the number of clients and families capable of delivering I.V. therapy independently.

Aspect: Vendor Relationships

Indicator: Vendors provided functioning equipment and correct pharmaceutical products on a timely basis.

Criteria:

1. Infusion pumps function correctly.
2. The client receives correct drug in appropriate solution with instruction on storage.
3. The client receives appropriate supplies for the delivery of intravenous therapy.

Monitors:

1. Documentation in client's record that equipment was in the home at the required time and in functioning order.
2. Documentation in the record that client received appropriate pharmaceutical products. Incident reports and on-call pager reports that document situations when equipment malfunctioned or incorrect products were delivered.
3. Record or statement of vendor's quality assurance plan on file.

Aspect: Incidents and Complications

Indicator: The delivery of I.V. therapy occurred without incident or complications.

Criteria:

1. I.V. therapy is delivered according to acceptable standards (NITA) in a timely fashion, as verified by documentation, a home visit made by the nurse's supervisor, and chart review.

2. The client or family demonstrate correct technique in the delivery of I.V. therapy, as verified by a home visit by the I.V. nurse.
3. All incidents and complications are recorded and analyzed. A corrective action plan is developed.

Monitors:

1. Specific I.V. record form that documents complications specific to the delivery of I.V. therapy (see Exhibit 14-1).
2. Quarterly review of incident reports (see Exhibit 14-2).
3. Report that analyzes the reason the event occurred and states corrective action plan.

EXTERNAL REVIEW PROCESS

In addition to the internal review process, the home care agency should develop a mechanism to substantiate its customers' satisfaction with the high-tech services it provides. Customers might include physicians, other referral sources, and clients and their families. One approach is to utilize a satisfaction survey germane to a particular customer's concerns (see Exhibit 14-3). This will give the agency a sense of how well the customer's needs were met and help it to modify its services appropriately. In today's competitive home care market, one must remember that an unsatisfied customer does not return to use the service again and often tells others that the service was unacceptable. The harsh reality of providing high-tech service is that the home care agencies that meet their customers' needs are the ones that will survive.

CONCLUSION

In *Megatrends*, John Naisbitt noted that "we are moving in the dual directions of high tech/high touch, matching each new technology with a compensatory human response."[1] The client receiving high-tech home care services generally requires an array of therapeutic supports, including complex equipment and skilled intervention by professionals. The attractiveness of high-tech home care is not necessarily the technology but the healing potential of the home environment. The need for "high touch," that is, the necessity of incorporating the human factor into the plan of care, must be reflected in the client-professional interaction. The balance between high tech and high touch is dependent on the home care provider's ability to personalize care and to use the mechanical devices to enhance and not obstruct the professional's clinical skills of caring for and with the client.

In an effort to monitor the relevant behaviors, each home care agency must develop and implement a quality assurance plan that will demonstrate the quality of its high-tech services, including the content of the services, the professional judg-

Exhibit 14-1 I.V. Record Form

Rush Home Health Service   I.V. Flow Sheet and Narrative Progress Note

Patient Name _____ ID# _____ Date _____

Left column	Right column

Allergies _____

Time _____ Temp. _____ Pulse _____ Resp. _____

B/P R _____ B/P L _____

Weight _____ Edema _____

Lungs R _____ Lungs L _____

Site change: Yes   No   Device used _____

Central line type _____

Site temp./color/location _____

_____

Dressing _____

Cap change _____

_____

Medication/Solution   Dose   Freq.

_____
_____
_____
_____
_____
_____

Flush _____

Administered by RN: Yes   No

Bowel/abdomen _____

Bladder/output _____

Appetite/diet _____

Lab work _____

_____
_____
_____
_____
_____

Complications of Infusion Therapy

	YES	NO
MECHANICAL:		
Obstructed or clotted catheter/device		
Vein thrombosis		
Infiltrated or dislocated catheter		
Faulty infusion pump/controller		
METABOLIC:		
Diarrhea		
Electrolyte imbalance		
Acid-base disorder		
Hyper/hypoglycemia		
Trace element deficiency		
Allergic reaction		
Fluid overload		
SEPTIC:		
Redness around catheter site		
Drainage from catheter site		
Temperature >101		
Positive culture of catheter tip		
JUDGMENTAL:		
Patient centered:		
Noncompliance		
Refusal of Rx/removal of device		
Patient/family inability to care for line		
Professional centered:		
Inappropriate drug/solution, admin.		
Duration of therapy too short for effective treatment		

Prob. No.   NARRATIVE PROGRESS NOTE

_____
_____
_____
_____
_____
_____
_____
_____
_____
_____
_____
_____
_____

if needed, cont. on Narrative Progress Note   RN Signature _____

Source: Courtesy of Rush Home Health Service, Chicago, Illinois.

---

ment of the providers of the service, and the agency's use of financial and human resources. A plan that includes program evaluation, appraisals from individuals who have used the service (e.g., clients, families, physicians, and vendors), and risk management and utilization reviews will consistently result in problem identification and resolution and improved client care. It is not enough merely to assume that the care provided is excellent; the care must be quantifiable, competently documented, and subjected to quality assurance monitors.

Exhibit 14-2 Incident Report

METHODOLOGY FOR DATA COLLECTION	CRITICAL ANALYSIS
Responsible person: Sample size: Data source: Acceptable level of conformance:	
CONCLUSION Extent of problem: Cause of problem: Significance of problem:	ACTION PLAN Responsible person: Date of evaluation of action plan:

Exhibit 14-3 Customer Satisfaction Survey

1. How did you first find out that you needed to have an I.V. at home?

   a. Were you or your family part of the decision-making process?

   b. Do you know why you needed to have an I.V. at home?

2. Did more than one nurse visit you concerning your I.V.?

3. Did you feel that the nurses visited often enough to help you with your I.V.?

4. If more than one nurse visited you during this time, did you feel that they used the same techniques (did things the same way) with your I.V.?

5. Did you ever have to contact the agency about a problem with your I.V.?

   a. If so, why?

   b. Had the home care nurse instructed you on how to call about the problem so you clearly understood how to do so?

   c. If you did call, did you reach a nurse easily?

   d. How long did it take to solve the problem once you called?

6. Were you (or your family) responsible for giving yourself any of the I.V. fluid or medication?

   a. If yes, what did you have to do?

   b. Do you feel that you were well instructed about what to do?

   c. If not, what didn't you understand?

   d. Do you feel that you needed more time with the nurses for this?

7. Were you instructed on what to do in an emergency concerning the I.V.?

   a. Do you feel that you understood this well?

   b. If not, what didn't you understand?

8. What was the best part of this experience?

   a. Was there a good part?

   b. What was the worst part?

   c. Was there anything that you didn't like about it?

9. Overall, on a scale of one to five, how satisfied were you with the I.V. nursing services you received?

10. Is there anything else that you would like to add?

NOTE

1. John Naisbitt, *Megatrends* (New York: Warner Books, 1982), 1.

REFERENCES

Gardner, C. ''I.V. Quality Assurance Provides Risk Management.''

Haddad, Amy. *High Tech Home Care: A Practical Guide*. (Rockville, Md.: Aspen Publishers, 1987).

NITA 8 (January-February 1985): 199–204.

NITA 7 (March-April 1984): 93.

Roebuck, M. ''The Effects of Quality Assessment on I.V. Therapy.'' *NITA* 7, no. 2 (March-April 1984): 103–104.

Nursing Standards of Practice: Home I.V. Therapy.

Chapter 15

Legal and Ethical Dilemmas Related to Quality Assurance

Ann Helm

Home health care, the fastest growing segment of the health care system, is in transition. Due to technological advances, government health policy, and changing consumer attitudes, the move to a different arena of delivery, namely the home, has presented unique and complex ethical and legal concerns for both the providers and consumers. The experience of caregivers in hospital settings provides a useful starting point for addressing some of these issues.

ETHICS COMMITTEES

The formation of ethics committees increased after the New Jersey Supreme Court ruling in the Karen Quinlan case; the ruling recommended that a "prognosis committee" should evaluate patients before life support systems could be withdrawn.[1] In March 1983, the President's Commission for the Study of Ethical Problems in Medicine and Biomedical and Behavioral Research emphasized the role of ethics committees again in *Deciding to Forego Life-Sustaining Treatment*.[2] This publication contains guidelines for the establishment of hospital ethics committees. Specifically, the commission believed ethics committees could provide a mechanism for decision making on behalf of incompetent patients and could improve the medical options available to dying patients.

The American Hospital Association (AHA) has also endorsed the concept of hospital ethics committees and has provided guidelines for their formation and performance.[3] The AHA guidelines indicate that everyone involved in a hospital, from trustees to volunteers, patients, and the families of patients, should have access to the ethics committee.

A survey conducted in 1985 by the AHA's National Society for Patient Representatives indicated that 59 percent of American hospitals had ethics committees. Only two years prior to that survey, the percentage was roughly 30 percent. Undoubtedly, even more hospitals have ethics committees today. *Ethics Committees in Hospitals*, published by the Kennedy Institute of Ethics, succinctly discusses the history, composition, and role of such committees.[4]

Typically the committees are multidisciplinary and serve in an advisory capacity with respect to policy, help to resolve ethical problems, and provide educational programs. Some institutions have "ethics rounds" or a system of on-call consultations. Typically the issues posed to ethics committees involve no code or Do Not Resuscitate concerns, withdrawal of life support, informed consent or refusal, living wills, access to health care, and determination of competency.

An ethics committee can help to meet the ethical and legal responsibilities of the hospital. Many areas of practice also have profession-specific codes of ethics, for example, *The American College of Physicians' Ethics Manual*.[5] The American Nurses Association,[6] Licensed Practical Nurse Association, and other bodies have also published profession-specific codes of ethics. While the AHA policy on patients' rights focuses on consumers' rights, the codes of practice indicate the obligations of health professionals. Earlier professional codes simply affirmed professional judgments in a very paternalistic style, but more recent codes stress the patient's right of autonomy.[7]

Ethics committees received wide support as an alternative to the court system for protecting client rights. However, as Dr. Lo states, "They must be perceived as fair as the courts," since the legal system affords due process and many other constitutional rights.[8] They must be viewed as providing assurance of client rights rather than being an institutional defense system. Ethics committees are not a panacea. They may raise more problems than they solve; they may give rise to peer pressure and group think or simply codify institutional politics and power.[9] If members are aware of these potential hazards, they can more genuinely assess issues brought before them.

Although the literature is generous with respect to ethics committees, very little exists that addresses the role of ethics committees in the area of home care. Ethics committees have been formed for specialized areas such as Baby Doe cases or nursing home issues but seldom for home health. However, the principles or recommendations for formation, composition, and role are to some extent transferable from the acute care setting to that of home health. Obviously, many ethical issues would change dramatically outside of the institutional environment.

Logistically, establishing an ethics committee for home health care may be more challenging than establishing one within an institution, since providers are working much more autonomously and in more diverse and possibly more complex environments than the hospital. However, the composition of a home health ethics committee is more likely to result in a genuine multidisciplinary forum than in the case of a hospital committee. Furthermore, home health ethics committees could serve to complement and support the autonomous practice and provide a source of risk management for decision making to balance the higher level of responsibility that home health practitioners agree to accept.[10]

CLIENT RIGHTS AND RESPONSIBILITIES

The AHA published "A Patient's Bill of Rights" in 1975 as a policy statement, and it has remained in effect since that date.[11] While that particular statement addresses rights, in reality rights co-exist in balance with responsibilities. Some states have incorporated patient rights into state statutes, giving these rights legislative weight. At a minimum, many states have enumerated specific patient rights (e.g., nursing home patient rights are articulated in most statutes concerned with nursing homes).

Regardless of the existence of the AHA policy and the state statutes, the foundation for most patient rights are within the U.S. Constitution. A state constitution can afford to recognize more rights than the U.S. Constitution, but not less. For instance, the right of privacy, which is woven into the U.S. Constitution's Bill of Rights, establishes the patient's right to informed consent *or* informed refusal, the right of confidentiality, and the right to have access to the medical record and related information. A specific right within the AHA policy statement that concerns home care is #10: "The right to expect reasonable continuity of care."

Client rights and responsibilities assume different dimensions in the home environment. Obviously the legal and eth-

ical rights of clients remain solidly intact. However, since the health care provider is on the client's turf, presumably more autonomy and less dependency exists.

Home health care more readily involves significant others and family members. At the same time, additional ethical dilemmas may arise with respect to the assumption of responsibility by caregivers. Caregivers need assessments and education from home care providers tailored specifically to the particular home environment, level of ability to assist in the care of the client, and coping ability. Caregivers and home care providers have an additional duty to identify when the client needs to return to the physician or institution.[12] It is up to the health care provider to assess the appropriate level of responsibility to be assumed by the client and the caregivers within the home.[13]

ETHICAL DILEMMAS

The study of bioethics provides exposure to ethical theories, principles, and rules and can assist health care providers and others in resolving ethical dilemmas. Many factors come into play in dealing with a dilemma, including professional norms, individual value systems, religious beliefs, allocation of scarce resources, and institutional values.

Two classic ethical theories exist. The first is utilitarianism, propounded by Hume, Bentham, and John Stuart Mill.[14] In summary, this theory holds that what is good supersedes right or duty, or that the end justifies the means. It also holds that an act is right if it leads to the utilitarian theory, greatest good for the greatest number, at least according to some interpretations. The other major ethical theory was developed by Kant. This theory holds that the concept of duty (or of right) is independent of the concept of good. In reality, the two theories are usually blended when dealing with ethical dilemmas.

Ethical dilemmas have been described as situations where there is no single right or wrong answer. Some of the ethical dilemmas frequently seen in health care institutions involve

- informed consent or refusal
- issues related to competency, confidentiality, and privacy
- truth telling
- use of placebos
- human experimentation
- Do Not Resuscitate orders
- decisions to withdraw life-sustaining treatment
- abandonment
- whistleblowing

Other ethical dilemmas in medicine involve gene splitting, genetic screening, the definition of death, access to health care, and compensation for research injuries. Defining death is presumably less of an issue in the home than in an institution. Research issues, as well as some of the other issues, are also conceivably less disconcerting to home care providers at this moment, but their importance could certainly increase significantly as home health care horizons rapidly expand.

Informed Consent

Informed consent is an ethical and a legal imperative. Capacity is a prerequisite of competency; capacity is established by age, by statute, and varies from state to state. The law assumes that all people are competent unless adjudicated otherwise through a court hearing and with the establishment of a guardian. Providers should assume that clients are competent. The legal determination of competency is, in general, much more generous than a psychiatric determination of competency. To establish informed consent or refusal, there must be (1) a competent client, (2) a voluntary consent or refusal, (3) information that a reasonable person would want or need in order to make a decision, (4) risks involved in the proposed treatment, (5) alternatives (including no treatment), and (6) risks involved in the alternatives. Voluntary consent can presumably be achieved more readily in the home, away from the paternalistic or potentially coercive hospital environment. Provision of care without informed consent could result in allegations of assault or battery (touching that is unconsented to).

"Blanket" consent has long been passé and is generally blatantly unethical. The duty to establish informed consent increases with the invasiveness of a procedure and the likelihood, frequency, and severity of the risks. However, it would be advisable to obtain consent at the outset of an agreement to provide home care and to incorporate in that consent specifically those procedures that are anticipated. Consent may designate a specific provider or procedure depending on the contractual arrangements for home care.[15] The Home Care Standards of the Joint Commission on Accreditation of Healthcare Organizations (Joint Commission) codify, in a sense, many of the legal and ethical rights of clients.[16] For instance, Standard #1 states that "the patient/client has the right to make informed decisions regarding his/her care." This clearly states the right to informed consent or refusal. The Home Care Standard #4 of the Joint Commission stipulates, "The patient/client is informed upon admission of the organization's mechanism for receiving, reviewing, and resolving patient/client complaints."

Confidentiality

Confidentiality is another client right. Confidentiality is based on the right to privacy, as is the legal and ethical right to informed consent and refusal. In an institutional setting, a health care provider may easily inadvertently (and inappropriately) share sensitive information regarding a patient. This may also occur in a home setting by giving information to family members or others not authorized by the client to receive it. For instance, the client may not wish to disclose the existence of terminal or self-inflicted conditions or of a positive HTLV test.

The Joint Commission's Home Care Standard #9 calls for policies "regarding the confidentiality of records and release of health information."

Professional Role

More so than the institutional environment, the home care setting may invite inappropriate provider-client relationships. If a provider returns to the home in another capacity or strives to serve as a friend as well as a health care provider, it is crucial to clearly establish what that role is and to indicate to the client that specific visits or interactions are outside of the formal health care process.

Whistleblowing

Providers have both a legal and an ethical duty to report incompetent colleagues, whether in an institutional or home care setting. Presumably, agency guidelines will exist for this process. Decisions about when and what to report must take into account the degree and frequency of incompetency. Failure to report may result in being charged as an accomplice to substandard care, elder abuse, and so forth. It may also result in agency liability.

Withdrawal of Life Support

As technology rapidly increases and allows for portability, classical dilemmas related to Do Not Resuscitate (DNR) orders and withdrawal of life support, including ventilator systems and nutrition, will often occur in the home setting. The incidence of chronic disease, the increase in the elderly population, rising health care costs, and the DRG movement will add to the frequency. Hospice care patients, AIDS patients, and terminally ill patients may indeed prefer the home over a high-tech environment. These issues intensify the responsibility of home health care providers to accurately assess caregivers' emotional, mental, and physical abilities to deal with the technology and the intensity of illness in the home setting. It is also critical to determine the client's wishes concerning a return to the hospital and the desired intensity of care should an acute episode develop.[17]

Abandonment

Just as the physician has the ultimate legal responsibility for discharge from the hospital, the home health care provider or agency has the responsibility for terminating care within an acceptable standard of practice. If the home care agency is affiliated with a hospital, the physician may well remain primarily responsible. Termination of care when the patient still needs that care can constitute ethical and legal abandonment, which can be a cause of action for a malpractice claim.

To avoid the client's perception of abandonment and to address the legal issues, the home care provider must be explicit with the client when care is being terminated and must document appropriately. If this is occurring because the client is noncompliant, the provider needs to indicate this clearly, refer the patient to other sources of care, and generally make an effort to assure continuity of care rather than allow care to end during a critical stage of illness.

More so than care providers in the hospital setting, the home care provider has a duty to identify any other conditions that may erupt in the immediate future. In the hospital, many other providers of different professions may identify respiratory distress, infections, contractures, and so forth; in the home, the health care provider has a duty to identify these events and make a referral back to the institution or physician.[18]

Scarce Resources

Home care providers commonly face dilemmas involving scarce resources, battling with the regulations and requirements of third party payers, federal and state governments, Medicare, and Medicaid. Too frequently, more money in itself may appear to be the "solution." Salladay raises what she believes is an important question: "Is there a responsibility to provide health care to people who cannot pay?"[19] In her case study, the patient's responsibility and level of compliance are thoroughly assessed and juxtaposed with the existing resources.

BIOETHICS: APPLICATION OF ETHICAL PRINCIPLES

Bioethics is the application of ethical principles in health care settings. One outcome of bioethics is the development of a larger range of options for problem solving. Applied ethics creates the opportunity for choice. Choice requires acting as a free moral agent. Decisions based on ethical theories are thus made in an intelligent, reflective manner instead of being mechanical, programmed, habitual, or discipline-determined.

With the assimilation of ethical decision making into one's repertoire of skills, ad hoc, emotive, or idiosyncratic decisions can be avoided. In turn, the underpinnings that allow one to live with the decision and oneself become stronger. Decision making requires responsibility, commitment, the weighing of risks and benefits, and the acceptance of accountability for choices. An ethical framework can provide the rationale for decisions while looking after the client's interests.

Bioethics has further implications for conflict resolution. Compared with avoiding conflict or abdicating decisions to other persons, playing an affirmative role in conflict resolution can promote individual and professional growth. In accepting and gaining responsibility, power is gained. Historical modes for conflict resolution fall into three basic types. One familiar mode is the use of force. Force is coercion or the exercise of authority without cooperation. Force is also used, although more subtly, in maintaining institutional, paternalistic norms and behaviors.

The second mode of conflict resolution is persuasion, for example, posing a good argument or using powers of persuasion. The final mode is democracy (or democratic decision making). This occurs in situations where clients, family members, and providers work as a team to resolve conflict and make care decisions. This mode can embrace dialogue, negotiation, and cooperation, and it can serve to diffuse the polarization brought about by an autocratic or traditional decision-making process. To take no action in conflict resolution is to abdicate power and autonomy as an individual.

Assessment of Ethical Dilemmas

Deciding what to do in an ethical dilemma requires an assessment of all the options. Typically, the health care provider will oversimplify the range of options because of a decrease in perceptual abilities resulting from the stress of undergoing a crisis. An ethical dilemma can be approached by using the following four-step process:

1. Gather as much information as possible in a value-free brainstorming effort. Keep in mind Bertrand Russell's observation that "we have an enormous talent for ignoring the obvious."
2. Determine the precise nature of the ethical dilemma in terms of ownership and source.
3. Decide what should be done and how it can best be done. This step involves attempting to use several different frameworks or the assessments of several people. Keep in mind that there are seldom "right" answers and that what is considered "best" will likely vary depending on perspectives of the provider, family, and client. The client's wishes should, with a few exceptions, be respected.
4. Do whatever has been decided upon.

Knowing ethical theories and being able to articulate and apply them can increase the quality of professional judgments and assist in meeting the unique challenges of home care. As Aristotle said, "Experience can promote ethical intelligence." Providers who can confidently involve themselves in difficult choices will help to humanize the health care environment. Appendix 15-A contains a bibliography for bioethics.

RISK MANAGEMENT: IMPLICATIONS FOR POLICY AND PRACTICE

While hospitals have had to adjust to the evolution of standards and accreditation requirements of the Joint Commission and other accrediting bodies, home care, actually a more traditional form of health care, has only recently come under public purview and entered the licensing and accreditation sphere. Home care providers at both individual and corporate levels are not necessarily starting at square one. Indeed, hearings before the Select Committee on Aging of the U.S. House of Representatives were conducted to ''highlight how little is known about the quality of care provided in the home and to draw public attention to the inadequacy of our current system of standards in quality assurance when it comes to home health care and supportive services.''[20] *The Black Box of Home Care Quality*, prepared by the American Bar Association for the select committee hearings, documents the lack of data on home care quality and inadequacy of the current system of standards.[21] It is at this stage that providers and agencies enter the arena.

Issues mentioned previously—the increasing elderly population, the high incidence of chronic disease, AIDS and other terminal diseases, the costs of health care, and the impact of DRGs—have all increased referrals to home care. The U.S. Senate Committee on Aging documented a 37 percent increase in home care referrals subsequent to the changeover to DRGs.[22] Also impacting the home care arena is the fact that many female members of households, who traditionally provided home care, are in the labor force. Implications for risk management policies and practices in home care amplify the need for a comprehensive approach to long-term care and illuminate the weaknesses in the Medicare and Medicaid system. Home care could easily become the cornerstone of a responsible national long-term care policy.

A detailed review of the congressional focus on this issue was published in *Caring*.[23] Obviously, risks are greater in some respects in the home environment due to the likely solitude of the health care provider in that setting, the diversity and potential complexity in the home itself, the distance from acute care resources, the variance in levels of support from caregivers in the home, the variance in the client's condition, and the existence of technology in the home. It is important to keep in mind, however, that the number of iatrogenic events in hospitals is tremendous, and there are strong arguments that hospitals are unsafe. Studies indicate that survival rates for persons receiving care at home are better than for those in institutions.[24]

Presumably, falls and other events that occur more readily in an unfamiliar environment can often be prevented in a client's home. To address risk management issues, home care agencies should develop explicit guidelines for standards of care. These guidelines should be approved by the agency or hospital providing care, and they should be consistent with the standards of quality assurance in the field. It is important that guidelines thoroughly address all areas of health care and set standards for dietitians, pharmacists, rehabilitation therapists, I.V. drug therapists, and biomed equipment manufacturers, as well as more traditional home care providers. While risk management is certainly important, focusing on each and every decision solely from a defensive perspective may entail the infringement of ethical principles.[25]

If decisions are made in good faith and according to current and reasonable professional standards of judgment, home health care providers can avoid the extension of defensive medicine into the home care environment.[26]

Agency and Corporate Liability

A home care agency has many potential liabilities. If it is hospital affiliated, it may ''steer'' hospital patients to its own home care program or that of a particular agency, possibly causing antitrust allegations. If the hospital owns a separate home health agency or has a substantial financial stake in it, a ''tying arrangement'' or monopoly may be alleged.[27]

The *Darling* case established corporate liability for hospitals; the legal theory could easily be extended to the home care environment. In brief, the home care agency can be sued for negligence if its providers practice substandard care. The employer is liable for the negligent acts of an employee under the doctrine of *respondeat superior*, and this can include volunteers. Medicare regulations for some programs classify volunteers as employees.[28] While historically immunity was granted to volunteers working within charitable organizations, more recently volunteer liability has been established. Essentially the more control an employer has over the volunteer, the more responsibility and liability may ensue. As with employees and volunteers, the home care agency may be legally responsible for contractors working with that agency, whether they are equipment providers, manufacturers, or other specialists.

As mentioned previously, opportunities for home care providers to establish relationships with patients as friends or volunteers are more common than in the hospital environment. Essentially, employees who act outside the scope of their employment do so at their own risk and the agency is not responsible for their actions, aside from the risk to the agency's public image.[29]

The Home Care Standards of the Joint Commission require every home care organization (1) to have a program designed to educate staff and clients in safety measures and (2) to develop what are essentially risk management policies.

Workers' Compensation

An employee could sue a home health agency if he or she contracted a communicable disease from a patient or another health care provider. One of the many unique features of home care is that the provider is under a duty to educate individuals in the home about safety procedures, including procedures to prevent the transmission of communicable disease, to prevent back injuries when lifting a client, and so forth.

It is imperative that home health agencies fully inform their employees and volunteers of the risks of employment to avoid allegations of fraud.[30] Risks may range from contracting contagious diseases such as AIDS to being attacked by a violent client. The risks of home care are increased as a result of the isolated setting in which providers work. The added risk can be addressed by agency guidelines mandating thorough client assessments with an emphasis on psychiatric symptoms.[31]

Formulation of a risk management policy or committee by the home health agency will clearly mitigate the potential liabilities. Such a policy should specifically identify a risk manager for the agency, granting this person sufficient authority and support from top management. The areas a risk management committee should routinely assess include

- documentation
- quality of care outcomes
- employee performance
- incidents
- malpractice allegations and awards
- employee injuries and claims
- client satisfaction surveys
- physician reports
- equipment malfunction reports
- infection rates
- unexpected deaths
- unscheduled hospitalizations
- turnover in staffing
- employee morale
- medication errors or adverse results
- caregiver proficiency
- on-call systems
- other high-risk, high-volume, or problem prone areas

In addition, it is crucial to implement appropriate corrective actions in these areas. Such actions may include (1) in-service education, (2) probation or termination of employees and volunteers, (3) renegotiation of contracts with independents, (4) reallocation of resources, (5) review of credentials and privileges, (6) revision of policies for staff selection and orientation, (7) increased staffing, and (8) enhanced communication systems through beepers and electronic monitoring.[32]

Employee Liability, Rights, and Responsibilities

Case law relating to the standard of care for home health is currently sparse. Therefore, the weight that courts and juries will give to the fact that care was provided in the home is unknown. As cases for failure to diagnose are increasing in the hospital setting, they likely will evolve in the home care setting, given the complexity of technology and the severity of illness of patients currently referred to home care.

To establish malpractice, the client must first establish the provider was a professional. Determination of this varies from state to state, according to case law interpretation or statute. The provider can be held responsible for negligence even if he or she had the best of intentions. Any citizen can be sued for negligence. For instance, if someone fell on ice covering your walkway, that person could sue you for negligence. Malpractice is a specific kind of lawsuit that concerns the conduct of professionals. To establish malpractice, the client would need to show that a client-provider relationship existed between the parties that gave rise to a duty and that that duty was breached through an omission or commission. In addition, the client would need to demonstrate actual physical harm from the

breach of duty and that the proximate cause of that harm was related to the provider's omission or commission. With respect to nurses' liability, R.N. student nurses are held to an R.N. or L.V.N./L.P.N. standard of practice. Faculty and educational institutions must respond to this responsibility. Contracts between institutions should clearly delineate all rights and responsibilities of students, faculty, educational institution, and home care givers.

To establish that malpractice occurred in court, there is usually expert testimony to validate that what the provider did met or failed to meet the standard of care. The length of time during which a client may sue the provider or agency varies from state to state, depending on the statute of limitations. The time period starts when the client either knew or should have known of the injury. In addition to suing for malpractice or negligence, the client may sue the provider for assault and battery if informed consent was not attained, for abandonment if termination of care was inappropriate, for invasion of privacy if confidential information was inappropriately released, for trespass if the provider came into the home without permission, and for misrepresentation if the provider failed to adequately identify him- or herself and the profession.[33]

As in the hospital setting, home health care providers may and should decline assignments for which they cannot assume full responsibility (i.e., cannot meet the standard of care).[34] A home care provider may also refuse to care for specific clients, such as AIDS patients or the terminally ill, if the provider is uncomfortable working with clients of that type. These issues need to be resolved prior to employment. It behooves providers to make sure that the agency they choose to work for is properly licensed and accredited for the state they choose to practice in. They should also make sure that the agency has (1) sufficient qualified staff, (2) staff orientation and education, (3) current and appropriate policies, and (4) properly functioning state-of-the-art equipment. The provider can respond to the increased risks in the home setting through (1) thorough home assessments, (2) ongoing assessments and instruction of clients and caregivers, (3) meticulous documentation, (4) preparation for the "unexpected," and (5) familiarity with agency policies and guidelines.[35]

It is recommended that the home health care provider carefully review the malpractice policy of the agency or hospital of employment and seriously consider obtaining personal professional liability insurance. The cost for such insurance in the area of home care is still low in comparison with acute settings, and there are situations in which the legal interests of the provider and the agency may diverge.[36]

Client Education and Documentation

With the increased availability of technology in the home, it is crucial that home care providers instruct clients on the appropriate use of equipment, generators, batteries, and backup systems, especially in the case of ventilators and respirators. One study discovered 31.4 percent of the noncompliant patients had inadequate discharge counseling about drugs.[37] Several studies have validated inadequate documentation of home care.[38]

This is an area where telephoning or electronically monitoring patients can substantially enhance the quality of care. One study indicated that a 48-hour postdischarge telephone assessment was a valuable tool for assessing the caregiver's knowledge of home care treatments and could possibly serve to prevent unscheduled readmissions.[39]

Documentation is undoubtedly the best defense against malpractice allegations; it is also good "insurance" for accreditation and other reviews of the provider and the agency. Portable dictating equipment can help ensure timely documentation between home visits.[40] In addition, while the home setting is certainly more informal than the hospital setting, this ought not to lead to "informal charting." For instance, derogatory comments regarding the home itself or the client's family can come back to haunt providers in court.

Product Liability and Knowledge of Equipment

Horsley describes a situation with a routine piece of equipment—a sphygmomanometer.[41] Although the glass had broken on the sphygmomanometer, the nurse felt she was still getting the same accurate reading as before, so she deferred getting it repaired. Subsequently, a patient developed transient ischemic attacks, with brief blackouts. Fortunately, the patient did not sustain residual injuries and the nurse's insurer settled for a small amount. This is an example, however, of how even "routine" equipment can set the stage for negligence. A provider may risk being held strictly liable in tort for using a defective piece of equipment. As Horsley emphasizes, the informal home environment lacks some of the routine safeguards of a hospital. For instance, the provider may need to interview the client to determine whether there are allergies to medications that the physician has prescribed. Appropriate action, such as notifying the physician or informing the client so he or she may do so, should be taken and documented in the client's record.

RESPONSIBILITIES OF THE AGENCY AND THE EMPLOYEE

Both the agency and employee have a duty to report certain situations to state health departments. The situations vary from state to state but they typically include instances of contagious disease. Reporting with respect to AIDS is in the developmental stage, and it behooves providers and agencies to keep up to date on state reporting laws. Among other situations, it is generally required to report suspected elder, child, or spouse abuse, which may include financial, emotional, or physical abuse or abandonment.

State law may exist to report dangerous or potentially dangerous clients or other individuals identified by the provider in the home setting. Case law exists to establish the duty of providers to report dangerous or potentially dangerous clients who threaten to harm the public at large or specific individuals. Anonymity is almost always assured for those complying with these reporting statutes; however, depending on the number of individuals coming into the home, the provider may feel vulnerable to exposure. Here an ethical dilemma may well arise, with the attendant soul searching.

While each of us has a right to privacy and confidentiality, this right is not absolute. It co-exists with a duty to protect the public. When a threat occurs to other individuals, whether it be exposure to contagious diseases or physical or emotional harm, the law establishes a duty to report the threat (even if it may be overreported). Providers and agencies also have duty to report any suspicious criminal behavior and divulge any evidence related to such. A duty to third parties exists in this area. For instance, a third party may sue the agency or the provider if the third party is indeed harmed by the client.[42]

ADMISSION AND DISCHARGE POLICIES

Continuity of care arrangements between the agency and the referring hospital or other health facility are extremely important for ensuring that a patient is discharged in a stable enough condition to tolerate the individual home environment and the support system. The intensity of care may be inappropriate for the family or for others in the home. While the home setting has many advantages that can enhance healing, inappropriate discharge, whether compounded by an inadequate home environment or not, may result in unscheduled readmissions to the acute care setting and potentially life-threatening complications. Many of the Home Care Standards proposed by the Joint Commission squarely address continuity of care, coordination, patient education, documentation, admission and discharge planning, and multidisciplinary teamwork in a home setting, including pharmacy, equipment, and nutrition services, among others.

A recent study indicated that patients who were readmitted to the hospital were less satisfied with the timing of their discharge and were good predictors of readmission. This study suggested readmission may be a result of inadequate aftercare.[43]

CONCLUSION

As standards of care are developed in home health care, the ethical and legal issues facing providers and consumers must be addressed. While Medicare law and regulations dominate the scope of the home health care industry, due to the absence of national standards of care, they furnish minimal protection for the provider and the consumer. Individual agencies must design written internal protocols, policies, and procedures that courts of law may cite as evidence of standards under which clients have a reasonable expectation of receiving care. Documenting the competency of agency employees and independent contractors as well as their individual rights and responsibilities is essential.

While responding to a variety of social, political, and economic factors, home health care agencies are also being squeezed financially by pressures exerted by government and private payers. In the absence of accepted national standards of care, the temptation is strong to reduce commitments to quality client care, even as acuity levels and the need for specialized care increase. One obvious solution is to have a coordinated process in which existing and potential ethical and legal issues impacting an agency, its employees, and the recipients of care can be identified and addressed by means of appropriate guidelines for practice.

NOTES

1. New Jersey Supreme Court, In Re: Karen Quinlan, 355 A2nd, 647 (March 31, 1976).

2. President's Commission for the Study of Ethical Problems in Medicine and Biomedical and Behavioral Research, *Deciding to Forego Life-sustaining Treatment: Ethical, Medical and Legal Issues in Treatment Decisions* (Washington, D.C.: GPO, March 1983).

3. American Hospital Association, Special Committee on Biomedical Ethics, *Values in Conflict: Resolving Ethical Issues in Hospital Care* (Chicago: Author, 1985), 30–35.

4. Pat McCarrick and Judith Adams, *Scope Note #3: Ethics Committees in Hospitals* (Washington, D.C.: Kennedy Institute of Ethics, June, 1987).

5. *American College of Physicians' Ethics Manual*, reprinted in *Annals of Internal Medicine* 101 (1984): 129–37, 263–74.

6. *Code for Nurses with Interpretive Statements* (Kansas City, Mo.: American Nurses' Association, 1976).

7. T.L. Beauchamp and J.F. Childress, *Principles of Biomedical Ethics*, 2d ed. (New York: Oxford University Press, 1983), 11.

8. Bernard Lo, "Behind Closed Doors: Promises and Pitfalls of Ethics Committees," *New England Journal of Medicine* 317, no. 1, (July 2, 1987) pp. 46–50.

9. Robert F. Weir, "Pediatric Ethics Committees: Ethical Advisors or Legal Watchdogs?" *Law, Medicine and Health Care* 15 (Fall 1987): 99–109.

10. Kaye Daniels, "Planning for Quality in the Home Care System," *Quality Review Bulletin* 12, no. 7 (July 1986): 247–51.

11. American Hospital Association, *Values in Conflict*, 77–79.

12. G.A. Kannoti, "STD, Home Care: A Shifting of Ethical Responsibilities," *Cleveland Clinic Quarterly* 52, no. 3, pp. 351–54.

13. Louis C. Feuer, "Discharge Planning: Home Care Givers Need Your Support Too," *Nursing Management* 18 (April 1987): 58–59.

14. Beauchamp and Childress, *Principles of Biomedical Ethics*, 19.

15. N. Connaway, "The Legalities of Home Care," *Home Health Care Nurse* 4, no. 1 (1986): 35–36.

16. Joint Commission on Accreditation of Healthcare Organizations, *Standards for the Accreditation of Home Care* (Chicago: Author, December 12, 1987, draft edition).

17. G. Lemieux, "Choices, Moral and Ethical Issues Involved with Life-Support Equipment When Used in the Home," *Home Health Care Nurse* no. 17, January-February 1984, pp. 12–14.

18. J. Horsley, "Caution: Home Visits Can Be Hazardous to Your License," *RN* September 1982, pp. 89–96.

19. S. Salladay, "An Ethicist Responds: Responsibility is the Issue When Patient Care and Medicare Conflict," *Journal of Christian Nursing*, Spring 1986, pp. 19–22.

20. U.S. Congress, House, Select Committee on Aging, *The Black Box of Home Care Quality* (Washington, D.C.: GPO, July 29, 1986), 1.

21. Ibid.

22. M. Cushman, "Meeting Needs and Protecting Rights: NAHC Priorities for Home Care," *Caring*, March 1986, pp. 8–10.

23. "U.S. Congress Speaks on Home Care: Statements From Legislative Leaders," *Caring*, March 1986, pp. 12–71.

24. V. Binciguerra, "Home Oncology Medical Extension (HOME): An Effective Alternative to Hospital Care," *Progress in Clinical and Biological Research* 120 (1983): 319–26.

25. M. Capp, "Law, Medicine and the Terminally Ill: Humanizing the Approach to Risk Management," *Healthcare Management Review* 2, no. 2 (1987): 37–42.

26. Ibid.

27. M. Phillip, "Home-Health Referral: Some Legal Guidelines," *Hospitals* 8 (December 1, 1985): 72–74.

28. *Federal Register* vol. 48.

29. Connaway, "Legalities of Home Care," 4, no. 2; 7–8.

30. R. Faden and T. Beauchamp, "The Right to Risk Information and the Right to Refuse Health Hazards in the Workplace," in *Contemporary Issues in Bioethics*, edited by T. Beauchamp and L. Walters, 2d ed. (Belmont, Calif: Wadsworth, 1982), 478–83.

31. P. Parris, "Psychiatric Assessment in the Home: Applications in Home Care," *Quality Review Bulletin*, April 1987, pp. 131–34.

32. J. Tehan and Colgrove, "Risk Management and Home Health Care: The Time Is Now," *Quality Review Bulletin*, May 1986, pp. 179–86.

33. L. Borden, "Patient Education and the Quality Assurance Process," *Quality Review Bulletin*, April 1985, pp. 123–27.

34. H. Creighton, "Legal Implications of Home Health Care," *Nursing Management* 18, no. 2, pp. 14–17.

35. J. Riffer, "Five Future Areas of Liability Risks Haunt Providers," *Hospitals*, November 29, 1986, pp. 48–53.

36. N. Connaway, "Should a Home Health Nurse Carry Her Own Professional Liability Insurance?" *Home Health Care Nurse* 4, no. 2, pp. 7–8.

37. R. Newcomer, J. Wood, and S. Sankar, "Medicare Prospective Payment: Anticipated Effect on Hospitals, Other Community Agencies and Families," *Journal of Health, Politics and Law* 10 (Summer 1985): 275–82.

38. S. Miller, "The Home Care Client Record Project: Model Forms and Comprehensive Guidelines," *Quality Review Bulletin*, May 1986, pp. 187–190.

39. S. Kun and D. Warburton, "Telephone Assessment of Parent's Knowledge of Home-Care Treatments and Readmission Outcomes for High-Risk Infants and Toddlers in Home Care Outcomes," *AHDC* 141 (August 1987): 882–92.

40. Horsley, "Caution," 91.

41. Ibid.

42. W. Julavits, "Psychiatric Home Care: An Evolving Legal Standard," *Psychiatric Clinics of North America* 8 (September 1985): 577–86.

43. C. Victor and N. Vetter, "The Early Re-admission of the Elderly to Hospital," *Age and Aging* 14 (January 1985): 37–42.

SUGGESTED READINGS

American Medical Association. "Principles of Medical Ethics." Adopted by AMA House of Delegates, July 1980.

American Nurses' Association. *Code for Nurses with Interpretive Statements*. Kansas City, Mo.: Author, 1976.

Cranford, Ronald, and Edward Doudera. *Institutional Ethics Committees and Health Care Decision Making*. Ann Arbor, Mich.: Health Administration Press, 1984.

International Covenants on Human Rights. New York: United Nations Office of Public Information, December 1967.

The World Medical Association, Third General Assembly. *The International Code of Medical Ethics*. London: Author, October 1949.

The Nuremberg Code. U.S. v. Karl Brandt et al. *Trials of War Criminals before Nuremberg Military Tribunals under Control Council Law No. 10*. (October 1946–April 1949).

Appendix 15-A

Health Law and Bioethics Bibliography

Journals

American Journal of Law and Medicine. American Society of Law and Medicine, 765 Commonwealth Avenue, Boston, MA 02215.

The Citation. A medicolegal digest published by the American Medical Association, 535 N. Dearborn Avenue, Chicago, IL 60611.

Hastings Center Report. The Hastings Center, 360 Broadway, Hastings-on-Hudson, NY 10706.

The Health Law Digest. National Health Lawyers Association, Suite 120, 522 21st Street, NW, Washington, DC 20006.

IRB: A Review of Human Subjects Research. Hastings Center, 360 Broadway, Hastings-on-Hudson, NY 10706.

The Journal of Legal Medicine. Shayer Publishing Co., 270 Lafayette Street, Suite 710, New York, NY 10012.

Kennedy Institute of Ethics Newsletter. Georgetown University, Washington, DC 20057.

Law, Medicine and Health Care. American Society of Law and Medicine, 765 Commonwealth Avenue, Boston, MA 02215.

Legal Aspects of Medical Practice. American College of Legal Medicine, Shayer Publishing Co., 270 Lafayette Street, Suite 710, New York, NY 10012.

The Regan Report on Nursing Law, published by Medical Press, Inc., 1231 Industrial Bank Building, Providence, RI 02903.

Western Bioethics Network. The Center for Bioethics, St. Joseph Health System, 440 South Batavia Street, Orange, CA 92668.

Books

American Hospital Association, Special Committee on Biomedical Ethics. *Values in Conflict: Resolving Ethical Issues in Hospital Care*. Chicago: Author, 1985.

Beauchamp, Tom and LeRoy Walters, eds. *Contemporary Issues in Bioethics*. 2d ed. Belmont, Calif.: Wadsworth, 1982.

Cassel, Chris and Ruth Purtillo. *Ethical Dimensions in the Health Professions*. Philadelphia: Saunders, 1981.

Cranford, Ronald and Edward Doudera. *Institutional Ethics Committees and Health Care Decision Making*. Ann Arbor, Mich.: Health Administration Press, 1984.

Hosford, B. *Bioethics Committees*. Rockville, Md.: Aspen Publishers, Inc., 1986.

Jonsen, R.A., M. Siegler, and W.J. Winslade. *Clinical Ethics*. Macmillan, 1982.

Robertson, John. *The Rights of the Critically Ill*. Cambridge, Mass.: Ballinger, 1983.

Guidelines

The following are sources for published guidelines for designing or advising bioethics committees.

American Academy of Pediatrics
141 Northwest Point Road
P.O. Box 927
Elk Grove Village, IL 60007

American Hospital Association
840 North Lake Shore Drive
Chicago, IL 60611

Judicial Council of AMA
American Medical Association
535 North Dearborn Street
Chicago, IL 60610

National Hospice Organization
1901 North Fort Meyer Drive
Suite 901
Arlington, VA 22209

Appendix 15-B

Publications of the President's Commission for the Study of Ethical Problems and Behavioral Research

Compensating for Research Injuries: The Ethical and Legal Implications of Programs to Redress Injured Subjects. Washington, D.C.; GPO, June 1982.

Deciding to Forego Life-sustaining Treatment: Ethical, Medical and Legal Issues in Treatment Decisions. Washington, D.C.: GPO, March 1983.

Defining Death: Medical, Legal and Ethical Issues in the Determination of Death. Washington, D.C.: GPO, July 1981.

"Guidelines for the Determination of Death." *Journal of the American Medical Association,* November 13, 1981.

Implementing Human Research Regulations: The Adequacy and Uniformity of Federal Rules and of Their Implementation. Washington D.C.; GPO, March 1983.

Making Health Care Decisions: The Ethical and Legal Implications of Informed Consent in the Patient-Practitioner Relationship. Washington, D.C.: GPO, October 1982.

Protecting Human Subjects: The Adequacy and Uniformity of Federal Rules and Their Implementation. Washington, D.C.: GPO, December 1981.

Screening and Counseling for Genetic Conditions: The Ethical, Social, and Legal Implications of Genetic Screening, Counseling, and Education Programs. Washington, D.C.: GPO, February 1983.

Securing Access to Health Care: The Ethical Implications of Differences in the Availability of Health Services. Washington, D.C.: GPO, March 1983.

Splicing Life: The Social and Ethical Issues of Genetic Engineering with Human Beings. Washington, D.C.: GPO, November 1982.

Summing Up: The Ethical and Legal Problems in Medicine and Biomedical and Behavioral Research. Washington, D.C.: GPO, March 1983.

Whistleblowing in Biomedical Research: Policies and Procedures for Responding to Reports of Misconduct. Washington, D.C.: GPO, September 1981.

Chapter 16

Home Health Aide and Home Companion Program

Sally Whitten

Visiting Nurse Services (VNS) is a voluntary, comprehensive home health agency that has been in existence since the mid-fifties. It has not been restructured to provide for a private duty or for-profit subsidiary. Since its beginning, its mission has been to respond to community needs. The agency's primary service area is Calhoun County, Michigan, which has a population of approximately 147,000 (the population percentage of seniors is slightly higher for the county than the state average). While there is no local office on aging in the county, there are a variety of services and programs available for seniors that are funded by a regional office on aging. VNS, throughout its history, has been the major provider of home health care in the county, although proprietary agencies created some competition when they came into existence in the early eighties. In keeping with its mission, VNS responded to a need in the community and developed the Home Companion Program. This chapter describes the evolution of this program and compares the roles and responsibilities of the home companion with the home health aide—two extremely vital roles in home health care today.

The Home Companion Program, developed and implemented in 1984 by VNS, was made possible by a three-year grant from the W.K. Kellogg Foundation. The agency saw a need for this program as a result of changes going on elsewhere in the health care community. With the advent of diagnostic related groups (DRGs) in hospitals, the nature of discharge planning changed drastically. Lengths of stay decreased and the need for more supportive care in the home increased. It became apparent that the type of service needed was not recognized by Medicare as falling under traditional reimbursement guidelines. A review of the literature, demographics, and service utilization alerted the agency to the fact that the need for in-home support care would increase. The Home Companion Program was developed in response to this coming need.

One of the goals cited in the grant was to have the home companion program become self-supporting by the time the grant period ended. More than a year after the end of the period, the program was still not self-supporting. However, the agency came to realize that the program was valuable in other ways that justified its continuation.

When the program was first conceived, it was decided that it would be a fee-for-service program. United Way money would not be utilized. Those who would benefit from the program were those who could afford to pay for it. The community did have another United Way agency providing similar services to seniors who did not have money to pay for the service. Thus, for the first two years of the program, it was necessary to interpret to the United Way and to the community the differences between the VNS's home companion program and the community's volunteer bureau. Job descriptions from the two agencies were compared and then revised to help clarify the differences. Both organizations worked together to make clear that while some services being delivered by the two agencies were the same or similar, the populations being served were different.

The following basic components of the home companion program will be discussed in further detail: (1) recruitment, (2) differentiating home companions and home health aides, (3) training, (4) services, (5) supervision, (6) assessments, (7) marketing, (8) evaluation, and (9) reimbursement.

RECRUITMENT

Initially, the qualifications for employees included having a high school diploma, being 18 years old or over, and possessing transportation. It was thought that older women who had cared for their own families and were now experiencing the "empty nest syndrome" would be ideal employees. Throughout the history of the program, the recruitment, selection, and retention of home companions have been major problems. These personnel issues contribute to the administrative costs of the agency and program. When there is not enough staff, clients are turned away; when volume is not increased, costs stay high.

The major methods of recruitment are the following:

- putting classified ads in the local daily newspapers
- distributing posters in area grocery stores and laundromats
- contacting area employment offices and social services departments
- displaying ads with coupons in the weekly shopper
- spreading the news by word of mouth

The last two methods have been the most successful.

In the third year of the program, it was decided that possession of a high school diploma was less significant than the successful completion of the training program. At present, the agency intends to approach vocational education programs in the hope of attracting employees in still another way. Also, a home companion class will be offered in a small city in the county 25 miles from the usual training site. The agency is hoping that by taking training out to prospective employees, recruitment will be more successful. Travel costs for enrollees from the area would be less. Ads in a local newspaper regarding a locally held home companion class might have greater impact on recruitment. Using familiar examples and local references in training might reinforce for trainees the significance of home companion services to the area's residents.

Home companions are paid hourly. Initially, they were hired at minimum wage. The starting wage was then raised to $3.45 per hour, and again to $4.00 per hour, in an effort to reduce turnover. Personnel policies were changed for the same reason. The changes provided for the following new benefits and opportunities: (1) health, life, and disability insurance; (2) uniform allowance; (3) educational tuition reimbursement; and (4) travel between cases on split shift assignments. All benefits are prorated for part-time employees. While employee satisfaction may have increased as a result of the changes in benefits, turnover has not been significantly reduced. Employee turnover is also the result of fluctuations in caseload and demand, which leads to inconsistencies in hours of work. Some turnover occurs because the agency cannot guarantee a minimum number of hours. During the three years of the grant (1984–1987), 95 home companions were recruited (i.e., enrolled in the home companion training). The retention rate is 18 percent. The costs and benefits of how home companions are recruited and paid are being re-evaluated. An inadequate number of staff is a major factor limiting the growth of this program.

The agency does encourage all personnel to seek further education and does encourage career advancement. Some home companions have been promoted to home health aides, while some could have been but chose not to, even though the pay is better. Home companions see themselves as having greater flexibility in meeting client needs, both in terms of services provided and in scheduling of visits. The home companions who stay with the agency like the flexibility. Ironically, that flexibility is what seems to frustrate other employees, causing a low retention rate.

HOME COMPANIONS VERSUS HOME HEALTH AIDES

VNS has differentiated the two positions in a number of ways. (See Appendixes 16-A and 16-B for job descriptions.)

In order to be a home companion, an individual must complete a training program defined by and usually provided by VNS. Home companion services may be independent of any other service delivered by VNS. The plan of care is developed by the agency with input and information from the client and family. The amount, the frequency, and the duration of services vary widely and are based on the needs of the clients and the resources of the agency. The home companion is intended to be a person supportive of the family and client in providing social, environmental, and community support services as well as health care services. The assignment sheets (plans of care) for the two positions are different. The sheet for the home health aide focuses more on clinical and skilled care support activities (Appendix 16-C); the sheet for the home companion focuses on personal and environmental support activities (Appendix 16-D). The words used on the assignment sheets were selected carefully. Periodic supervision of home companion services is based on a policy set by the agency rather than by a regulating body. Fees are set by the agency.

While both types of employees at times may provide similar services, the approach and the focus are different. A home health aide will not visit a patient in the home without delivering specific care to that patient. A home companion, on the other hand, may provide a wide variety of services that are supportive of the client, yet never provide any personal care to the client. Note, too, that the agency refers to "patients" served by home health aides and "clients" served by home companions.

TRAINING

The home companion training program spreads 30 hours of instruction over a two-week period. Content includes personal care, housekeeping services, first aid, the basics of confidentiality and recordkeeping, and so forth. Training is not a replacement for agency orientation. The format of training includes lectures, slides, books, speakers, and demonstrations.

While VNS had the Kellogg grant, participants were paid $100 upon successful completion of the training. Not only was VNS committed to developing the home companion program, but it was trying to make available to the community a pool of persons capable of providing a high level of care. It was thought that families would come to learn more about caring for their own members. This proved not to be true. Now persons being trained pay VNS $15 to attend the classes. There are fewer in the classes, but the overall employment and retention rates for VNS have not changed significantly since this change was made.

The first instructor for the program was the home companion supervisor. Later other nurses on staff who had been certified to be Red Cross instructors conducted the program. For the participants, the most significant factor seems to be the positive attitude of the instructor.

It is interesting to note that in the community there were a few individuals who thought the junior college should be doing the training. They thought provider agencies should stay out of teaching. While there were some discussions held to consider the alternative, it was determined that the cost of a more formal educational approach would be a barrier to recruitment.

SERVICES

Initially home companions were mainly needed for personal care and in-home support, such as light housekeeping and errand running. The target population consisted of seniors, as noted in the agency's job description (Appendix 16-A) and samples of home companion promotional literature (Appendixes 16-E and 16-F). When the service began to be utilized, suggestions for additional services came from the clients by way of requests, from employees themselves, and from VNS board members. The program has been expanded to include the full population. The agency's pediatric nurse practitioner has been providing in-service education on infant and child care. An agency staff member was the first to utilize a home companion for child care. She had a son at home who had broken his leg, and she wanted a responsible caretaker with the child so she could return to work. It was an agency board member who suggested that the agency should promote a traveling companion service. The board member rightly pointed out that there are many people who have the money and time to travel, but refrain for fear they cannot manage their health affairs while traveling. Home companions can assist in medication supervision, ambulation, or wheelchair support and can provide other kinds of support, thus enabling people to improve their quality of life through travel. Several travel agencies have expressed interest in working with the agency to expand and promote the traveling companion service.

SUPERVISION

Initially, home companions had their own nurse supervisor, who did the greater part of recruitment, selection, and training as well as the actual supervision of the employees. There was also a home companion coordinator, who worked on the scheduling and management issues of the program. The supervisor left the agency during the program's second year. As a temporary measure, the agency's home health aide supervisor was asked to assume temporary responsibility for the supervision of home companions. When the agency realized it was necessary to make some critical changes for cost containment, the combination of the two supervisory positions into one became final. The position of home companion coordinator was eliminated as another cost containment measure. The scheduling and management responsibilities have been transferred to patient information specialists. There are several individuals in the agency who have that job title, and they are capable of backing each other up.

From the standpoint of the program, there were both positive and negative aspects to these changes. When the home companion program had its own supervisor and coordinator, home companions had two individuals in management they knew were assigned exclusively to their program. The employees received a great deal of support from these individuals. Clients also knew immediately whom to relate to—by title if not by name. One of the positive aspects of the changes is that there is now more than one individual who has knowledge of the management requirements. The cost implications are obvious. At present, the program cannot afford its own supervisor and coordinator and it continues to share the home health aide supervisor. There is no evidence that the program has suffered in terms of quality or client satisfaction. It is probable that quality and satisfaction may have even improved, because of closer interaction with the skilled and intermittent programs. Some in-service programs have been held jointly with the home health aides. As a result of the same individual being responsible for the home health aide and the home companion programs, greater promotion and understanding of the two programs have occurred. The distinction between skilled care and personal care services is clearer, thus helping to reduce Medicare denials.

ASSESSMENTS

From the very beginning of the program, it was understood that home companion clients would have the benefit of a functional assessment. The particular tool to be utilized was developed by means of another grant from the W.K. Kellogg Foundation (Appendix 16-G). Originally all area health care providers and institutions that serve seniors were going to use this instrument. At this writing, it is only being used by VNS. The major problem seems to be the length of each assessment. VNS does acknowledge that doing this type of assessment is a time-consuming process, and since there is not substantial evidence that it contributes significantly to the well-being of the client, functional assessments might be discontinued. In addition to the functional assessment, clients also receive a physical and psychosocial assessment. The home environment is assessed. A plan of care is developed with the client.

Clients were initially reassessed by the program supervisor. At the completion of the first program evaluation, it was determined that frequent assessments were of questionable value. The interval between assessments was expanded.

The agency has a strong commitment to the value of assessments done by professional nurses. However, the final program evaluation—carried out at the end of the grant period—documented that clients themselves questioned the value of assessments. While clients appreciated having assessments available when indicated or requested, they placed a greater value on the services delivered directly by the home companions as well as on the excellent reputation of the agency. It became evident that having routine nursing and functional assessments of home companion clients had greater value and meaning for the agency's nurses. After reviewing these findings, the agency established the following new policies (effective July 1, 1987):

1. If a home companion client has been receiving skilled VNS service, the VNS staff nurse will (if possible) carry out home companion admission procedures at the time of discharge from skilled care.
2. An L.P.N., an R.N., or the home health aide–home companion supervisor will carry out admission procedures when VNS has no previous knowledge of the client.
3. The need for an initial nursing assessment visit for clients discharged from either skilled care or the home companion program within the past 30 days will be re-evaluated.
4. Designated L.P.N.s may carry out home companion procedures for re-admission and home companion supervisory visits for cases that are stable and uncomplicated.
5. A home companion supervision visit will take place at least once every 90 days.
6. Functional assessments will be redone at least every 6 months.

The revised policy on the frequency of supervision visits is being reassessed.

MARKETING

The marketing focus for the home companion program has been on physicians, hospital discharge planners, patients and families, and the public at large. The marketing process has included a marketing audit, market research, a marketing plan, branding (development of a logo and slogan), communications, and evaluation.

The agency has been fortunate to have a relationship with an excellent marketing and public relations firm. That firm has worked with the agency in the development of materials and strategies and in helping the agency's staff to become more aware of their roles and responsibilities in marketing the agency and its services.

EVALUATION

All home companion clients are encouraged to evaluate the service at the time of discharge (Appendix 16-H). The evaluation may be anonymous. The agency director and program supervisor review all returned evaluations. While comments are generally positive, feedback on one such form helped VNS to realize some further in-service training was needed in the area of nutrition and meal preparation.

In the second year of operation, a formal program evaluation was carried out. An agreement to conduct this quasi-formal research program was entered into with a doctorate-prepared nurse from the University of Michigan. Evaluation activities were carried out by means of personal and telephone interviews and written questionnaires specific to the group surveyed (Appendix 16-I).

The groups targeted for input in the evaluation were home companions (former and present), VNS staff, discharge planners, physicians, and home companion clients (former and present). If a client was not available, family members participated in the evaluation.

The evaluation also included a detailed review of program costs, revenue, and service statistics. As a result of this first program evaluation, internal changes were made in supervision, employee selection, and retention procedures. In addition, a record audit system was developed and implemented, and marketing was redirected at physicians with the hope of increasing their understanding and utilization of the program.

In the third year (at the conclusion of the grant period), a final program evaluation was carried out using strategies similar to those used in the previous year. In general, the evaluation yielded similar results. The program's strengths were that it provided needed services to clients, prevented or delayed institutionalization, helped to maintain a higher quality of life, had caring and competent staff, and provided support and respite for the family. Its weaknesses were that it had high employee turnover, its programs were nonreimbursable (some of the population could not afford the services), its services had a high cost, and there was a shortage of home companions given the demand.

REIMBURSEMENT

From the very beginning of the program, it was recognized that the service would not be affordable for everyone. The agency chose to keep it on a private pay basis to avoid creating an overwhelming need for United Way money. When the agency increased the charge in the second year, clients on the caseload did not immediately drop the service, although some stated they discontinued the service sooner than they might have preferred.

This program was the agency's first nonregulated private pay program. The need for more definitive reimbursement policies became clear. Services are billed monthly, bimonthly, or weekly, depending on the frequency of service. The following new policies became effective in July 1987:

1. Clients will be billed for a minimum of two hours.
2. Clients who have failed to make payment after two billing periods may be discharged from the service.
3. Clients who request the service, receive the admission services, and then change their minds may be billed at the rate of a skilled nursing visit.
4. Rates for packages of services may be negotiated with third party payers.

The most frustrating reimbursement issue is that there are clients whose needs would be well met by this program, but most reimbursement sources will only pay for more costly services (home health aide services). One HMO has recently acknowledged that it may be willing to pay for home companion services, and one self-insured union is already willing to pay for these services. The agency will continue to try to educate all payers about the value of home companions in terms of both quality and cost containment.

SUMMARY

At a time when reimbursement policies and utilization patterns are changing throughout the health care industry, agencies are continually studying all their services with regard to costs and benefits. The benefits provided to clients by VNS's home companion program have been documented repeatedly. The costs are in excess of revenue. Internal review revealed the fact that the program does carry significant overhead. Should the program be dropped, all the overhead would not disappear with it. For example, the agency's building costs, now spread to all programs, would be spread to one less. The remaining programs would have to carry a proportionately higher burden. Further, the home companion program has value as a referral source for other agency programs. Physicians and discharge planners rely on VNS to address the support needs as well as the skilled care needs of their clients.

Clearly, the future of VNS's program is dependent on many issues, including reimbursement sources for long-term care, the cost of home care versus institutional care, and the degree to which payers can see the value of preventive and supportive services. The fact that the program adds substantially to its clients' quality of life unfortunately may not matter much in this era of cost containment.

Appendix 16-A

Home Companion Job Description*

Title: Home Companion
FLSA Status: Nonexempt
Supervised by: Home Health Aide/Home Companion Supervisor
Workers Supervised: None
Summary Statement:

Under a care plan established by the agency and the client, Home Companions provide valuable supportive services of personal care, light housekeeping, and personal companionship enabling the client to remain at home and/or to be cared for and/or provided companionship in the setting specific to the client's plan for care. The service may or may not be to individuals who are under current medical care. The service is usually provided for 2 to 4 hours a day but may be for shorter periods and as long as 24 hours a day. Clients served by home companions receive a periodic assessment, thereby facilitating a current and appropriate client care plan and the home companion's place on the total agency health care team.

Principle Duties and Responsibilities:

1. Assist with or provide personal care services such as bed, tub, or shower bath, shampoo, caring for teeth or dentures, and skin care. If indicated, assist clients getting in and out of bed and in taking medications that are ordinarily self-administered.
2. Following formal classroom instruction and supervised field experience, performs simple, uncomplicated supportive procedures for clients according to care plan (e.g., temperature-pulse-respirations, simple cleansing enema, change uncomplicated nonsterile dressing, empty or refill humidity bottles on O_2 equipment).
3. Assist clients with normal elimination activities.
4. Plan, prepare and serve nutritious meals according to diet. If indicated, assist client in eating. Do dishes and keep kitchen in good order.
5. Carry out light housekeeping for client and household if so assigned. For example, do laundry, vacuum, sweep and dust.
6. Provide support services outside the home such as shopping for the client and accompanying client to appointments for health care.
7. Provide companionship promoting the client's physical and emotional comfort. Examples of appropriate supportive activities are, if indicated, assisting the client with ambulation, writing letters or carrying out hobbies, reading to client, or playing games with client.
8. Transport client according to agency policies.
9. Communicate with the client in such a way as to provide encouragement toward the goal of independent living.
10. Document observations and services provided on each client's chart daily. Notify the Home Health Aide/Home Companion Supervisor immediately of any change in client's condition which may need agency and/or professional intervention.
11. Participate in staff meetings, in-service education programs, and other opportunities for learning.
12. Carry out work according to agency policies and procedures and in such a manner as to reflect appropriately agency standards for timeliness, appearance, and behavior. Maintain confidentiality of client and agency information.

---

*Courtesy of Visiting Nurse Services of Calhoun County, Inc.

Qualifications and Requirements:

Home Companions must have:

1. An observable interest in people and in home care.
2. The ability to follow oral and written instructions.
3. The ability to make reports.
4. The ability to work effectively as a member of a team.
5. The ability to accept and utilize supervision.
6. The ability to work independently in an effective and efficient manner, according to a prescribed time frame.

It is preferred, but not required, that Home Companions be high school graduates or have the equivalent. They must attend and successfully complete a Home Companion training course. They must have a current driver's license and proof of automobile insurance.

Approved: _____   _____
                 Executive Director   Date

This description is intended to describe the type and level of work being performed by a person assigned to this job. It is not an exhaustive list of all duties and responsibilities required of a person so classified.

Appendix 16-B

Home Health Aide Job Description*

Title: Home Health Aide
FLSA Status: Nonexempt
Supervised by: Home Health Aide/Home Companion Supervisor
Workers Supervised: None
Summary Statement:

Under a professional care plan established by the agency, Home Health Aides provide valuable supportive services to patients whose health status is unstable and/or who require skilled professional services. Home Health Aides take vital signs, provide personal care and specifically defined nonskilled health care services, and provide a clean and orderly environment for the patient. On cases assigned, Home Health Aides work under the supervision of an R.N. or R.P.T. Their service is given in combination with one or more skilled services to enable the patient to remain at home.

Principle Duties and Responsibilities:

1. Provide and document personal care services such as bed, bath, skin care, shampoo, hair set and comb out, caring for the teeth or dentures, giving bed pan, helping patient in and out of bed, bed making and assist with medications or procedures ordinarily self-administered (or by family member) as prescribed by physician.
2. Support the skilled plan of care by carrying out and recording specific nursing care procedures such as giving a cleansing enema, applying heat and cold, changing uncomplicated nonsterile dressings, emptying catheter and colostomy drainage bags, measuring and recording intake and output, measuring weight gain or loss, and providing emotional support and encouragement to terminally ill, acutely ill, or recovering patients.
3. Help patient in his plan of rehabilitation by assisting with transfers, walking, ROM exercises, and other physical, speech or occupational therapy activities as established by the therapist for the purpose of increasing muscle strength, self-care, and independence. May utilize a Hoyer lift in assisting with transfers.
4. Give support and encouragement necessary for the patient to strive to achieve the goals established by the staff under the direction of the patient's physician.
5. Document observations and services provided on each client's chart daily. Report observations and activities to the primary nurse or therapist responsible for the patient. Notify the primary nurse immediately of any change in client's condition which may need agency and/or professional intervention.
6. Participate in in-service education programs, staff meetings, and other opportunities for learning provided.
7. Carry out work according to agency policies and procedures and in such a manner as to reflect appropriate agency standards for timeliness, appearance and behavior. Maintain confidentiality of client and agency information.

Qualifications and Requirements:

Applicant must have interest in caring for the sick at home.

Applicant must have the ability to follow oral and written instructions, establish and maintain effective working relationships, function effectively as a member of the health care team, make simple reports, and accept and utilize supervision.

*Visiting Nurse Services of Calhoun County, Inc.

High school graduate or equivalent. Successful completion of a Home Health Aide Training course is required prior to or early in the weeks of regular employment. Must possess current driver's license and carry proof of automotive personal and property liability insurance.

Preference is given to applicants with successful work experience as nurse aides.

Approved: _____   _____
                        Executive Director   Date

This description is intended to describe the type and level of work being performed by a person assigned to this job. It is not an exhaustive list of all duties and responsibilities required of a person so classified.

Appendix 16-C

Home Health Aide Assignment Sheet*

Name _____
Date _____
AR# _____
Diagnosis _____
Goal _____

Frequency, Duration & Length of Visits_____

1. PERSONAL CARE — CHECK AND NOTE FREQUENCY

☐ BATH— ASSIST _____ COMPLETE _____ BED _____ TUB _____ SHOWER _____

☐ MOUTH CARE DENTURES _____ ROUTINE _____ MOUTH SWAB _____

☐ HAIR CARE— SHAMPOO _____ GROOMING _____

☐ SKIN CARE— ROUTINE _____ SPECIAL _____

☐ SHAVING— FACIAL _____ AXILLIARY _____ LEGS _____

☐ NAIL CARE— TRIMMING _____ CLEANING _____ FILING _____ SOAK FEET _____ NO _____

☐ TOILETING— BEDPAN _____ B/S COMMODE _____ URINAL _____ BATHROOM _____

☐ OTHER _____

2. TREATMENTS AND/OR OBSERVATIONS

VITAL SIGNS: ACCEPTABLE RANGES

☐ TEMPERATURE _____ ☐ PULSE _____ ☐ RESPIRATION _____ ☐ BLOOD PRESSURE _____ ☐ WEIGHT _____

☐ MEDICATIONS— ASSIST WITH MEDICATIONS _____

☐ ENEMA— FLEET.(REG) _____ FLEET(OIL) _____ SOAP SUDS _____ SUPPOSITORY _____ TAPWATER _____ OTHER _____

☐ ORAL INTAKE _____ ☐ URINARY OUTPUT _____ TIME FRAME _____ ☐ OTHER _____

☐ WOUND CARE—PROCEDURE _____

☐ ASSIST WITH OSTOMY — PROCEDURE _____

☐ DECUBITI CARE — PROCEDURE _____

☐ CATHETER CARE — PROCEDURE TYPE _____

☐ SITZ BATH/PERINEAL FLUSH _____

☐ OTHER _____

3. EXTENSION OF THERAPY — CHECK AND NOTE FREQUENCY

☐ ENCOURAGE ADL'S— SPECIFY _____

☐ AMBULATION/TRANSFER ACTIVITIES _____

☐ EXERCISES— SPECIFY _____

☐ APPLICATION OF IMMOBILIZER _____ LOCATION _____

☐ APPLICATION OF HEAT/COLD _____ LOCATION _____

☐ RESPIRATORY EQUIPMENT — CLEANING _____ CHECKING SUPPLIES _____

☐ OTHER _____

4. NUTRITION/FOOD/HOUSEHOLD SERVICE

☐ MEAL PREPARATION _____   ☐ CHANGING BED LINEN _____

☐ ASSIST WITH FEEDING _____   ☐ CLEANING PT. AREA _____

☐ TUBE FEEDING _____   ☐ LAUNDRY _____

☐ OTHER _____

continues

*Visiting Nurse Services of Calhoun County, Inc.

5. ADDITIONAL ACTIVITIES AND COMMENTS

_____
_____
_____
_____

6. OBSERVATIONS/CHANGES TO BE REPORTED IMMEDIATELY TO PRIMARY CLINICIAN

_____
_____
_____
_____
_____

SIGNATURE OF PATIENT/CARE GIVER   SIGNATURE OF CLINICIAN   DATE

VNS 1012 9/87

Appendix 16-D

Home Companion Assignment Sheet*

Date: _____

Client's Name: _____

AR # _____

Frequency & Length of Visits_____

1. PERSONAL CARE — CHECK AND NOTE FREQUENCY

☐ Bath - Assist _____ Complete _____ Bed _____ Tub _____ Shower _____

☐ Mouth Care — Dentures _____ Routine _____ Mouth Swab _____

☐ Hair Care — Shampoo _____ Grooming _____

☐ Skin Care — Routine _____ Other _____

☐ Shaving — Facial _____ Axilliary _____ Legs _____

☐ Nail Care — Trimming _____ Cleaning _____ No _____

☐ Toileting — Bedpan _____ B/S commode _____ Urinal _____ Bathroom _____

☐ Other _____

2. TREATMENTS — CHECK AND NOTE FREQUENCY

VITAL SIGNS: ACCEPTABLE RANGES

☐ Temperature _____ ☐ Pulse _____ ☐ Respiration _____ ☐ Weight _____

☐ Medications - Assist with Medications _____

☐ Enema - Fleet (Reg) _____ Fleet (Oil) _____ Soap Suds _____

☐ Oral Intake _____ ☐ Urinary Output _____ Time Frame _____

☐ Wound Care - Procedure: _____

☐ Assist with Ostomy - procedure _____

☐ Decubiti care - procedure _____

☐ Catheter Care - Clean around catheter _____ Empty Cath. Bag _____

☐ Sitz Bath/Perineal Flush _____

☐ Other _____

3. PROMOTION OF INDEPENDENT FUNCTION

☐ Encourage ADL'S - Specify _____

☐ Ambulation/Transfer Activities _____

☐ Exercises - Specify _____

☐ Application of Heat/Cold _____ Location _____

☐ Other _____

4. NUTRITION/FOOD/HOUSEHOLD SERVICE

NUTRITION

☐ Plans/prepares/serves/meals according to diet _____

☐ Feeds/Assists w/feeding _____

☐ Wash & Dry All Dishes _____

☐ Grocery Shopping _____

LAUNDRY

☐ Launder clothing/Bed, _____

☐ Kitchen, Bath, Linen _____

☐ Iron if Requested _____

☐ Delivery or Pick-up of Dry Cleaning _____

continues

*Visiting Nurse Services of Calhoun County, Inc.

LIGHT HOUSEKEEPING

☐ Dust/Tidy the following Rooms: _____

_____

☐ Vacuum the carpet _____

☐ Sweep the Floor _____

☐ Mop Floors _____

☐ Clean Sinks and Tubs _____

☐ Replenish supplies: Notify family when supplies are low_____

☐ Make beds and change linen _____

☐ Report Mech. failure to V.N. _____

SHOPPING

☐ Shop for needed items _____

☐ Transportation _____

☐ Other: (Specify) _____

☐ Observation and Recording_____

☐ Report change in Pt. condition (Specify) _____

_____

_____

_____

_____
Signature of Patient Caregiver

Signature of Clinician

Date

VNS 1100 9/87

Appendix 16-E

Home Companion Program Advertisement

Courtesy of Visiting Nurse Services of Calhoun County, Inc.

Appendix 16-F

Home Companion Program Advertisements

When you want to stay home, but need a little help.

See how a Home Companion can make things easier for you.

A Home Companion can
- Assist with personal care
- Prepare meals
- Do light housework
- Assist with medical care
- Do the shopping
- Be a companion

Program includes nursing assessment

Patient Care - Homestyle

VISITING NURSE SERVICES
of Calhoun County, Inc.

181 North Avenue
Battle Creek, MI 49017
616/962-0303 or 616/781-2507
A United Way Agency

© 1985 VNS

Do you need help with personal care or housekeeping?

See how a home companion from Visiting Nurse Services can make things easier for you.

A home companion can
- Assist with personal care
- Prepare meals
- Do light housekeeping
- Assist with medical care
- Do the shopping
- Provide care for sick infants and children
- Provide transportation (in patient's car)
- Provide respite care
- Give assistance to new mothers
- Do the laundry
- Provide traveling companionship
- Provide one-on-one attention to a hospitalized patient
- Care for someone in the family's absence
- Simply provide wanted companionship

Program includes nursing assessment

Patient Care—Homestyle

VISITING NURSE SERVICES
of Calhoun County, Inc.

181 North Avenue
Battle Creek, MI 49017
616/962-0303
1-800-622-9822
A United Way Agency

Courtesy of Visiting Nurse Services of Calhoun County, Inc.

Appendix 16-G

Functional Assessment Form*

FUNCTIONAL STATUS

PATIENT IDENTIFICATION

For each activity listed, check (✔) the description which most accurately represents the patient's performance at the time of admission. If the patient requires help or performance can't be measured, indicate the pre-admission performance level as well. This information is needed to provide the appropriate amount and kind of assistance, to determine rehabilitation potential and to encourage the inclusion of rehabilitation goals in the plan of care. To promote consistency in describing performance, definitions are included. Keep original in chart and send duplicate to facility where patient is being transferred.

A. BATHING gets to or obtains water; washes/dries body.
B. TOILETING gets to/from, on/off, cleanses after, adjusts clothes.
C. DENTITION the number, kind, and arrangement of teeth in the jaw.
D. EATING gets food into body from plate, cup, etc.

E. WHEELING Moves by a wheeled device (wheelchair, stretcher).
F. MOBILITY LEVEL describes the total movement of patient.
G. DRESSING fastens/unfastens, obtains, replaces items from storage area.

H. TRANSFERRING gets in/out of bed or chair.
I. WALKING process of ambulation and moving about
J. CLIMBS STAIRS process of going up and down stairs from one floor to another.

Date Directions: Place date in small square each time an assessment is done.

DATE OF ASSESSMENT					
2/8/85	4/9/85	1/11/86			

DATE OF ASSESSMENT

A. BATHING	AT ADM	PRE ADM			
1. Without help of any kind					
2. Using assistive device(s)					
3. With help of another person					
4. Device and help of another					
5. Is bathed by others					
B. TOILETING	AT ADM	PRE ADM			
1. Without help of any kind					
2. Using assistive device(s)					
3. With help of another person					
4. Device and help of another					
5. Does not use toilet room					
C. DENTITION	AT ADM	PRE ADM			
1. All/most teeth present					
2. Some opposing teeth					
3. No opposing teeth					
4. Difficulty chewing					
5. Dentures					
a. Upper					
b. Lower					
c. Other					
6. No teeth					
D. EATING/FEEDING	AT ADM	PRE ADM			
1. Without help of any kind					
2. Using assistive device(s)					
3. Eats finger foods					
4. With help of another person					
5. Device and help of another					
6. Spoon, tube, or I.V. fed					
7. Supplements					
E. WHEELING	AT ADM	PRE ADM			
1. Does not wheel - walks					
2. Without help of any kind					
3. Using assistive device(s)					
4. With help of another person					
5. Device and help of another					
6. Is wheeled by others					
7. Is not wheeled					
F. MOBILITY LEVEL	AT ADM	PRE ADM			
1. Goes out without help					
2. Goes out with help					
3. Confined to house					
4. Confined to bed-chair					

DATE OF ASSESSMENT

G. DRESSING/UNDRESSING	AT ADM	PRE ADM			
1. Without help of any kind					
2. Using assistive device(s)					
3. With help of another person					
4. Device and help of another					
5. Is not dressed					
H. TRANSFERRING	AT ADM	PRE ADM			
1. Without help of any kind					
2. Using assistive device(s)					
3. With help of another person					
4. Device and help of another					
5. Is transferred by others					
6. Is not transferred					
I. WALKING	AT ADM	PRE ADM			
1. Without help of any kind					
2. Using assistive device(s)					
3. With help of another person					
4. Device and help of another					
5. Does not walk					
J. CLIMBS STAIRS	AT ADM	PRE ADM			
1. Without help of any kind					
2. Using assistive device(s)					
3. With help of another					
4. Device and help of another					
5. Does not climb stairs					

Describe devices and assistance needed:

Describe any paralysis, contractures, paresis, etc. (include location):

*Courtesy of Visiting Nurse Services of Calhoun County, Inc. Designed with funding from W.K. Kellogg Foundation.

FUNCTIONAL ASSESSMENT

K. BOWEL FUNCTION the process of elimination of feces from the body

L. BLADDER FUNCTION process of eliminating urine from the body.

M. BEHAVIOR PATTERNS is the manner of conducting one's self within one's environment.

N. MENTAL STATUS awareness of an individual within his/her environment in relation to time, place, and person.

O. SOCIAL CONTACT/SUPPORT refers to social contacts the individual has and his/her participation in activities

	DATE OF ASSESSMENT				
K. BOWEL FUNCTION	AT ADM	PRE ADM			
1. Continent					
2. Incontinent					
3. Ostomy					
a. Self-care					
b. Non-self care					
4. Bowel training					
L. BLADDER FUNCTION	AT ADM	PRE ADM			
1. Continent					
2. Incontinent					
3. Gets up at night to urinate					
4. Catheter					
5. External devices					
6. Ostomy					
a. Self care					
b. No self care					
7. Bladder training					
M. BEHAVIOR PATTERNS	AT ADM	PRE ADM			
1. Aggressive					
2. Abusive					
3. Anxious					
4. Uncooperative					
5. Demanding					
6. Depression					
7. Forgetful					
8. Inappropriate					
9. Independent					
10. Manipulative					
11. Noisy					
12. Talkative					
13. Suspicious/Guarded					
14. Withdrawn					
15. Appropriate					

	DATE OF ASSESSMENT				
N. MENTAL STATUS	AT ADM	PRE ADM			
S=sometimes; O=not at all;					
A=all the time (Place appropriate letter in space)					
1. Oriented					
a. Time					
b. Place					
c. Person					
2. Comatose					
3. Semi-comatose					
4. Lethargic					
5. Restraint used					
6. Safety device used					
O. SOCIAL CONTACT/SOCIAL SUPPORT	AT ADM	PRE ADM			
1. Family					
2. Children					
3. Friends					
4. Guardian					
5. Religious Personnel					
P. OTHER SERVICES NEEDED	AT ADM	PRE ADM			
1. Financial					
2. Housekeeping					
3. Laundry					
4. Meal preparation					
5. Shopping					
6. Transportation					

Living Arrangement in Community (describe briefly)

Home health care or "chore-provider" needed:?

How frequently or consistently are safety or restraint devices needed?

FUNCTIONAL ASSESSMENT

Q. COMMUNICATION making known to others one's needs/desires - transmits information.

R. VISION act, faculty or process of seeing.

S. HEARING act, faculty or process of perceiving sound through the ear.

T. SLEEPING HABITS describes how the individual maintains rest/sleep patterns.

U. SKIN the condition of the outer covering of the body.

	DATE OF ASSESSMENT					
Q. COMMUNICATION	AT ADM	PRE ADM				
1. Speaks						
2. Writes						
3. Reads						
4. Follows directions						
5. No communication						
R. VISION	AT ADM	PRE ADM				
1. Impairment						
2. No impairment						
3. Does not see						
4. Wears glasses						
5. Wears lens						
6. Has glass eye						
S. HEARING	AT ADM	PRE ADM				
1. Hears						
2. Hears with hearing aid						
3. Does not hear						
T. SLEEPING HABITS	AT ADM	PRE ADM				
1. Sleeps all night						
2. Sleeps during day						
3. Wanders at night						
4. Sleep aids (non-medicine)						
5. Sleeps only with medication						

	DATE OF ASSESSMENT					
U. SKIN	AT ADM	PRE ADM				
1. Lacerations						
2. Decubiti						
3. Bruises						
4. Abrasions						
5. Rash						
6. Ulcer						

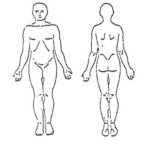

Locate skin conditions on figures above.
Describe below.

V. List any professional therapies patient has had in past six (6) months (i.e., speech, occupational, physical, other.)

W. Add any pertinent comments. (Please date each comment.) May include dressings, patient teaching, oxygen, tracheostomy (and care), etc.

FUNCTIONAL ASSESSMENT

Pertinent/Significant Findings

Height _____

Weight _____

Significant findings (include any laboratory, x-ray, E.K.G., etc. findings that are significant). Please include date.

Smoker ☐
Non-smoker ☐

Therapeutic Diet (Specify)

_____
_____
_____
_____

Assessor Name/Title/Date

_____
_____
_____
_____

Medications

Start date

Stop date

Date

Immunizations

Pneumonia

Flu

Other

Allergies

_____
_____
_____

Nursing Diagnosis

_____
_____
_____
_____

Medical Diagnosis

_____
_____
_____
_____

Appendix 16-H

Home Companion Program Evaluation Form*

Visiting Nurse Services

181 North Avenue   of Calhoun County, Inc.
Battle Creek, Michigan 49016
1-616-962-0303

To Our Home Companion Clients:

We are asking those who have received assistance from our Home Companion program to help in evaluating our services.

We would appreciate your taking a few moments of your time to answer the following questionnaire and return it to us in the envelope provided (no postage necessary). You will not need to sign your name.

1. How did you hear about the Home Companion program?
   A. Doctor   _____
   B. Visiting Nurse Services   _____
   C. Hospital   _____
   D. Relative or friend   _____
   E. Advertisement (radio, newspaper, telephone, book, poster—please circle appropriate ad).   _____
   F. Other (specify) _____

2. Who referred you to the program?
   A. Doctor   _____
   B. Hospital   _____
   C. VNS employee   _____
   D. Self   _____
   E. Relative or friend   _____
   F. Other (specify) _____

3. A VNS nurse did the following (check all that apply):
   Explained the Home Companion program   Yes _____ No _____
   Explained Home Companion duties   Yes _____ No _____
   Conducted a health check (i.e., took temperature and blood pressure, reviewed medical history)   Yes _____ No _____
   Instructed Home Companion about your care   Yes _____ No _____

4. The Home Companion did the following (check all that apply):
   Provided the service I expected   Yes _____ No _____
   Was on time for work   Yes _____ No _____
   Was organized and thorough in her/his work   Yes _____ No _____
   Made it easier for me to remain at home   Yes _____ No _____

5. Do you have family members nearby who knew that you had Home Companion services?   Yes _____ No _____
   If yes, do you believe the Home Companion services you received made your family's life easier?   Yes _____ No _____

---

*Courtesy of Visiting Nurse Services of Calhoun County, Inc.

6. On the average, would you say the care you received was:
   A. Excellent   ____
   B. Good   ____
   C. Fair   ____
   D. Poor   ____
7. Would you recommend the Home Companion program to others?   Yes ____ No ____
8. Why was the Home Companion service discontinued?

_____

_____

9. How could the Home Companion program be improved?

_____

10. Would you choose Visiting Nurse Services again to help you?   Yes ____ No ____
11. Would you be interested in joining the VNS auxiliary (a group of volunteers supporting VNS services by helping with mailings, phone calls, clinics, typing, etc.)?

Thank you for your help.

_____   _____
            Date   Signature (Optional)

Appendix 16-I

Home Companion Program Client Satisfaction Interview Form*

Now I would like to ask you a few questions about yourself and then about the services you received from the Home Companion Program.

#_____

1. Respondent:
    - 1a. Patient __ Caregiver __ Other (specify) __
    - 1b. Age __
    - 1c. Female __ Male __
2. Patient:
    - 2a. Age of patient __
    - 2b. Female __ Male __
    - 2c. Caucasian __ Black __ Hispanic __
    - 2d. Does the patient live:
        - alone   __
        - with spouse   __
        - with other relative __
        - with other person   __
3. How did you hear about the Home Companion Program? From:
    - VNS employee (specify) _____
    - Physician/doctor   _____
    - Nurse   _____
    - Social worker   _____
    - Family   _____
    - Friend   _____
    - DSS   _____
    - Hospital   _____
    - Newspaper   _____
    - Radio   _____
    - Other (specify) _____
4. Who advised you to contact the Home Companion Program?

Self	_____	Hospital	_____
Nurse (not VNS)	_____	DSS	_____
Physician/doctor	_____	Extended care facility	_____
VNS employee	_____	Other	_____
Social worker	_____		
Family	_____		
Friend	_____		

5. Overall, how would you describe the service you received? Would you say:

1	2	3	4
Poor	Fair	Good	Excellent

_____

*Visiting Nurse Services of Calhoun County, Inc.

6. During her/his visit, which of the following activities did the Home Companion Nursing Supervisor do?

		Yes	No
6a.	Explained the Home Companion Program	____	____
6b.	Explained the Home Companion duties	____	____
6c.	Conducted a health check (temperature, blood pressure, medical history)	____	____
6d.	Introduced the Home Companion to you	____	____
6e.	Instructed the Home Companion about your care	____	____

7. What kinds of services did you *expect* that the Home Companion would provide?

		Yes	No
7a.	Personal care	____	____
7b.	Prepare meals	____	____
7c.	Light housework	____	____
7d.	Do laundry	____	____
7e.	Do shopping	____	____
7f.	Run errands	____	____
7g.	Help with medical care	____	____
7h.	Be a companion	____	____
7i.	Other (specify) _____		

8. What kinds of services did you *receive* from the Home Companion?

		Yes	No
8a.	Personal care	____	____
8b.	Prepare meals	____	____
8c.	Light housework	____	____
8d.	Do laundry	____	____
8e.	Do shopping	____	____
8f.	Run errands	____	____
8g.	Help with medical care	____	____
8h.	Be a companion	____	____
8i.	Other (specify) _____		

9. In terms of organization, would you say the Home Companion Program (from the time you first had contact with it to the end/now) is:

1	2	3	4
Very Disorganized	Disorganized	Organized	Very Organized

10. How often did you feel the Home Companion listened to you regarding your feelings, needs, etc.?

1	2	3	4
Never	Seldom	Sometimes	Always

11. How many different Home Companions visited you? _____

12. How many times a week did a Home Companion come to your home?

_____

13. On the average, how many hours did the Home Companion spend on each visit? _____

14. How long a period of time did you receive Home Companion Services?

_____

15. What was the *most* valuable service the Home Companion provided for you?

_____

16. What was the *least* valuable/helpful service the Home Companion provided for you?

_____

17. Are there any services that the Home Companion did not provide that you would have liked to have had?
    17a. Yes _____ No _____
    17b. If yes, what are they?

18. What do/did you like *best* about the Home Companion Program?

_____

19. What do/did you like *least* about the Home Companion Program?

_____

20. Would you recommend the Home Companion Program to a friend or relative?

    20a. Yes _____ No _____

    20b. If no, why not? _____

21. How did you pay for the Home Companion services?

    Insurance _____   Out of pocket   _____

    Medicaid _____   Other (specify) _____

22. Would you be willing to pay more money per hour, say, $9.00 to $15.00, for Home Companion Services?

    Yes _____ No _____

23. If a Home Companion came to your home and helped you with your personal care, assisted you with your medication, cooked a meal, did some laundry, ran errands, helped with house cleaning and spent time visiting with you, how much would you be willing to pay per visit?

_____

24. Would you be willing to pay a price differential (a higher price for Home Companion services on the weekend)?

    Yes _____ No _____

25. What difference did/does having a Home Companion make for you? (For example, did it help you stay in your own home, make you feel better, make you not feel lonely, help your family, etc.)

	Yes	No
25a. Made it easier for me to remain in my home	_____	_____
25b. How? _____		
25c. Made me feel better	_____	_____
25d. How? _____		
25e. Made me feel not as lonely	_____	_____
25f. How? _____		
25g. Helped my family	_____	_____
25h. How? _____		
25i. Other (specify) _____		

26. Where do you think you would be today were it not for the Home Companion Services?

_____

27. What do you think your state of health would be today were it not for the Home Companion Services?

_____

28. What impact do you believe the Home Companion services have had on your family?

_____

29. How often did the Home Companion Supervisor visit you while you received Home Companion services, including the initial visit?

_____

30. Did you feel comfortable in asking the Home Companion to do different things for you?

    30a. Yes _____ No _____

    30b. Please explain or give examples:

31. If you wanted to complain about or praise a Home Companion, did you know whom to call?

    31a. Yes _____ No _____

    31b. Did you feel free to call?

    Yes _____ No _____

32. Did you complete the VNS Home Companion evaluation form?

    Yes _____ No _____

33. Are you currently using Home Companion services?

    33a. Yes _____ No _____

    33b. If no, why not? _____

    33c. If no, would you use the Home Companion services again in the future?

    Yes _____ No _____

    33d. If no, why not? _____

    33e. If yes, what would prompt you to do so? _____

34. What was the major reason you hired a Home Companion through the VNS rather than hire a caretaker on your own or through another agency?

_____

35. We are always interested in improving services to our clients. What suggestions do you have to improve the Home Companion Program?

_____

_____

36. Overall, how satisfied are/were you with the Home Companion services you received?

1	2	3	4
Very Unsatisfied	Unsatisfied	Satisfied	Very Satisfied

Do you have any other comments or suggestions about our services that you would like to share with us?

Thank you very much for the time you've spent answering our questions. This information will be very useful to us in planning services for clients in situations like yours.

Chapter 17

Role of the Family Caregiver in the Home

Lynn Rew

When considering issues of quality assurance in home health care, special attention must be directed to family and other significant members of the recipient's support system (hereafter they will be referred to as *family caregivers*). Specifically, the family caregivers who are expected to provide ongoing care to a person recently discharged from the hospital or other health-related institution are also in need of support, education, and care from health professionals. In order to assure that quality of care is provided to the home care recipient, specialized needs of the family caregiver must also be addressed. This chapter provides a general description of the role of the family member as caregiver. Unique needs and problems associated with filling this role are identified as they relate to the structure, process, and outcomes of quality assurance in home care. Finally, strategies to enhance the quality of care of the designated care recipient through attending to the needs and problems of the family caregiver are discussed.

ROLE OF THE FAMILY CAREGIVER

The shift of an individual's convalescent care from a hospital or another health care institution to the home places new demands on other family members. While this shift to home care is often praised as a measure to contain the escalating costs of health care, it is also blamed for creating new burdens and strains on family members who are expected to take on roles as caregivers. The strain of providing ongoing nursing care to a family member often places the caregiver at risk for developing health problems of his or her own.

When the decision is made to discharge a hospitalized individual to home care, health care professionals often assume that some family member is both able and willing to accept the role of caregiver. Like other roles, that of caregiver evokes expectations from the person providing and the person receiving the care. Similarly, health care professionals and other members of society also have expectations regarding someone who fills that role. These expectations ultimately affect issues of quality assurance in home care. Consumer and provider, in this case both members of the same family, anticipate outcomes that are not always easy to assure.

The concept of role and role theory are familiar to nurses, physicians, social workers, and psychologists. According to Banton, society consists of individuals who interact within a system of roles.[1] A role indicates how a person occupying the role is expected to behave. Roles may be assigned or achieved. Banton points out that when an individual changes roles through the assignment or achievement of a new role, this change requires that he or she knows the rights and responsibilities associated with the new role. Further, other people in the social environment must also recognize the change in the person's role and modify their behavior toward that person accordingly.

Biddle provides further discussion of expectations, identities, and behaviors in role theory.[2] He identifies reciprocal roles as those in which some of the behaviors expected of a person in one role act as sanctions for behaviors expected of a person in the reciprocal role. Reciprocal roles of mother and child and of caregiver and care recipient are likely to be very specific and the behaviors associated with each role tend not to overlap. Biddle adds that role strain, role ambiguity, and role overload are associated with stressful experiences concerning roles. Role strain is associated with expectations that are unrealistic, role ambiguity occurs when the stated expectations for a particular role are incomplete or unclear, and role overload results when a person is faced with a role that is too complex to master.

Role and role theory may also be understood in relation to the developmental stages of the life span. Primary, secondary, and tertiary roles are described in relation to various developmental stages and tasks. Primary roles are performed by the individual on a routine basis and are related to individual attributes such as age, sex, and stage of development. For example, a 6-month-old female would occupy a primary role of "baby girl." Secondary roles are also related to the individual's developmental stage and are generally positions of achievement. For example, a secondary role is achieved when the 22-year-old male completes a baccalaureate degree, successfully passes the state board of nursing examination, and then occupies the role of registered nurse.

Tertiary roles are also usually positions of achievement, but tend to be related to short-term tasks associated with a specific goal.[3] The 50-year-old female who is elected president of a professional organization to which she belongs is expected to fill a tertiary role. In the role of president, certain expectations regarding her behavior are implicit. Furthermore, it is assumed that she will fulfill this role in a particular time frame (e.g., one year) and that filling this role is essential to meeting a goal (e.g., the smooth running of the organization). Tertiary roles are accepted in addition to the secondary and primary roles that an individual already has assumed. A young mother who provides specialized care for a child on a respirator occupies a primary role of young woman, a secondary role of mother, and a tertiary role of caregiver.

Although the role of caregiver is considered to be a tertiary one, the parameters for expected behaviors associated with this role are not as clear or explicit as the ones in the example of the 50-year-old president of a professional organization. Many family caregivers are given little choice about taking on this role.[4] When a 65-year-old man is sent home to recuperate from a total hip replacement, it may be assumed by health professionals planning for his discharge that because he has a wife, she will become the caregiver. In order to plan for quality care for this man, his wife must be included in the decisions about his home care. Does his wife have the necessary resources in terms of her own health and lifestyle to adjust to the particular demands associated with providing his care? Is she motivated to continue special tasks that require acquisition of new skills and diligence in adhering to medical and nursing protocols? While she may be eager to have her husband back home, it is easy to overlook many of the daily activities that may need to be altered in order to provide his care. Even with regular visits from a home health nurse or homemaker, the burden of responsibility may fall on the wife. The wife turned caregiver may be ill prepared to assume this new role and may have a very unrealistic idea of what will be expected of her.

In providing quality care in the home, health professionals must consider the family caregiver and his or her physical surroundings, including environmental resources such as space, time, and equipment, as constituting the structural component of service.[5] Preparation for home care must include an assessment of the family caregiver's motivation and resources for filling this role, and this must be done prior to planning for the discharge of the care recipient from the hospital. Family members who agree to assume the caregiver role must be able to make an informed decision about this role. This decision must be based on a realistic appraisal of the amount of time the family member will need to devote to the behaviors expected for that role and of the demands associated with other roles already in place. Alternate caregivers should be considered and strengths and weaknesses of each evaluated carefully. The future health and well-being of both family members—care recipient and caregiver—must be appraised before a final decision about home care is made.

THE AFFIRM MODEL

A detailed set of interventions for preparing the family caregiver for this new role is provided in the AFFIRM model.[6] AFFIRM is an acronym for availability, formulation, factual information, referrals, and monitoring. Based on their experiences with providing home health care, a group of graduate nurses and their faculty developed this set of interventions to promote role mastery in the family member who accepts the role and responsibilities of the caregiver. In their review of the literature, the authors of the model identify the impact of technology on the caregiver and discuss how the adjustment to dialysis machines, ventilators, and intravenous infusion equipment leads to role confusion in family members who become caregivers. Similarly, others describe the change in the family lifestyle that is brought about by the addition of complex equipment into the home environment.[7] For example, when an infant is sent home with special equipment, older children in the family may be expected to grow up quickly and take on additional responsibilities, such as for housekeeping.[8]

The process of quality assurance in home care focuses on specific tasks to be performed for the home care recipient. Using the AFFIRM model, nurses can help a family caregiver make the adjustment to having complex technical equipment in the home and to learn the specialized skills needed to operate this equipment. The AFFIRM model is based on principles of affirmation and encouragement and emphasizes the importance of adult learning principles. Application of the model as a series of nursing interventions is facilitated by the use of a booklet (Appendix 17-A) that can be introduced by a hospital-based discharge planning nurse or by a home health nurse.

Availability

The first step is to assist the family caregiver in assessing the *availability* of resources in the home environment and community. The AFFIRM booklet contains a page with a list of resources that the family caregiver will need to have available in providing the projected care for the care recipient.[9] The list of resources includes equipment, space, time, medications, finances, social support, and the caregiver's motivation for assuming the role of caregiver. The nurse is encouraged to complete this step of the intervention with the caregiver prior to the transfer of the family care recipient to the home setting. At this time the nurse can also help the family caregiver to clarify the decision to accept the role of caregiver and, through an assessment of the available resources, make other arrangements to facilitate the caregiver's ability to master the role and provide quality care.

Formulation

The second step of the AFFIRM model consists of *Formulation*, that is, formulating a daily schedule of caregiver activities to meet care recipient needs. By completing the second page of the booklet, the nurse and family caregiver can identify potential conflicts in the day-to-day activities that are planned for the care recipient.[10] Again, this permits both the nurse and the family caregiver the opportunity to consider alternate care plans and care providers that might ease the conflicts that would otherwise emerge. It also is an opportunity to reinforce and encourage the caregiver in the decision that he or she has made.

Factual Information

After agreeing to take on the role of caregiver, a family member may need to learn specialized skills, such as those required to change a dressing or to operate highly complex equipment. In the AFFIRM model, this step is identified as *factual information* and is based on adult learning principles.[11] Health professionals must remember that learning styles vary and an individualized teaching plan should be developed. Again, to assure quality of care, objective evaluation and adequate reinforcement of the teaching of the caregiver is required. The caregiver may easily demonstrate how to change a dressing immediately after instruction in the hospital but be totally confused about performing this skill under different conditions at home. Client and caregiver manuals, with written instructions for specific procedures and high-tech equipment, are useful reinforcers.

In addition to applying principles of motivation and learning styles to the teaching of the family caregiver, principles of reinforcement and transfer of learning to another environment must be kept in mind by the individual who is planning for the discharge. Expected outcomes for the care recipient's health status must be identified and behaviors of the family caregiver that are intended to facilitate this must be encouraged and reinforced. An important consideration in applying the principles of reinforcement and transfer of learning is that time for this must be included in the schedule of the nurse making the initial home visits. Although this time may not be accounted for in the description of direct care provided to the care recipient, it is essential for the quality of care delivered.

In the AFFIRM booklet the caregiver is given brief factual information about the relationship of stress to the caregiver's new role. Whether role conflict or role overload occurs, such experiences are stressful to the caregiver and may lead to greater vulnerability to fatigue and illness. Several stress management suggestions, such as deep breathing, relaxation techniques, and talking to friends and nurses, are provided. Because the family caregiver is a vital part of the care recipient's daily environment, it is essential that the health and well-being of this person be protected. Principles of health promotion for the family caregiver will contribute to the overall high quality of care received.

Referrals

The fourth step of the AFFIRM model is the construction of a list of *referrals*. This list of additional resources includes names, addresses, and phone numbers of a wide range of services available in a specific community setting. In addition to family and friends, the list includes hospital personnel that may provide home health services, physicians, home health nursing agencies, emergency medical services, pharmacies, durable medical equipment companies, support groups, counseling services, electric and gas companies, fire departments, and rescue services within the community. This step of the intervention is especially helpful when the home health nurse takes additional time to assist the family caregiver in identifying those family members and friends who may be called on for specific aid over the weeks and months ahead. Many family caregivers are reluctant to call on these resources, believing instead that they should be able to manage "on their own." However, when a list of resources is constructed in such a way that all potential resources are identified and the specific kinds assistance associated with each are enumerated, family caregivers feel strengthened and empowered by the realization they have access to support. This may be especially helpful to individuals who are facing a prolonged period of caregiving and to those with limited access to community resources (such as persons in rural areas) and to third party reimbursement benefits.

Monitoring

The final step of the AFFIRM model involves *monitoring* the progress of both the care recipient and the family caregiver in the home setting. Monitoring includes an evaluation of the recipient's care and the caregiver's success in role mastery. However, rather than being a single step in which a list of criteria are checked off at a certain time, monitoring is a dynamic process of ongoing observation, communication, and suggestion. In home care, the home health nurse or case manager may be responsible for observing care received in the home and in communicating information among nurses, physicians, the care recipient, and the family caregiver. Similarly, close communication by way of the telephone provides information about the care recipient's recuperation and the family caregiver's mastery of the caregiver role. If problems or concerns exist, suggestions for alternative support for care recipient or caregiver can be made.

In the AFFIRM booklet, the family caregiver is reminded of scheduled times for the care recipient to be seen by the physician and for home visits to be made by the nurse. In addition, the caregiver is encouraged to keep in touch with the nurses at the hospital who were instrumental in the acute care of the care recipient. Further, the caregiver is encouraged to monitor his or her own progress toward mastery of the caregiver role. The booklet contains six questions to help assess such progress. Three of the questions reflect role mastery while the other three focus on whether the caregiver is experiencing fatigue, lack of time for his or her own interests, and conflict with other roles and responsibilities. The family caregiver is encouraged to call for help if the answers to the last three questions are affirmative.

POTENTIAL FOR ABUSE AND NEGLECT

Any discussion of the quality of home care and the role of the family caregiver is incomplete without a consideration of the actual and potential problems of patient abuse, neglect, and maltreatment. Although these harmful practices are defined in many different ways, for the purpose of this discussion a broad definition is provided. Care that is essential to the health and well-being of the patient (i.e., food, housing, financial support, and adequate medical care) may be omitted, given with psychological undertones that are destructive (e.g., insulting the person or using humiliating names), or provided in ways contrary to the safe standards determined for professional health care providers. Thus, when considering the overall quality of care received by a home care recipient, these types of mistreatment must be assessed. Further, inclusion of health professionals as potential perpetrators of abuse and neglect is essential in monitoring quality of home care.

Three groups of particularly high risk for abuse, neglect, or maltreatment are children, the elderly, and the mentally retarded. Members of these groups are especially vulnerable to all forms of abuse because they tend to be physically smaller than their caregivers, have less physical or mental capability than their caregivers, and are economically and emotionally dependent on their caregivers.[12] Children who have brain damage and physical handicaps, who were illegitimate, and whose families experience high levels of stress are the most vulnerable to abuse, neglect, and maltreatment.[13] Indications of possible abuse or neglect among these at-risk care recipients include bruises, lacerations, broken bones, and burns as well as evidence of malnourishment and dehydration.

In monitoring, the progress of the care recipient in the home assessments of both the caregiver and care recipient must be made. The relationship between the caregiver and recipient may provide clues that require a follow-up investigation, for example, in cases where the care recipient is extremely compliant or unduly afraid of the family caregiver, the care recipient sits far away from the caregiver, or the care recipient is isolated or passive and attributes injuries to improbable causes.[14] Further, the caregiver may also exhibit hostility, ascribe blame to the care recipient, attempt to discipline the care recipient, or fail to make eye contact with the care recipient, all of which behaviors warrant investigation.

In order to promote optimal health among home care recipients, continued monitoring of the relationship between caregiver and care recipient is essential. Procedures for reporting possible abuse, neglect, and maltreatment of care recipients must be in place. When suspected, abuse or neglect must be reported to the appropriate authorities and other plans made to provide the care recipient with a more supportive environment. This same monitoring should still be conducted even when the caregiver is a professional.

STRATEGIES TO ENHANCE QUALITY OF CARE

Strategies to enhance the quality of care given and received in the home must include those aimed at the family caregiver as well as the professional health provider. As suggested earlier, the decision of a family member to assume the role of caregiver must be an informed choice. The discharge planning nurse at the hospital or the care manager of the home health team can provide value clarification exercises to help the family member make this decision (see Exhibit 17-1 for an example).

CONCLUSION

Application of the AFFIRM model to provide basic elements of the nursing process to home care recipients and their family caregivers is one method of enhancing the quality of home care. The structure of home care includes the family caregiver as well as all of the environmental resources available to the care recipient. Encouragement and affirmation of the caregiver by home health professionals contribute to the

Exhibit 17-1 Value Clarification Exercise for Family Caregiver

A member of your family was hospitalized recently and plans to return home in a few days. He/she still needs nursing care at home. This care requires time and skill from a caregiver.

1. Make a list of family members you think might be able to provide such care.
2. Re-arrange the list in the order of whom you think would best provide it.
3. What other resources does the family have for caregiving (e.g., friends, relatives, ability to pay for professional services).
4. What are the advantages and disadvantages for each of these caregiving resources?
5. If you are high on the re-arranged list (Step 2), list three reasons why you would be a good caregiver.
6. Whom else would you like to consult before making a decision to accept the role of caregiver?

overall quality of this structure. Continued monitoring of the relationship between caregiver and care recipient is essential for promoting high-quality care as well. Efforts to prevent the abuse, neglect, or maltreatment of home care recipients must be included in criteria for quality assurance in home care. When role strain, role conflict, or role overload are assessed, plans may be made to provide respite care. This strategy provides relief for the family caregiver and a change of pace for the care recipient. Without occasional respite, the potential for abuse, neglect, and maltreatment increases, as does the potential for development of illness in the family caregiver.

Having agency nurses on call also provides a source of backup information and expertise to the caregiver, who may be uncertain or confused about specific procedures or care routines. Receiving assurance via the telephone supports the caregiver as well as decreases the potential for client injuries. Although an agency's liability for the caregiver who initially appeared competent but, with added burdens, becomes physically or emotionally distraught is currently ambiguous, it is likely that a court of law would find a home health agency responsible for injury caused by a caregiver determined to be incompetent. The judicial system has clearly established that custom does not necessarily determine whether the standard of care has been met;[15] lack of clear standards or inadequate reimbursement are not plausible excuses.

When health care is provided through institutions such as hospitals and nursing homes by educated health care professionals and trained ancillary personnel, quality assurance programs address structure, process, and outcomes. When health care is provided in the home, these same components of quality care also must be addressed. The family caregiver is an integral part of the structure, the process, and the outcome. Criteria that address this unique human role are essential to promoting continuity of care and having home care of the highest quality.

NOTES

1. M. Banton, *Roles: An Introduction to the Study of Social Relations* (New York: Basic Books, 1965).

2. B.J. Biddle, *Expectations, Identities, and Behaviors* (New York: Academic Press, 1979).

3. K.A. Nuwayhid, "Role Function: Theory and Development," in *Introduction to Nursing: An Adaptation Model*, ed. S.C. Roy, 2d ed. (Englewood Cliffs, N.J.: Prentice-Hall, 1984).

4. L. Rew et al., "AFFIRM: A Nursing Model to Promote Role Mastery in Family Caregivers," *Family and Community Health* 9, no. 4 (1987): 52–64.

5. S.L. Salloway, "Quality Assurance," in *Community Health Nursing*, ed. W. Burgess (Norwalk, Conn.: Appleton-Century-Crofts, 1983).

6. Rew et al., "AFFIRM."

7. E.F. Banaszak et al., "Home Ventilator Care," *Respiratory Care* 26 (1981): 1262–67.

8. E.A. Feinberg, "Family Stress in Pediatric Home Care," *Caring* 4 (1985): 38–41.

9. Rew et al., "AFFIRM."

10. Ibid.

11. Ibid.

12. M.F. Pollick, "Abuse of the Elderly: A Review," *Holistic Nursing Practice* 1, no. 2 (1987): 43–53.

13. M.E. Broome and D. Daniels, "Child Abuse: A Multidimensional Phenomenon," *Holistic Nursing Practice* 1, no. 2 (1987): 13–24.

14. Pollick, "Abuse of the Elderly."

15. Darling v. Charleston Community Memorial Hospital, 33, Ill.2d 326 (1965).

SUGGESTED READINGS

Bader, J.E. "Respite Care: Temporary Relief for Caregivers." *Health Needs of Women* 10, no. 2–3 (1985): 39–52.

Baines, E. "Caregiver Stress in the Older Adult," *Journal of Community Health Nursing* 1 (1984): 257–63.

Britton, J.G., and D.M. Mattson-Melcher. "The Crisis Home." *Journal of Psychosocial Nursing and Mental Health Services* 23, no. 12 (1985): 18–23.

Cantor, M.H. "Strain among Caregivers: A Study of Experience in the United States." *Gerontologist* 23 (1983): 597–604.

Capuzzi, D., L. Gossman, S. Whiston, and J. Surdam. "Group Counseling for Aged Women." *Personnel and Guidance Journal* 57 (1979): 306–9.

Choi, T., L. Josten, and M.L. Christensen. "Health-Specific Family Coping Index for Noninstitutional Care." *American Journal of Public Health* 73, no. 11 (1983): 1275–1277.

Clark, N.M., and W. Rakowski. "Family Caregivers of Older Adults: Improving Helping Skills." *Gerontologist* 23 (1983): 637–42.

Coleman, J.R., and D.S. Smith. "DRGs and the Growth of Home Health Care." *Nursing Economics* 2 (1984): 391–95, 408.

Crouch, M.A. "Role Reversal of the Elderly and Their Middle-aged Children: Emotional Fusion across the Life Cycle." *Family and Community Health* 9, no. 4 (1987): 65–76.

Ewing, W.A. "Domestic Violence and Community Health Care Ethics: Reflections on Systemic Intervention." *Family and Community Health* 10, no. 1 (1987): 54–62.

Feldman, G., and P.G. Tuteur. "Mechanical Ventilation: From Hospital Intensive Care to Home." *Heart and Lung* 11 (1982): 162–65.

Fengler, A. and N. Goodrich, "Wives of Elderly Disabled Men: The Hidden Patient." *Gerontologist* 19 (1979): 175–82.

Finkelhor, D., R.J. Gelles, G.T. Hotaling, and M.A. Straus. *The Dark Side of Families*. Beverly Hills, Calif.: Sage Publications, 1983.

Fox, J. "Chronic Respiratory Patients: A New Challenge for Home Health Nursing." *Home Healthcare Nurse* 3, no. 2 (1985): 13–16.

Foxall, M.J., J.Y. Ekberg, and N. Griffith. "Adjustment Patterns of Chronically Ill Middle-Aged Persons and Spouses." *Western Journal of Nursing Research* 7 (1985): 425–44.

Goldman, H. "Mental Illness and Family Burden." *Hospital and Community Psychiatry*, 1982, 33: 557–560.

Goldstein, V., G. Regnery, and E. Wellin. "Caretaker Role Fatigue." *Nursing Outlook* 29, no. 1 (1981): 24–30.

Gutierrez, K. "Home Is Where the Care Is." *Nursing* 11 (1985): 49.

Hays, J.C. "Hospice Policy and Patterns of Care." *Image: Journal of Nursing Scholarship* 18, no. 3 (1986): 92–97.

Herman, C.M., and K. Krall. "University Sponsored Home Care Agency as a Clinical Site." *Image: The Journal of Nursing Scholarship* 16 (1984): 71–75.

Johnson, C.L., and D. J. Catalano. "A Longitudinal Study of Family Supports to Impaired Elderly." *Gerontologist* 23 (1983): 612–18.

Kane, C. "The Outpatient Comes Home: The Family's Response to Deinstitutionalization." *Journal of Psychosocial Nursing and Mental Health Services* 22 (1984): 19–25.

Knight, B., and D.L. Walker. "Toward a Definition of Alternatives to Institutionalization for the Frail Elderly." *Gerontologist* 25 (1985): 358–63.

Kopacz, M.A., and R.M. Wright. "Multidisciplinary Approach for the Patient on a Home Ventilator." *Heart and Lung* 13 (1984): 255–62.

Landis, K., and S. Smith. "The Mechanically Ventilated Patient: A Comprehensive Care Plan." *Critical Care Quarterly* 6, no. 2 (1983): 43–52.

Medeiros, C., and G. Barreto-Vega. "Projecting Need for Home Health Services: Analysis of Need and Demand." *Home Health Review* 4 (1981): 32–42.

Montgomery, R.J.V., J.G. Gongea, and N.R. Hooyman. "Caregiving and the Experience of Subjective and Objective Burden." *Family Relations* 34 (1985): 19–26.

Newcomer, R., J. Wood, and A. Sankar. "Medicare Prospective Payment: Anticipated Effect on Hospitals, Other Community Agencies, and Families." *Journal of Health Politics, Policy, and Law* 10 (1985): 275–82.

Newman, S.J. "Housing and Long-term Care: The Suitability of the Elderly's Housing to the Provision of In-Home Services." *Gerontologist* 25 (1985): 35–40.

Oleske, D.M., D.M. Otte, and S. Heinze. "Development and Evaluation of a System for Monitoring the Quality of Oncology Nursing Care in the Home Setting." *Cancer Nursing* 10, no. 4 (1987): 190–198.

Parmelee, P.A. "Spouse versus Other Family Caregivers: Psychological Impact on Impaired Aged." *American Journal of Community Psychology* 11 (1983): 337–49.

Petrosino, B.M. "Characteristics of Hospice Patients, Primary Caregivers, and Nursing Care Problems: Foundation for Future Research." *Hospice Journal* 1 (1985): 3–19.

Phillips, L.R., and V.F. Rempusheski. "Caring for the Frail Elderly at Home: Toward a Theoretical Explanation of the Dynamics of Poor Quality Family Caregiving." *Advances in Nursing Science* 8, no. 4 (1986): 62–84.

Potasznik, H., and G. Nelson. "Stress and Social Support: The Burden Experienced by the Family of the Mentally Ill Person." *American Journal of Community Psychology* 12 (1984): 589–607.

Robinson, B. "Validation of a Caregiver Strain Index." *Journal of Gerontology* 36 (1983): 344–48.

Robinson, K.M. "A Social Skills Training Program for Adult Caregivers." *Advances in Nursing Science* 10, no. 2 (1988): 59–72.

Sexton, D.L., and B.H. Munro. "Impact of a Husband's Chronic Illness (COPD) on the Spouse's Life." *Research in Nursing and Health* 8 (1985): 83–90.

Shanas, E. "The Family as a Social Support System in Old Age." *Gerontologist* 19 (1979): 169–74.

Soreff, S.M. "Indications for Home Treatment." *Psychiatric Clinics of North America* 8 (1985): 563–75.

Splaingard, M.L., R.C. Frates, G.M. Harrison, et al. "Home Positive-Pressure Ventilation: Twenty Years Experience." *Chest* 84 (1983): 376–82.

Stengel, J.C., D.W. Echeveste, and G.C. Schmidt. "Problems Identified by Registered Nurse Students in Families with Apnea-monitored Infants." *Family and Community Health* 8 (1985): 52–61.

Stetz, K.M. "Caregiving Demands During Advanced Cancer: The Spouse's Needs." *Cancer Nursing* 10, no. 5 (1987): 260–268.

Stone, R., G.L. Cafferata, and J. Sangl. *Caregivers of the Frail Elderly: A National Profile.* Washington, D.C.: U.S. Department of Health and Human Services, 1986.

Stuifbergen, A.K. "The Impact of Chronic Illness on Families." *Family and Community Health* 9, no. 4 (1987): 43–51.

Teusink, J., and S. Mohler. "Helping Families Cope with Alzheimer's Disease." *Hospital and Community Psychiatry* 35, no. 2 (1984): 152–156.

Thomas, J.L. "Adult Children's Assistance as a Health Care Resource: The Older Parent's Perspective." *Family and Community Health* 9, no. 4 (1987): 34–42.

Zarit, S.H., K. Reever, and J. Bach-Peterson. "Relatives of the Impaired Elderly: Correlates of Feelings of Burdens." *Gerontologist* 20 (1980): 649–55.

Appendix 17-A

The AFFIRM Model Booklet*

AFFIRM
YOUR
NEW ROLE AS
CAREGIVER
- - - - - - -
YOU are about to begin
a new role as CAREGIVER.
This booklet was designed
to offer encouragement and
support.

ON THE FOLLOWING PAGES YOU WILL
FIND INFORMATION TO HELP YOU
PLAN FOR CHANGES WHICH MAY BE
NEEDED IN YOUR HOME OR IN YOUR
DAILY ROUTINE. YOU WILL BE TAUGHT
ANY NEW SKILLS, IF NEEDED, AND WHOM
TO CONTACT IF YOU NEED HELP.

Availability

On this page you will find a list of resources which you will need to have available to you when caring for your family member at home. The nurse will help you identify what is needed and how to obtain necessary items.

EQUIPMENT:

SPACE:

MEDICATIONS:

FINANCES:

SOCIAL SUPPORT:

YOUR MOTIVATION:

Formulation

This formulation is a plan of the daily schedule of the family member for whom you will be caring and of your daily activities. This will give you an idea of how your daily routines may need to be adjusted.

PATIENT'S DAILY SCHEDULE   YOUR DAILY SCHEDULE

6:00 a.m.

NOON

6:00 p.m.

MIDNIGHT

Factual Information

This page is to help you identify specific factual information which you will need in order to perform the role of caregiver.

WHAT:

WHEN:

WHO:

HOW:

In addition to the above information, we would like for you to know the following things about taking care of yourself:

Being a CAREGIVER may be a new role for you. Learning new roles sometimes leads to feelings of STRESS. It is impor-

---

*Adapted from *Family & Community Health,* Vol. 9, No. 4, pp. 62–64, Aspen Publishers, Inc., © February 1987.

tant that you make time for yourself and continue many of the activities which have always brought you PLEASURE and RELAXATION. Deep breathing, listening to music, and walking outdoors may be helpful. A phone call to a friend or to one of the nurses may also be helpful.

Referrals

The following referrals consist of various organizations which you may need to call for additional supplies or services.

EMS

PHYSICIANS

HOSPITAL

HOME HEALTH AGENCY

PHARMACY

DURABLE MEDICAL EQUIPMENT

ELECTRIC COMPANY

FIRE DEPARTMENT

COUNSELING

SUPPORT GROUP

FRIENDS/RELATIVES

Monitoring

Following the progress of you and the patient is important. Plans for return visits to the physician and/or visits from the home health nurse are listed below. Please do not hesitate to call one of the nurses here at the hospital or the home health nurse if you need assistance before the planned visits.

RETURN TO PHYSICIAN(S):

HOME NURSE TO VISIT:

NURSES AT HOSPITAL:

YOU may want to MONITOR your own progress in living with the new role of CAREGIVER. Answer the following questions at intervals and call for help if you answer ''yes'' to # 4–6:

1. I feel confident in providing the patient's daily care.
2. I feel knowledgeable about the care I'm giving.
3. I feel satisfied with this new role.
4. I feel overworked and tired much of the time.
5. I find I don't have enough time for myself.
6. I feel conflict with my other roles and responsibilities.

Chapter 18

Assuring Continuity of Care: Managing the Transition from Hospital to Home

Sister Ann M. Schorfheide

The rapid transition from hospital to home (quicker and sicker) is a challenge to health care providers and health care receivers as well as to their formal and informal support systems. There must be planning, coordinating, communicating, referral, and follow-up to achieve continuity of care and meet the health care needs and maximize the potential of the individual client. Planning for continuity of care through discharge planning is an integral part of quality assurance. Discharge planning is intended to facilitate the transition from one level of health care to another. The goal of discharge planning is to assure that clients receive the care they need to maintain or regain as normal or productive a role in life as possible in the most appropriate environment.

This chapter addresses societal forces affecting continuity of care, strategies for continuity of care planning, and barriers to effective continuity of health care. The conclusion urges research validation to assure quality care.

SOCIETAL FORCES AFFECTING CONTINUITY OF CARE

In reviewing the contemporary forces affecting discharge planning for continuity of care, the 1965 Medicare and Medicaid amendments to the Social Security Act stand out. The implementation of Medicare (Title XVIII) and Medicaid (Title XIX) on July 1, 1966, required the establishment of utilization review committees in all participating hospitals to evaluate the appropriateness of services rendered and the lengths of stay. In August 1966, the Steering Committee of the Division of Nursing Services, National League for Nursing, composed of members of the departments of hospital and public health nursing, promulgated a statement recommending that every hospital, nursing home, and home care agency take steps to assure the existence of a program of continuity of nursing care.[1] They strongly recommended that each agency

- charge one individual, preferably on a full-time basis, to assist staff members in developing plans for the next stage of care during the present stage
- develop well-defined, clearly written procedures for client referral and interpret them to the entire staff
- invest administrative authority on the appointed person to conduct the continuity program by effectively planning and communicating with appropriate agencies[2]

In 1974, two additional federal sources provided significant input. The first was the Skilled Nursing Facility Medicare and Medicaid Rules (revised), which provided more detailed guidelines on discharge planning.[3] The second was the Department of Health, Education and Welfare's publication of guidelines for professional standard review organizations (PSROs), which were intended to monitor the necessity for, and cost of, medical care. The PSRO manual included a section on discharge planning.[4]

In 1975, the American Nurses' Association published their statement on the need for continuity of care and discharge planning programs in institutions and community agencies.[5] In 1984, the American Hospital Association (AHA) published guidelines for discharge planning in order for hospitals to maintain high-quality, cost-effective client care.[6]

As the nation continued to experience overwhelming health care costs along with a rapidly growing federal budget deficit, both voluntary and regulatory efforts were directed at cost containment by decreasing the lengths of stay and rates of re-admission in health care facilities. The dramatic movement in 1983 to the prospective payment system (PPS) for reimbursement for in-hospital services provided to Medicare clients on the basis of diagnosis related groups (DRGs) may prove to be the most significant economic and social transformation since the enactment of Medicare itself.[7] With this system, hospitals have financial incentives to hold costs down and to send clients home sooner. Closely associated with the PPS are peer review organizations (PROs), implemented in 1984 to replace the PSROs, which were generally considered ineffective in controlling costs.[8] Effective September 15, 1986, the revised conditions for hospital participation in Medicare and Medicaid programs included a standard on quality assurance and mandated that the hospital have "an effective, ongoing discharge planning program that facilitates the provision of follow-up care."[9]

In introducing the Omnibus Budget Reconciliation Act (OBRA) of 1986, the Health Care Financing Administration (HCFA) clearly mandated that home health care agencies be brought under the umbrella of the PROs beginning on October 1, 1987. Contracts between home care agencies and PROs, which are paid by the federal government, involve reviews for medical necessity, appropriateness, and quality of treatment for Medicare clients. A uniform needs assessment (to be developed by January 1, 1989) is to be used by "discharge planners, hospitals, nursing facilities, other health care providers, and fiscal intermediaries in evaluating an individual's need for posthospital extended care services, home health services, and long-term care services of a health related or supportive nature."[10]

In enforcing a client's right to be informed and involved in decision making and planning for posthospital care, the Medicare Quality Protection Act of 1986 (S. 2331 and H.R. 4638) viewed discharge planning as a quality of care issue.

The need for appropriate discharge planning was further reinforced by the standards of the Joint Commission on Accreditation of Healthcare Organizations (Joint Commission). In 1987, the Joint Commission further refined its standards for services and functions, which include continuing care and discharge planning as responsibilities of several disciplines and services.[11]

Indeed, these declarations from governmental and professional sources make continuity of care through discharge planning of considerable importance in any multidisciplinary team approach. Quality care and utilization review standards create expectations that make it mandatory to consider the least restrictive alternatives for the provision of quality health care.

THE STRATEGIES OF CONTINUITY OF CARE PLANNING

Continuing care planning is a process of working with the client and his or her family to facilitate the move from one health setting or level of care to another while taking into consideration their unique health care and personal needs (Exhibit 18-1).

Assessment

Discharge planning follows the same steps as the nursing process and begins with a holistic assessment. The initial steps should occur as soon as possible—before or at the time of admission, especially with high-risk clients. High-risk factors include (1) age, (2) disability or illness, (3) mental status, (4) living situation, and (5) reason for admission. The assessment should be holistic and take into account the client's direct physical care needs and health education needs as well as other biological, psychological, social and cultural needs.

Assessment of the family and other support systems might include investigating the client's living arrangements and determining who could and would be able to provide assistance to the client. If the client lives alone, are there caretakers or other support systems that could be of assistance? How suitable is the home environment? Is the setting accessible and safe? Are necessary facilities accessible—bed, toilet, bath, kitchen, laundry? Does the client need special equipment?

Appropriate community resources must also be assessed. Hospital discharge planners must be aware of the diversity and quality of services a home care agency can provide. Can the

---

Exhibit 18-1 Continuity of Care Discharge Planning Guide

Assessment

    Home environment and support system
    Personal daily living needs
    Medical and health problems
    Psychosocial and behavioral needs
    Skilled nursing, health education, and coordination of care needs
    Community resource service capability
    Resources for assistance after professional home care

Planning

    Team approach (providers, client, family)
    Realistic, mutually acceptable goals and expected outcomes
    An ongoing process

Implementation

    Skilled professional care
    Supportive services
    Coordination of activities
    Use of independent nursing interventions
    Accurate documentation

Evaluation

    Written progress and outcomes
    Patient and family satisfaction
    Input from providers, client, and family
    Follow-up of unmet needs
    Status of the caregiver

agency provide such services as I.V. therapy, ventilator care, physical, occupational, and speech therapy, and so forth? If necessary, are private duty nurses, homemakers, companion sitters, Meals on Wheels, volunteers, or support groups available? How can needed equipment be secured?

Needs vary with each client, family, setting, and collection of resources. The above questions and statements are meant to be only illustrative, not exhaustive. A number of tools and checklists have been developed for the assessment of discharge planning needs, and they are readily available in the literature (see Exhibit 18-2 for an example of such a checklist). Some authors have validated their instruments by testing the psychometric properties relating to validity and reliability for more authentic use in both research and practice.[12,13]

Planning

The planning step involves developing both a medical plan and a nursing plan, which include roles for the client, family, and the other appropriate health care providers. Realistic, mutually acceptable goals should be set for the short and the long term. This can be done through either a formal or informal process. The formal process should include scheduled

Exhibit 18-2 Discharge Planning Checklist

PATIENT DISCHARGE STATUS

Instructions: √ all items that apply.

	√	HEALTH/MEDICAL PROBLEMS
1		End-stage disease with poor prognosis (cancer, COPD, end-stage renal, CHF, etc.)
2		Enteral or parenteral nutrition
3		IV therapy
4		Right atrial catheter (Broviac, Hickman, Leonard)
5		Open wound(s) and/or draining/non-draining tubes
6		Unresolved pain control
7		Needs frequent post-hospitalization monitoring of lab values/vital signs/health status/or self-medications
8		Recent dependency in activities of daily living (hemiplegic, paraplegic, quadriplegic, total body case, amputee, etc.)
9		Recent body image change (ostomy, trach, disfiguring surgery, etc.)
10		Health status significantly impacts on normal growth and development
11		Other (please specify)
12		Status reviewed, no service needs observed
		PSYCHOSOCIAL/BEHAVIORAL PROBLEMS
13		Patient and/or family non-acceptance of disease/prognosis
14		Patient and/or family making inappropriate or inadequate plans for post-hospitalization care
15		Emotional, behavioral or mental health problems substantially impairing daily functioning
16		Evidence or suspicion of lack of compliance with or understanding of care plan
17		Other (please specify)
18		Status reviewed, no service needs observed
		EDUCATION/COORDINATION OF CARE NEEDS
19		Additional patient and/or family education is needed to provide self-care after discharge
20		Care needs to be coordinated with other services (e.g., P.T., O.T., home health aide, etc.) or other agencies
21		Lack of competent care provider in the home if patient is dependent on self-care
22		Home needs physical modifications for care of patient
23		Patient and/or family needs help with obtaining medical equipment
24		Other (please specify)
25		Status reviewed, no service needs observed
		COMMENTS:

Source: Reprinted from *Public Health Nursing*, Vol. 4, No. 4, p. 214, with permission of Blackwell Scientific Publications, Inc., © December 1987.

team conferences in the hospital prior to discharge and/or in the home. During these conferences, appropriate health care providers can share their unique perspectives on the client's progress and future needs. The conferences should include the client and family or other support systems to ensure understanding of the real and perceived needs of the client and family. In the informal process, information is shared appropriately, but not necessarily with all team members present. It may be indiscreet to share everything with all team members; client and family wishes must be honored. It is important to include the client and family in all planning phases, both in the hospital and in the home. Their varied perceptions of needs are crucial for establishing goals and enhancing positive outcomes.

Implementation

Written plans and progress notes are necessary in order for client progress to be monitored. Implementation requires accurate documentation, in narrative notes or flow sheets, of goals and progress toward goals by each team member. Aside from reimbursement and legal reasons, documentation is the main indicator for evaluating staff performance, utilization of services, and quality of care provided. The professional, serving as case manager, coordinates and facilitates care. Client and family input are critical in accurately documenting the quality of care provided.

When the author of this chapter worked with graduate students preparing to become clinical nurse specialists in a program involving high-tech home care, it was noted that the technical aspects of client care were managed rather easily by clients and families, with appropriate support.[14] However, the psychosocial aspects of the illness caused continuing problems, including feelings of powerlessness and dependency and confusion resulting from role reversals and other lifestyle disruptions. These problems created opportunities for nurses to use a variety of independent nursing interventions. Among these independent interventions were relaxation methods, stress management, guided imagery, contracting, and so forth. While implementing a plan of care, professional caregivers must be willing and able to deal with a variety of client and family needs.

Evaluation

Evaluation should be written and ongoing. Input should come from the caregiving professionals as well as the client and family. Appropriate forms or a standard format help to identify the expected goals and to determine if the goals are being met, the client's status has altered or improved, and the client and family are satisfied with the care. Since unmet needs can surface during the care process, goals are added or changed to meet the new challenges. A successful outcome is dependent on an orderly, systematic, well-documented process.

Another issue that should be addressed when evaluating home care is the status of the client caregivers. Caring for the caregiver is unfortunately often neglected. It is essential to support and show concern for the client caregiver, which minimizes stress and maximizes independence. The caregiver is critical to continuity of care. (Chapter 17, "The Role of the Family Caregiver in the Home," discusses this issue in great detail.)

BARRIERS TO EFFECTIVE CONTINUITY OF HEALTH CARE

Several factors can be identified as impacting the continuity of care.[15] They can be categorized as provider, client, and resource factors.

Provider Factors

Interagency and interprofessional competition for health care dollars, territorial jealousies, and lack of trust can seriously complicate coordination of health care services as well as interfere with communications. Too often, providers' perspectives on health care are limited by their setting, values, and the concerns of the moment, and they remain unaware of the planning and home care needs of clients and of the services available for continued care in the community. Unfortunately, this narrowness of perspective can occur both inside and outside of the institutional setting.

Client Factors

The client, the family, and members of other support systems need to understand and be part of the goal-setting process. They must have access to information to make informed choices from among care alternatives. Failure to include the client and family as interactive participants in the decision-making process can result in formidable barriers to quality care. Understanding how the client, the family, and significant others view their roles and responsibilities is crucial to effective planning and positive outcomes. Client and family priorities, awareness of problems, motivation to change or alter behaviors, and readiness and ability to act are essential. An understanding of the various cultural and environmental factors obstructing or enhancing interventions should be incorporated into client care.

In addition, sometimes clients wish to receive services, but financial barriers exist. When Medicare and other third party payers deny reimbursement, clients may not be willing or able to pay for the services privately.

Resource Factors

In addition to affordability, the availability and accessibility of appropriate resources is essential to goal attainment. Consideration of the client's or family's previous experience with a resource will enhance utilization of it, whether it is a service, a piece of equipment, or some other resource. If the client or family has had a negative experience in utilizing the resource, there may be resistance to using this resource again—or any other community resource. Perceptions, attitudes, and feelings must be handled appropriately.

DISCHARGING FROM HOME CARE: PROMOTING CONTINUITY OF CARE

Concern for quality care demands the development of discharge planning programs within home health care agencies. With Medicare and many private and commercial insurance carriers defining home care as skilled, intermittent care provided to essentially homebound clients, agencies must have written policies concerning the acceptance of clients into home care and the discharge of clients or termination of services.

As case managers, home care agency personnel have the responsibility to begin preparing for withdrawal of services upon admission of a client to the agency. The Medicare conditions of participation mandate that there be a discharge policy and discharge summary as well as the standardized plan of treatment forms (commonly referred to as Forms 485, 486, and 487). In order to maximize the effectiveness of the plan of treatment, the client and the family must participate in planning for discharge. Documentation must reflect the client's goals and the progress toward those goals as well as the continued needs of the client and plans for meeting those needs. Proper after-care referrals to reasonable care alternatives (e.g., appropriate family and community resources) must occur in order to avoid the charge of abandonment (refer to Chapter 15).

CONCLUSION

Continuity of care and discharge planning are critical components of health care delivery. Continuity of care involves the client, family, and various members of the health care team participating in the planning, implementation, evaluation, and revision of client care based on reliable information continually flowing between the appropriate individuals. A mutually acceptable and mutually determined process of discharge planning enhances the goal of maintenance or attainment of optimum health for clients. The strategy is to optimally and cost-effectively utilize health care resources for which there is a demonstrated client need. From an administrator's perspective, effective discharge planning is essential to the financial viability and survival of the organization. While nurses in every setting are crucially placed to assure continuity of care, success will depend on administrative approval and support. In today's competitive health care environment, effective discharge planning can be a strong public relations tool for the marketing of a caring organization.

Unfortunately, only a small amount of research data exists concerning the effectiveness of discharge planning.[16] Most studies reported in the literature are descriptive in nature and focus on the number of discharge referrals, lengths of hospital stay, operationalizing various discharge planning models, transfer of information, client knowledge, and client and provider satisfaction. Indeed, additional research is needed to validate the effectiveness of the service and the process. It is only with this validation that quality continuing care can be assured.

NOTES

1. *National League for Nursing Statement on Continuity of Nursing Care* (New York: National League for Nursing, August 1966).
2. Ibid.
3. *Federal Register* (May 1, 1974), vol. 39, no. 85, p. 15232.
4. U.S. Department of Health, Education and Welfare, *PSRO Program Manual* (Washington, D.C.: GPO, 1974).
5. American Nurses' Association, *Continuity of Care and Discharge Planning Programs in Institutions and Community Agencies*, pub. code NP-493000 (Kansas City, Mo.: Author, 1975).
6. American Hospital Association, *Discharge Planning Guidelines*, catalogue no. 004170 (Chicago: Author, 1984).
7. *Public Law 98-21, Title VI, Prospective Payment for Medicare In-Patient Hospital Services* (Washington, D.C.: GPO, 1983).
8. T.F. Cahill, "Peer Review Organization (PRO): Medicare and Medicaid Programs," *Discharge Planning Update* 5 (Fall 1984).
9. *Federal Register* (June 17, 1986), vol. 51, no. 116, pp. 22042–52.
10. *Ibid.*
11. Joint Commission on Accreditation of Healthcare Organizations, *Accreditation Manual for Hospitals, 1987* (Chicago: Author, 1987).
12. J. Garrard et al., "A Checklist to Assess the Need for Home Care: Instrument Development and Validation," *Public Health Nursing* 4 (December 1987): 212–18.
13. T.S. Inui et al., "Needs Assessment for Hospital Based Home Care Services," *Research in Nursing and Health* 3 (September 1980): 101–6.
14. C.E. Smith, A.M. Schorfheide, and N.R. Lackey, "Acute to Home Care: Managing the Transition," *The Kansas Nurse* 60 (November 1985): 9–11.
15. B.U. Tebbitt, "What's Happening in Continuity of Care?" *Supervisor Nursing* 12 (March 1981): 22–26.
16. S.L. Shamansky, J.C. Boase, and B.M. Horn, "Discharge Planning, Yesterday, Today and Tomorrow," *Home Healthcare Nurse* 2 (May-June 1984): 14–21.

REFERENCES

Archer, S.E., and R.P. Fleshman. *Community Health Nursing*. 3d ed. Monterey, Calif.: Wadsworth Health Sciences, 1985.

Bulechek, G.M., and J.C. McCloskey. *Nursing Interventions*. Philadelphia: Saunders, 1985.

Clemen-Stone, D.G. Eigsti, and S.L. McGuire. *Comprehensive Family and Community Health Nursing*. 2d ed. New York: McGraw-Hill, 1987.

Lubkin, I.M. *Chronic Illness Impact and Interventions*. Boston: Jones and Bartlett Publishers, 1986.

O'Hare, P.A., and M.A. Terry. *Discharge Planning: Strategies for Assuring Continuity of Care*. Rockville, Md.: Aspen Publishers, 1988.

Snyder, M. *Independent Nursing Interventions*. New York: Wiley, 1985.

Zarle, N.C. *Continuing Care*. Rockville, Md.: Aspen Publishers, 1987.

Chapter 19

Examples of Existing Quality Assurance Programs in Home Health Care

Donna Amblers Peters and Rhoda Regenstreif

CASE STUDY 1: A HOSPITAL-BASED AGENCY*

The ultimate purpose of any quality assurance program is to serve as a vehicle to make certain that quality care is delivered to groups of consumers within the mandates of state and federal regulations. In order to attain this goal, there must be an organized, systematic plan to evaluate (1) the structure within which these services are offered, (2) the delivery of these services by professionals and nonprofessionals, (3) the actual care received by consumers, and (4) the outcome of the provided services. However, before any evaluation can take place, quality must be defined.

Defining quality is no easy task. To define quality is to make value judgments regarding degrees of excellence. Quality can be measured only by establishing written standards, which by definition set acceptable levels of practice or delineate conditions that need to be in place. Nursing organizations, state boards of nursing, and regulatory agencies have all developed standards in an attempt to define quality care. Unfortunately, these groups differ in their ideas about what standards are, how they should be developed, and what they should contain.[1] The result is confusion, with many agencies either having no standards, too many standards, poorly written standards, standards that are disorganized, or standards that are too limited in scope. Without appropriate standards, there is no adequate basis to evaluate quality. Thus, many quality assurance programs are doomed to failure before they start.

It is this same lack of appropriate standards that contributes to the costliness of a quality assurance program. If standards are lacking, disorganized, or ill-defined, then the measurement of those standards will also be disorganized, poorly defined, inefficient, ineffective, and wasteful of human resources, all of which add up to lost time and dollars.

This chapter is devoted to describing the quality assurance program that our small hospital-based agency developed in order to provide a logical, comprehensive approach to the problem of defining and measuring quality while using a minimum of staff time and resources. The program consists of three parts: (1) a conceptual practice model that defines the scope of community nursing practice and articulates standards, (2) an organized committee structure that both facilitates and monitors compliance with the established standards and takes corrective action where indicated, and (3) an established evaluation plan that delineates the specific areas to be monitored or audited and by whom. Each of these parts will be described in detail.

The Conceptual Practice Model

The idea of using a conceptual model to guide clinical practice is not a new one. Currently, the Neuman Systems Model, the Roy Adaptation Model, and the Orem Self-Care Model of Nursing, among others, are being applied and analyzed in various practice settings.[2] Smith-Marker states that a model is necessary in order to (1) provide a comprehensive framework, (2) organize all the components of practice,

*This section is by Donna Ambler Peters. The author wishes to acknowledge the contributions of Carol C. Sylvester, M.S., C.R.N.P., and Stephanie S. Poe, R.N., B.S.

The views expressed in this section are solely those of the author, and official endorsement by the Robert Wood Johnson Foundation is not intended and should not be inferred.

252

(3) define the practice of nursing and, (4) prevent confusion over terminology.[3]

Instead of using an existing model, our agency elected to adapt the unique conceptual framework for nursing practice that had been developed by the nursing staff at the hospital with which we are affiliated.[4] This model was developed by an expert panel of clinical and administrative nurses, who identified and integrated the essential components of nursing practice as it exists within the institution. It was modified to accommodate the scope of community health nursing practice.

The key components of the framework are as follows: (1) external influences, (2) philosophy, (3) standards of practice, (4) standards of care, (5) tools for practice, and (6) outcomes. For heuristic purposes, the framework can be visualized as having the shape of a dome (Figure 19-1).

External Influences

Community health practice is influenced by a variety of external and internal factors. These include consumer and provider expectations, legal mandates, and regulatory and professional directives (e.g., Medicare regulations, state licensing laws for home health agencies, and nurse practice acts). Because these factors must be considered when rendering care, they are acknowledged as boundaries or limitations in our definition of care.

Philosophy

The framework is built upon our philosophy of nursing, which includes the principles underlying primary nursing. This foundation maximizes our professional role by holding us

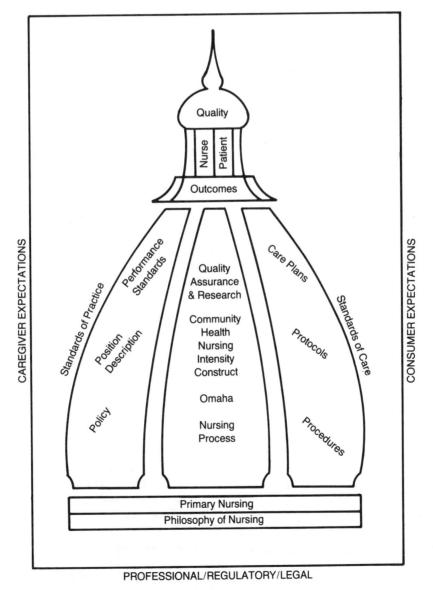

Figure 19-1 Conceptual Framework for Community Health Practice at Johns Hopkins Hospital. *Source:* Adapted from *Journal of Nursing Quality Assurance*, Vol. 2, No. 1, p. 31, Aspen Publishers, Inc., © November 1987.

accountable to our clients, to our profession, and to the community.

Standards

Nursing practice and patient care become more definitive with the addition of standards to the framework. Standards define, qualitatively and quantitatively, the minimum level of care to be achieved within our agency. As such, they are the means by which we define and measure quality nursing practice and patient care.

Standards of practice focus on the nurse and are directed toward the performance of specified nursing behaviors. Although they exist as discrete entities (e.g., the standards published by the American Nurses' Association),[5] they are also operationalized through policies, position descriptions, and performance standards.

Standards of care focus on the clients and are directed toward specified client outcomes. Client populations change and their care requirements become increasingly more complex; standards of care provide a guide for client care and allow staff to keep up with the changing requirements. Standards of care are operationalized through procedures, protocols, and care plans. Generic standards of care are currently being developed for each of 15 community health parameters identified in our Community Health Nursing Intensity Construct.

Tools for Practice

The framework integrates standards of practice and standards of care with certain useful tools. These tools include the nursing process, the Omaha Classification Scheme (OCS), the Community Health Nursing Intensity Construct, and nursing quality assurance and research. The OCS is a nursing diagnosis taxonomy for community health nursing that was developed by the Visiting Nurse Association of Omaha and provides a means to articulate areas of concern in community health to others.[6] It organizes community health nursing into four domains: environmental, psychosocial, physiological, and health behaviors.

The Community Health Nursing Intensity Construct (Exhibit 19-1) defines 15 community health parameters that provide a structure for staff to organize their care. The parameters were originally developed as the basis for a patient classification system for community health.[7] Since the classification system encompassed community health nursing, the content of the parameters was extracted to describe the practice of community health nursing and form the Community Health Nursing Construct. The 15 community health parameters are organized using the same four domains as the OCS. The parameters are finances; housing (safety, health); community networking; family system; emotional response; individual growth and development; sensory function; respiratory/circulatory function; neuromusculoskeletal function; reproductive function; digestion/elimination; structural integrity; nutrition; personal habits; and health management. See Exhibit 19-1 for the definition of each parameter.

The last two tools in the framework are quality assurance and research. The quality assurance program is the means by which compliance to standards is monitored or audited. The research component is important for validating standards.

Outcomes

The integration of standards of practice and standards of care using the unifying tools results in quality outcomes. These outcomes are described in terms of the performance of the professional and the status of the client.

The Quality Assurance Structure

The purpose of quality assurance is to provide a system for monitoring and measuring compliance with agency standards and state and federal regulations. In addition, we believe that quality assurance (1) involves improvement actions (proactive) as well as evaluation (reactive), (2) coordinates and communicates issues and findings to all levels within the agency, and (3) results in changes within the agency. Finally, because we are a hospital-based agency, our quality assurance program must also interface appropriately with the hospital quality assurance program. The organizational structure that we use to accomplish these goals reflects a comprehensive approach to quality assurance (Figure 19-2).

Our quality assurance structure consists of an integrated network of six standing committees. Each of these standing committees reports to the Professional Advisory Committee. Recommendations from the Professional Advisory Committee are given to agency administration to assure future compliance. Standing committees include the policy and administrative review, utilization review, standards, budget, and research committees. Each has particular responsibilities with respect to quality assurance. In addition, agency administration is also charged with certain quality assurance activities.

Professional Advisory Committee

The Professional Advisory Committee is a group of professional persons charged with establishing and reviewing all agency policies. It is also responsible for evaluating the quality assurance program and subsequently recommending modifications as appropriate. It reports to the agency's governing body. For each service provided by the agency, the committee has a professional who represents that service (e.g., physical therapy, occupational therapy, social services, etc.). In addition, membership includes other professionals from important hospital linkages, such as discharge planning, pharmacy, nursing, and the medical staff. A consumer is also represented. With the inclusion of these members, this committee is able to provide a communication link between hospital services and home care.

Policy and Administrative Review Committee

The primary responsibility of the Policy and Administrative Review Committee is the annual agency self-evaluation.

Exhibit 19-1 Community Health Nursing Intensity Construct Parameter Definitions

	Environmental Domain
Finances	Available financial resources, including employment status, of an individual/family; reflects the adequacy/availability of income with regard to financial obligations.
Housing: safety, health	Condition of patient's home/neighborhood, including availability of necessary facilities and transportation to those facilities.
	Psychosocial Domain
Community networking	Individual's/family's knowledge and use of community resources/services.
Family system	Interpersonal relationships within the household (primary unit) and/or with relatives, friends, and significant others outside the household, such as church members, social group members and fellow employees. This parameter does not reflect the family's ability to render skilled care unless that ability is marred due to interpersonal problems.
Emotional response	Expression of feelings, including sexual concerns, spiritual beliefs, depression, anxiety, and behavioral outcomes that arise from an individual's/family's perception of self as it relates to a change in health status.
Individual growth and development	Early/adult life development of cognitive, physical, and social tasks, including ability to speak, read, and write.
	Physiological Domain
Sensory function	The body function concerned with the use of senses, including vision, hearing, taste, touch, smell, proprioception, and an individual's perception of pain.
Respiratory/ circulatory function	The body function concerned with (1) the transfer of gases to meet ventilatory needs and (2) the supply of blood to body tissues via the cardiovascular system.
Neuromusculo- skeletal function	The body function concerned with integration and direction of body regulatory processes related to gross and fine motor movements, including level of consciousness, mental status, speech patterns, muscle strength, coordination, skeletal integrity, and degree of physical independence/mobility.
Reproductive function	The body function concerned with menstruation, family planning, fertility, pregnancy, lactation, and impediments to sexual activity. Included are sexual organs and secondary sexual characteristics such as breasts.
Digestion/ elimination	The ability to ingest food and fluids, utilize nutrients, and excrete waste products from the body.
Structural integrity	The character and intactness of the body's protective mechanisms, including skin and/or the immunological system.
	Health Behaviors Domain
Nutrition	An individual's/family's selection, preparation, and consumption of nutrients, including significant cultural and health factors.
Personal habits	An individual's/family's management of personal health–related activities. It includes sleep activity patterns, personal hygiene, and avoidance of harmful materials. It addresses patient/family habits or preferences, not ability to do ADLs.
Health management	An individual's/family's management of their own health status, including their perception of health and their motivation to strive for an optimal level of wellness as demonstrated by (1) regular participation in recommended health screenings/examinations appropriate for age and physical condition, (2) participation in technical procedures, and (3) adherence to prescribed therapeutic plans.

Because our agency is hospital based, we utilize the self-survey tool of the Joint Commission on Accreditation of Healthcare Organizations (Joint Commission). Thus, in addition to fulfilling the mandate to evaluate the agency, we also prepare ourselves for Joint Commission accreditation. The areas of agency functioning that are audited include client rights, client care, safety and infection control, documentation, quality assurance, administration, the governing body, patient services, and support services. Results of the self-audit are presented to the Professional Advisory Committee at the end of each fiscal year.

Utilization Review Committee

The Utilization Review Committee is responsible for the concurrent and retrospective review of clinical records for the purpose of determining the appropriateness of the agency's service utilization. It is composed of at least one representative from each profession delivering services in the agency. Standards of practice are used to measure appropriateness. These standards most often take the form of administrative policies and position descriptions.

Standards Committee

The Standards Committee has two main roles. The first is to recommend and revise standards of practice and standards of care as appropriate. The second role is to audit compliance with these standards. In addition, because most audit data is retrieved through chart review and is therefore affected by adequacy of documentation, the Standards Committee makes recommendations related to documentation formats. These three roles constitute a large task for one committee. However, it was decided to assign these roles to one committee because

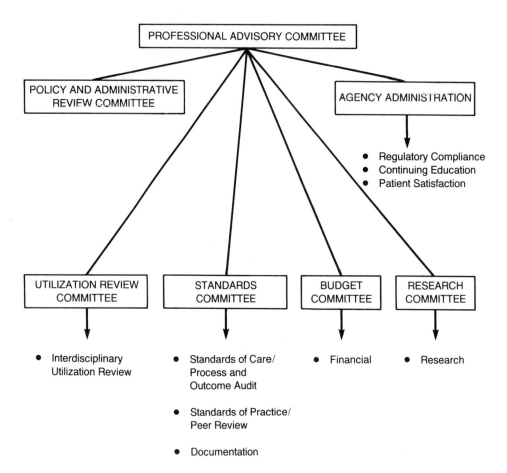

Figure 19-2 The Quality Assurance Structure and Functions of the Department of Home Care and Services, The Johns Hopkins Hospital. *Source:* Courtesy of Johns Hopkins Home Care Agency.

we are a small agency with few staff. Larger agencies might want to consider having one committee for writing new standards (standards committee) and one for monitoring compliance (quality assurance committee)—or one committee for standards of practice and one for standards of care. A separate documentation committee could also be established. Because of our belief that quality assurance is everyone's responsibility, the membership of this committee includes clinical staff people.

Budget Committee

The Budget Committee is responsible for overseeing the budget planning process, monitoring expenditures and revenues, and advising the agency on general financial planning issues. Its position within the quality assurance structure is supportive and represents a monetary quantification of the agency's definition of quality.

Research Committee

The Research Committee is responsible for the development and coordination of research activities within the agency. It provides a mechanism for incorporating scientific inquiry into the quality assurance program. Its mission is to promote scientific inquiry that involves quantifying and qualifying

nursing practice and establishing the foundation for future trends in nursing care. In addition, research plays a key role in the validation of standards.

Agency Administration

The final component of the quality assurance structure is the agency administration. Administrative personnel have a dual role in the quality assurance process. First, they are responsible for consumer input, especially the patient satisfaction survey, which is conducted no less than twice a year. Second, they are responsible for the overall implementation of the quality assurance plan, including initiating corrective actions based on the recommendations of the Professional Advisory Committee. Such actions can include (1) enforcing existing standards, (2) formulating new or revised standards (this task could be delegated to the appropriate committee), (3) implementing new or revised standards, (4) eliminating inappropriate standards, and (5) providing the necessary education to staff so that they have the information they need to comply with existing standards.

This entire quality assurance structure provides for communication and networking on several levels. Because staff are included in committees, they are kept informed of agency activities. Communication is also open between agency personnel and the hospital community since there are hospital staff on the Professional Advisory Committee, to which all other committees report. Some of the standing committees, such as the policy and administrative review, utilization review, and the budget committees, have Professional Advisory Committee members as part of their membership. Finally, networking also occurs within the hospital quality assurance structure by virtue of common committee membership. Designated members of the research and standards committees represent home care on similar hospital quality assurance committees. There is a member of the hospital quality assurance program on the Professional Advisory Committee. For any hospital quality assurance committees that do not have home care counterparts, the agency administration represents home care. For example, an agency administrator is a member of the hospital nursing quality assurance steering and program committees.

The Quality Assurance Monitoring Plan

Even with defined standards and an established committee structure, the question remains, how does the process work? It begins with the establishment of a monitoring or auditing plan that incorporates the agency's scope of care and definition of quality, which have been identified through the conceptual practice model. The monitoring plan (Table 19-1) includes all quality assurance activities within the agency. It consists of a list of various aspects of care; indicators for these aspects of care; and how, by whom, and how often each indicator is to be monitored or measured.

Aspects of care are defined as those major clinical or administrative functions that are either high volume or prone to problems. An indicator is an observable characteristic of client care or agency administration that can predict or identify potential problem areas. For example, one clinical aspect of care is appropriateness (i.e., was the right care given to the patient in the right amount?). An indicator for appropriateness

is service utilization. One way of monitoring service utilization is by chart review, and the designated reviewer is the Utilization Review Committee. Frequency of chart review is monthly.[8] This is a straightforward example, but it shows how to develop the monitoring plan.

The monitoring plan is important for several reasons. First, it identifies all the areas that need to be monitored or audited within the defined scope of agency practice. Second, it identifies all the indicators of quality being monitored by the agency. Many quality assurance measures are so much a part of agency operations that they are often overlooked as quality assurance activities (e.g., the monitoring of current professional licenses). Third, the plan identifies which committee (or component of agency administration) is responsible and accountable for monitoring each indicator. The responsible committee is also helped by this, because its charge is clearly delineated. In the example above, it would be very clear to members of the Utilization Review Committee that they were to review charts on a monthly basis in order to determine appropriateness (i.e., compliance with established standards of practice in the form of policies and position descriptions). After chart review, any cases that do not meet standards are dealt with directly by the committee, using a response form that explains the problem deviation to the staff member involved and requires a response in regard to the action taken or a comment. A summary of findings is submitted quarterly to the Professional Advisory Committee and to the agency administration noting any trends or recurring problems. The agency administration would also be informed of required changes (e.g., revising a standard, informing staff of existing policy, or counseling repeat offenders) so that it could implement them.

A similar process exists in regard to the Standards Committee. For example, the monitoring plan may have identified professional practice as an aspect of care. An indicator for this aspect of care is consistent use of the nursing process. This would include appropriate use of the OCS, since our agency uses that taxonomy of nursing diagnoses. One way of monitoring this indicator is by chart review, using a nursing process audit tool developed for this purpose. By retrospectively

Table 19-1 Quality Assurance Monitoring Activities

Aspects of Care	Indicators	Monitoring	Reviewer	Frequency
Major clinical or administrative activities or functions. Diagnostic and therapeutic modalities most important to the quality of patient care. High-risk, high-volume, or problem-prone activities.	Major dimensions of an aspect of care. Critical elements of nursing care that, if properly monitored, can predict or identify potential problem areas. Critical elements of nursing practice that are significant enough to be used as a basis for performance measurement.	Systematic, routine process of gathering data about indicators. Information sources for monitoring can include minutes, incident reports, interviews, observations, rounds, case reviews, or reports.	Individual, role or committee that will be accountable for reviewing indicators.	How often information will be collected in order to track trends and make decisions about deviations from established standards.

Source: Adapted from *Journal of Nursing Quality Assurance*, Vol. 2, No. 2, p. 35, Aspen Publishers, Inc., © February 1988.

reviewing a chart using this tool, the committee can evaluate the degree to which the OCS has been used in identifying client problems. For example, one criterion found in the tool is the requirement for documented evidence of an initial assessment related to each of the four OCS domains.[9] The designated committee for this review is the Standards Committee (or quality assurance committee), and the frequency of review is quarterly. Here again, cases requiring follow-up are dealt with directly by the committee. Since the membership of the committee consists of staff nurses, a system of peer review is provided. (Refer to Chapter 9 for staff nurse perspective regarding peer review.) This system helps remind staff of existing standards, making compliance easier and making quality assurance a part of everyone's responsibility rather than "a separate program." A summary of findings is submitted to the Professional Advisory Committee, with notification of required changes or disciplinary actions being sent to the agency administration.

Summary

Successful quality assurance programs are becoming more and more important as home health agency directors find themselves faced with the challenge of providing quality services to a greater variety of very ill clients with a minimum of resources. Unfortunately, most quality assurance programs are costly and do little more than meet the mandated requirements. Our agency found that quality assurance became more meaningful by (1) defining practice by using a conceptual model to organize, define, and write standards; (2) developing an organized committee structure to both improve and evaluate agency activities; (3) using the committee structure to network with staff, hospital personnel, and the community; and (4) writing a plan that outlines what aspects of care are to be measured and by whom. With all these elements in place, everybody has a well-defined role in assuring quality and quality becomes an integral part of agency service rather than a costly separate program.

The Quality Assurance Program in Alberta is the result of efforts by members of the Home Care Standards Committee* and outside consultants** who have assisted in various phases

*The Home Care Standards Committee Membership includes representatives from six health units: Judy Cameron, South Peace Health Unit, Helen Dueck, Barons-Eureka-Warner Health Unit, Brenda Hannah, Calgary Health Services, Alice Mah-Wren, Edmonton Board of Health, Lois Sorgen, Edmonton Board of Health, Gloria Leraand, Vegreville Health Unit and Sharon Tell, Leduc-Strathcona Health Unit and members of the Home Care Unit in the Department of Community and Occupational Health; Sheila Weatherhill, Manager, Home Care/Long Term Care Unit, Rhoda Regenstreif, Grace Whitehouse, and former members, Carol Blair, and Jean Schmidt.

**Dr. Carol Lindemann, Dean of Nursing, Oregon Health Sciences University; Evelyn Shapiro, Associate Professor of Social and Preventative Medicine, University of Manitoba; Management Analysis and Planning Services (MAPS), Alberta Hospital Hospital Association; Dr. Barbara Horn, Dr. Martha Herriott and Dr. Bernadette Lalonde, University of Washington; and Dr. Nancy Staisey, Price-Waterhouse Associates.

of the project. The development of the client outcome–focused quality assurance program has truly taken place because of the collaborative efforts of all those involved.

Above all else, this work was made possible by the support of the Department of Community and Occupational Health in the Provincial Government of Alberta.

CASE STUDY 2: A COORDINATED HOME CARE PROGRAM*

The Coordinated Home Care Program (CHCP) was introduced in Alberta in July 1978. The program is funded by the Department of Community and Occupational Health and administered and delivered through 27 local health units in Alberta (Appendix 19-A). The program is designed to assess the need for and arrange the delivery of coordinated health and support services (homemaking and personal care) to clients in the home; support and enhance the capacity of families in caring for ill or elderly family members at home; improve, maintain, or delay deterioration of health status and level of independence and prevent, delay, or reduce institutionalization (Appendixes 19-B and 19-C).

The program provides a range of health and support services to selective clients who meet the eligibility and admission criteria outlined in provincial legislation (the Coordinated Home Care Program Regulation under the Public Health Act). Although these services may vary from one health unit to another, all programs provide nursing, homemaking, and personal care services. In addition, they may provide physiotherapy, occupational therapy, nutrition counseling, speech therapy, respiratory therapy, friendly visiting, handyman services, heavy housework services, meals on wheels (or wheels to meals), and transportation.

There are 2,100,000 people in Alberta, with 189,000 over 65 years of age. As of December 1987, the active monthly caseload of CHCP was 14,212 people. About 85 percent of the caseload consists of people 65 years or older, and most require long-term care.

Referrals to the program are accepted from anyone in the community, including the family physician, a public health nurse, community agencies, relatives, friends, or the client him- or herself. Upon receipt of a referral to home care, a home care assessor, usually a nurse or an occupational or physical therapist, carries out a comprehensive assessment of the client and the client's environment to determine eligibility for admission, to identify the client's and family's needs, to estimate the type and amount of services required, and to arrange for and coordinate the necessary services.

A person may be admitted to a program when a physician whose care the person is under states in writing that the person

*This section is by Rhoda Regenstreif.

has a medical condition which limits that person's ability to function independently. Furthermore, the manager of the home care program must be satisfied that the person requires a health or support service; that the program is the most suitable means of providing the amount, level, and type of service; that the resources and the budget of the program are sufficient to meet the assessed needs of the person; and that the cost of providing the service to the person will not exceed the cost of providing a similar level of care in a health care facility.

Overview of Quality Assurance

A quality assurance program, as it relates to service delivery, is a plan of action. Its goal is to guarantee a certain degree of excellence in service delivery, which entails identification of the degree of excellence to be achieved. Such a program has two requirements: (1) The current level of practice must be evaluated and (2) actions must be performed to maintain or improve the quality of care.

There have been several changes in society in the last decade that have produced a growing demand for the evaluation of all public services. In the health care field, three major factors currently reinforce each other and stimulate the development of programs to maintain or improve existing services.

The first factor is the increased *expense* of health care. The demands for sophisticated health care services are increasing and financial resources are limited. Stringent cost containment programs are being imposed. Health care professionals worry that the quality of care will be reduced as attempts are made to cut costs. Since there is little hard data about the effects of cost containment on the quality of health care, there is an urgent need to find ways to accurately measure these effects. Also, competition for the dollar (e.g., should government spend more on highway safety or health care?) is causing service delivery programs to evaluate the results of their programs and to demonstrate they provide quality care for the dollars expended.

The second factor is *consumerism*. In the past, control of quality of health care was in the hands of health care professionals. The right of the practitioner to be the sole judge of the quality of care is being challenged by individual citizens, organized consumer groups, nonmedical boards of health care agencies, and governments. People want a part in planning a system that delivers the right care in the right amount to the right place at the right time for the right price. The development of quality assurance programs is being stimulated by the demand of consumers to be included in the planning and evaluation of health care services. The third factor is increased *professionalism* among health care workers, both collectively and individually. They are demonstrating their accountability to the public through a variety of activities, such as developing standards to direct and evaluate professional practice, implementing programs to monitor the safety of practice, participating in health care planning at various levels of government, assisting with the development of standards for use in indi-

vidual agencies, and conducting peer reviews to evaluate patient care and the competency of coworkers. They are demanding a clearly defined, easily understood, and unified approach to the delivery of care that will indicate how various activities and programs fit together to demonstrate public accountability.[10]

The Quality Assurance Framework

Quality Assurance is a continuous, cyclical process. The steps described below are interrelated and sequential. However, there is flexibility in the process. The first four steps are part of a systematic evaluation of the current level of service delivery, which is the first requirement of any quality assurance program. The last four steps are necessary to ensure that appropriate actions are taken to maintain or improve the quality of service provided, which is the second requirement of a quality assurance program.

Step 1. Beliefs about care are determined by values held by patients (consumers), health care professionals, agency administrators, board members, the public at large, and government representatives. Reaching a consensus on which values pertain to quality of care is essential, because it forms the basis for selecting the measurement criteria and for developing the standards used to judge care.

Step 2. Based on knowledge and the values identified, these two questions must be answered: What aspects of care are to be evaluated? What is the acceptable level or degree of performance for each aspect of care? Since it is always impossible to evaluate all aspects of care, decisions must be made as to which are the most relevant indicators of care. (This is very difficult: What can be measured to assess patient outcomes?) After the criteria are chosen, standard statements may be written which make explicit the level or degree of performance expected. In our approach, after the criteria are chosen, we attempt to measure the criteria to obtain baseline data that will in turn, and in time, enable us to write our standards.

Step 3. Approval of and commitment to the established criteria and standards must be obtained before it is reasonable to expect achievement of the desired results.

Step 4. Data obtained are used to make judgments about how current care compares with the established standards.

Step 5. The factors that have contributed to the existing level of care should be identified. A variety of factors influence quality, for example, the professionals' knowledge and skills, the availability of human and material resources within the agency, the need for research, the date of evaluation, etc.

Step 6. The most cost-effective actions to maintain or improve the quality of care should be determined. Maintaining desirable levels of care should not be neglected while correcting deficiencies.

Step 7. The corrective actions should be implemented. Time should be allowed for the actions to take effect before reevaluation occurs.

Step 8. It is important to collect new data about care, compare them with the standards and results of the previous evaluation, and make judgments about whether or not the quality of care was maintained or improved.

Evaluation in Quality Assurance Program: The Assessment of Quality

Given the definition and general model of quality assurance, the process might seem relatively straightforward. Obviously, the purpose of evaluation in quality assurance is to compare the current level of care with the expected standards. The methods of evaluation used for quality assurance must be practical in terms of required resources and the significance of findings. Evaluation results in quality assurance programs should be analyzed immediately and be used to maintain or improve the level of care. However, very early in the development of a quality assurance program, the program developers will find themselves faced with some major conceptual issues. These issues need to be addressed, as they greatly influence the direction of a program's quality assurance activities. (For example, the issue of how to assess quality is very basic and will influence ongoing decisions and activities.) A review of the health sciences literature related to evaluation of patient care and quality assurance discloses three classical approaches to assessing quality: structure, process, and outcome. (Donabedian is known in quality assurance circles as the person who first began to link structure, process and outcome.)

Structure

At one time hospitals, nursing homes, and other health care providers concentrated on assessing quality through the structural approach. Evaluation of structure focuses on the setting in which care is given and includes an appraisal of the facility itself (the equipment and supplies, manpower, support services, and finances). Traditional methods of evaluation studied agency structure based on the assumption that excellent resources will result in excellent care. Evaluation of agency structure is necessary to ensure that necessary resources are available for the delivery of safe, efficient care. When structure is evaluated in isolation, decisions may be made about the efficiency of the operation. However, little research is available to document that structural excellence ensures excellence in care. Indeed, it was soon discovered that structural components did not guarantee expected positive patient outcomes. They may increase or decrease the probability of such outcomes,[11] but it seems that once minimum standards are met, other factors have a much greater influence on outcomes.[12]

Process

The factors that were thought to influence outcomes most were those involved in the process of care. The process approach to assessing quality examines the activities of the caregivers. It involves studying observable behaviours (e.g., performing procedures and interacting with patients) and also the results of nonobservable behaviours like decision making. This approach is based on the assumption that if a caregiver is competent and performs care activities effectively, high-quality care will result. This approach is often the most acceptable, because it focuses on activities performed in the actual delivery of care. Technical aspects of care (e.g., the adequacy of diagnostic workups and treatment; the volume of care) and the subjective, value-based qualitative aspects of care (e.g., concern and consideration for clients on the part of professional care providers) were both considered to be important in the measurement of quality. The reasoning appeared to be that if the technical aspects of care were attended to and if the care was delivered in a warm, caring manner, then quality care would be guaranteed. Accordingly, health care providers developed general process case management standards (e.g., all clients will have a written plan of care; all clients will be assessed within one week of referral and reassessed at three-month intervals) or specific accepted methods of treatment for specific presenting problems (i.e., standardized care plans).

The use of process as the only approach to evaluation has some disadvantages. Many of the standards used to measure process are based on expert opinion and not on research data. Therefore, many activities thought to be essential to quality care have never been proved to be of great import. When evaluation indicates that deficiencies exist, time and money may be spent on activities that may not rectify the deficiencies.

Also, data about process are collected directly by making observations while care is being given or indirectly by reviewing documentation of care on the health record. The first method, observation of the care provider, is costly because of the time involved and may introduce the observer's bias. The second, reviewing the documentation of the care provider, is limited to reliance on charts for evidence that process procedures have been adhered to. Charts pose major problems, however, for they are often not kept up to date and a great deal of extraneous information must be sifted through. Many times, not all presenting problems are listed in a chart, and where more than one presenting problem is identified, it is sometimes difficult to know which procedures were done for which problem. Problem-oriented records offer a solution to some of these problems, but the possibility still exists that what is listed in the chart may have no resemblance to what was actually done. Also, when one reviews a chart, one can only determine if certain processes were done, not how well they were done. Furthermore, evaluation of the process without reference to the effects on the patient may be an end in itself rather than a means to an end. Similarly, evaluation of the caregiver without consideration of the setting may result in unfair judgments about performance, safety, and efficiency.

Outcome

The third approach focuses on patient outcomes and utilizes evaluations of the changes in the health status of the patient as a result of care. Outcomes offer an answer to the question, What happens to our clients as a result of being in our program? Since outcome measures relate quality to actual concrete results of service, this approach tends to be regarded as being more objective or scientific than the structure or process approaches. Certainly, consumers, third party insurance carriers, and other holders of the purse strings tend to judge the worth of a program by the results it obtains with its clients. This does not necessarily mean that all clients have to get better. This would be a very unreasonable requirement for nursing homes and programs such as the CHCP, for they serve many clients who will not get better. It does mean, however, that the expected outcomes for clients should be realized.

Although outcomes "remain the ultimate validators of the effectiveness and quality of medical care,"[13] they too are not without problems. The main problem is that outcomes are not always the result of the care given. This is particularly true for care provided in a person's home. If the expected outcome for a client was complete recovery, but he or she died, it would be grossly unfair to automatically assume that quality care was not provided. A perusal of the chart might reveal that all necessary procedures were followed and that the client died as a result of some unexpected disease factors beyond the control of the caregiver. Outcome results, then, can be "dangerously sterile because when process is not also examined one cannot know what caused the favourable or unfavourable outcomes."[14] The outcome approach has therefore caused the most controversy. It is recognized that patient outcomes are affected by the care of many professionals and by factors in the setting and that evaluation of outcomes in isolation can be very misleading.

The above are the three main approaches to assessing quality. There have been many attempts to determine which of them—structure, process, or outcome—provides the most valid assessments. The answer is important for two reasons. First, one tends to get very different quality results depending on the assessment method used. High process scores do not necessarily guarantee high structure or outcome assessment scores. Second, if the type of assessment affects quality ratings and if appropriate corrective actions or policy decisions are to be made on the basis of the assessment results, it would be important to know which assessment approach yields the most valid results. Unfortunately, there is no firm answer from researchers; their research has yielded conflicting results. The best advice is to use an appropriate combination of all three components and to view each as a necessary but not sufficient element of quality assurance.[15]

The most recently devised approach to evaluation of care coordinates the three classical approaches. It is based on the belief that the quality of care is affected by three interrelated and interdependent variables: the patient, the caregiver, and the setting. This approach could potentially have a great impact on the health care system because it is conducive to the study of interrelationships among patient outcomes, the caregiver process, and the agency structure. After patient outcomes are validated and rated according to their importance in health or wellness, the most cost-effective aspects of both process and structure may be validated and used. In addition, the role of each discipline in achieving desired outcomes may

be clarified. The drawbacks to this approach are that it is complex and that it requires a multidisciplinary approach to the delivery of health care.

Development of a Quality Assurance Program in Alberta

Home Care Standards Committee Established

CHCP embarked on the development of a quality assurance program in 1980 with the formation of the Home Care Standards Committee, which is composed of representatives from the health units and the Department of Community and Occupational Health (Appendix 19-D). The purpose of the committee is to develop and promote provincial home care standards for delivering safe and consistent home care services across the province.

The Home Care Standards Committee has taken the view that an appropriate combination of structure, process and outcome measurements is necessary to assess quality of care.

Quality Assurance Defined

The Home Care Standards Committee defined quality assurance as the promise or guarantee made by the CHCP to itself, its clients, its clients' families, and the provincial government that certain standards of excellence would be met.

Quality Assurance Program Goals

1. To provide a multidisciplinary team at the local level with data regarding the quality of care for individuals or small homogeneous subsets of clients.
2. To provide a multidisciplinary team at the local and provincial levels with aggregate data to address issues regarding the delivery of home care.
3. To provide the framework for linking outcomes with both structure and process within an outcome-focused quality assurance program.
4. To utilize computerizable data generated through routine data collection procedures.
5. To utilize data collection tools and procedures that meet relevant and acceptable psychometric or measurement standards.
6. To provide an efficient quality assurance program that relies on minimum data and minimizes the variability in tools used to support quality assurance action at the local and provincial levels.

The Conceptual Framework[16]

In this case study, the phrase *conceptual framework* refers specifically to a framework used to guide the development of a client outcome–focused quality assurance program for home care. The framework is a blending of the mental representation of the care process and of the quality assurance process specific to the CHCP. The diagram of the conceptual framework (Figure 19-3) displays the assumptions unique to the Alberta

CARE PROCESS

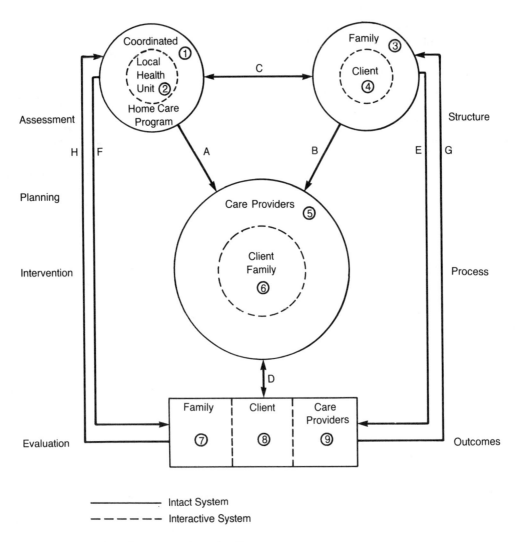

Figure 19-3 The conceptual framework for a client outcome–focused quality assurance program.

program while indicating program features common to health care in general. Both the phenomena considered significant to quality assurance and the assumed relationships among the phenomena are shown in the diagram. It is also likely that once the quality assurance system is in operation, the conceptual framework used to guide its development will need revision, as it reflects numerous undocumented assumptions.

In developing the conceptual framework, the following assumptions were considered significant:

1. The health status and attitudes of the client and family at the time of admission to the program directly influence client and family outcomes.

2. The client and family are active partners of the home care staff at every point in the care process.

3. There is continuous interaction among the client's environment, health status, family, and care so that out-

comes must be viewed as the result of a complex, interactive process involving numerous variables.

4. The care provided by the home care staff is best conceptualized as the product of multidisciplinary team efforts rather than the result of particular actions by particular professionals.

5. The outcomes of care during the process of providing care do influence the home care staff and thereby create another feedback loop influencing the care provided.

6. Health care provider outcomes are a legitimate component of a client outcome–focused quality assurance program.

7. Theoretical rather than empirical linkages among concepts were used in creating the framework along with the assumption that clear-cut causal relationships that can be supported empirically are unlikely to materialize in the near future.

Structural Standards Developed

The Home Care Standards Committee began the task of developing home care structural standards to be used as guidelines by local home care programs. They developed explicit standards reflecting basic expectations regarding the organizational structure, contracts with service agencies, staffing development, equipment and supplies, staff qualifications, and so forth.

These structural standards have been implemented as statements of intent to assist local home care programs in establishing appropriate local policies and procedures. In developing initial standards, consideration was given to what could realistically be expected of all local health units. They were stated in broad terms to allow flexibility for adapting to local circumstances. Local health units could elaborate these standards to meet local needs. It was the intent of the Home Care Standards Committee to ensure that where the CHCP is responsible for service provided, these standards would foster service delivery of a high caliber.

Process Audit Developed

Problem-oriented recording has been implemented in local home care programs. General case management process standards were developed by the Home Care Standards Committee and incorporated into a process tool (chart audit tool).[17] This tool was piloted initially in two local home care programs (Red Deer and Calgary) and was subsequently piloted in three other sites. These five programs have appointed a quality assurance program committee for peer review of client assessments and care planning. The benefits of this system have already become apparent: The chart audit has generated an awareness, on the part of staff, of quality of care and quality assurance. Staff have developed and implemented a number of care indicators in the form of program policies and procedures. The chart audit tool was revised following pilot site feedback in September 1984 and has been available to other home care programs for implementation on a voluntary basis.

In July 1986, a survey of all home care programs was carried out to monitor their progress in developing quality assurance procedures and to determine how the chart audit tool was being implemented.[18] The main issues addressed in the survey were these: Who is responsible for chart auditing? What structures are in place to carry out a chart audit? Who is responsible and what structures are in place for quality assurance?

Fifteen of the 27 health units reported having a structure in place to implement a chart audit and 10 reported having a tool in place. The various structures and procedures used included

- having monthly audits completed by quality assurance committee members

- giving all charts of clients discharged during a particular month to a data control assistant, who lists them and redistributes them to the case coordinator

- having chart audits completed every two months on a random basis and routinely on discharge

- reviewing charts yearly to determine if
  —there is a signed medical authorization or progress note completed within the last six months
  —there is evidence of review of the medications record within the last six months

- having the committee perform chart audits routinely while the tool and the guide are being developed

Of the 27 programs, 16 reported having conducted a chart audit. However, of these 16, only 9 conduct audits regularly while 7 perform their chart audits occasionally. The actual number of audits reported varied from 1 audit to ongoing monthly audits. Two units performed 1 audit. Three performed monthly audits. The remaining programs performed between 2 and 12 audits.

In outlining the procedures followed for auditing charts, respondents specified who audits the charts and how the charts are selected. Several responses were received concerning who audits the charts. One or a combination of the following parties were listed as responsible for auditing charts: the case coordinator, the area coordinator, all professional staff, clinical and program managers, a committee, the director of home care, the medical officer of health, teams of staff, the quality assurance committee, home care nurses, and the nursing coordinator. The most frequent auditors were the case coordinator (used by 3 units), a committee (used by 4 units), and the director of home care (used by 2 units).

Several responses were also received concerning how the charts are selected. One or a combination of the following procedures were indicated: charts were selected from admissions, charts were selected randomly from all current charts, all charts were reviewed, current charts were selected, some charts were selected from discharges, and spot audits were performed. The Alberta West Central Unit used a computerization acceptance test as one means of auditing charts for completeness of records. As part of the procedure to test a new software package, this unit volunteered to supply selected fictitious and real client charts. Any items found incomplete while selecting the charts were corrected, and thus this procedure was considered by the unit to be a type of audit. The most frequently used technique is random selection. Six units select the charts for auditing in this manner.

In reporting who was responsible for quality assurance in the different programs, the program director was most often mentioned. Ten units reported the program director alone or in combination with others was responsible for quality assurance. The quality assurance committee was indicated by 7 programs. One or a combination of the following parties were also reported to be responsible for quality assurance: the program manager, standards committee, home care coordinator, assistant director, area manager, and the case coordinator. In some cases there was no formal process.

Various structures were reported to be in place for the purpose of quality assurance. The most frequently cited structure was a standards manual (or a policy and procedures manual), which was mentioned by 7 of the home care programs. Chart audits were reported by 5 of the units as a structure for quality assurance.

Numerous activities have been undertaken by the different home care programs with respect to quality assurance. One or a combination of the following techniques were employed:

- in-service instruction on charting
- surveys to determine client satisfaction
- periodic reviews of policy and procedures
- performance appraisals
- methods of tracking client outcomes
- structural standards
- chart audits
- full monthly reports to the director and area coordinator
- in-service training and continuing education
- case conferences with the program director
- family visits
- reviews of nurses' records and rehabilitation and volunteer staff records and reports
- follow-up on client complaints
- one-on-one evaluation of staff performances
- spot checks
- general supervision
- discussion at team management meetings
- monitoring of quality of care

Chart auditing was the most frequently cited method of quality assurance.

In summary, although programs have not specifically been encouraged to undertake chart audits, many have conducted audits or have a structure in place to do so. Conducting audits can be of great benefit, since charts will be used to identify relevant outcome criteria for clients who will be subject to outcome measurement. The quality and accuracy of the chart is of concern, and it is thus advantageous to have a chart auditing structure in place.

Outcome Standards Developed

When the Home Care Standards Committee made the decision in 1981 to develop a client outcome–focused quality assurance program, a conceptual framework for the program had not yet been articulated. With the assistance of outside experts in quality assurance development, the initial efforts led to the identification of 75 outcome criteria within 15 dimensions. (Table 19-2 presents 4 of the dimensions and 12 of the criteria.)

The task of narrowing the 75 outcome criteria to a number of outcomes that could be measured and that would provide an indicator of care was overwhelming. However, we probably

Table 19-2 Outcome Dimensions and Criteria

Dimension	Criterion
Body integrity	1. Condition of oral cavity
	2. Integrity of skin around/over stoma, shunts, implants
	3. Skin integrity (including nails, hair, scalp, mucous membranes, skin)
Communication	4. Comprehension of messages
	5. Reception of messages
	6. Transmission of messages
Comfort	7. Physical pain/discomfort
Compliance	8. Carries out treatment regime (excluding medications)
	9. Eats a nutritious diet
	10. Modifies activities of daily living
	11. Modifies household activities
	12. Takes prescribed medications

had included in this list all the outcomes and many of the measures that were to be developed later. For example, within the dimension Body Integrity, the criterion Skin Integrity is now in one of our measurement modules under physiological outcomes. Unfortunately, we did not have a clear idea of which outcomes were important to measure.

The next step involved a brainstorming session to find out what it was that we valued in home care.[19] Members of the Home Care Standards Committee, with the help of an outside facilitator, identified client, family, and caregiver values specific to home care. The values for clients included being as independent as possible and controlling pain. For the family, they included having the client remain at home, maintaining as normal a life as possible, and knowing whom to call in a crisis. A list of values identified in the brainstorming session follows.

1. What clients value
   - to stay in the home/community/familiar surroundings
   - to receive support or care from family/friends/community
   - to be as independent as possible (physically, psychosocially)
   - to make decisions or to be involved in decision making
   - to control or be free of pain
   - to have caring help available as needs change
   - to maintain relationships and as normal a life as possible
   - to be informed
   - to be shown respect
   - to be given choices
   - to cope adequately with loss of function or grief
   - to have control
   - to have access to service (or have service readily available)
   - to have good mental health

2. Family values
   - value the help—dependable—coordinated in assessing the individual to remain at home (be as independent as possible) in redesigning roles (assistance in adapting to new role)
   - possibility of maintaining as normal a life as possible
   - recognizing their contribution to care
   - value having someone to talk to as professional opinion/teaching/counseling
   - advocacy role of caregiver
   - individualization of service
   - nonjudgmental about social and personal lives by caregiver
   - information
   - role of program to help individual to adapt to changed roles and responsibilities (with definition of role and how to cope with the change)
   - help in accepting and maintaining new relationships
   - security of knowing who to call in crisis and availability of resources (reassurance)—value reassurance (even though may not be receiving service)
   - responsibility
   - the services are coordinated (from one place/who to call)
   - concentration on health/assets not only on illness/deficits
   - keeping them involved/informed on circumstances of situation

3. Values as caregivers
   - try to keep up-to-date using current knowledge to provide best service
   - use professional judgment based on education and experience
   - access to variety of resources
   - contributing to valuable component to continuum of care
   - being able to help people stay home in their communities
   - opportunity to be related to more than the client (i.e. family unit and environment)
   - participation in coordinated program approach to care
   - joint approval (family and program) to care
   - value uniqueness of home care; home care is not a health program nor social program but both
   - multidisciplinary approach—contribution of other caregivers to needs of each client
   - contribution of volunteers, family, friends, neighbors, etc. to our efforts
   - (re-assessed needs) value assessment—fit service to person rather than vice versa
   - families have limits that we are able to identify

- concentrate on health, not illness
- concentrate on social and emotional needs

These values were then translated by the Home Care Standards Committee into objective statements unique to home care.

Objective Statements Unique to Home Care

1. The client will
   - stay in the home/community/familiar surroundings
   - maintain normal roles, relationships, and functioning at home and in the community (to the extent possible)
   - be as independent as possible in activities of daily living in the home
   - maintain appropriate control (e.g., physiologic, decision making) in the home environment
   - have required supports provided in the home by family, friends, and the community
   - cope adequately with loss and grief while being maintained within the home environment
   - have easy access to a range of community services
   - receive individualized care that responds to the client's perceived needs in the home

2. The family will
   - maintain normal roles, relationships, and functioning at home and in the community (to the extent possible)
   - have easy access to a range of community services available for the client in the home through
     —service coordination provided by home care
     —information about available resources
   - receive appropriate help when needed to maximize their contributions and maintain the client in the home
   - receive recognition for their contributions to maintenance of the client in the home
   - receive nonjudgmental support that is sensitive to the unique stresses experienced by virtue of having the client in the home
   - cope adequately with loss and grief within the home environment

3. Caregivers will
   - assist clients to stay in their homes and communities
   - incorporate current technology and professional practices into the home and environment
   - exercise professional judgment in independent settings
   - provide a coordinated and integrated approach to care by
     —incorporating the services of a multidisciplinary team of professionals and paraprofessionals into the home care process
     —incorporating the contributions of family, friends, neighbors, and volunteers into a plan of activities within the home and community

—utilizing a variety of community resources
- ensure that any care plan established is mutually agreeable
- achieve and maintain a healthful living pattern within a client's ecosystem and encourage maximal independence in meeting health, social, emotional, physical, and safety needs
- provide a service tailored to the client's and family's needs, goals, and value systems
- provide an assessment in the home of
  —the client and the ecosystem
  —the potential for the client's continuance in the home
- provide an opportunity for professionals and paraprofessionals to achieve role satisfaction through
  —interactions with the client and significant others
  —interactions in the home and community setting
- assist the client and family with loss and grief while the client is maintained in the home environment

These statements were translated into a long list of outcome criteria and then condensed into 20 client-related and 8 family-related and caregiver-related outcomes. These criteria related directly to the values identified in the brainstorming sessions.[20]

Client-related Outcome Criteria

1. maintenance at home
2. comfort: pain management, symptom management
3. disposition at discharge
4. death at home
5. early discharge from hospital
6. activities of daily living
7. instrumental activities of daily living
8. knowledge of diagnosis and treatment
9. application of knowledge, diagnosis, treatment, and skill to care for oneself
10. knowledge of appropriate community resources
11. utilization of appropriate community resources
12. control, choice, involvement in plan of care
13. acceptance of responsibility for health
14. client satisfaction
15. selected physiological indicators
16. cognitive status
17. moral/life satisfaction
18. continuity of social relations
19. goal attainment
20. client coping with stress/strain

Family-related and Caregiver-related Outcome Criteria

1. family strain
2. family cohesiveness

3. moral/life satisfaction
4. knowledge of family members' diagnosis and treatment
5. application of knowledge of family members' care
6. knowledge of appropriate community resources
7. utilization of appropriate community resources
8. family/caregiver satisfaction with service

The Home Care Standards Committee met once a month and went through a process of reducing the list to 13 outcome criteria. The committee then sought tools for measuring these criteria. The outcomes had to be ones for which data was easily obtainable from either the client or the client's chart. The process for reducing the list of criteria included evaluating the outcomes for appropriateness (i.e., high, medium or low) and determining the relative importance of each criterion.

Outcome indicators are difficult to measure. Tools must be sensitive, as it is necessary to know the differences among outcomes. Tools must also be valid and reliable in order to give meaningful data. Data not only will help set standards, but will also help in assessing where a program is in relation to the standards.

As expected, some criteria viewed as highly appropriate for the CHCP were not considered very important (e.g., death at home). Based on the ratings, a shorter list of the most appropriate and important criteria were selected for immediate attention.

Final approval was given to the 8 client-related and 4 family-related outcome criteria presented in Table 19-3. Criteria for implementation needed to be selected according to several yardsticks:

1. Are the criteria essential and/or appropriate?
2. Will they be relatively easy to implement?
3. Are they reliable, valid measures available at the time at which the data would need collecting? (For example, reliable and valid ADL measures are readily available.)
4. Does each item apply to every patient for which the tool is intended?
5. Is it possible for every patient being measured to obtain a high score?
6. Is there variation within the patient group or over time? (Variation is essential if measurement is to have meaning.)
7. Are items related specifically to particular disciplines or caregivers?

Defining Criteria

Explicit conceptual definitions of the outcome criteria had to be prepared and adapted. The development of the definitions is an iterative process. The development of measurement items on the tool in accordance with the definitions is difficult if the intent of the outcome is not explicit. For example, we needed to clarify that we wanted to know the "ability" of the client and family to implement actions in a manner and degree satisfactory to them.

Table 19-3 Client-related and Family-related Outcome Criteria

Outcome Criterion	Definition	Rationale
Pain management	The ability of the client/family to implement actions designed to manage pain and associated symptoms in a manner and to the degree satisfactory to the client	Pain management is an important aspect of care. The inability to keep a client comfortable at home could in itself lead to transfer. Interventions associated with this outcome include education regarding medication and other therapeutic options; monitoring effectiveness of client/family; and consultation with the physician.
Symptom control (excluding pain)	The ability of the client/family to implement actions designed to maintain maximum functional capacity through management of symptoms (irreversible and reversible) associated with an acute or chronic illness	Control of symptoms generating from a pathological state is a major force of care and necessary to enable the client to remain at home with the same degree of comfort available in other care settings. Interventions associated with this include education regarding activities, therapeutic interventions, environment monitoring, and monitoring of progress.
Physiological health status	The actual state of the client's physical well-being in relationship to norms for healthy people and to norms for comparably ill populations	The client is admitted to the program because of a health problem. The optimum management of that problem, given the constraints of the client's condition, is a major goal of the program. Skin care, nutrition counseling, diabetic care, etc., are examples of interventions that affect this outcome. The measures used will have to be specific to the client or diagnostic category.
Activities of daily living	The ability of the client to perform activities that relate to self-care and mobility	Activities of daily living may be a critical variable in determining whether a client stays at home or is institutionalized. Interventions are aimed at developing, maintaining, or redeveloping these skills or arranging for services to be provided by family or others. Interventions include educational activities, occupational therapy, physical therapy, environment modification, and acquisition of necessary aids and equipment.
Instrumental activities of daily living	The ability of the client to perform activities that relate to the conduct of household and environmental management	Clients require completion of these activities if they are to remain at home. Interventions are aimed at developing, maintaining, or redeveloping these skills or arranging for services to be provided by family or others. Interventions include those listed for activities of daily living plus assistance through homemakers, home help, etc.
Sense of well-being*	Client's perception of his/her state of well-being given the realities of his/her health status (locus of control and feeling of self-worth are important elements)	The client's sense of well-being may influence the home care services provided. This outcome may be mediated by other outcomes, such as activities of daily living and pain control. The outcome is affected by attitudes of family and staff (personnel) as well as the success of other interventions.
Goal attainment	The degree to which the client achieves or surpasses the expected outcomes of care as depicted by the problems recorded in the client's record	Goals are established through interactions. The achievement of those goals is the essence of the home care program. The goals must be client specific to be meaningful. Interventions that affect this outcome include all services provided, individually and collectively.
Knowledge (client and family)	The client's and family's ability to identify and describe diagnoses, treatment regimes, management regimes, skills to implement treatment and management regimes, and safety issues in the home environment	Although knowledge is not sufficient to ensure compliance, it is a prerequisite. A substantial amount of time is devoted to teaching the client and the family, with the intent of providing the greatest amount of independence.
Application of knowledge (client and family)	The actual performance of the client and family in implementing the prescribed treatment and management regimes, including what is done, how it is done, when it is done, and how it is modified in response to unanticipated health events/problems	This criterion represents the ultimate goal of the teaching interventions. The intent is to enable the client and family to do what needs to be done and to establish a level of motivation that will encourage consistent implementation of care requirements. The purpose of education interventions is to have the client/family apply the knowledge gained thereby.

continues

Table 19-3 continued

Outcome Criterion	Definition	Rationale
Satisfaction with services (client and family)	Satisfaction refers to the subjective evaluation of the adequacy and acceptability of services in relation to the value or importance ascribed to that service	Although there are many variables other than home care that could alter satisfaction, it is important to have some measure of public acceptance of the program. Interventions include the services provided as well as how they are provided. Inclusion of the client and family in the decision-making process as well as good communication skills should have a positive influence on satisfaction.
Family strain	Self-perceived psychosocial and physical impact upon the family caregivers of caring for a family member at home	Home care should minimize family strain through recognition of poor coping strategies and stress. Any breakdown in this area is likely to result in the client being institutionalized. Interventions include identification of necessary support services, providing psychological support, encouraging communication, and respite care.
Maintenance at home†	The perception of the client and the family that • institutionalization was postponed • during the postponement, the client's condition was maintained at an adequate level (or above)	Home care does assist people in staying at home and prevents institutionalization.

*This outcome was rejected or questioned by a minority. The main issue was whether it was directly or indirectly affected by home care and to what degree.
†This criterion is difficult to define in any way that even suggests how it could be measured without designing a specific randomized clinical trial study. However, it is listed here because as many people voted to keep it in as to throw it out.

Source: Adapted from "The Development of a Home Care Quality Assurance Program in Alberta" by Lois Sorgen in *Home Health Care Services Quarterly*, Vol. 7, No. 2, with permission of Haworth Press, Inc., 75 Griswold St., Binghamton, New York, © Summer 1986.

By means of the definition process, the short-listed client outcomes were further short-listed—on the basis of whether they were relevant and responsive to home care services (e.g., sense of well-being was deleted on this basis) and whether they had understandable definitions (e.g., cognitive status [reality orientation] was deleted on this basis). The outcome of cognitive status was questioned by several people, since it was unclear what impact home care could have on this and what was expected in the way of client behavior or results. Sense of well-being was also debated, since it was unclear what was meant—quality of life, depression, morale?

Also used as a basis for reducing the list was the potential for measurement. In the case of sense of well-being, it was unclear what would be measured.

Finally, knowledge and application of knowledge was deleted due to the impracticality of collecting this information given the number of diagnostic conditions and health behaviors that could be taught. It may be preferable to do targeted studies using a specific condition such as diabetes rather than collect ongoing data.

As a result of the definition process and a final critique of the linkage of structure and process to outcome, a decision was made to measure only the following eight outcomes:

1. pain management
2. symptom control
3. physiological health status
4. activities of daily living
5. activities of household management
6. client satisfaction with services
7. family satisfaction with services
8. family strain

Tool Development

The next major piece of work was the actual development of the tool. It was decided that we would have an independent module for each of the criteria. Existing outcome tools that were believed to be applicable to community living home care clients or similar clients (e.g., the rehabilitation population) were reviewed.

Criteria for Selection of the Outcome Measurement Instruments[21]

The list below represents the general criteria used in guiding the selection of measurement tools, scales, or items for addressing each of the outcome areas. These criteria describe characteristics of the optimal measurement instrument. It was unlikely that tools meeting all of these criteria were available for each outcome area, but these criteria were intended to describe desirable characteristics of the instruments.

The criteria that had to be met were these:

1. minimizes response burden of the client or family
2. demonstrates reliability (.80) and face validity
3. not diagnosis specific
4. majority of items are applicable to home care

5. applicable for adults
6. sensitive to clinically important differences in outcome
7. written in language which is easily understood by the general population
8. produces interval data (if possible)

The criteria that were desirable were these:

1. not knowingly touches client or family sensitivities or raises ethical questions
2. developed for use with noninstitutionalized populations
3. minimizes client response time
4. minimizes staff administration time
5. easily coded and compatible with computerization
6. requires minimal training to administer
7. resistant to response bias
8. resistant to manipulation
9. cost-efficient to implement
10. able to be integrated with case management procedures
11. uses available information when possible
12. minimizes paper burden

After the review, a decision was made to use two existing tools (ADL and family strain) to modify two others (pain and activities of household management) and to construct from existing sources three others (symptom control, physiological status, and client/family satisfaction). The criteria and modules were subjected to content validity testing, in which the modules were assessed as to how well they represented the universe they sampled. Construct validity was assessed to ensure that the outcome criteria, measurement module, scale, and items were consistent with the values and with the program's objectives.

Intervening Variables

Client outcomes are affected not only by the quality of home care but also by factors independent of home care. The outcome obtained may be affected by characteristics of the client, the client's family, or the service provision system. For example, while one of the objectives of CHCP is to "reduce admissions to health care institutions," the quality of home care services alone does not determine whether the client can be maintained at home; support provided by relatives and the availability of funds for specialized services or equipment may also influence this outcome. Unpredictable accidents may also occur. The following is a list of intervening variables pertaining to the client, the client's family, and the service provision system.

1. client
   - physical
     —change in condition unrelated to illness
     —change in condition related to illness
     —hospitalization of client
   - social/environmental
     —change in residence of client
   - psychological
     —rejection of service(s)
2. caregiver (family member, significant other, informal support)
   - physical/psychological
     —change in the level of support/care provided by family
   - social/environmental
     —change in family constellation
        due to hospitalization of caregiver
        due to death of caregiver
        due to change in residence of caregiver
        due to illness of caregiver
        due to rejection of service(s)
3. service provision
   - home care services
     —lack of availability of appropriate resources (e.g., funding, personnel)
     —change in level/frequency of home care services
     —change in administrative policies/procedures
   - other services
     —change of medical authorization or support for home care
     —change in level/frequency of other non–home care support services
     —change in availability of other home care support services

Quantification of Factors Composing the Tool

Another issue addressed was the type of data that we wanted to collect. We decided to use interval data so that we could do statistical analysis and also could aggregate or summarize the data at local and provincial levels. Every measurement scale developed has a number that corresponds to the degree at which the attribute occurs.

Reliability Testing

Reliability testing is necessary to ensure that the tool is consistent in its use (i.e., that anyone trained to use it would use it in the same way as another person). We decided to test its reliability through both interrater reliability and test-retest reliability.

Validity Testing

Validity testing is necessary to determine the extent to which a tool actually measures what it seeks to measure. We decided to test concurrent validity given that the standards committee had already assessed content validity.

Scoring

Equal weighting was given to all items (the assumption was that they were equally relevant). Following data analysis,

Table 19-4 Sample of Potential Outcome Standards

Variable	Method of Measurement	Standard
Pain: The ability of the client/family to implement actions designed to manage pain and associated symptoms in a manner and to a degree satisfactory to the client.	Pain Module: 13 Likert-type items using a 1–5 response scale and representing five subscales. Range for total scores is 0–52. Data are obtained through interviews and are self-reported.	100% of the clients will have total scores of at least 26, which represents average or midpoint pain management. 75% of the clients will have total scores of at least 39, which represents above average pain management.
Physiological Status: The attainment and/or maintenance of the physiological status of the client within acceptable levels.	Physiological Health Module: Items include blood pressure, pulse, blood glucose, and weight and are scored as either in or out of the desired range. Data are taken from the chart.	75% of the clients will have recordings within the desired range for any problem identified on assessment/reassessment.
Symptom Control: The ability of the client/family to implement actions designed to maintain maximum functional capacity through management of symptoms associated with an acute, chronic, or terminal illness.	Symptom Control Module: Symptoms include nausea, loss of appetite, fatigue, bowel, bladder, sleep, weakness, stiffness, cough, dizziness, and breathing. Symptoms are evaluated through self-reports and items using a five-point response scale.	100% of the clients for whom the symptom was a problem on assessment will report at least midpoint ability to manage the symptom. 75% of the clients for whom the symptom was a problem on assessment will report above midpoint ability to manage the symptom.

weighting will be re-examined and probably be adjusted (e.g., the ability to manage, satisfaction, and impact may be weighted more than other items).

Pilot Testing of the Client Outcome Tool (COT)

Four health units representing urban and rural sites were involved. Pretesting was done to finalize the COT for testing. Most of the issues arising out of pretesting related to the need for more complete instructions on use of the tool (i.e., training). Four hundred clients (or their families) were sampled; 175 were measured twice for interrater reliability. The sample was stratified by type of care (acute, chronic, rehabilitative, and palliative). It included recent discharges (within the last month) and clients receiving services for at least three months. The tool was completed in a structured interview with the client (or client's family) by a case coordinator who was not familiar with the case. Client and family satisfaction surveys were left for completion and then mailed in. Concurrent validity was completed by having a case coordinator who did not have access to the previously completed COT but was familiar with the case complete a COT based on the chart, service providers, clients, and family. Four hundred and thirty-three COTs were completed. Data has not yet been analyzed. Based on piloting experience, the issues that will need further discussion include

- the suitability of modules for some types of clients (e.g., pain control for palliative care)
- the comprehensiveness of some modules
- difficulties in answering questions (e.g., family strain and dissatisfaction with services)
- COT procedures (e.g., when should COTS be done)

The next steps involve (1) staff training and development of local committees, (2) creation of outcome standards, and (3) implementation and monitoring of the quality assurance

system, including studies to begin to link structure, process, and outcome. Data analysis is currently being completed. Preliminary results show that only minor changes will need to be made to the COT, so that it can be implemented provincewide. An example of how we envision translating the variables into standards that can be measured is shown in Table 19-4.

CONCLUSION

Quality assurance programs in health care are used to systematically evaluate the effectiveness of existing programs of care and to provide data that may be used by providers and consumers to make decisions about what to maintain or change in the present system. When an agency accepts responsibility for setting standards, its members (staff) become accountable for meeting these standards. Thus, a quality assurance program is a mechanism for consistently directing service delivery toward achieving standards and ensuring that the program is directed toward the improvements required. In Alberta, the ongoing effort to establish a comprehensive quality assurance program has been an exciting learning experience. The collaboration between government and local program staff has proven that combining local and provincial energies and perspectives is mutually beneficial.

NOTES

1. C.G. Smith-Marker, ''The Marker Model: A Hierarchy for Nursing Standards,'' *Journal of Nursing Quality Assurance* 1, no. 2 (1987): 7–20.

2. C.F. Capers, ''Some Basic Facts about Models, Nursing Conceptualizations, and Nursing Theories,'' *Journal of Continuing Education in Nursing* 16, no. 5 (1986): 149–54.

3. C.G. Smith-Marker, ''Setting Standards for Professional Nursing: The Marker Model'' (Presentation at The Johns Hopkins Hospital, Baltimore, 1987).

4. S.S. Poe and J.C. Will, ''Quality Nursing-Patient Outcomes: A Framework for Nursing Practice,'' *Journal of Nursing Quality Assurance* 2, no. 1 (1987): 29–37.

5. American Nurses' Association, *Standards of Community Health Nursing Practice* (Kansas City, Mo.: Author, 1974).

6. D.A. Simmons, *Classification Scheme for Client Problems in Community Health Nursing*, DHHS Publication no. HRA 80-16 (Washington, D.C.: GPO, 1980).

7. D.A. Peters, "Development and Testing of a Community Health Nursing Intensity Rating Scale for Patient Classification" (Ph.D. diss., University of Pennsylvania, 1987).

8. D.A. Peters and S.S. Poe, "Using Monitoring in a Home Care Quality Assurance Program." *Journal of Nursing Quality Assurance* 2, no. 2 (1988): 32–37.

9. P. Cell et al., *Components for the Successful Use of the Omaha Classification System* (Princeton, N.J.: Home Health Assembly of New Jersey, 1987).

10. Carol Blair and Jean Schmidt (Presentation given to the Metropolitan Toronto Home Care Program, March 1985).

11. A. Donabedian, *Explorations in Quality Assessment and Monitoring* (Ann Arbor, Mich.: Health Administration Press, 1980), vol. 1, *The Definition of Quality and Approaches to Its Assessment*.

12. Margaret W. Linn, Lee Gurel, and Bernard S. Linn, "Patient Outcome as a Measure of Quality of Nursing Home Care," *Journal of Public Health* 67 (April 1977).

13. A. Donabedian, "Evaluating the Quality of Medical Care," *Milbank Memorial Fund Quarterly* 44 (1966): 166–206.

14. D. Block, "Evaluation of Nursing Care in Terms of Process and Outcome: Issues in Research and Quality Assurance," *Nursing Research* 24: 256–63.

15. Donabedian, "Evaluating the Quality of Medical Care"; M.Q. Thorne, "Models of Quality Assurance Programs in Rural Community Mental Health Centers," in *Quality Assurance in the Ambulatory Setting: Nine Papers,* ed. R.S. Kessler (St. Albans, Vt.: Institutional Industries Press, 1977); J. Woy,

D. Lund, and C. Attkisson, "Quality Assurance in Human Service Program Evaluation," (New York: Academic Press, 1978).

16. Dr. Carol Lindeman, Dean of Nursing, Oregon Health Sciences University, assisted the Home Care Standards Committee in developing the conceptual framework for the quality assurance program as outside consultant.

17. The chart audit tool was developed by Management, Analysis and Planning Services, Alberta Hospital Association, in 1982.

18. The home care programs survey results were completed by Price Waterhouse Associates, July 25, 1986.

19. Evelyn Shapiro was the outside consultant for the brainstorming session, which occurred on May 13, 1983.

20. The Home Care Standards Committee completed this phase of the project with the assistance of Dr. Barbara Horn, Dr. Martha Herriot, and Dr. Bernadette Lalonde.

21. This phase of the project was done with the assistance of Dr. Nancy Staisey, a Price Waterhouse consultant.

REFERENCES

Case Study 2

Lalonde, Bernadette I.D. "Quality Assurance." In *Handbook on Mental Health Administration*, edited by M.J. Austin and Hershey. San Francisco: Jossey-Bass, 1982.

Lindeman, C. "Measuring Quality of Nursing Care." Parts 1, 2. *Journal of Nursing Administration* 6 (June, September 1976): 7–9, 16–19.

Sorgen, Lois M. "The Development of a Home Care Quality Assurance Program in Alberta." *Home Health Care Services Quarterly* 7 (Summer 1986): 13–28.

Appendix 19-A

Health Units within the Province of Alberta

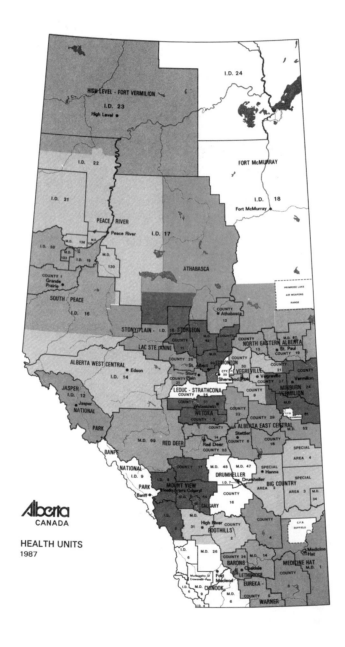

Source: Produced by the Alberta Bureau of Surveying and Mapping © 1987.

Appendix 19-B

The Coordinated Home Care Program Statement of Philosophy*

A statement of program philosophy is a statement of beliefs which provides guidance for staff in achieving the objectives of the Program. For the Coordinated Home Care Program, the statement of philosophy finds its roots in the Ministerial Statement of Home Care, delivered by the Honourable Helen Hunley in March 1978 and in the statement of philosophy and purpose for community health services (January 1980). The statement of philosophy, the Home Care Regulation, and the goals of the Program are mutually consistent. Similarly, any statement of philosophy adopted by a Local Health Authority must be compatible with them.

The Home Care Directorate, together with local Coordinated Home Care Programs, believe that:

1. Home Care, while accepting that health is a community concern, must encourage the individual to take responsibility for maintaining his/her health.
2. The preferred method of delivering Home Care services is on a decentralized basis, through the Local Health Authorities.
3. Home Care is an integral component in any comprehensive health care delivery system.
4. Home Care should be available to persons throughout the Province for whom this is the most appropriate health care mode.
5. Home Care services must enhance the existing resources of the client, family, and community to enable them to achieve and/ or maintain optimal level of functioning.
6. The multi-disciplinary health care team approach, which emphasizes the role of the client and family in care planning, is the appropriate method of providing home care service to the client.
7. In providing services to clients, it is essential that the local Coordinated Home Care Program coordinate the activities of Home Care staff, in order that they are integrated with other works and volunteer groups in the community.

Prepared by
Home Care Directorate
in consultation with
Local Health Authorities
Alberta Social Services
and Community Health
September 1980

---

*Courtesy of Alberta Coordinated Home Care Program, Department of Community and Occupational Health.

Appendix 19-C

Alberta Coordinated Home Care Program (CHCP) Objectives*

1. To coordinate the provision of Home Care services to persons meeting the admission criteria, particularly the elderly and adult handicapped, in order to
   a. improve, maintain or retard deterioration of health status and level of independence
   b. reduce admission to health care institutions
   c. facilitate early discharge of patients in health care institutions, thereby reducing their length of stay;
2. To develop, maintain and upgrade standards of care so that Home Care services are provided in an efficient, effective and humane manner;
3. To make available throughout the province all services listed in the Home Care Regulation, Section 2 (3) and (4), so as to meet the needs of potential Home Care recipients;
4. To increase the capacity of families and other social networks to provide care for persons in need;
5. To promote cooperation among health and social services agencies in the community so that:
   a. services for Home Care recipients and referrals by the Home Care program to other agencies are effective, efficient, and timely, and
   b. community services are not unnecessarily duplicated;
6. To involve volunteers in the provision of Home Care services;
7. To advise decision makers on program changes needed to meet the needs of client groups; and
8. To determine the extent to which CHCP objectives are being met.

Prepared by
Home Care Directorate
Alberta Social Services
and Community Health
May 23, 1979
(HCIB 1979-6)

---

*Courtesy of Alberta Coordinated Home Care Program, Department of Community and Occupational Health.

Appendix 19-D

Terms of Reference for the Home Care Standards Committee*

A Sub-Committee of the Home Care Program Standing Committee

1. *Purpose of Committee*
   a. The general purpose of the Home Care Standards Committee is to develop and promote Provincial Home Care Standards (allowing for local autonomy) for recommendation to the Home Care Program Standing Committee. In this regard, the Home Care Standards Committee provides a forum for discussion of the common concerns of the Home Care Programs relating to the need for standards in delivering safe and consistent Home Care services, the development of standards and recommendation of the standards to support decision-making at the level of the Home Care Program Standing Committee and the Meeting of Directors. The Home Care Standards Committee has four main responsibilities.
      I) To develop basic structural standards which can be applied in each local program.
      II) To act as a steering committee to outside contracted consultant who will develop process and outcome standards which can be applied in each local program so that quality of care can be measured.
      III) To submit the standards for approval to the Home Care Program Standing Committee and the Meeting of Directors.
      IV) To promote the implementation of the Home Care Standards in each local program.

2. *Committee Membership*
   a. *Non-rotating Members*
      I) Manager of Home Care Unit, Professional Services Branch.
      II) The Home Care Unit Nursing Consultant, Professional Services Branch.
      III) The Home Care Unit Rehabilitation Consultants, Professional Services Branch.
      IV) The Home Care Unit Support Service Consultant, Professional Services Branch.
   b. *Rotating Members*
      I) One representative from either Calgary or Edmonton Home Care Program (alternating between Edmonton and Calgary).
      II) There shall be five representatives from Local Health Authorities, including a mix of Home Care Coordinators and care providers.
      III) One representative from Meeting of Directors.
   c. Others may attend committee meetings by committee request as a resource to the committee or others may request an invitation from the chairman to attend.
   d. Pilot Projects shall have membership on Home Care Standards Committee.

3. *Appointment and Tenure*
   a. When Committee vacancies occur, the Committee Chairman will send a letter to each Home Care Coordinator (with a copy to each Director of a LHA) notifying him/her of a vacancy on the Committee, and soliciting applications for membership. Interested Home Care Coordinators will be encouraged to submit their name to the Committee after they received permission to do so from their employers. The Committee will select new members from the applications received. These appointments shall be ratified by the Home Care Program Standing Committee.
   b. Under 2(b) I & II, Home Care Coordinators may nominate a representative to the Committee.
   c. Term of office for rotating committee members shall normally be for a minimum two years. Rotating Committee members shall change their term of office in January and June. Normally no more than two rotating committee members would change at any one rotation.

---

*Courtesy of Alberta Coordinated Home Care Program, Department of Community and Occupational Health.

    d. Rotating Committee members may be reappointed for a second term.

    e. When a committee member or alternate fails to attend for three consecutive meetings, the member will be asked to resign.

4. *Accountability*

    a. A Chairman and Vice-Chairman shall be selected by the Committee, and appointed for a term of one calendar year, starting on January 1st. These appointments do not have to be ratified by the Home Care Program Standing Committee.

    b. The Committee, through its Chairman, shall be directly responsible to the Home Care Program Standing Committee which in turn is accountable to the Meeting of Directors.

    c. Committee workplans shall be approved yearly in advance by the Home Care Program Standing Committee and the Meeting of Directors.

5. *Budget*

    a. Travel and subsistence expenses incurred as a result of Committee membership shall be reimbursed by the Department according to current government regulations.

    b. Cost incurred by the Committee in carrying out its mandate shall be defrayed by the Department, providing those costs have been authorized in advance by the Manager of Home Care.

6. *Meeting Format and Frequency*

    a. The frequency of meetings shall be determined by the Committee.

    b. Meeting format shall be determined by the Committee. Minutes shall be recorded by the Home Care Unit, and provided to each Committee member by the Home Care Unit.

    c. The Chairman is responsible for preparing an agenda and circulating it in advance of the next meeting.

    d. Decisions shall be reached by consensus among Committee members present.

    e. One-half of regular members constitutes a quorum.

7. *Reporting*

    a. Reports on the work of the Committee will be given at Home Care Program Standing Committee meetings on a regular basis.

    b. Minutes of meetings will be tabled with the Meeting of Directors at their request.

    c. Minutes of meetings will be submitted to the Home Care Program Standing Committee.

    d. Abstracts of Committee minutes will be included in Home Care Information Bulletins, where deemed appropriate by the committee.

    e. Direct communications with users may be undertaken by the Committee from time to time, e.g., surveys, questionnaires, reports.

8. *Revisions of Terms of Reference*

    a. These Terms of Reference may be revised, provided revisions are consistent with Departmental policies and regulations, and approved by both the Program Standing Committee, and the Meeting of Directors.

    b. These Terms of Reference shall be reviewed annually by the Committee.

Quality Assurance Glossary for Home Health Care

Abstract. Summary of a client's medical data that provides a basis for classifying the client according to treatment, age, discharge status, or any of an extensive number of client attributes.

Acceptability. From the point of view of the population served, the degree to which the provided service meets the health care need and is pleasing.

Accessibility. Degree of ease with which the individual or the population can enter, that is, gain needed admittance to, the various segments of the health care delivery system.

Accountability. Condition of being responsible for providing a reckoning to the persons who gave the authority to act; an obligation to reveal, explain, and justify through broad reporting what one does and how one discharges one's responsibilities. Such an accounting might be made to the public, a review committee of peers, or an employer.

Accreditation. Acknowledgment by a voluntary, nongovernmental agency (e.g., Joint Commission, NLN) that the institution or individual meets some predetermined structure, process, and outcome standards of practice; required for third party reimbursements, etc.

Activity. Action that results in change.

Actual practice data. Entries in client's medical records and other home care records of diagnostic and therapeutic care rendered, including observations, physical, laboratory findings, assessment modes, client responses, etc.

Adequacy. Degree to which the total need or the portion of the total need that is specified in the program objectives is met.

Affordability. Degree to which the service has a monetary cost that is within reasonable reach of the population served.

Appropriateness. Degree of importance and priority of the objectives that are specified for a particular program when compared with other possible objectives for the particular program or for other programs.

Assess. To estimate or judge characteristics, qualities, or attributes.

Assure. To guarantee; to give confidence in.

Audit. To examine the record of transactions and attest to the excellence of these transactions. Also called a *Study*. The *study sample* is the selected group of clients whose care is reviewed in a study and is therefore considered representative of the care provided to other clients covered by the study topic. The *study topic* is the subject of a study; it may be a diagnosis, problem, procedure, or a critical process of care.

Capitation. Method of payment for health services in which an individual or institutional provider is paid a fixed per capita amount for each person served without regard to the actual number or nature of services provided to each person.

Care. Actions and behaviors taken to fulfill the responsibility for causing or maintaining the well-being of persons.

Caregiver, primary. Individual in the home (spouse, family member, friend or significant other) responsible for assisting the client's return to maximal functioning.

Case management. The coordination of services provided by a home health care agency, including client/family referrals to appropriate community resources and liaison with other individuals (e.g., the client's physician and/or community services involved in client care), to meet the ongoing identified needs of the client, to assure implementation of the plan of care or service, and to avoid unnecessary duplication of services.

Case mix. Categories of clients (types and volume) treated by a home health care agency; the case mix represents the complexity of the agency's caseload.

Certification. Process by which a nongovernmental agency or association identifies that an individual licensed to practice a profession has met certain predetermined standards specified by that profession for specialty practice.

Charges. Prices assigned to units of health care services, such as visits by a nurse or aide. Charges for services may not be related to the actual costs of providing the services.

Client classification system. The grouping of clients according to some observable or inferred properties or characteristics and quantification of these categories as a measure of the professional staff effort; a descriptive system that can objectively assess a client's needs for services and deliver an outcome that predicts types and intensity of services to be delivered.

Clinical. Pertaining to actions (actual observations and treatment) by health care practitioners—physicians, nurses, therapists, etc.

Competency. A demonstrable ability; does not necessarily imply proficiency or expertise.

Concurrent monitor. Device that allows continual or frequent monitoring of a procedure, policy, person, or area of service to assure that action taken to resolve problems disclosed by retrospective audit is having its desired effect or to identify problems that require further investigation.

Concurrent review. Monitoring activity that occurs during the provision of services. PRO activity that certifies the necessity, appropriateness, and quality of services during a home care episode.

Concurrent study. Type of client or medical care evaluation study performed while a client is still receiving services; involves process or intermediate outcome criteria and continuous data collection. One advantage is that client care can be altered during the process.

Conditions of participation (COP). Ten requirements (standards) that must be met by a home health care agency in order to become a certified provider eligible to receive Medicare and Medicaid funds.

Continuing education. Programs designed to enhance overall professional growth and development.

Continuity. Course or procession or the continuous, orderly, forward-moving arrangement of persons or things. In delivery of health care, continuity is the sequence of events in the delivery of care, the coordination among different segments of the system, and the integrated action among members of the team.

Costs. Actual expenses incurred in the provision of services or goods.

Credentialing. A process in which a qualified agent reviews an individual, program, or organization and publically recognizes that minimum standards have been met at the time of review.

Criteria mapping. A process evaluation method to assess clinical decision making based on the presence or absence of certain signs, symptoms, and client needs.

Criterion. Standard, model, norm, test, or rule used in comparisons. An indicator that represents a desired level of client care used for the purpose of screening large numbers of client records to determine the quality of care provided. In study methods, a criterion consists of an *element* (minimum essential evidence of an aspect of care), *standard* (desired occurrence [100 percent] or nonoccurrence [0 percent] of the element), and an *exception* (acceptable reasons or circumstances that account for the presence or absence of an element in a client's record).

Criterion, outcome. The desired results in terms of maintenance or change in health status.

Criterion, process. Elements of appropriate clinical management.

Criterion, structural. Desired home care and medical care organization and resources for the provision of care.

Data retrieval. Gathering of information from medical records or other sources relevant to client care.

Deficiency. A given variation from an audit criterion determined by an auditor or a committee to be a sign of deficient performance by the agency or by individuals responsible for care.

Diagnosis related groups (DRGs). Hospital (inpatient) classification scheme that categorizes patients who are medically related with respect to diagnoses and treatment and who are statistically similar with respect to length of stay. There are 23 major diagnostic categories, 467 diagnostic subgroups (effective October 1, 1983, for Medicare patients). Related to the prospective payment system (PPS).

Discharge planning. The process of assessing needs and obtaining or coordinating appropriate resources for clients as they move through the health care system.

Discharge summary. A written record including the (1) date and reason for discharge, (2) status of problems identified on admission and subsequently, (3) overall status of the client, and (4) summary of the care or services provided.

Distributions. Display of numerical data from a study showing the proportions of cases that do or do not meet a given criterion and arranged in such a way as to help identify patterns of care.

Documentation variation. Variation so designated because documentation is absent, insufficient, or too ambiguous to determine whether actual practice conformed to a criterion. Documentation variations are treated in all other respects like practice variations.

Effectiveness. Degree to which specified objectives are attained as a result of activities.

Efficiency. Cost of the resources used appropriately to attain specified objectives.

Evaluate. To determine the outcome achieved by an activity (or activities) designed to attain a valued objective. Can also be applied to measurement of the quality of other parameters, such as activities, continuity, and resources.

Evaluation study. A systematic, in-depth appraisal of care accomplished by utilizing predetermined structure, process, or outcome criteria and a wide variety of data collection techniques, such as interviewing, observation, reviewing client records, and performing client satisfaction surveys.

Exception. Clearly defined reason, instance, or circumstance that, if documented in the client medical record, accounts for the absence (or presence) or an element in the client medical record; alternate secondary evidence that is acceptable to a committee.

Feedback. Communication to an individual or group of individuals involved in the subject area of the communication, usually about an identified problem.

Follow-up. Deliberate action taken to ensure the continuing resolution of a problem.

Generic screen. Review and display of client records that utilizes criteria that apply equally to all clients, regardless of sources of or persons responsible for care ordered or provided.

Goal. The desired end toward which activities are directed.

Governing body. A group of individuals responsible for adopting written governing policies (e.g., bylaws, mission statement) detailing services to be provided and management of the agency, including overseeing the quality of care provided to clients by employed staff and individuals under contract.

HMO (health maintenance organization). Prepaid medical insurance based on an ambulatory care–preventive medicine model. There are three basic organizational types: (1) staff, where each practitioner is employed by the HMO; (2) group practice, where a group practice involving different specialties enrolls clients on a prepaid basis; and (3) independent practice association, where physicians in a single area (but at different locations) include HMO membership as an option for their clients.

Home health care agency. An organization that offers a program of health services in a client's residence or other community setting to persons of all ages. Such services may include, but are not limited to, physician, nursing, social, therapy, nutrition, laboratory and x-ray, homemaker, and medical supply and equipment services.

Home health care. That component of comprehensive health care in which services are provided to individuals and families in the home for the purpose of promoting, maintaining, or restoring health or minimizing the effects of illness and disability. Services appropriate to the needs of the individual client and family are planned and coordinated by an agency using employed staff or contractual agreements.

Homebound. Generally speaking, homebound status implies that the client's health is impaired to the extent that he or she could not seek services outside the home.

Incident report. Formal reporting mechanism through which exceptional occurrences taking place within the agency are identified.

Indicator. Aspect of the health care process that signals whether or not the appropriate practitioner interventions were provided.

In-service education. Programs designed to maintain or enhance the knowledge and skills required to provide care to clients (i.e., job-related programs).

Intermittent care. The provision of services less than 8 hours a day and less than a total of 40 hours per week. Also called *part-time care*.

Instrument. A written form used in the evaluation process to identify the data to be collected and directions for recording data. Also called a *tool*.

JCAHO (Joint Commission). Joint Commission on Accreditation of Healthcare Organizations. Formerly Joint Commission on Accreditation of Hospitals (JCAH).

Justification. Category of criteria for evaluating the appropriateness of medical intervention; also a clinically supportive reason that renders a record acceptable with respect to audit criteria, thereby permitting the record to pass committee review and eliminating it from further study.

Levels of care/staging. An outcome-oriented evaluation method to determine the severity of medical problems or functional limitations at time of admission.

Licensure. A process by which an agency of the state government grants permission to individuals accountable for the practice of a profession and prohibits all others from legally practicing it. *Home health care agency licensure* is the process by which a state recognizes and authorizes an agency to operate. The agency must meet minimum operational standards (varying in each state), comply with the state's certificate of need (CON) (in states where applicable), and disclose names and addresses of the director and each officer of the agency.

Measurable. Being objectively quantifiable or assessable by means of standard measuring devices.

Measure. Device for gauging by comparison the quantity and quality of some aspect of health services.

Measurement validity. Absence of random or systematic measurement error.

Medicaid (Title XIX). Government program of health insurance for the eligible indigent and disabled. Medicaid is financed by both state and federal governments.

Medical care evaluation (MCE). Process of studying the effectiveness and efficiency of medical care delivered to clients with the purpose of making recommendations for changes beneficial to clients, staff, facility, and community; required by governmental bodies.

Medical record. Permanent documentation of an individual's health care; it includes client identification, diagnoses, care needs, plans of treatment, outcomes, and other data required by external and internal review bodies.

Medicare (Title XVIII). Government program of health insurance for the eligible aged and disabled; financed by the federal government.

Multidisciplinary study. Type of client or medical care evaluation study in which representatives of two or more professional disciplines develop criteria and analyze variations from criteria pertinent to their respective disciplines. Also called a *combined study*. A *parallel study* is one in which more than one discipline studies the same topic, but, while utilizing the same client populations and the same data sources, each discipline sets its own criteria and reviews the variations and establishes corrective actions separately from the other disciplines.

Objective. A measurable activity that is performed in order to achieve a goal.

Orientation. Program designed to acquaint all employees with the agency *prior* to providing client care; includes information on policies and procedures of agency; job description and performance expectations; roles and relationships of various health personnel employed by agency; resources in community, including medical services; ethics, confidentiality of client information; and client rights.

Outcome. End result of care; measurable change in client's health status within a specific period of management.

Outliers. Clients displaying atypical characteristics relative to other clients.

Client satisfaction survey. An evaluation method to determine client's perceptions of the appropriateness and acceptability of care received.

Pattern of care. Overall statistical performance profile of the clinical behavior of all persons involved in the care of the clients in a study or of the agency as a whole.

Peer. An equal. In delivery of care, peers are those who have a high degree of expertise and are involved together in goal-directed care transactions with a very specific client population.

Peer review. Review of individuals by their colleagues.

Peer review organization (PRO). Successor of PSRO. Organization having contract with home health care agencies to monitor quality of reasonable and medically necessary services; reviews validity of diagnosis and procedures and appropriateness of admission and discharge.

Plan of treatment (POT). The proposed plan of care for the client written by the attending physician or by a nurse and countersigned by a physician; the plan includes a description of the types of services to be provided, the frequency and duration of treatment, the diagnosis, any functional limitations, the extent of homebound status, medications and diet, needed medical supplies, and the expected outcome of treatment.

Problem. Deviation from accepted standard of client care.

Process. Whole or totality of the service; it includes the outcomes, activities, continuity, resources, and population dimensions.

Process audit. Evaluation based on process measures; conducted during the period of time services are being provided.

Profile analysis. Retrospective review in which aggregate client care data are compiled to analyze the patterns of health care services.

Program. Prearranged plan for an action or group of actions that will result in change.

Professional advisory body. A group of individuals (a practicing physician, a nurse, and appropriate representatives from other professional disciplines who are neither owners nor employers of the agency) who review annually and make recommendations to the governing body concerning the scope of the agency's services, admission and discharge policies, medical supervision and plans of treatment, emergency care, clinical records, personnel qualifications, program evaluations, and the maintenance of connections with other health care providers in a community information program.

Prospective reviews. Review of the need for home care services prior to admission to determine if they are medically necessary and if the home care agency can provide the appropriate level of care.

Quality. The distinguishing characteristics that determine the value, rank, or degree of excellence.

Quality assurance. Distinguishing characteristics that determine the value or degree of excellence and the mechanisms to efficiently and effectively monitor client health care.

Quality assurance program. A set of monitoring and evaluation activities designed to identify, promote, and enhance the delivery of quality health care.

Report. Presentation of generic screen data compiled once a month (monthly) or every three months (quarterly) and displayed cumulatively on a yearly basis for the purpose of making decisions regarding the quality of care provided.

Randomization. Distribution of individuals such that all have an equal chance of being selected in proportion to their frequency or occurrence within the population under study.

Reimbursement, cost-based. Amount of payment based on the cost to the provider of delivering the service. The actual payment may be based on any one of several different formulas, such as full cost, full cost plus additional percentage, allowable cost, or fraction of cost.

Reimbursement, prospective. Payment method in which home care rates are set prospectively (before services are rendered) and are based upon expected types and volumes of clients.

Reimbursement, retrospective. Payment to providers by a third party carrier for costs or charges actually incurred by subscribers in a previous time period.

Reliability. Reproducibility of findings; the degree to which a tool consistently generates the same results when measuring a like situation.

Resources. The human and material means that give assistance or support.

Restudy. Subsequent complete study of a topic audited previously to assess the impact of the first study's corrective measures on the identified problems.

Retrospective review. Review of care after it has been provided.

Review. Prospective, concurrent, or retrospective formal critical examination with a view to improvement.

Review committee. Any medical staff, department, or other professional group charged with the responsibility of assessing the quality or utilization of health care.

Risk management. Control of those circumstances of home health care that pose a threat to the safety and comfort of clients; a set of activities designed to identify and prevent or control all potential and real risks of economic loss.

RUGS (resource utilization groups). A case mix methodology being developed by Yale University for the purpose of evaluating and providing reimbursement for "activities of daily living" in long-term health care facilities.

Screening. Method by which charts in a study that conform to explicit, predetermined criteria are excused from further scrutiny. When a chart conforms, it can be said to have "passed through the screen"; if it does not conform, it is "screened out" for individual attention.

Sentinel. An outcome evaluation method based on an epidemiological approach that monitors all factors which contribute to an unnecessary identified disease, disability, or complication.

Skilled nursing service. Care provided by or under the direction of a registered nurse according to the plan of treatment. Such care may include catheter changes, dressing changes and wound care, I.V. therapy, and client and family teaching.

Standard. Any established measure of extent, quantity, quality, or value; an agreed-upon or expected level of performance; a degree of care excellence that is established; the percentage of time an aspect of care should occur (0–100%).

Structural evaluation. A method designed to assess administrative organization, facilities, equipment, range of services, qualifications of health care providers, and client mix.

Structure. Arrangement and functional union of the related parts so that they form a whole. For monitoring and evaluation purposes, a structure may include the number, mix, qualifications, and organization of staff, equipment, material, facilities, and financial resources.

Supervisory visit. A method of evaluation. A visit to a client's home, conducted by a registered nurse or other appropriate professional, for the purpose of determining the progress toward pre-established goals, observing and assessing relationships, and determining the appropriateness of continued or alternative services for meeting the ongoing needs of the client. Such visits are conducted at least once every 60 days or as often as deemed appropriate in order to monitor and evaluate care.

Tracers. A process and outcome evaluation method best suited to evaluate care provided to a group of clients by an agency rather than an individual professional. Tracers measure how the components of a system work together to affect health status.

Utilization review. A clinical record review; concurrent or retrospective formal critical examination of appropriateness of admissions and discharges, use of personnel, and utilization of services.

Validity. The degree to which an instrument (tool) actually measures what it is intended to measure.

Index

A

Abandonment, 206–07
Abstract, 277
Abuse, potential for, 242
Abused patients, social work referrals and, 164–65
Acceptability, 277
Accessibility, 277
Accident reports, 38
Accountability, 277
Accreditation, 57–59, 277
  definition of, 57
  Joint Commission program of, 58, *59*
  National Home Caring Council program of, 58–59
  National League for Nursing program of, 57–58
  requirement of, 15
Accrediting agency, viewpoint of, 15
Acquired immunodeficiency syndrome (AIDS), care for patients with, 152
Action report(s)
  form, 135
  reassessment of, 124–25
Activity(ies), 277
  evaluation process, 42–43
  monitoring process, 42–43
    form, 45–46
  quality assurance
    format for, 44
    log for, 48–51
Actual practice data, 277
Adequacy, 277
Administration, 65
  agency program evaluation, 67
  agency standards, 66–67
  federal certification, 67
  incident reports, 67
  intake process, 66
  patient satisfaction, 67

  problem identification in, 66–67
  productivity, 67
  referral process, 66
  state licensing requirements, 67
  utilization review, 67
Admission
  definition of, 176
  policies, 210
AFFIRM model, 240–42
  availability of resources, 240–41
  booklet, 245–46
  factual information, 241
  formulation of daily schedule, 241
  monitoring progress, 241–42
  referral list, 241
Affordability, 277
Agency. *See* Home health care agency
Agency liability, 208
AIDS, care for patients with, 152
Alberta, Canada
  health units within, 272
  quality assurance program in, 258–70
Alcoholism, social work referrals and, 166
American College of Physicians'(ACP), position of, 153
American Medical Association (AMA)
  Home Health Care Report, 152–53, 160
  Journal of the American Medical Association, 153–54, 154*n*
  Physician Guide to Home Health Care, 153, 160
  support for home health care, 152–53
American Nurses Association (ANA)
  definition of standards, 55
  model for quality assurance, 56, *56*
  standards of home health nursing practice, 60, *61*
Annual Program Evaluation Policy, 15, *19*
Annual reports, 39
Appropriateness, 277

Around-the-clock services, 198
ASCO calendar card, 188–90, *189*
Assess, 277
Assurance, definition of, 13
Assure, 277
Audit, 277
  as method of data collection, 73

B

Benefits, social work referrals and, 165–66
Bioethics, 207
  bibliography, 212
"Black Box" of Home Care Quality, The (American Bar Association), 56, 57
"Blanket" consent, 206
Brewster, Mary, 6

C

Capitation, 277
Care, 277. *See also* Home health care
  clinical, 18, *25*
  levels of, 151–52, 279
Caregiver(s). *See also* Family caregiver(s)
  concerns of, 165
  primary, 277
  professional competence of, 163–64
  related outcome criteria, 266
  values as, 265
Case management, 277–78. *See also* Nursing process
  initiation of care, 140–41
  staff nurses and, 140–44
Case mix, 278
Certification, 278
  individual, 60–61
  paraprofessional, 57
  requirement of, 15
Certification of need (CON), 57

283

Certifying agencies, viewpoint of, 15
Charges, 278
Chavigny, K. H.
  Home Health Care Report, 152–53, 160
Checklist, as method of data collection, 73
Circulatory function, *255*
Client(s)
  classification system, 278
  education, 209–10
  related outcome criteria, 266, *267–68*
  related variables, 22
  responsibilities of, 205
  rights of, 205
  satisfaction survey, 280
  standards, 61–62
  values for, 265
Client outcome tool (COT), pilot testing
  of, 270
Clinical, 278
Clinical data, 15–18
Clinical note form, *108–14*
Clinical progress notes, 86, *107–14*
  influence of, on clinical record, 85
  questions, *85*
Clinical record
  discharge summary and, 86
  discipline-specific care plans and, 84
  incident reports and, 86
  physician's plan of treatment and, 84
  progress notes and, 85, *85*
  reports to third party payers and, 86
  societal influences on, 84–86
Clinical specialist, as member of home
  care team, 154
Code for nurses, 60
Committee Agenda/Minutes form, 47
Communication flow, 38
  chart, *39*
Community Health Intensity Rating Scale
  (CHIRS), 77
Community Health Nursing Intensity
  Construct, 254
  parameter definitions, *255*
Community networking, *255*
Competency, 278
Complications, 198–99
Computerized quality assurance system, 76
Concurrent monitor, 278
Concurrent review, 278
Concurrent study, 278
Conditions of participation (COP), 278
Confidentiality, 206
Conflict resolution, 207
Consultant pharmacy service, 190
Consultation, social workers and, 170
Consumer, viewpoint of, 13–14
Consumerism, 259
Contacts, social workers and, 169
Continuing education, 278
  analysis of, 23–24
Continuity, 278

Continuity of care
  assessment for, 248–49
  client factors and, 250
  discharge planning guide, *248*
  effective, barriers to, 250–51
  evaluation for, 250
  implementation for, 250
  planning strategies, 248–50
  promotion of, 251
  provider factors and, 250
  resource factors and, 250–51
  societal forces affecting, 247–48
Coordinated Home Care Program (CHCP),
  258–70
  assessment of, 260–61
  caregiver-related outcome criteria, 266
  client outcome tool, 270
  client-related outcome criteria, 266,
    267–68
  defining criteria, 266, 268
  development of, 261–68
  evaluation of, 260–61
  family-related outcome criteria, 266,
    267–68
  framework of, 259–60
    conceptual, 261–62, *262*
  goals of, 261
  intervening variables, 269
  objectives of, 274
  objective statements, 265–66
  outcome, 260–61
    measurement instruments, 268–69
    standards, 264–65, *264*
  overview of, 259
  potential outcome standards, *270*
  process, 260
    audit, 263–64
    scoring, 269–70
  standards committee, 261
  statement of philosophy, 273
  structural standards, 263
  structure of, 260
  tool development, 268–70
    testing, 269
Corporate liability, 208
Costs, 278
  of home care, 158–59
County medical societies, role of, 158
Credentialing, 278
Crisis intervention, social work referrals
  and, 166
Criteria
  definition of, 176, 266, 268
  mapping, 278
    as method of data collection,
    73
  types of, 176
Criterion, 73, 278
Criterion, outcome, 278
Criterion, process, 278
Criterion structural, 278

Critical Incident Report, 52–53
Customer Satisfaction Survey, *202*

D

Daily Intake Report, *40*
Data
  analysis of, 176–77
  collection, 72–73
    definitions, 73
    measures, 74–78
    mechanisms, 73–79
    methods of, 73–74
    outcome measures, 76–78
    process, 74–76, *75*
    resources, 78–79
    sources, 73
    structure, 74
  definition of, 73
  derivations of, 73
  financial, 15–18
  origins of, 73
  retrieval, 278
  sources of, 73, 176
Daubert's Patient Classification Outcome
  Criteria System (PCO), 77
Deficiency, 278
Delphi technique of problem identification,
  69-70
Department of Health and Human
  Services (DHHS), definition of home
  health care, 3
Diagnosis related groups (DRGs), 278
Dietitian, as member of home care team,
  155
Digestion/elimination, *255*
Direct observation, as method of data
  collection, 73
Discharge
  definition of, 176
  patient questionnaire, 14, *14*
  planning, 278
    checklist, *249*
  policies, 210
  summary, 86, 278
    clinical records and, 86
    form, *115–17, 146*
    social workers and, 169
Discipline-specific plan of care, 84, 86,
  90–106
Distributions, 278
District nursing, 5
Documentation, 81, 209–10
  content guidelines for, 83
  fiscal imperatives and, 83–84
  influences on, 82–84
  legal influences on, 83
  professional standards and,
    82–83
  social workers and, 168–69
  technical guidelines for, 83

types of, 82
variation, 278
"Do Not Resuscitate" Monitor Summary, 131
Drug(s)
ASCO calendar card, 188–90, *189*
compliance packaging, 188
distribution systems, 188–90
elderly and, 187
problems of, 187–88
regimen, example of, *189*
risks of, 187–88

E

Education Program Summary, *26*
Effectiveness, 278
Efficiency, 279
Elimination, *255*
Emotional response, *255*
Emotional status of clients, 166
Employee(s)
competency of, 66
injury reports, 66
liability of, 209
orientation, 66
recruitment of, 65
responsibilities of, 209, 210
retention of, 65
rights of, 209
training, 66
Employment, 64
criteria, 21–22
problem identification, 65–66
Environment(s)
standards and, 56–57
unsafe, 165
Equipment, knowledge of, 210
Ethical issues
abandonment, 206–07
admission policies, 210
agency liability, 208
agency responsibilities, 210
assessment of, 207
client education, 209–10
confidentiality, 206
corporate liability, 208
discharge policies, 210
documentation, 209–10
employee liability, 209
employee responsibilities, 209, 210
employee rights, 209
informed consent, 206
knowledge of equipment, 210
product liability, 210
professional role, 206
publications on, 213
reassessment of, 125
scarce resources, 207
whistleblowing, 206

withdrawal of life support, 206
workers' compensation, 208–09
Ethical principles, application of, 207
Ethics committees, 204–05
Evaluate, 279
Evaluation activities, 42–43
Evaluation study, 279
Exception, 279
Expense of health care, 259
External review process, 200

F

Family. *See also* Family caregiver(s)
related outcome criteria, 266, *267–68*
relationships, 168
system, *255*
values for, 265
Family caregiver(s)
abuse potential and, 242
AFFIRM model for preparation of, 240–42
neglect potential and, 242
role of, 239–40
value clarification exercise for, *242*
Federal certification, 67
Feedback, 279
Field Agency Agreement, 28–29
Finances, *255*
Financial aspects, 158–59
analysis of resources, 24–26
merging of data, 15–18
reimbursement, 192
Fiscal imperatives, documentation and, 83–84
Focus groups, problem identification and, 68
Follow-up, 279
Forms, effectiveness of, 123–24
Functional assessment form, 229–32

G

Generic, definition of, 176
Generic screen, 279
Goal, 279
Governing body, 279

H

Health care system, history of, 150–51
Health law bibliography, 212
Health maintenance organization (HMO), 279
Health management, 255
Henry Street Settlement House, 6
High-tech home care, 197
accurate initial assessment, 198
acute, 151
around-the-clock services, 198
characteristics of, 197–99

competent staff, 198
complications and, 198–99
incidents and, 198–99
intravenous therapy, 199–200
ongoing assessment, 198
referral response time, 198
risk management, 198–99
services offered by, 197
staff, 198
teaching, 198
vendor relationships, 198
Holistic care, staff nurses and, 140
Homebound, 279
Home care patient. *See* Patient(s)
Home care services. *See* Home health care
Home Care Standards Committee, terms of reference for, 275–76
Home care team, 154–55
Home companion(s), 214
assignment sheet, 225–26
job description, 219–20
versus home health aides, 215
Home Companion Program, 214
advertisements, 227–28
assessments, 216–17
basic components of, 214
client satisfaction interview form, 235–38
evaluation, 217
form, 233–34
marketing, 217
recruitment, 215
reimbursement, 217–18
services, 216
supervision, 216
training, 215–16
Home health agency. *See* Home health care agency
Home health aide(s), 214
assignment sheet, 223–24
job description, 221–22
promotion to, 215
versus home companions, 215
Home health care, 279
ACP's position on, 153
advantages of, 156
barriers to acceptance and use of, 157
consultant pharmacy services in, 190
continuity of, 66
costs of, 158–59
definitions of, 3, 151, 173
development of, 4–5
in United States, 5–7
disadvantages of, 156–57
discharging from, 251
elements of, 64–65
future, 159
future prospects of, 9–10
glossary, 277–81
history of, 4–5
therapy, 173–74

important aspects of, 64–65
merging clinical and financial data for
    improvement of, 15–18
objective statements unique to, 265–66
pharmacist role in, 188–90
physician in
    renewed interest of, 152
    role of, 155–56
quality assurance programs in, examples
    of, 177–83, 252–70
quality of
    definitions of, 55
    monitoring of, 153–54
    outcomes as measure of, 76–78
rewards of, 159
standards of, 66
summary of, 10–11
support of organized medicine for, 152–53
today, 7–9
use of, barriers to, 157
Home health care agency(ies), 279
    accreditation of, 57–59
    certification of, 59
    employees, 209
    liability of, 208
    medical director, 157–58
    problem identification, 66–67
    professional standards of, 82–83
    program evaluation, 67
    responsibilities of, 210
    selection of, 157
    staff nurses and, 140
    standards, 57–59
    state regulation of, 57
    viewpoint of, 15
Home Health Care Report (Chavigny),
    152–53, 160
Home health therapist. See Therapist(s)
Home hospice care, 152
Homemaker-home health aide, 154
Housing
    health, 255
    inadequate, 165
    safety, 255
    social work referrals and, 165–66
Human resources
    analysis of, 18–20, 21–24
    continuing education, 23–24
    employment criteria, 21–22
    in-service education, 23–24
    peer review, 23
    service-education collaboration, 18–19, 21
    staffing patterns, 22–23

I

I.V. Record Form, 201
Illness
    adjustment to, 166
    terminal, 165
Inadequate housing, 165

Incident(s), 198–99
    description of, 52
Incident report(s), 38, 202, 279
    form, 133–34
    influence of, on clinical record, 86
    problem identification and, 67
    reassessment of, 124–25
Indicator, 279. See also Quality indicators
Individual growth and development, 255
Industrial nursing, 6
Informed consent, 206
In-service education, 279
    analysis of, 23–24
Instrument, 279
Interdisciplinary studies, 175–76
Intermittent care, 279
Interview, as method of data collection, 73
Intravenous therapy, 199–200, 201

J

Johns Hopkins Hospital
    conceptual framework for community
        health practice at, 253
    Department of Home Care and Services,
        quality assurance structure and
        functions of, 256
Joint Commission (JCAHO), 279
    accreditation program of, 58, 59
    definition of standards, 55
    standard criteria of, 74
Joint Commission on Accreditation of
    Healthcare Organizations. See Joint
    Commission (JCAHO)
Journal of the American Medical
    Association (American Medical
    Association), 153–54, 154n
Justification, 279

L

LaLonde, Bernadette
    Quality Assurance Manual of the Home
        Care Association of Washington, 78, 80
Language therapist, 155
Legal influences on documentation, 83
Legal issues
    abandonment, 206–07
    admission policies, 210
    agency
        liability, 208
        responsibilities, 210
    client
        education, 209–10
        rights and responsibilities, 205
    confidentiality, 206
    corporate liability, 208
    discharge policies, 210
    documentation, 209–10
    employee
        liability, 209

    responsibilities, 209, 210
    rights, 209
    informed consent, 206
    knowledge of equipment, 210
    malpractice, 209
    product liability, 210
    professional role, 206
    reassessment of, 125
    scarce resources, 207
    whistleblowing, 206
    withdrawal of life support, 206
    workers' compensation, 208–09
Levels of care/staging, 279
Licensure, 279
    agency, 57
    individual, 60
Life support, withdrawal of, 206
Likert-type rating scale, 74
Living arrangements, 166
Long-term care, 151–52

M

Malpractice, defense against allegations of, 210
Managing for Quality in Home Health
    Care: Effective Business Strategies
    (Wagner), 64–65
McDowell, Ian, Measuring Health: A
    Guide To Rating Scales and
    Questionnaires, 78, 80
Measurable, 279
Measure, 73, 279
Measurement validity, 279
Measuring Health: A Guide to Rating
    Scales and Questionnaires, (McDowell
    and Newell), 78, 80
Medicaid (Title XIX), 279
    affect of, on continuity of care, 247, 248
    conditions of participation, 59
Medical care evaluation (MCE), 279
Medical director, role of, 157–58
Medical record, 279–80
Medical social worker, 155
Medical update form, 118–20
Medicare (Title XVIII), 280
    conditions of participation, 59
    continuity of care and, 247, 248
    quality assurance and, 174
Medication(s). See also Drug(s)
    record, 190–92
        contents of, 190–91
        review of, 192
    regimen, example of, 189
Medication record review form, 191
Mental competency, social work referrals
    and, 164
Metropolitan National Nursing
    Association, emphasis of, 5
Monitoring activities
    process for, 42–43
    quality assurance form, 45–46

Montefiore Hospital Home Care
  Program, 7
Multidisciplinary study(ies), 175, 280
Multiple-diagnoses patients
  intervention outcomes of, *185*

N

National Home Caring Council,
  accreditation program of, 58–59
National League for Nursing (NLN)
  approach to use of standards, 55–56
  criteria for home care, *58*
  definition of standards, 55
  program for accreditation, 57–58, *58*
National Organization for Public Health
  Nursing, provisions of, 7
Neglect
  potential for, 242
Neuromusculoskeletal function, *255*
  social work referrals and, 164–65
Newell, Claire, *Measuring Health: A
  Guide to Rating Scales and
  Questionnaires*, 78, 80
Nominal group meeting, procedures for
  conducting, 68–69
Nurses, professional, as member of home
  care team, 154
Nursing care plan form, *90–97*
Nursing diagnoses
  for Group V—Terminal Illness, *24*
  recap, *25*
Nursing history and assessment form,
  99–106
Nursing home placements, 164
Nursing process, 141–44. *See also* Nursing
  staff
  assessment, 141
  coordination, 143
  counseling, 142–43
  direct client care, 142
  discharge from agency, 143–44
  evaluation, 143–44
  interventions, 142–43
  planning, 141–42
  teaching, 142
Nursing staff, 139. *See also* Nursing
  process
  agency and, 140
  case management and, 140–44
  commitment of, 139–40
  holistic care and, 140
  initiation of care and, 140–41
  patterns, 144–47
  peer review, 147–48
  perspective of, 139–48
  productivity, 144–147
  professional development of, 140
  quality care and, 139
  supplemental personnel, 147
Nutrition, *255*

O

Objective, 280
Observation, direct, 73
Occupational therapist, 155
Occupational therapy
  diagnostic analysis of, *184*
  outcomes of, 183–84
  visits, *184*
Older Americans Act, conditions of
  participation, 59
On-call patient data base form, *145*
On-site evaluation form, *184*
Orientation, 280
Outcome(s), 55, 280
  assessment of, 170
  definition of, 73, 176
  description of, 163, 175
  criteria, *264*, 266
  dimensions, *264*
  as measure of quality, 76–78
Outliers, 280

P

Patient(s)
  abused, 164–65
  care, 151–52
    services, 64–66
    characteristics of, *188*
    classification system, *23*, 25
  flow sheet, *181*
  neglected, 164–65
  outcome goals, *25*
  satisfaction, 67
    survey, 74, 126–27
  standards, 61–62
  survey form, *178*
Pattern of care, 280
Peer, 280
Peer review, 23, 280
  as method of data collection, 73
  staff nurses and, 147–48
Peer review organization (PRO), 280
Performance appraisal form for home care
  physical therapists, 182–83
Personal habits, *255*
Personnel, supplemental, 147. *See also*
  Nursing staff
Persuasion, 207
Phaneuf Nursing Audit, 74
Pharmaceutical services, 190
  reimbursement for, 192
Pharmacist(s)
  as member of home care team, 155
  perspective on, 187–93
  role of, 188–190
  state-of-the-art services offered by, *193*
Physical therapist
  as member of home care team, 154
  performance appraisal form, *182–83*

Physical therapy
  evaluation and care plan form, *98*
  evaluation form, *107*
Physician(s)
  assessment of patient, 155–56
  guidelines for, 155
  as member of home care team, 154–55
  payment for services of, 158–59
  perspective of, 150–59
  renewed interest in home care, 152
  responsibilities of, 156
  role of, 155–56
Physician Guide to Home Health Care
  (American Medical Association), 153, 160
Physician's plan of treatment. *See* Plan of
  treatment
Physician Satisfaction Survey, 128
Plan of treatment (POT), 86, 280
  examples of, *87–89*
  clinical record and, 84
Policymakers, viewpoint of, 14–15
Practice standards, 60–62
President's Commission for Study of
  Ethical Problems and Behavioral
  Research, publications of, 213
Private insurance program standards, 60
Problem, 280
Problem identification, 65–67, 177
  in administration, 66–67
  in agency program evaluation, 67
  in agency standards, 66–67
  basis for, 64–65
  in caregiver competency, 66
  in case management, 66
  in continuity of care, 66
  delphi technique of, 69–70
  employee injury reports and, 66
  in employment, 65–66
  federal certification and, 67
  focus groups and, 68
  group techniques of, 67–70
  in incident reports, 67
  in intake process, 66
  nominal group technique of, 68–69
  orientation of employees and, 66
  in patient care services, 66
  in patient satisfaction, 67
  pretesting, 67
  in productivity, 67
  quality circles and, 69
  in recruitment of employees, 65
  in referral process, 66
  in retention of employees, 65
  in standards of care, 66
  state licensing requirements and, 57
  summary of, 70
  training of employees and, 66
  in utilization review, 67
Process, 55, 280
  assessment of, 170
  audit, 280

concern, 163
definition of, 73, 176
description of, 163, 175
measurement, 74
as measure of quality, 74–76, *75*
Productivity, problem identification and, 67
Product liability, 210
Professional(s)
    advisory body, 280
    development, 140
    role, 206
    standards, 82–83
    viewpoint of, 15
Professionalism, 259
Profile analysis, 280
Program, 280
    standards, 59–60
Progress
    notation of, 169
    note sheet, *144*
Prospective reviews, 280
Psychological counseling, 155
Psychological status of clients, 166

Q

Quality, 280
    care
        improvement of, 15–18
        staff nurse and, 139
    circles, 69
    components of, 73
    indicators, 64–67
        administration, 66–67
        employment, 65–66
        objectives of use of, 67
        patient care services, 66
        pretesting, 67
        problem identification, 65–67
    measurement of, 72–73
Quality assurance, 3–4, 8–9, 13, 280
    accrediting agencies viewpoint of, 15
    activities log, 48–51
    activity format, 44
    calendar, 15, *22*
    certifying agencies viewpoint of, 15
    committee
        effectiveness of, 125
        yearly calendar, *123*
    computerized, 76
    consumer's viewpoint of, 13–14
    definition of, 174, 261
    description of, 3
    generic model for, 174–77, *175*
        analyze data, 176–77
        collect data, 176
        committee, 175–76
        evaluate results of action plan, 177
        identify criteria, 176
        identify problems, 176–177
        institute corrective action, 177

method, 175
    ratify criteria, 176
    time frame, 176
    topic, 174–75
glossary, 277–81
growth of, 13–15
home health agency viewpoint of, 15
influence of medicare on, 174
legislative and regulatory viewpoint of,
    14–15
monitor(ing), 123–24
    activity form, 45–46
    do not resuscitate form, 131
    plan, *257*
    summary form, 130
    timely initial service form, 132
outcome indicators for, *10*
perceptions of, 13–15
policy, 15, *16–18*
policymakers viewpoint of, 14–15
process indicators for, *10*
professional's viewpoint of, 15
regulatory viewpoint of, 14–15
risk management and, 35
structure indicators for, *10*
studies on, 76–78
summary of, 26
survival of, 13–15
third party payer's viewpoint of, 14
utilization review and, 34–35
written plan, 122
*Quality Assurance Manual of the Home
    Care Association of Washington*
    (LaLonde), 78, 80
Quality assurance program(s), *36–38*,
    280. *See also* Coordinated Home Care
    Program (CHCP)
    assessment of, 34, *35*
    communication flow and, 38, *39*
    conceptual framework for, *262*
    Coordinated Home Care Program
        example of, 258–70
    designing of, 33–53
        planning, 33–34
    development of, 34
    evaluation of effectiveness of, 122–25
    examples of, 177–83, 252–70
    goals of, 33–34, 261
    hospital-based example of, 252–58
        administrative review committee,
            254–55
        agency administration, 256–57
        budget committee, 256
        conceptual practice model, 252–54
        external influences, 253
        monitoring plan, 257–58
        outcomes, 254
        philosophy, 253–54
        policy review committee, 254–55
        professional advisory committee, 254
        research committee, 256

standards, 254
    standards committee, 255–56
    structure, 254–57
    tools for practice, 254
    utilization review committee, 255
reasons for, 13
summary of, 41
Quality measurement mechanisms. *See*
    Data collection mechanisms
Quality of care. *See* Home health care,
    quality of
Quality of life index (QLI), 77
Quality Patient Care Scale (Qual pacs), 74
Quarterly Record Review for Home Health
    Aide, 15, *20–21*

R

Randomization, 280
Referral
    definition of, 176
    response time, 198
Referral Source Satisfaction Survey, 129
Regulation, 57
Rehabilitation Services of Wisconsin
    (RSW), quality assurance program of,
    182–83
Reimbursement, 280
Reliability, 281
Report(s), 38–39, 280
    action
        form, 135
        reassessment of, 124–25
    annual, 39
    incident
        clinical record and, 86
        form, 133–34
        reassessment of, 124–25
    to third party payers, 86
Reporting mechanisms, 38–39
    effectiveness of, 124
Reproductive function, *255*
Resources, 281
    as measure of quality, 78–79
    scarce, 207
Resource utilization groups (RUGs), 281
Respiratory function, *255*
Restudy, 281
Retrospective review, 281
Review, 281
Review committee, 281
Risk management, 35, 198–99, 207–08, 281
Risser Patient Satisfaction Scale, 78
Role theory, 239–40

S

Satisfaction tools, 124
Schmadl, John C.
    definition of quality assurance for
        nursing, 174

Schmele instrument to measure process of nursing practice in community nursing service (SIMP), 74–75
    representative items from, *75*
Schmele's standards implementation model, 56, *56*
Screening, 281
Self-evaluation, 73
Sensory function, *255*
Sentinel, 281
    as method of data collection, 74
Service-education collaboration analysis of, 18–19, 21
Services, eligibility for, 165–66
Single-diagnosis patients, intervention outcomes of, *185*
Skilled nursing service, 281
Slater Nursing Competency Scale, 74
Socialization needs, 168
Social services
    progress note, *167*
    quality assurance audit, *171*
Social Services Block Grant (Title XX), conditions of participation, 59
Social worker(s)
    appropriate referrals, 164–68
    assessments and, 170
    competence of, 163–64
    consultation and, 170
    contacts and, 169
    discharge summary and, 169
    documentation and, 168–69
    general considerations for, 168
    initial assessment and, 168–69
    need for, 164
    notations and, 169
    outcome assessment and, 170
    perspective of, 163
    problems and, 164–68
    process assessment and, 170
    progress and, 169
    teamwork and, 169–70
    treatment plan and, 169
    visits and, 169
Social work referral(s)
    abused patients and, 164–65
    adjustment to illness and, 166
    alcoholism and, 166
    caregiver's concerns and, 165
    clients' socialization needs and, 168
    crisis intervention and, 166
        eligibility for services or benefits and, 165–66
    emotional status of client and, 166
    family relationships and, 168
    form, *165*
    housing arrangements and, 166
    inadequate housing and, 165
    living arrangements and, 166

    mental competency and, 164
    neglected patients and, 164–65
    nursing home placements and, 164
    planning for future needs and, 168
    psychological status of client and, 166
    substance abuse and, 166
    terminal illness and, 165
    unsafe environments and, 165
Societal influence(s)
    on clinical record, 84–86
    dealing with, 86–120
Speech therapist, 155
Staff
    high-tech, 198
    productivity, 22
Staffing patterns, analysis of, 22–23
Staff nurse. *See* Nursing staff
Staging
    levels of, 279
    as method of data collection, 74
Standard(s), 54–62, 281
    agency, 57–59
        problem identification and, 66–67
    American Nurses Association, 60, *61*
    of care, 66
    client/patient, 61–62
    conclusion on, 62
    and criteria, 55
    definitions of, 54–55, 73
    description of, 54
    development of, 55
    environment and, 56–57
    framework for, 55
    implementation of, 55–56
    levels of, 57–62
    model program, 59–60
    practice, 60–62
    professional, 82–83
    program, 59–60
    uses of, 62
State licensing requirements, 67
State medical societies, role of, 158
State-of-the-art pharmacy services, *193*
State regulation, 57
Structural evaluation, 281
Structural integrity, *255*
Structure, 55, 281
    definition of, 73, 176
    description of, 163, 175
    as measure of quality, 74
Substance abuse, 166
Supervisory evaluation, 73
Supervisory visit, 281

T

Teamwork 169–70
Terminal illness, 165
Therapist(s)
    language, 155
    occupational, 155, 185

    performance appraisal form, 182–83
    perspective of, 173–85
    physical, 154, 185
    role of, 174
    speech, 155
Therapy
    future of, 185
    history of, in home care, 173–74
    occupational, 183–84, *184*
Third party payer(s)
    reports to, 86
    viewpoint of, 14
Timely initial service monitor summary, 132
Title XIV, conditions of participation, 59
Title XIX. *See* Medicaid program
Title XX. *See* Social Services Block Grant
Tools, effectiveness of, 123–24
Tracers, 281
    as method of data collection, 74
Trajectory, 74
Transition from hospital to home, 247. *See also* Continuity of care
Travel-related variables, 22

U

Unsafe environment, 165
Utilization review, 34–35, 281
    form, *179–80*
    problem identification and, 67

V

Validity, 281
Value(s)
    as caregivers, 265
    for clients, 264
    for family, 265
Vendor relationships, 198
Visiting Nurse Association of New Haven, quality assurance program of, 184–85
Visiting Nurse Association of Orange County, quality assurance program of, 177–82
Visiting nurses, 5
Visiting Nurse Services (VNS), 214
Visiting Nurse Society of Philadelphia, 5, 6
Visits, notation of, 169
Voluntary consent, 206

W

Wagner, Donna M., *Managing for Quality in Home Health Care: Effective Business Strategies*, 64–65
Wald Lillian, 6
Whistleblowing, 206
Workers' compensation, 208–209

Y

Yearly plan (calendar), 122–23, *123*